American Happiness and Discontents

ALSO BY GEORGE F. WILL

American Happiness and Discontents

The Unruly Torrent, 2008–2020

George F. Will

hachette BOOKS

NEW YORK

Copyright © 2021 by G.F.W. Inc.

Cover design by Terri Sirma
Cover copyright © 2021 by Hachette Book Group, Inc.

Hachette Books
Hachette Book Group
1290 Avenue of the Americas
New York, NY 10104
HachetteBooks.com
Twitter.com/HachetteBooks
Instagram.com/HachetteBooks

First Edition: September 2021

Published by Hachette Books, an imprint of Perseus Books, LLC, a subsidiary of Hachette Book Group, Inc. The Hachette Books name and logo is a trademark of the Hachette Book Group.

The Hachette Speakers Bureau provides a wide range of authors for speaking events. To find out more, go to www.hachettespeakersbureau.com or call (866) 376-6591.

The publisher is not responsible for websites (or their content) that are not owned by the publisher.

Print book interior design by Sean Ford.

Library of Congress Cataloging-in-Publication Data has been applied for.

ISBNs: 978-0-306-92441-5 (hardcover); 978-0-306-92440-8 (ebook)

Printed in the United States of America

LSC-C

Printing 1, 2021

For Sarah Walton
To whom I am indebted for her many years of
indispensable assistance.
And to whom the nation is indebted.

(see page 492)

Contents

CONTENTS

Introduction

"In order to master the unruly torrent of life the learned man meditates, the poet quivers, and the political hero erects the fortress of his will."

—José Ortega y Gasset

But a journalist, whose job is to chronicle and comment on the torrent, knows that this is not amenable to being mastered. That is what it means to be unruly. Besides, the enjoyment of life is inseparable from life's surprises, and hence from its contingencies. Surprises and contingencies have propelled this columnist through a happy half century of arriving at his office each morning impatient to get on with the pleasure of immersion in the torrent.

For a third of a century my office has been in a narrow, three-story townhouse built in 1810 in what is now Washington's Georgetown section. It was here in 1814 when marauding British troops burned the White House and part of the Capitol. I purchased the building in 1987 from a small, sprightly, sparrow-like woman, then in her nineties, who had lived there since her childhood. She said that her parents recalled seeing Abraham Lincoln's son Robert walk past the house on his way to the corner saloon to purchase a pail of beer. This is plausible. Back then, beer was often sold in pails. And Robert, although frail at age seventy-eight, haltingly made his way up the steps of the memorial to his father at the dedication of it on May 30, 1922.

Because of where I live and work, the continuity of America's institutions and arguments is never far from my mind, as is the truth of William Faulkner's statement that "the past is not dead. It is not even past." That is why this book begins with some writings about American history. Were I a benevolent dictator, I would make history the only permissible college major in order to equip the public with the stock of knowledge required for thinking clearly about how we arrived at this point in our national narrative.

The poet E. E. Cummings—or as he's remembered, e.e. cummings— wrote of a "footprint in the sand of was." As a Washingtonian, I live immersed in was—in history. I have spent almost all of my adult life in Washington and still am stirred by its grand vistas and monuments. And by the fact that the bricks of Georgetown's sidewalks have been trod by politicians, jurists, and statesmen who have made American principles vivid and the American project successful.

I have now completed five decades as a columnist, and a few readers might be interested in learning how someone could have the good fortune to tumble into such a delightful career. In September 1958, four months after my seventeenth birthday, I came out of the Illinois wilderness to matriculate at Trinity College in Hartford. Soon thereafter I did what a young man from Central Illinois would naturally do: I took the train to New York City. Arriving in the splendor of Grand Central Terminal, I plunked down a nickel for a New York tabloid in order to see what was going on in Gotham. This purchase of a *New York Post* was a life-changing event because in it I found a column by Murray Kempton.

I do not remember what his subject was that day, but his subjects generally were of secondary importance to his style, which reflected his refined mind and his penchant for understated passion, mordantly expressed. Here, for example, is a sentence from his October 26, 1956, report on President Dwight David Eisenhower campaigning for re-election:

In Miami he had walked carefully by the harsher realities, speaking some 20 feet from an airport drinking fountain labeled "Colored" and saying that the condition it represented was more amenable to solution by the hearts of men than by laws, and complimenting Florida as "typical today of what is best in America," a verdict which might seem to some contingent on finding out what happened to the Negro snatched from the Wildwood jail Sunday.

This seventy-five-word sentence—sinewy, ironic, and somewhat demanding—paid a compliment to his readers: He knew they could and would follow a winding syntactical path through a thought so obliquely expressed as to be almost merely intimated. Kempton understood that the swirling, stirring society in which Americans are at all times immersed is constantly clamoring for their attention, plucking at their sleeves and even grabbing them by the lapels with journalism, politics, advertising, and other distractions. Furthermore, Kempton knew that reading newspaper columns is an optional activity, so a writer must make the most of his ration of words—in Kempton's case, often fewer than 700 of them. Reading a columnist's commentary on political and cultural subjects is an acquired taste, and a minority taste: It will only be acquired if it is pleasant, even fun.

However, the fact that most Americans do not read newspapers, let alone the commentary columns, is actually emancipating for columnists. The kind of people who seek out written arguments are apt to bring to the written word a fund of information and opinions. Having a self-selected audience of intellectually upscale readers allows the columnist to assume that his or her readers have a reservoir of knowledge about the world. So, he can be brief—most of the writings in this book are approximately 750 words long—without being superficial.

Today, America has a much more clamorous media environment than Kempton knew. New technologies—cable television, the Internet, social media—produce a blitzkrieg of words, written and spoken. The spoken words are often shouted by overheated individuals who evidently believe that the lungs are the seat of wisdom. Here, however, is the good news: Amid the cacophony, and because of it, there is an audience for something different, for what Kempton exemplified and some of us aspire to—trenchant elegance.

My path from my Grand Central Terminal epiphany to a life practicing the columnists' craft was circuitous. After college, I studied for two years at Oxford. As I prepared to leave that magical place of "dreaming spires," I was undecided about my preferred career path—law, or teaching political philosophy. (My father was a professor of philosophy, specializing in the philosophy of science.) So, I applied to a distinguished law school and to Princeton's graduate school. I do not remember all the reasons I chose Princeton, but I suspect they included this one: Princeton is located between New York and Philadelphia, two National League baseball cities. My father, a philosophy professor, was a born academic; I obviously was not.

Still, having earned a PhD, I was teaching at the University of Toronto in the autumn of 1969 when Everett Dirksen from Pekin, Illinois, who was minority leader of the U.S. Senate, died. (Pekin, which is about eighty miles from my hometown of Champaign, was a sister city of Peking, China, as Beijing was then known. The sports teams at Pekin High School, from which Dirksen graduated, were called the Chinks. Times change, and aren't we glad.) Senate Republicans shuffled their leadership and someone of whom I knew nothing, Colorado's Gordon Allott, was elected chairman of the Republican Policy Committee. He decided he wanted to hire a Republican academic to write for him. In the late 1960s the phrase "Republican academic" was not quite an oxymoron, but then as now such creatures were thin on the ground. Allott, however, found me north of the border and brought me to Washington.

After three years on the Senate staff, I called William F. Buckley, with whom I was acquainted and for whose *National Review* I had written a few things. I told Bill that I thought his magazine, which was then and still is produced in New York, needed a Washington editor. He made a practice of collecting young writers, and was probably inured to their impertinence. His characteristically generous reply to me was: You're right, I do, and you're it. In January 1973 I began writing columns for *NR* and also for the *Washington Post*, which was just starting a syndication service. Fifty years and 6,000 or so columns later I number myself among the fortunate few who have lived this familiar axiom: If you love your work, you will never work a day in your life.

So, as a believer in free markets, and hence in the price system's rational allocation of society's resources and energies, I am amused by the fact that this system has made a mistake regarding me. Under sensible pricing of labor, people should be paid the amount necessary to elicit their work. I, however, am paid to do what I would do without pay. Writing—forming sentences and paragraphs, producing a felicitous phrase in the service of a well-made argument—is, for me, a metabolic urge, and more fun than I can have anywhere outside of a major league ballpark.

Peter De Vries—novelist, fiction editor of the *New Yorker*, and the wittiest American writer since Mark Twain—said, "I write when I'm inspired, and I see to it that I am inspired at nine o'clock every morning." I am at my desk before eight o'clock every morning, so eager am I for another day of the pleasures of my craft.

It might seem peculiar to derive pleasure from working in a Washington that for many years has been sunk in visceral, mindless partisanship. And, truth be told, the bitterness is often inversely proportional to the stakes. Furthermore, it might seem perverse to enjoy writing cultural criticism at a time when the culture is increasingly coarse and silly. However, one reason the temperature of the nation's discourse is high is that the stakes are high. Today's fights are not optional and they are worth winning.

In recent years, colleges and universities have received from the public increased attention and decreased admiration. This is because America's most dispiriting intellectual phenomenon is the degradation of higher education, which is being swept by two plagues to which it should be immune—fads and hysterias. But because some of the noblest achievements of American civilization, our great research universities, are imperiled, the nation's future is, too.

Although there are many kinds of colleges and universities, the *idea* of a university is inherently aristocratic: Higher education is not for everyone, and it is not primarily vocational or even "practical," as this is commonly understood. Rather, institutions of higher education—some much more than others—should be answers to a question posed by Alexis de Tocqueville. His *Democracy in America*, which has rightly been called the greatest book about a nation written by a citizen of another nation, implicitly but insistently asked this: Can a nation so thoroughly committed to equality cultivate and celebrate excellence, which distinguishes the few from the many? Much depends on our being able to answer this question in the affirmative. Much depressing evidence suggests that we cannot.

The book you are holding includes a substantial selection of pieces illustrating the role of courts in contemporary American governance. The fact that courts are increasingly central to the nation's political arguments explains the ferocity of the struggles over the confirmation of presidential nominations to the U.S. Supreme Court. Many thoughtful people think courts have become too important. I disagree, for reasons that will, I hope, become clear in the pieces dealing with various instances in which basic rights have routinely been imperiled by majoritarian institutions, but have been protected by judicial ones.

There is much in this book about cultural matters, broadly construed, including the interesting fact that "parent" has become a verb, and sexual mores have…well, let Peter De Vries explain: "A hundred years ago Hester Prynne of *The Scarlet Letter* was given an A for adultery. Today she would rate no better than a C-plus." There is very little in this book about recent presidents. What William Wordsworth felt about the world—that it is "too much with us"—is how I feel about almost all presidents. They permeate the national consciousness to a degree that is unhealthy and, strictly speaking, unrepublican and anti-constitutional. Entire forests are felled to produce the paper for books about presidents. What we more urgently need, always, is attention paid to the ideas that have consequences as presidents come and go. They are all temporary; the Constitution and the American creed bide.

Many selections in this book are about books. The more fuss is made about new media—the Internet, Google, Facebook, Instagram, and so on, and on—the more I am convinced that books remain the primary transmitters of ideas. In fact, *because* of what makes the new media so enchanting to so many, the importance of books is increasing. When television was a new medium, the witty Fred Allen, whose career was in radio, quipped that television enabled you to have in your living room people you would not want in your living room. The new media enables the instantaneous and essentially cost-free dissemination of thoughts, most of which should never have been thought, let alone given written expression. The velocity imparted by the new media somehow is an incentive for intemperate discourse. Books, however, have long gestations and, usually, careful editors. One of the most demanding and satisfying facets of this columnist's craft is taking the many hours required to distill to its essence a worthy book that took another author many years to write; to offer just one example, to be able to acquaint a large readership with the lapidary sentences and mind-opening nuggets of information in Rick Atkinson's military histories—a specialty now almost extinct in the academy.

It has been well said that the United States is the only nation founded on a good idea, the proposition that people should be free to pursue happiness as they define it. In recent years, however, happiness has been elusive for this dyspeptic nation, in which too many people think and act as tribes and define their happiness as some other tribe's unhappiness. As a quintessentially American voice, that of Robert Frost, said, "The only way out is through." Perhaps the information, the reasoning, and, I hope, the occasional amusements in this book can help readers think through, and thereby diminish, our current discontents.

They will diminish if, but only if, Americans adhere to two categorical imperatives: They should behave as intelligently as they can, and should be as cheerful as is reasonable. The pursuit of individual happiness, and of a more perfect union, never reaches perfect fulfillment, but never mind. "The struggle itself toward the heights," wrote Albert Camus, "is enough to fill a man's heart. One must imagine Sisyphus happy." For Americans, the pursuit of happiness is happiness.

SECTION 1

THE PATH TO THE PRESENT

FROM RUNNYMEDE TO STELLE'S HOTEL

June 14, 2015

WASHINGTON—Americans should light 800 candles for the birthday of the document that began paving the meandering path to limited government. Magna Carta laid down the law about "fish weirs" on English rivers, "assizes of darrein presentment," people being "distrained to make bridges," and other "liberties...to hold in our realm of England in perpetuity." But what King John accepted at Runnymede meadow on June 15, 1215, matters to Americans because of something that happened 588 years later in the living room of Stelle's Hotel in Washington, where the Library of Congress now sits.

Although the "great charter" purported to establish certain rights in "perpetuity," almost everything in it has been repealed or otherwise superseded. Magna Carta led to parliamentary supremacy (over the sovereign—the king or queen) but not to effective limits on government. The importance of the document was its assertion that the sovereign's will could be constrained.

In America, where "we the people" are sovereign and majority rule is celebrated, constraining the sovereign is frequently, but incorrectly, considered morally ambiguous, even disreputable. Hence the heated debate among conservatives about the role of courts in a democracy. The argument is about the supposed "countermajoritarian dilemma," when courts invalidate laws passed by elected representatives: Does the democratic ethic require vast judicial deference to legislative acts?

The first memorial at Runnymede was built in 1957 by, appropriately, the American Bar Association. It is what America did with what

Magna Carta started that substantially advanced the cause of limited government.

The rule of law—as opposed to rule by the untrammeled will of the strong—requires effective checks on the strong. In a democracy, the strongest force is the majority, whose power will be unlimited unless an independent judiciary enforces written restraints, such as those stipulated in the Constitution. It is "the supreme law" because it is superior to what majorities produce in statutes.

Magna Carta acknowledged no new individual rights. Instead, it insisted, mistakenly, that it could guarantee that certain existing rights would survive "in perpetuity." British rights exist, however, at the sufferance of Parliament. In America, rights are protected by the government's constitutional architecture—the separation of powers *and by the judicial power to stymie legislative and executive power.*

Early in 1801, as John Adams's presidency was ending, a lame-duck Congress controlled by his Federalists created many judicial positions to be filled by him before Thomas Jefferson took office. In the rush, the "midnight commission" for William Marbury did not get delivered before Jefferson's inauguration. The new president refused to have it delivered, so Marbury sued, asking the Supreme Court to compel Jefferson's secretary of state, James Madison, to deliver it.

Chief Justice John Marshall, writing for the court, held that the law authorizing the court to compel government officials to make such deliveries exceeded Congress's enumerated powers and hence was unconstitutional. Jefferson, who detested his distant cousin Marshall, was surely less pleased by the result than he was dismayed by the much more important means by which Marshall produced it. Marshall had accomplished the new government's first exercise of judicial review—the power to declare a congressional act null and void.

Although the Constitution does not mention judicial review, the Framers explicitly anticipated the exercise of this power. Some progressives and populist conservatives dispute the legitimacy of judicial review. They say fidelity to the Framers requires vast deference to elected legislators because Marshall invented judicial review ex nihilo. Randy Barnett of Georgetown University's law school supplies refuting evidence:

At the 1787 Constitutional Convention, Madison acknowledged that states would "accomplish their injurious objects" but they could be "set aside by the national tribunals." A law violating any constitution "would be considered by the judges as null and void." In Virginia's ratification convention, Marshall said that if the government "were to make a law not warranted by any of the [congressional] powers enumerated, it would be considered by the judges as an infringement of the Constitution which they are to guard.... They would declare it void."

With the composition of the Supreme Court likely to change substantially during the next president's tenure, conservatives must decide: Is majority rule or liberty—these are not synonyms, and the former can menace the latter—America's fundamental purpose? Because one ailing justice was confined to Stelle's Hotel, it was there that Marshall read aloud *Marbury v. Madison*. This made February 24, 1803, an even more important date in the history of limited government, and hence of liberty, than June 15, 1215.

A NATION NOT MADE BY FLIMSY PEOPLE

June 6, 2019

> By the rude bridge that arched the flood,
> Their flag to April's breeze unfurled,
> Here once the embattled farmers stood
> And fired the shot heard round the world.
> —Ralph Waldo Emerson, "Concord Hymn"

WASHINGTON—After the morning bloodshed on Lexington green, on the first day of what would become a 3,059-day war, there occurred the second of what would be eventually more than 1,300 mostly small

5

military clashes. Rick Atkinson writes: "A peculiar quiet descended over what the poet James Russell Lowell would call 'that era-parting bridge,' across which the old world passed into the new." Here again is Atkinson's felicity for turning history into literature.

Many who have read his Liberation Trilogy on U.S. forces in World War II's European theater (*An Army at Dawn*, *The Day of Battle*, *The Guns at Last Light*) will already have immersed themselves in his just-published *The British Are Coming: The War for America, Lexington to Princeton, 1775–1777*, the first of what will be his Revolution Trilogy. It is a history of the combat in which the fate of a continent, and an idea, was determined by astonishingly small numbers of combatants, and one astonishing man.

As London came to terms with the fact that Boston is farther from Charleston than London is from Venice, it slowly dawned on Britain's government that it was fighting not just a nascent army but also a nation aborning. And that it had the daunting, and ultimately defeating, logistical challenge of maintaining an army across an ocean in the age of sail. When its North American commander asked London for 950 horses, more than 400 died en route and others, weakened by the voyage, died on shore.

America's shores—most Americans lived within twenty miles of Atlantic tidewater—were home to people made restive, then violently belligerent by a vibrant print culture: "Philadelphia…boasted almost as many booksellers—77—as England's top 10 provincial towns combined." The war would be won largely by the deft retreating of George Washington who, as Atkinson demonstrates, several times came "within a chin whisker of losing the war."

Approximately 250,000 Americans served for some period in some military capacity, and more than one in ten died, a higher proportion of the nation's population than perished in any conflict other than the Civil War. They died from battle, disease, or vile British prisons. Few battles produced mass carnage (one in eight of the British officers who would die in the eight years of war died in four hours at Bunker Hill). Inaccurate muskets (Atkinson says, "The shot heard round the world likely missed") often were less lethal than the primitive medicine inflicted on the victims of muskets, cannons, and bayonets. Only the fortunate wounded got "their ears stuffed with lamb's wool to mask the sound of the sawing." Amputations above the knee took thirty seconds; about half the amputees survived the ordeal or subsequent sepsis.

Washington rarely had more than 20,000 soldiers and often had fewer: On one December day during his late-autumn 1776 retreat from New York City across New Jersey, he lost about half his "threadbare and dying" army to expiring enlistments, and he crossed the Delaware into Pennsylvania with less than 3,000. Later that month, however, he recrossed the river with 2,400 and in less than two hours at Trenton (where Lt. James Monroe was wounded) and, eight days later, in an hour at Princeton, saved the idea of a continental nation based on republican ideals.

One lesson of *The British Are Coming* is the history-shaping power of individuals exercising their agency together: the volition of those who shouldered muskets in opposition to an empire. Another lesson is that the democratic, sentimental idea that cobblers and seamstresses are as much history-makers as generals and politicians is false. A few individuals matter much more than most. Atkinson is clear: No George Washington, no United States.

Washington, writes Atkinson, learned that "only battle could reveal those with the necessary dark heart for killing, years of killing; that only those with the requisite stamina, aptitude, and luck would be able to see it through, and finally—the hardest of war's hard truths—that for a new nation to live, young men must die, often alone, usually in pain, and sometimes to no obvious purpose." The more that Americans are reminded by Atkinson and other supreme practitioners of the historians' craft that their nation was not made by flimsy people, the less likely it is to be flimsy.

NEWS BULLETIN: THE AMERICAN
REVOLUTIONARY WAR WAS VIOLENT

July 2, 2017

PHILADELPHIA—Some American history museums belabor visitors with this message: You shall know the truth and it shall make you feel ashamed of, but oh-so-superior to, your wretched ancestors. The new Museum of the American Revolution is better than that. Located near Independence Hall, it celebrates the luminous ideas affirmed there 241 Julys ago, but it does not flinch from this fact: The war that began at Lexington and Concord fourteen months before the Declaration of Independence was America's first civil war. And it had all the messiness and nastiness that always accompany protracted fratricide.

Among its many interesting artifacts—weapons, uniforms, documents— the museum's great possession is the tent George Washington used from 1778 to 1783, which on its long, winding path to the museum was owned by Robert E. Lee's wife and was later sold to raise money for Confederate widows. The museum makes rather more than is necessary of the Oneida Indian Nation's contributions to American independence but, then, the Oneidas are now in the casino business and contributed $10 million to the museum.

The museum has one of those "immersive" exhibits wherein visitors hear the cannon and feel the vibrations of battle. It would, however, be a more convincing experience of war if enemies were trying to impale the visitors with this war's most lethal device, the bayonet. Never mind. There are limits to what realities a museum can, or should try to, convey. This probably bothers those who are properly intent on making us face the worst facts. Consider, for example, Holger Hoock's recently published *Scars of Independence: America's Violent Birth*.

He writes in the manner of current academics, who are forever "unmasking" this and that. He offers "an unvarnished portrait" of revolutionary violence in order to purge the "popular memory" of "romanticized notions" and end the "whitewashing and selective remembering and forgetting" and—herewith the inevitable academic trope—the "privileging" of patriots' perspectives.

Hoock is, however, right to document the harrowing violence, often opportunistic and sadistic, that was "fundamental" to how both sides experienced "America's founding moment." The war caused "proportionately more" deaths—from battle, captivity, and disease—than any war other than that of 1861–1865. The perhaps 37,000 deaths were five times more per capita than America lost in World War II. Sixty thousand loyalists became refugees. "The dislocated proportion of the American population exceeded that of the French in their revolution." The economic decline "lasted for 15 years in a crisis unmatched until the Great Depression."

After the second civil war, William Tecumseh Sherman declared that "war is hell." Hoock demonstrates that this was true even when battle casualties (only twenty-three patriots died at Yorktown) were small by modern standards. He is, however, mistaken in suggesting that he is uniquely sensitive to our founding mayhem. Consider two recent books that examine the anarchic violence on both sides.

Nathaniel Philbrick's *Bunker Hill: A City, a Siege, a Revolution* (2013) recounts a patriot mob's long torture, in January 1774, of loyalist John Malcom, a Boston customs officer, who was tarred and feathered: The crowd dislocated his arm while tearing off his clothes, then daubed his skin with steaming tar that parboiled his flesh. Paraded for many hours through Boston's two feet of snow, beaten, whipped, and finally dumped "like a log" at his home, where "his tarred flesh started to peel off in 'steaks.'"

Alan Taylor's *American Revolutions: A Continental History* (2016) hammers home the war's human costs. A Connecticut critic of the Continental Congress was tarred, carried to a sty, and covered with hog's dung, some of which was forced down his throat. Connecticut loyalists were imprisoned in a copper mine, in darkness 120 feet underground. Georgia patriots knocked a loyalist unconscious, "tied him to a tree, tarred his legs, and set them on fire" and then partially scalped him. Some courts ordered loyalists "branded on the face or cut off their ears" to make them recognizable.

This small, efficient new museum will stimulate public understanding by quickening interest in books like these. Its bookstore includes *The Last Muster*, a treasure of photographs displayed in the museum. They are of people who were born before the Revolution and lived to sit in front of cameras. An unquenchable dignity radiates from the visage of nattily dressed Caesar, who was born in 1737, and was owned as a slave by four generations of a New York family until his death in 1852, shortly before a new birth of freedom in our complicated country.

U. S. GRANT, AND THE WRITING OF HISTORY, RESCUED

November 5, 2017

WASHINGTON—Evidence of national discernment, although never abundant, can now be found high on the *New York Times* combined print and ebook best seller list. There sits Ron Chernow's biography of Ulysses Simpson Grant, which no reader will wish were shorter than its 1,074 pages. Arriving at a moment when excitable individuals and hysterical mobs are demonstrating crudeness in assessing historical figures, Chernow's book is a tutorial on measured, mature judgment.

It has been said that the best biographer is a conscientious enemy of his or her subject—scrupulous but unenthralled. Chernow, laden with honors for his biographies of George Washington and Alexander Hamilton, is a true friend of the general who did so much to preserve the nation. And of the unjustly maligned president—the only one between Andrew Jackson and Woodrow Wilson to serve two full consecutive terms. He nobly, if unsuccessfully, strove to prevent the war's brutal aftermath in the South from delaying, for a century, freedom's arrival there.

After reluctantly attending West Point and competently participating in the war with Mexico, his military career foundered on alcohol abuse exacerbated by the aching loneliness of a man missing his family. His civilian life was marred by commercial failures. Then the war came. Four years after he was reduced to selling firewood on St. Louis streets, he was leading the siege of Vicksburg. Six years after Vicksburg fell he was president.

And a good one. He was hopelessly naive regarding the rascality unleashed by the sudden postwar arrival of industrialism entangled with government. But the corruptions during his administration showed only his negligence, not his cupidity. More importantly, Grant, says Chernow, "showed a deep reservoir of courage in directing the fight against the Ku Klux Klan and crushing the largest wave of domestic terrorism in American history." He ranks behind only Abraham Lincoln and Lyndon Johnson as a presidential advancer of African-American aspirations.

After the presidency, he was financially ruined by his characteristic misjudgment of the sort of miscreants who abused his trust when he was president. His rescuer from the wreckage inflicted by a nineteenth century Madoff was Mark Twain, who got Grant launched on his memoirs. This taciturn, phlegmatic military man of few words, writing at a punishing pace during the agony of terminal cancer, produced the greatest military memoir in the English language, and the finest book published by any U.S. president.

Chernow is clear-eyed in examining and evenhanded in assessing Grant's defects. He had an episodic drinking problem but was not a problem drinker: He was rarely incapacitated, and never during military exigencies or when with Julia. Far from being an unimaginative military plodder profligate with soldiers' lives, he was by far the war's greatest soldier, tactically and strategically, and the percentage of casualties in his armies was, Chernow says, "often lower than those of many Confederate generals."

Sentimentality about Robert E. Lee has driven much disdain for Grant. Chernow's judgment about Lee is appropriately icy: Even after failing to dismember the nation he "remained a southern partisan" who "never retreated from his retrograde views on slavery."

Chernow's large readership (and the successes of such non-academic historians as Rick Atkinson, Richard Brookhiser, David McCullough, Nathaniel Philbrick, Jon Meacham, Erik Larson, and others) raises a question: Why are so many academic historians comparatively little read? Here is a hint from the menu of presentations at the 2017 meeting of the Organization of American Historians: The titles of thirty included some permutation of the word "circulation" (e.g., "Circulating/Constructing Heterosexuality," "Circulating Suicide as Social Criticism," "Circulating Tourism Imaginaries from Below"). Obscurantism enveloped in opacity is the academics' way of assigning themselves status as members of a closed clerisy indulging in linguistic fads. Princeton historian Sean Wilentz, who is impatient with academics who are vain about being unintelligible, confesses himself mystified by the "circulating" jargon. This speaks well of him.

Chernow leans against today's leveling winds of mindless egalitarianism—the belief that because greatness is rare, celebrating it is undemocratic. And against the populist tear-them-down rage to disparage. The political philosopher Harvey Mansfield, Harvard's conservative, says education should teach how to praise. How, that is, to recognize excellence of character when it is entwined, as it always is, with flaws. And how to acknowledge excellence of achievement amid the contingencies that always partially defeat good intentions. Chernow's *Grant* is a gift to a nation presently much in need of measured judgments about its past.

FREDERICK DOUGLASS, A CLASSICAL LIBERAL BORN AT SIXTEEN

February 1, 2018

WASHINGTON—It was an assertion of hard-won personal sovereignty: Frederick Douglass, born on a Maryland plantation 200 years ago this month, never knew on what February day because history-deprivation was inflicted to confirm slaves as non-persons. So, later in life, Douglass picked the fourteenth, the middle of the month, as his birthday. This February, remember him, the first African-American to attain historic stature.

In an inspired choice to write a short biography of this fierce defender of individualism, Washington's libertarian Cato Institute commissioned the Goldwater Institute's Timothy Sandefur, who says that Douglass was, in a sense, born when he was sixteen. After six months of being whipped once a week with sticks and rawhide thongs—arbitrary punishment was used to stunt a slave's dangerous sense of personhood—Douglass fought his tormentor. Sent to Baltimore, where he was put to work building ships—some of them slave transports—he soon fled north to freedom, and to fame as an anti-slavery orator and author. His 1845 *Narrative of the Life of Frederick Douglass* is, as Sandefur says, a classic of American autobiography.

Abolitionists such as William Lloyd Garrison said there should be "no union with slaveholders," preferring disunion to association with slave states. They said what the Supreme Court would say in its execrable 1857 *Dred Scott* decision—that the Constitution was a pro-slavery document. Douglass, however, knew that Abraham Lincoln knew better.

"Here comes my friend Douglass," exclaimed Lincoln at the March 4, 1865, reception following his second inauguration. After the assassination forty-two days later, Lincoln's widow gave Douglass her husband's walking stick. After Appomattox, Douglass, who had attended the 1848 Seneca Falls Convention on behalf of women's suffrage, said: "Slavery is not abolished until the black man has the ballot." If so, slavery ended not with the Thirteenth Amendment of 1865 but with the Voting Rights Act of 1965.

Douglass opposed radical Republicans' proposals to confiscate plantations and distribute the land to former slaves. Sandefur surmises that "Douglass was too well versed in the history and theory of freedom not to know" the importance of property rights. Douglass, says Sandefur, was not a conservative but a legatee of "the classical liberalism of the American founding." His individualism was based on the virtue of self-reliance. "He was not," Sandefur says, "likely to be attracted to any doctrine that subordinated individual rights—whether free speech or property rights—to the interests of the collective."

Although Douglass entered the post–Civil War era asking only that blacks at last be left to fend for themselves, he knew that "it is not fair play to start the Negro out in life, from nothing and with nothing." A twentieth-century Southerner agreed. In 1965, President Lyndon Johnson said: "You do not take a person who, for years, has been hobbled by chains and liberate him, bring him to the starting line of a race and then say, 'you are free to compete with all the others,' and still justly believe that you have been completely fair." As Martin Luther King Jr. knew: In 1965, he met Alabama sharecroppers who, having been paid all their lives in plantation scrip, had never seen U.S. currency. Peonage had followed slavery in sharecropper society.

By the time of Douglass's 1895 death, the nation was saturated with sinister sentimentality about the nobility of the South's Lost Cause: The war had really been about constitutional niceties—"states' rights"—not slavery. This, Sandefur says, was ludicrous: Before the war, Southerners "had sought *more* federal power, not less, in the form of nationwide enforcement of the Fugitive Slave Act and federal subsidies for slavery's expansion."

Nevertheless, in the South, monuments to Confederate soldiers were erected and Confederate symbols were added to states' flags. In the North, the University of Chicago's Charles Edward Merriam, a leading progressive, wrote in a widely used textbook that "from the standpoint of modern political science, the slaveholders were right" about some people not being entitled to freedom. As an academic, Woodrow Wilson paid "loving tribute to the virtues of the leaders of the secession, to the purity of their purposes." As president, he relished making *The Birth of a Nation*, a celebration of the Ku Klux Klan, the first movie shown in the White House.

Douglass died thirty years before 25,000 hooded Klansmen marched down Pennsylvania Avenue. That same year, Thurgood Marshall graduated from Baltimore's Frederick Douglass High School, en route to winning *Brown v. Board of Education*. Douglass, not Wilson, won the American future.

AN ILLINOIS POGROM

August 10, 2008

WASHINGTON—The *Oxford English Dictionary* dates the word "pogrom" from 1905, the year hundreds of Russian Jews were massacred in Odessa. In 1908, there was a pogrom of sorts in Illinois. It occurred in Springfield one hundred years ago this week. So, consider the phenomenon of progress, which at the moment seems more contingent than it did just a decade ago.

On the night of August 13, Mabel Hallam, a pretty young white woman whose husband, Earl, was working the night shift as a streetcar conductor, retired early. Around 11:30 p.m. she was awakened by a man's weight on her. "Why, Earl," she said, "what is wrong with you?" The man, who was not Earl and was black, said, "I am drunk." He raped her and fled. So she said.

"Negro's Heinous Crime" and "Dragged From Her Bed and Outraged by Negro" were the next day's headlines. As Jim Rasenberger reconstructs events in his fine book *America 1908*, police plucked black men from the streets of Hallam's neighborhood until she identified one, George Richardson, as her assailant. By five p.m. the jail was surrounded by a mob of at least 4,000 baying for blood. Eighty-nine blacks would be lynched in America in 1908.

Springfield's sheriff enlisted a leading citizen—owner of the city's largest restaurant, and of a fast automobile—to spirit Richardson and another black man also accused of rape out of town. This further inflamed the mob, which destroyed the restaurant—a white patron was killed by a stray bullet—piled its furnishings on the owner's overturned automobile, and burned the pile.

For the next six hours the rioters, fueled by liquor looted from the restaurant, sacked two black neighborhoods, setting fires and blocking fire wagons and cutting their hoses. Forty black homes were destroyed, as were twenty-one black and several Jewish businesses. Thousands of Springfield's blacks fled into the countryside; some never returned.

After beating an elderly black man and a paralyzed black man, at two a.m. the mob seized a fifty-six-year-old black barber from his home, beat him unconscious, hanged him from a tree, and mutilated his body. Souvenir hunters carved away bits of the tree, which was entirely gone by the end of the day.

The next night a mob of 500 brought a rope and proceeded to the home of a prominent and wealthy eighty-four-year-old black man who, standing in front of his house, inquired, "Good evening, gentlemen. What can I do for you?" He was beaten, slashed with a razor, hanged from a tree too supple to bear his weight. He was alive when troops from the state militia reached him. He died that night.

The next day's *New York Times* headline read:

"RIOTERS HANG ANOTHER NEGRO
   Mobs in Springfield, Ill., Defying 3,000 Soldiers,
   String Up Old and Innocent Victim"

One hundred seventeen rioters were indicted. One was fined twenty-five dollars for petty larceny; another, a teenager, was sent to a reformatory. Mrs. Hallam later admitted that she invented the attack to explain to her husband some bruises inflicted by her boyfriend.

Now, fast forward to ten years ago, when Americans were intoxicated by fumes from myriad triumphs. The Cold War had been won, the Gulf War had been a cakewalk, Russia was democratizing, China was locked in the logic of the Starbucks Postulate (give people a choice of coffees, and a choice of political parties will soon follow), and everyone was becoming rich with technology stocks. The exhaustion of various fighting faiths—fascism, communism, socialism—meant there was no remaining ideological rival to the American model for organizing a modern society. Few Americans anticipated aggression from people who despise modernity.

Today, Russia's government is despotism leavened by assassination, China will achieve universal emphysema before meaningful universal suffrage, and Americans, in a slough of despond about economic diffi-culties that have not yet even reached a recession, gloomily embrace an inversion of the Whig Theory of History, which holds, or once did, that progress—steadily enlarged and ennobled liberty—is the essence of the human story.

So, remember Springfield. The siege of the jail, the rioting, the lynching and mutilating all occurred within walking distance of where, in 2007, Barack Obama announced his presidential candidacy. What-ever you think of his apotheosis, it illustrates history's essential promise, which is not serenity—that progress is inevitable—but possibility, which is enough: Things have not always been as they are.

LET US NOW PRAISE PRESIDENT TAFT

May 27, 2018

WASHINGTON—No elaborate catechism is required to determine if someone is a conservative. A single question, as simple as it is infallible, suffices: For whom would you have voted in the presidential election of 1912?

That year, a former president and a future president ran against the incumbent president, who lost, as did the country, which would have been much better off giving another term to William Howard Taft. In-stead it got Woodrow Wilson and the modern imperial presidency that had been prefigured by Taft's predecessor and second major opponent in 1912, Theodore Roosevelt. Taft won fewer electoral votes (eight, from Utah and Vermont) than any other incumbent president; Roosevelt carried six states, Wilson forty.

Taft's presidency was bracketed by Roosevelt's and Wilson's, the progenitors of today's imperial presidency. Jeffrey Rosen, law professor at George Washington University and CEO of the National Consti-tution Center in Philadelphia, began writing his new appreciation of the twenty-seventh president (*William Howard Taft*, the latest in the series of slender books on "The American Presidents," now edited by Princeton historian Sean Wilentz) in January 2017, when the forty-fifth president began inadvertently doing something useful—validating nostalgia for Taft, whom Rosen calls "the only president to approach the office in constitutional terms above all."

Wilson was the first president to criticize the American founding, particularly for the separation of powers that crimps presidential supremacy. Roosevelt believed that presidents are free to do whatever the Constitution does not forbid. Taft's constitutional modesty held that presidents should exercise only powers explicitly granted by the document.

Romanticizers of Roosevelt ignore his belief that no moral equivalent of war could be as invigorating as the real thing, and they celebrate him as a trustbuster taming corporate capitalism and a pioneering environmentalist. Rosen notes, however, that Taft "extended federal environmental protection to more land than Roosevelt"—and he created ten national parks—"and brought more antitrust suits in one term than Roosevelt brought in nearly two." One of Roosevelt's excuses for trying to regain the presidency was that Taft, who in 1911 brought an antitrust action against U.S. Steel (world's first billion-dollar corporation, then producing a quarter of the world's steel), was too aggressive in trust-busting. Roosevelt thought that, in industry, big was beautiful (because efficiently Darwinian) if big government supervised it.

Taft signed the first revision of tariffs, which are regressive taxes, since the 1890s, when they were raised by an average of 57 percent. His tariff message to Congress was just 340 words because he thought the Constitution and traditional political practice allowed presidents to recommend, but not lobby for, congressional action. Such was his constitutional reticence, in his inaugural address he referred to tariff reform as "a suggestion only."

Taft unsuccessfully resisted President William McKinley's entreaties that he become governor of the Philippines ("I have never approved of keeping the Philippines"). Others wanted him to be president much more than he did. His aspiration, achieved after the presidency, was to be chief justice of the United States. As a reluctant president, he demonstrated that reluctance, which is vanishingly rare, is a recommendation for the office.

In 1912, Roosevelt's "New Nationalism" promised populism rampant and a plebiscitary presidency untethered from constitutional inhibitions: "I don't think that any harm comes from the concentration of powers in one man's hands." And "I believe in pure democracy," the purity being unmediated, unfiltered public opinion empowered even to overturn state court decisions by referendums. This galvanized Taft's determination to resist Roosevelt ("my closest friend") in the name of judicial independence. Taft had vetoed the legislation admitting New Mexico and Arizona to statehood because the latter's constitution provided for the recall of judicial decisions. Arizona removed this quintessentially populist provision—then restored it once safely inside the Union.

Taft correctly compared Roosevelt to the first populist president (whose portrait would be hung in the Oval Office in 2017 by a populist president): "There is a decided similarity between Andrew Jackson and Roosevelt. He had the same disrespect for law when he felt the law stood between him and what he thought was right to do."

The 1912 strife between conservative and progressive-populist Republicans simmered until Ronald Reagan's election in 1980 sealed conservatism's ascendancy in the party. This lasted thirty-six years, until it was supplanted by its antithesis, populism, 104 years after Taft resisted Roosevelt. This, for a while, prevented America from having only a populist Republican Party to oppose a progressive Democratic Party—an echo, not a choice.

AMERICA'S DARK HOME FRONT DURING WORLD WAR I

April 9, 2017

> "War is the health of the state. It automatically sets in motion throughout society those irresistible forces for uniformity, for passionate cooperation with the government in coercing into obedience the minority groups and individuals which lack the larger herd sense."
>
> —Randolph Bourne (1886–1918)

WASHINGTON—One hundred years ago, two events three days apart set the twentieth century's trajectory. On April 9, 1917, in Zurich, Vladimir Lenin boarded a train. Germany expedited its passage en route to Saint Petersburg—known as Leningrad from 1924 to 1991—expecting him to exacerbate Russia's convulsions, causing Russia's withdrawal from World War I, allowing Germany to shift forces to the Western Front. Lenin boarded the train three days after the United States, responding to Germany's unrestricted submarine warfare and other provocations, declared war. Soon 2 million Americans would be in Europe. They, and the promise of many more, compelled Germany to accept an armistice at the eleventh hour of the eleventh day of the eleventh month of 1918.

Monday night and the next two nights, PBS's *American Experience* will present a six-hour documentary, "The Great War." Watch it and wince. It covers familiar diplomatic and military events, before and after America's bloodiest battle, the Meuse-Argonne Offensive, in which American fatalities averaged 550 a day for forty-seven days.

Woodrow Wilson imposed and incited extraordinary repressions: "There are citizens of the United States...born under other flags...who have poured the poison of disloyalty into the very arteries of our national life....Such creatures of passion, disloyalty and anarchy must be crushed out.... They are infinitely malignant, and the hand of our power should close over them."

His Committee on Public Information churned out domestic propaganda instructing the public how to detect pro-German sympathies. A twenty-two-year-old Justice Department official named J. Edgar Hoover administered a program that photographed, fingerprinted, and interrogated 500,000 suspects. Local newspapers published the names of people who were not buying war bonds or otherwise supporting the war. People were fired or ostracized for insufficient enthusiasm. The Espionage Act of 1917 made it a crime to "collect, record, publish or communicate" information useful to the enemy.

In Illinois, Robert Prager, a German-American coal miner suspected of spying, was stripped, marched through the streets, and hanged. The *Washington Post* deplored such "excesses" but applauded the "healthful and wholesome awakening in the interior part of the country."

Josef Hofer and his two brothers were South Dakota Hutterites whose faith forbade any involvement in war, including wearing a military uniform. They were arrested in March 1918, and a week after the armistice they were sent to Fort Leavenworth, Kansas. Arriving at the military prison around midnight, they stood naked for hours in a seventeen-degree November night. Then they were suspended naked from the bars of their cells, their feet barely touching the ground, refusing to wear the uniforms left in their cells. Fed only bread and water, after two weeks David Hofer was allowed to telegraph to Josef's wife, telling her that her husband was dying. He died the morning after she arrived. Prison guards mocked his corpse by dressing it in a uniform.

The U.S. military was the world's seventeenth largest in April 1917, smaller (less than 250,000) than Romania's, and smaller than Britain's casualties in one battle. America's military became a melting pot for a nation in which one-third of the population had been born abroad or whose parents had been. Forty-three languages were spoken in one Army division raised in New York. One group was ineligible for melting. Printed at the bottom of draft registration cards were these words: "If person is of African descent, tear off this corner."

The African-Americans from around the nation who joined New York's 15th National Guard Regiment, the Harlem Hellfighters, included Leroy Johnston from Phillips County, Arkansas. He spent nine months in French hospitals recuperating from wounds suffered in the Meuse-Argonne, then in 1919 returned to an Arkansas seething with fears of an African-American insurrection because a returning African-American veteran had formed a union of black sharecroppers. The narrator of "The Great War" says that as groups of white men "roamed the countryside, killing hundreds of black people, a train pulled into the station. A crowd rushed aboard and dragged out four unsuspecting black men. They were Leroy Johnston and his three brothers." After a melee, "the mob shot the Johnston brothers to pieces."

The war unleashed a flu pandemic that killed more people in a year—somewhere between 20 million and 50 million—than the war killed in four years. The flu's victims included Randolph Bourne.

THE SOMME: THE HINGE OF WORLD WAR I, AND HENCE OF MODERN HISTORY

June 30, 2016

> "See that little stream? We could walk to it in two minutes. It took the British a month to walk to it—a whole empire walking very slowly, dying in front and pushing forward behind."
> —F. Scott Fitzgerald, *Tender Is the Night*

WASHINGTON—The walk began at 7:30 a.m., July 1, 1916, when British infantry advanced toward German trenches. In the first hours, eight British soldiers fell per second. By nightfall 19,240 were dead; another 38,230 were wounded. World War I, the worst manmade disaster in human experience, was the hinge of modern history. The war was the incubator of Communist Russia, Nazi Germany, World War II, and innumerable cultural consequences. The hinge of this war was the battle named for "that little stream," the river Somme.

The scything fire of machine guns could not be nullified even by falling curtains of metal from creeping artillery barrages that moved in advance of infantry. Geoff Dyer, in *The Missing of the Somme*, notes: "By the time of the great battles of attrition of 1916–1917 mass graves were dug in advance of major offenses. Singing columns of soldiers fell grimly silent as they marched by these gaping pits en route to the front-line trenches."

William Philpott's judicious assessment in *Three Armies on the Somme: The First Battle of the Twentieth Century* is that the Somme was "the cradle of modern combat," proving that industrial war could only be won by protracted attrition. And hence by the new science of logistics. The thirty-one trains a day required to supply the British at the Somme became seventy when the offensive began. The romance of chivalric warfare died at the Somme, which was what the Germans called *Materialschlacht*, a battle of materials more than men. Geographic objectives—land seized—mattered less than the slow exhaustion of a nation's material and human resources, civilians as well as soldiers.

In the next world war, the distinction between the front lines and the home front would be erased. In 1918, Randolph Bourne, witnessing the mass mobilization of society, including its thoughts, distilled into seven words the essence of the twentieth century: "War is the health of the state." Relations between government, the economy, and the individual were forever altered, to the advantage of government.

Military necessity is the most prolific mother of invention, and World War I was, Philpott writes, "a war of invention," pitting "scientific-industrial complexes" against each other: "Gas, flame-throwers, grenade-launchers, sub-machine guns, trench mortars and cannon, fighter and bomber aircraft, tanks and self-propelled artillery all made their battle-field debuts between 1914 and 1918."

Attritional war had begun in earnest at Verdun, which occupies in France's memory a place comparable to that of the Somme in British memory. And the Somme offensive was begun in part to reduce pressure on Verdun and to demonstrate that Britain was bearing its share of the war's burden.

In December 1915, Winston Churchill, then forty-one, said, "In this war the tendencies are far more important than the episodes. Without winning any sensational victories we may win this war." The war itself may have been begun by a concatenation of blunders, but once begun it was worth winning, and the Somme, this "linear siege" (Philpott), set the tendency for that. Germany, trying to slow the trans-Atlantic flow of matériel, resorted to unrestricted submarine warfare, which, five months after the Somme ended, brought the United States into the war and, in a sense, into the world.

Thomas Hardy's description of the 1813 Battle of Leipzig—"a miles-wide pant of pain"—fit the battle of the Somme, where a soldier wrote, "From No Man's Land…comes one great groan." The Somme ended on November 18, with men drowning in glutinous lakes of clinging mud sometimes five feet deep. This was the war that British poet Rupert Brooke had welcomed as God's gift to youth awakened from sleeping, "as swimmers into cleanness leaping." By November a million men on both sides were dead—72,000 British and Commonwealth bodies were never recovered—or wounded. Twenty-two miles of front had been moved six miles.

But because of this battle, which broke Germany's brittle confidence, the war's outcome was discernible. Not so its reverberations, one of which was an Austrian corporal whose Bavarian unit deployed to the Somme on October 2. Adolf Hitler was wounded on his third day in the line.

The battle of the Somme is, in Dyer's words, "deeply buried in its own aftermath." As is Europe, still.

PROHIBITION'S UNINTENDED CONSEQUENCES

July 8, 2010

WASHINGTON—The evening of January 16, 1920, hours before Prohibition descended on America, while the young assistant secretary of the Navy, Franklin Roosevelt, drank champagne in Washington with other members of Harvard's class of 1904, in Norfolk, Virginia, evangelist Billy Sunday preached to 10,000 celebrants: "The reign of tears is over. The slums will soon be only a memory..." Not exactly.

Daniel Okrent's darkly hilarious *Last Call: The Rise and Fall of Prohibition* recounts how Americans abolished a widely exercised private right—and condemned the nation's fifth-largest industry—in order to make the nation more Heavenly. Then all Hell broke loose. Now that ambitious government is again Hell-bent on improving Americans—from how they use salt to what light bulbs they use—Okrent's book is a timely tutorial on the law of unintended consequences.

The ship that carried John Winthrop to Massachusetts in 1630 also carried, Okrent reports, 10,000 gallons of wine and three times more beer than water. John Adams's morning eye-opener was a tankard of hard cider; James Madison drank a pint of whiskey daily; by 1830, adult per capita consumption was the equivalent of ninety bottles of eighty-proof liquor annually.

Although whiskey often was a safer drink than water, Americans, particularly men, drank too much. Women's Prohibition sentiments fueled the movement for women's rights—rights to hold property independent of drunken husbands; to divorce those husbands; to vote for politicians who would close saloons. So the United States Brewers' Association officially opposed women's suffrage.

Women campaigning for sobriety did not intend to give rise to the income tax, plea bargaining, a nationwide crime syndicate, Las Vegas, NASCAR (country boys outrunning government agents), a redefined role for the federal government, and a privacy right—the "right to be let alone"—that eventually was extended to abortion rights. But they did.

By 1900, per capita consumption of alcohol was similar to today's, but mere temperance was insufficient for the likes of Carry Nation. She was "six feet tall, with the biceps of a stevedore, the face of a prison warden, and the persistence of a toothache," and she wanted Prohibition. It was produced by the sophisticated tenacity of the Anti-Saloon League, which at its peak was spending the equivalent of 50 million of today's dollars annually. Okrent calls it "the mightiest pressure group in the nation's history." It even prevented redistricting after the 1920 census, the first census to reveal that America's urban—and most wet—population was a majority.

Before the Eighteenth Amendment could make drink illegal, the Sixteenth Amendment had to make the income tax legal. It was needed because by 1910 alcohol taxes were 30 percent of federal revenues.

Workmen's compensation laws gave employers an interest in abstemious workers. Writes Okrent, Asa Candler, founder of the Coca-Cola Company, saw "opportunity on the other side of the dry rainbow." World War I anti-German fever fueled the desire to punish brewers with names like Busch, Pabst, Blatz, and Schlitz. And President Woodrow Wilson's progressivism became a wartime justification for what Okrent calls "the federal government's sudden leap into countless aspects of American life," including drink.

And so Prohibition came. Sort of. Briefly.

After the first few years, alcohol consumption dropped only 30 percent. Soon smugglers were outrunning the Coast Guard ships in advanced speedboats, and courts inundated by violations of Prohibition began to resort to plea bargains to speed "enforcement" of laws so unenforceable that Detroit became known as the City on a Still.

Prohibition agents cherished $1,800 jobs because of the bribes that came with them. Fiorello La Guardia taunted the government that it would need "150,000 agents to watch the first 150,000." Exemptions from Prohibition for church wine and medicinal alcohol became ludicrously large—and lucrative—loopholes.

After thirteen years, Prohibition, by then reduced to an alliance between evangelical Christians and criminals, was washed away by "social nullification"—a tide of alcohol—and by the exertions of wealthy people like Pierre du Pont, who hoped that the return of liquor taxes would be accompanied by lower income taxes. (They were.) Ex-bootleggers found new business opportunities in the southern Nevada desert. And in the Second World War, draft boards exempted brewery workers as essential to the war effort.

The many lessons of Okrent's story include: In the fight between law and appetite, bet on appetite. And: Americans then were, and let us hope still are, magnificently ungovernable by elected nuisances.

WHEN AMERICA REACHED PEAK STUPIDITY

June 30, 2019

> Wide open and unguarded stand our gates,
> And through them presses a wild motley throng...
> O Liberty, white Goddess! is it well
> To leave the gates unguarded?
> —Thomas Bailey Aldrich (1892)

WASHINGTON—If you think we have reached peak stupidity—that America's per-capita quantity has never been higher—there is solace, of sorts, in Daniel Okrent's guided tour through the immigration debate that was heading toward a nasty legislative conclusion a century ago. *The Guarded Gate: Bigotry, Eugenics, and the Law That Kept Two Generations of Jews, Italians, and Other European Immigrants Out of America* provides evidence that today's public arguments are comparatively enlightened.

Late in the nineteenth century, immigration surged, as did alarm about it, especially in society's upper crust, particularly its Boston portion, which thought that the wrong sort of people were coming. Darwinian theory and emerging genetic science were bowdlerized by bad scientists, faux scientists, and numerous philistine ax-grinders with political agendas bent on arguing for engineering a better stock of American humans through immigration restrictions and eugenics—selective breeding.

Their theory was that nurture (education, socialization, family structure) matters little because nature is determinative. They asserted that even morality and individuals' characters are biologically determined by race. And they spun an imaginative taxonomy of races, including European "Alpine," "Teutonic" (aka "Nordic"), and "Mediterranean" races.

Racist thinking about immigration saturated mainstream newspapers (the *Boston Herald*: "Shall we permit these inferior races to dilute the thrifty, capable Yankee blood...of the earlier immigrants?") and elite journals (in the *Yale Review*, recent immigrants were described as "vast masses of filth" from "every foul and stagnant pool of population in Europe"). In the *Century* monthly, which published Mark Twain, Henry James, Rudyard Kipling, W. E. B. Du Bois, and H. G. Wells, an author informed readers that "Mediterranean people are morally below the races of northern Europe," that immigrants from Southern Italy "lack the conveniences for thinking," that Neapolitans were a "degenerate" class "infected with spiritual hookworm" and displaying "low foreheads, open mouths, weak chins…and backless heads," and that few of the garment workers in New York's Union Square "had the type of face one would find at a county fair in the west or south." The nation's most important periodical, the *Saturday Evening Post*, devoted tens of thousands of words to the braided crusades for eugenics and race-based immigration policies. Popular poet Edgar Lee Masters (*Spoon River Anthology*) wrote "The Great Race Passes":

> *On State Street throngs crowd and push,*
> *Wriggle and writhe like maggots.*
> *Their noses are flat,*
> *Their faces are broad…*

Eugenics was taught at Boston University's School of Theology. Theodore Roosevelt, who popularized the phrase "race suicide," wrote to a eugenicist that "the inescapable duty of the good citizen of the right type is to leave his or her blood behind him in the world, and that we have no business to permit the perpetuation of citizens of the wrong type." Woodrow Wilson warned against the "corruption of foreign blood" and "ever-deteriorating" genetic material.

Amateur ethnologists conveniently discovered that exemplary southern Europeans (Dante, Raphael, Titian, Leonardo da Vinci) were actually from the north. One wrote, "Columbus, from his portraits and from his busts, *whether authentic or not*, was clearly Nordic." (Emphasis added.) Okrent writes: "In an Alabama case, a black man who married an Italian woman was convicted of violating the state's anti-miscegenation law, then found surprising absolution when the conviction was vacated by an appellate court's provocative declaration: 'The mere fact that the testimony showed this woman came from Sicily can in no sense be taken as conclusive evidence that she was therefore a white woman.'"

The canonical text of the immigration-eugenics complex, Madison Grant's *The Passing of the Great Race*, is available today in at least eight editions and is frequently cited in the Internet's fetid swamps of white supremacy sites. At the 1946 Nuremberg "Doctors' Trial," Nazi defendants invoked that book as well as the U.S. Supreme Court's *Buck v. Bell* decision upholding states' sterilization of "defectives" (Justice Oliver Wendell Holmes, a eugenics enthusiast: "Three generations of imbeciles are enough") and America's severely restrictive Immigration Act of 1924. It based national quotas on 1890 immigration data—before the surge of the "motley throng." Okrent writes, "These men didn't say they were 'following orders,' in the self-exonerating language of the moment; they said they were following Americans."

Four years before the 1924 act, 76 percent of immigrants came from Eastern or Southern Europe. After it, 11 percent did. Some of those excluded went instead to Auschwitz.

"TELL THAT TO MRS. COOLIDGE"

February 14, 2013

WASHINGTON—Before Ronald Reagan traveled the sixteen blocks to the White House after his first inaugural address, the White House curator had, at the new president's instruction, hung in the Cabinet room a portrait of Calvin Coolidge. The Great Communicator knew that "Silent Cal" could use words powerfully—fifteen of them made him a national figure—because he was economical in their use, as in all things.

Were Barack Obama, America's most loquacious president (699 first-term teleprompter speeches), capable of learning from someone with whom he disagrees, he would profit from Amity Shlaes's biography *Coolidge*, whom she calls "our great refrainer" with an "aptitude for brevity," as when he said, "Inflation is repudiation." She says that under his "minimalist" presidency, he "made a virtue of inaction." As he said, "It is much more important to kill bad bills than to pass good ones." During the sixty-seven months of his presidency, the national debt, the national government, the federal budget, unemployment (3.6 percent), and even consumer prices shrank. The GDP expanded 13.4 percent.

In 1898, at twenty-six, he won his first of ten public offices, a seat on the City Council of Northampton, Massachusetts. Like Reagan, Coolidge benefited from being underestimated: The letter of reference he carried to Boston when elected to Massachusetts's General Assembly said, "Like the singed cat, he is better than he looks." Tougher, too. During the chaos of the 1919 Boston police strike, Governor Coolidge electrified the nation with these fifteen words: "There is no right to strike against the public safety by anybody, anywhere, any time."

Nine months later, Republican leaders in the famous "smoke-filled room" in Chicago's Blackstone Hotel decided to nominate for president Ohio Senator Warren Harding, whose dreadful rhetoric ("not nostrums, but normalcy…not surgery, but serenity") drove H. L. Mencken to rhapsodies of disgust: "It reminds me of a string of wet sponges; it reminds me of tattered washing on the line; it reminds me of stale bean soup, of college yells, of dogs barking idiotically through endless nights." The convention produced a rhetorically balanced ticket by stampeding for Coolidge as vice president. He wrote to his father: "I hope you will not mind."

Harding was a reprobate with bad judgment about friends but good instincts about policy. The former produced unpleasantness about Naval Petroleum Reserve Number 3, aka Wyoming's Teapot Dome. The latter produced prosperity.

When Harding died in August 1923, Coolidge had not seen him since March, but the new president, assisted by a splendidly named former congressman, C. Bascom Slemp, continued Harding's program of cutting taxes, tariffs, and expenditures. "I am for economy. After that I am for more economy," said the thirtieth president, whose administration's pencil policy was to issue one at a time to each bureaucrat, who if he or she did not entirely use it up had to return the stub. Coolidge and Treasury Secretary Andrew Mellon advocated "scientific taxation," an early iteration of the supply-side economics theory that often lowering rates will stimulate the economy so that the government's revenue loss will be much less than the taxpayers' gain. Soon Coolidge was alarmed that economic growth was producing excessive revenues that might make government larger.

He met his wife, the vivacious Grace, after hearing her laughter when she saw through a window him shaving while wearing a hat. Shlaes's biography would be even more engaging had she included this oft-repeated anecdote:

When President and Mrs. Coolidge were being given simultaneous but separate tours of a chicken farm, Grace asked her guide whether the rooster copulated more than once a day. "Dozens of times," she was told. "Tell that to the president," she said. When told, Coolidge asked, "Same hen every time?" When the guide said, "A different one each time," the president said: "Tell that to Mrs. Coolidge."

In 1924, after the lingering illness and death of his sixteen-year-old son from blood poisoning, Coolidge demonstrated—if only our confessional culture could comprehend this—the eloquence of reticence: "When he was suffering he begged me to help him. I could not."

Coolidge, says Shlaes, thought his office "really was one of 'president,' literally one who presided." And "the best monument to his kind of presidency was no monument at all." This absence, however, is a kind of admonitory presence for him who said, "It is a great advantage to a president, and a major source of safety to the country, for him to know he is not a great man." The 1933 funeral service for this man of brevity lasted twenty-two minutes.

1940: WHEN THE REPUBLICAN
ESTABLISHMENT MATTERED

June 19, 2016

WASHINGTON—Months before the 1940 Republican convention nominated Wendell Willkie, Alice Roosevelt Longworth, Theodore Roosevelt's waspish daughter, said that Willkie's support sprang "from the grass roots of a thousand country clubs." There actually was a Republican establishment in 1940, when GOP elites created a nominee ex nihilo.

According to Charles Peters's book *Five Days in Philadelphia*, three months before the convention, Willkie registered zero percent in polls measuring public sentiment about potential Republican nominees. This was not surprising: He was a businessman—president of Commonwealth & Southern Corporation, the nation's largest electric utility holding company—who had given substantial support to Franklin Roosevelt in 1932. Willkie had never sought public office and had not registered as a Republican until late 1939 or early 1940.

And he was not an isolationist regarding European events. Eighty percent of Americans were more or less isolationist, as were the three strongest Republican candidates—Ohio Senator Robert Taft, Michigan Senator Arthur Vandenberg, and New York prosecutor Thomas Dewey, just thirty-eight but favored by 60 percent in early 1940 polls. Herbert Hoover hoped a deadlocked convention would turn to him.

The Republicans' "Eastern establishment," however, was interventionist to the extent of favoring aid to Britain. The adjective "Eastern" was superfluous: Two-thirds of Americans lived east of the Mississippi (California's population was under 7 million) and the South was solidly Democratic.

The Republican establishment had power and the will to exercise it. As the convention drew near, "Willkie Clubs" suddenly sprouted like dandelions, but not spontaneously. Their growth was fertilized by Oren

Root, a lawyer with the Manhattan law firm of Davis, Polk, Wardwell, Gardner & Reed, whose clients included the J. P. Morgan banking empire. Root began seeking support for Willkie with a mailing to Princeton's class of 1924 and Yale's class of 1925. Another close Willkie adviser was Thomas Lamont, chairman of the board of J. P. Morgan & Co. Root's uncle Elihu had been a U.S. senator and Theodore Roosevelt's secretary of war. By opposing his friend TR's bid to defeat President William Howard Taft for the 1912 Republican nomination, Elihu Root helped to rescue the country from having both parties devoted to progressivism.

One of the few politicians among Willkie's early backers was Sam Pryor, Republican national committeeman, whom the candidate met at the Greenwich Country Club, naturally. Willkie's top adviser was Russell Davenport, managing editor of Henry Luce's *Fortune* magazine, which together with *Time* and *Life* made Luce, an ardent interventionist, a mass media power unlike anyone before or since. The April issue of *Fortune* was almost entirely devoted to praise of Willkie. *Look* magazine, second only to *Life* in importance, chimed in, as did *Reader's Digest*, which had the nation's largest magazine circulation.

On April 9, Dewey won a second of the few primaries—and Hitler invaded Norway and Denmark, with Belgium, Holland, and France soon to follow. Willkie said he would vote for FDR over a Republican opposed to aiding Britain and France.

Willkie, "the barefoot boy from Wall Street," cultivated an Indiana aura but had become a Manhattan fixture, and by 1937 his criticism of the New Deal had *Fortune* applauding his "presidential stature," and the letters column of the *New York Herald Tribune*, the Republican establishment's house organ, concurred. In May, the *Atlantic Monthly* carried a Willkie essay, in June it was the *Saturday Evening Post*'s turn. In July, *Time* featured a celebratory cover story on him. Madison Avenue titans of advertising—Bruce Barton of BBDO and John Young of Young and Rubicam—joined the effort. Root would have a meeting for Willkie, "under the clock at the Biltmore," followed by another at the University Club or Century Club. Between May 8 and June 21, Willkie's support rose from 3 percent to 29 percent.

Willkie also was lucky: In May, the Taft man in charge of tickets had a stroke and was replaced by a Willkie man who would pack the gallery with raucous Willkie supporters, including a Yale law student named Gerald Ford. The *Herald Tribune* endorsed Willkie in its first front-page editorial, and tens of thousands of pro-Willkie telegrams inundated delegates in one day. Delegates heard from their hometown bankers, who had heard pro-Willkie instructions from New York bankers. He won on the sixth ballot.

Willkie's nomination neutralized much Republican opposition to FDR's war preparations and was crucial to the narrow congressional approval of conscription. Willkie lost the election, but the coming war would be won. Time was, party establishments had their uses.

AMERICA'S LAST MASS LYNCHING

June 7, 2020

WASHINGTON—Back in the day, post-lynching souvenir hunting— fragments from the hanging tree; victims' body parts—was a hobby for some. A student who found a victim's tooth at Moore's Ford Bridge in July 1946 gave it to his girlfriend for her charm bracelet. The past really is another country.

On July 25, 1946, Roger Malcom, a black twenty-four-year-old, was released from jail on bail after the charge against him was reduced from murder to attempted murder because the white man he had stabbed during an altercation was going to live. Malcom, his wife, and another black couple were being driven home by the white farmer who had posted the bail, and who before the lynching was heard to say, "All these damn [N-word] been to the army and come back and think themselves something." The car was stopped by more than twenty armed white men, none of them masked, at the bridge over the Apalachee River about sixty miles from Atlanta. The mob evidently planned to murder only Malcom until his wife called out the name of someone in the mob, which then took both couples to the riverbank and shot them all at least sixty times.

The South was simmering in 1946, as nearly half a million African-American soldiers returned to the region with uniforms, decorations, and attitudes dangerous to social norms of subjugation. On February 12, Sergeant Isaac Woodard Jr. was blinded by a South Carolina police chief who slammed his nightstick into Woodard's eyes, news of which horrified President Harry Truman. On February 25, a veteran's insufficient deference ignited a riot that destroyed the black business district in Columbia, Tennessee.

On May 9 in Georgia, the Ku Klux Klan staged a mass cross-burning on Stone Mountain. After a 1944 U.S. Supreme Court decision overturning all-white primaries, black Georgians were eligible to vote on July 17, and Eugene Talmadge, who bragged of flogging his black farm workers, was campaigning (successfully) for a fourth term as governor, warning that if he lost, white politicians would henceforth have to "go to [blacks'] homes and knock on their doors with hat in hand, shake hands with all of them, and kiss the babies."

FBI agents questioned 2,790 locals in the Moore's Ford killings, filled 10,000 pages of investigative reports, and issued 106 subpoenas to a December grand jury (twenty-one white men; two black men). It concluded: "We have been unable to establish the identity of any person" in that mob of undisguised men who called one another by their names, and whose leader, according to the driver of the car, said, "Git them women. Bring 'em over here. They know too much."

This story, or as much of it as can presently be known, is meticulously told in *Fire in a Canebrake: The Last Mass Lynching in America* (2003) by Laura Wexler, who picked up the baton of the late historian Anthony Pitch. Wexler is supporting the effort of Joseph J. Bell, a New Jersey lawyer, to make public the only extant information about this atrocity: the grand jury records. In 2017, a federal court ruled that those records should be unsealed. In March, however, the U.S. Court of Appeals for the Eleventh Circuit held that federal courts have no authority over district courts' supervision of grand jury proceedings. There is, however, disagreement among the circuits, so there will be an appeal to the Supreme Court.

Government secrecy is essential to protect the sources, methods, and fruits of intelligence-gathering, and to facilitate deliberative processes. But all government secrecy is, as Daniel Patrick Moynihan said, regulation. Most regulations tell us what we cannot do; secrecy tells us what we cannot know. Regarding Moore's Ford, we cannot know about the social dynamics that obstructed justice in the most lurid crime in the year that lit the fuse that blew up Jim Crow.

In 2011, Attorney General Eric Holder's Justice Department recommended amending the Federal Rules of Criminal Procedure "to allow district courts to permit the disclosure, in appropriate circumstances, of archival grand-jury materials of great historical significance." The reasons for grand jury secrecy are compelling, Holder said, but "do not forever trump all competing considerations." And "most other categories of historically significant federal records, including classified records, eventually become part of the public historical record."

Today, Bell, Wexler, and others ask about the Moore's Ford lynching: When is a cold case that should be, but is not, part of our national memory too cold to learn more about? Their correct answer: never.

A YEAR IN U.S. HISTORY AS DISRUPTIVE AS 2020

July 26, 2020

"War, like every other human ailment, tends to leave the body politic folded along ancient creases and festering old sores."

—W. E. B. Du Bois

WASHINGTON—Few Americans have memories of the only year in U.S. history comparable to 2020 for sudden and comprehensive disruption of Americans' lives. To place today's myriad social traumas and dislocations in perspective, read Tracy Campbell's *The Year of Peril: America in 1942*.

Pearl Harbor had catapulted the nation into total war when just two years earlier its army was smaller than Portugal's, and its population was so ravaged by malnutrition and negligible health care during the Depression that half of the Army's first recruits were deemed unfit. The armed forces—and blood supplies—would remain racially segregated, although in 1940 President Franklin D. Roosevelt had told civil rights leader A. Philip Randolph that African Americans could be musicians on Navy ships "because they're darned good at it."

The saccharine myth that "everything changed" in a nation united by the sense of "all being in this together" was belied by lynchings and violent killings, such as that in Sikeston, Missouri, of an African American accused of assaulting a white woman.

After he was tied by his feet to a truck and dragged to his death, the local newspaper said this would "protect the wives of soldier boys." When some black soldiers in Oklahoma City were forced to ride on segregated trains for twenty-four hours without food while white soldiers were fed, an indignant FBI Director J. Edgar Hoover investigated the African American who reported this. In the epicenter of the Arsenal of Democracy, aka Detroit, rioting, gun-toting whites persuaded the city to rethink integration of public housing.

In California, General John "A Jap Is a Jap" DeWitt said of the 112,000 Japanese Americans on the West Coast, "There are indications these are organized and ready for concerted operation." The indications were the absence of indications. This, DeWitt said, indicated secret plotting, so these Americans were sent to concentration camps. Including Fred Korematsu, who had tried to enlist. His challenge to internment reached the Supreme Court, where he lost. In 2018, the court repudiated this decision.

In 1942, in New Haven, Connecticut, Anne Miller, having developed a blood infection after a miscarriage, became the first person successfully treated with penicillin. By 1945, U.S. pharmaceutical companies were producing 650 billion units of it a month.

In 2020, vilification of such companies has paused, presumably to be resumed after they find a COVID-19 vaccine.

In 1942, the War Production Board banned cuffs and pleats on men's trousers to save cloth. Daylight saving time became a national law in order to save 736 million kilowatt hours of electricity. Rationing of gasoline, automobile tires, sugar, coffee, and much else impended, but Congress, which never misses an opportunity to miss the point, voted itself pensions. After two months of hearing the vox of an unamused populi, it repealed them.

Tracy Campbell, a University of Kentucky historian, says that in 1942 the War Rumor Project "began systematically monitoring Americans," relying on "barbers, bartenders, doctors, hairdressers, police officers, and drugstore owners to eavesdrop on their neighbors." Many rumors arose from preexisting prejudices: A poll found that 42 percent of Americans thought "Jews have too much power and influence."

When a foolhardy regent suggested canceling the University of Georgia's football season, Governor Eugene Talmadge (D) said that before doing that, they would try "putting our debutantes to hoeing potatoes." The Bulldogs won the national championship.

Seventy-eight years later, some football factories, aka universities, might be more apt to have football Saturdays than weekday classes.

Few debutantes but many other women powered war production in places such as Ford's plant in Willow Run, Michigan, which eventually assembled a B-24 bomber every hour. An economic "stabilization" law partially exempted health benefits from restrictions on "wages," thereby decisively shaping today's health-care system, which is centered on employer-provided insurance.

In 1942's off-year elections, the president's party took a drubbing. James Farley, former chairman of the Democratic Party, said: "The American people just got a little tired of being pushed around."

Disrupting crises can be history's accelerants. In January 1942, in the Philippines, the U.S. Army conducted the last mounted cavalry charge in U.S. history. In December, beneath the University of Chicago's football stands, there occurred the first sustained nuclear chain reaction, a harbinger of nuclear weapons.

On New Year's Eve, FDR watched a not-yet-released movie, *Casablanca*. Eleven days later, he became the first president to leave the country during wartime, going to meet Winston Churchill in Casablanca.

THE PERVERSE FECUNDITY OF A PERFECT FAILURE

September 15, 2013

WASHINGTON—At four a.m. on January 1, 1959, an hour when there never were commercial flights from Havana, David Atlee Phillips was lounging in a lawn chair there, sipping champagne after a New Year's Eve party, when a commercial aircraft flew low over his house. He surmised that dictator Fulgencio Batista was fleeing because Fidel Castro was arriving. He was right. Soon he, and many others, would be spectacularly wrong about Cuba.

According to Jim Rasenberger's history of the Bay of Pigs invasion, *The Brilliant Disaster*, Phillips was "a handsome 37-year-old former stage actor" who "had been something of a dilettante before joining the CIA." There, however, he was an expert. And in April 1960, he assured Richard Bissell, the CIA's invasion mastermind, that within six months radio propaganda would produce "the proper psychological climate" for the invasion to trigger a mass Cuban uprising against Castro.

The invasion brigade had only about 1,400 members but began its members' serial numbers at 2,500 to trick Castro into thinking it was larger. Castro's 32,000-man army was supplemented by 200,000 to 300,000 militia members. U.S. intelligence was ignorant of everything from Castro's capabilities to Cuba's geography to Cubans' psychology.

Fifty-two years and many misadventures later, the invasion still fascinates as, in historian Theodore Draper's description, "one of those rare events in history—a perfect failure." It had a perverse fecundity.

It led to President John Kennedy's decision to demonstrate toughness by deepening U.S. involvement in Vietnam. Rasenberger writes that three weeks after the April 1961 invasion, Kennedy sent Vice President Lyndon Johnson to Saigon: "Johnson's assignment was to deliver a message to [South Vietnam's President Ngo Dinh] Diem that the United States intended to fully support the South Vietnamese effort to beat the Communists." (Thirty months later, the United States was complicit in the military coup—regime change—in which Diem was murdered.) The Bay of Pigs led to Nikita Khrushchev's disdainful treatment of Kennedy at the June summit in Vienna, and to Khrushchev being emboldened to put missiles in Cuba.

In 1972, the Bay of Pigs made a cameo appearance in the Watergate shambles, which involved some Cubans and Americans active in the invasion. On the June 23 "smoking gun" Oval Office tape, Richard Nixon directs his aide H. R. Haldeman to urge the CIA to tell the FBI to back off from investigating the burglary by saying, "Look, the problem is that this will open the whole Bay of Pigs thing."

Surely this "thing" should be studied as deeply as possible. Unfortunately, the CIA, which you might think had made every mistake possible regarding the invasion, is now making another. It is resisting attempts to force the release of the fifth and final volume of its official history of it.

This autumn, a federal appeals court is expected to hear arguments about disclosing the document written in 1981 by CIA historian Jack Pfeiffer, who retired in 1984 and died in 1997. The National Security Archive, a private research institution and library, is arguing that no important government interest is served by the continuing suppression of a thirty-two-year-old report about a fifty-two-year-old event.

The CIA admits that the volume contains only a small amount of still-classified information. It argues, however, that it should be covered by the "deliberative process privilege" that makes it exempt from release under the Freedom of Information Act. The argument is that, for some unclear reason, release of this volume, unlike the release of the first four volumes, would threaten the process by which the CIA's histories are written. Supposedly candid histories will not be written if the writers know that, decades later, their work will become public.

This unpersuasive worry—an excuse for the selective censorship of perhaps embarrassing scholarship—is surely more flimsy than the public's solid interest in information. And the government's interest.

In his 1998 book *Secrecy: The American Experience*, Senator Daniel Patrick Moynihan argued that secrecy makes government stupid by keeping secrets from itself. Information is property and government agencies hoard it. For example, in the 1940s, U.S. military code breakers read 2,900 communications between Moscow and its agents in America. So, while the nation was torn by bitter disagreements about whether Alger Hiss and the Rosenbergs committed espionage, the military *knew* they had. But it kept the proof from other parts of the government, *including President Harry Truman.*

America needs all the caution its history of misadventures—a record recently enriched by Syria—should encourage. Since the Bay of Pigs, caution has been scarcer than information justifying it.

THE TRANSFORMATION OF A MURDER, AND OF LIBERALISM

October 10, 2013

> "Ex-Marine Asks Soviet Citizenship"
> —*Washington Post* headline, November 1, 1959
> (concerning Lee Harvey Oswald)

> "He didn't even have the satisfaction of being killed for civil rights. It's—it had to be some silly little Communist."
> —Jacqueline Kennedy, November 22, 1963

WASHINGTON—She thought it robbed his death of any meaning. But a meaning would be quickly manufactured to serve a new politics. First, however, an inconvenient fact—Oswald—had to be expunged from the story. So, just twenty-four months after the assassination, Arthur

Schlesinger Jr., the Kennedys' kept historian, published a thousand-page history of the thousand-day presidency without *mentioning* the assassin.

The transformation of a murder by a marginal man into a killing by a sick culture began instantly—before Kennedy was buried. The afternoon of the assassination, Chief Justice Earl Warren ascribed Kennedy's "martyrdom" to "the hatred and bitterness that has been injected into the life of our nation by bigots." The next day, James Reston, the *New York Times* luminary, wrote in a front-page story that Kennedy was a victim of a "streak of violence in the American character," but especially of "the violence of the extremists on the right."

Never mind that adjacent to Reston's article was a *Times* report on Oswald's communist convictions and associations. A Soviet spokesman, too, assigned "moral responsibility" for Kennedy's death to "Barry Goldwater and other extremists on the right."

Three days after the assassination, a *Times* editorial, "Spiral of Hate," identified Kennedy's killer as a "spirit": The *Times* deplored "the shame all America must bear for the spirit of madness and hate that struck down" Kennedy. The editorialists were, presumably, immune to this spirit. The new liberalism-as-paternalism would be about correcting other people's defects.

Hitherto a doctrine of American celebration and optimism, liberalism would now become a scowling indictment: Kennedy was killed by America's social climate whose sickness required "punitive liberalism." That phrase is from James Piereson of the Manhattan Institute, whose 2007 book *Camelot and the Cultural Revolution: How the Assassination of John F. Kennedy Shattered American Liberalism* is a profound meditation on the reverberations of the rifle shots in Dealey Plaza.

The bullets of November 22, 1963, altered the nation's trajectory less by killing a president than by giving birth to a destructive narrative about America. Fittingly, the narrative was most injurious to the narrators. Their recasting of the tragedy in order to validate their curdled conception of the nation marked a ruinous turn for liberalism, beginning its decline from political dominance.

Punitive liberalism preached the necessity of national repentance for a history of crimes and misdeeds that had produced a present so poisonous that it murdered a president. To be a liberal would mean being a scold. Liberalism would become the doctrine of grievance groups owed redress for cumulative inherited injuries inflicted by the nation's tawdry history, toxic present, and ominous future.

Kennedy's posthumous reputation—Americans often place him, absurdly, atop the presidential rankings—reflects regrets about might-have-beens. To reread Robert Frost's banal poem written for Kennedy's inauguration ("A golden age of poetry and power of which this noon-day's the beginning hour") is to wince at its clunky attempt to conjure an Augustan age from the melding of politics and celebrity that the Kennedys used to pioneer the presidency-as-entertainment.

Under Kennedy, liberalism began to become more stylistic than pro-grammatic. After him—especially after his successor, Lyndon Johnson, a child of the New Deal, drove to enactment the Civil Rights Acts, Medicare, and Medicaid—liberalism became less concerned with mate-rial well-being than with lifestyle, and cultural issues such as feminism, abortion, and sexual freedom.

The bullets fired on November 22, 1963, could shatter the social consensus that characterized the 1950s only because powerful new forces of an adversarial culture were about to erupt through society's crust. Foremost among these forces was the college-bound population bulge—baby boomers with their sense of entitlement and moral superiority, vanities encouraged by an intelligentsia bored by peace and prosperity and hungry for heroic politics.

Liberalism's disarray during the late 1960s, combined with Americans' recoil from liberal hectoring, catalyzed the revival of conservatism in the 1970s. As Piereson writes, the retreat of liberalism from a doctrine of American affirmation left a void that would be filled by Ronald Reagan seventeen years after the assassination.

The moral of liberalism's explanation of Kennedy's murder is that there is a human instinct to reject the fact that large events can have small, squalid causes; there is an intellectual itch to discern large hidden meanings in events. And political opportunism is perennial.

JFK: NOT SO ELUSIVE

November 21, 2013

> What he was, he was:
> What he is fated to become
> Depends on us.
>
> —W. H. Auden, "Elegy for JFK" (1964)

BOSTON—He has become fodder for an interpretation industry toiling to make his life malleable enough to soothe the sensitivities and serve the agendas of the interpreters. The quantity of writing about him is inversely proportional to the brevity of his presidency.

He did not have history-shaping effects comparable to those of his immediate predecessor or successor. Dwight Eisenhower was one of three Americans (with George Washington and Ulysses Grant) who were world-historic figures before becoming president, and Lyndon Johnson was second only to Franklin Roosevelt as a maker of the modern welfare state and second to none in using law to ameliorate America's racial dilemma.

The *New York Times*'s executive editor calls Kennedy "the elusive president"; the *Washington Post* calls him "the most enigmatic" president. Most libidinous, certainly; most charming, perhaps. But enigmatic and elusive? Many who call him difficult to understand seem eager to not understand him. They present as puzzling or uncharacteristic aspects of his politics about which he was consistent and unambiguous. For them, his conservative dimension is an inconvenient truth. Ira Stoll, in *JFK, Conservative*, tries to prove too much but assembles sufficient evidence that his book's title is not merely provocative.

A *Look* magazine headline in June 1946 read: "A Kennedy Runs for Congress: The Boston-bred scion of a former ambassador is a fighting-Irish conservative." Neither his Cold War anti-communism, which was congruent with President Harry Truman's, nor his fiscal conservatism changed dramatically during his remaining seventeen years.

Visitors to the Kennedy Presidential Library and Museum here, on the salt water across which his ancestors came as immigrants and on which he sailed his yacht, watch Kennedy press conferences, such as that of September 12, 1963, when, responding to a question about Vietnam, he said his policy was to "win the war there"—"That is why some 25,000 Americans have traveled 10,000 miles to participate in that struggle." He added: "We are not there to see a war lost." His answer was consistent with a 1956 speech calling Vietnam "the keystone to the arch, the finger in the dike," adding: "This is our offspring—we cannot abandon it."

A few years later, with the war going badly, several Kennedy aides claimed that he had been planning to liquidate the intervention. But five months after the assassination, Robert Kennedy told an oral history interviewer that his brother "had a strong, overwhelming reason for being in Vietnam and that we should win the war in Vietnam."

Interviewer: "There was never any consideration given to pulling out?"
RFK: "No."
Interviewer: "The president was convinced that we had to keep, had to stay in there…"
RFK: "Yes."
Interviewer: "…And couldn't lose it."
RFK: "Yes."

As president, JFK chose as treasury secretary a Republican Wall Street banker, C. Douglas Dillon, who thirty years after the assassination remembered Kennedy as "financially conservative." Kennedy's fiscal policy provided an example and ample rhetoric for Ronald Reagan's supply-side tax cuts. Kennedy endorsed "a creative tax cut creating more jobs and income and eventually more revenue." In December 1962, he said:

The federal government's most useful role is…to expand the incentives and opportunities for private expenditures.…It is a paradoxical truth that tax rates are too high today and tax revenues are too low and the soundest way to raise the revenues in the long run is to cut the rates now.

John Kenneth Galbraith—Harvard economist, liberal polemicist, and Kennedy's ambassador to India—called this "the most Republican speech since McKinley." It was one of many. Kennedy was driving to the Dallas Trade Mart to propose "cutting personal and corporate income taxes." Kennedy changed less during his life than liberalism did after his death.

The Kennedy library here where he lived draws substantially fewer visitors than does Dallas's Sixth Floor Museum at Dealey Plaza, where he was murdered. This is emblematic of a melancholy fact: How he died looms larger in the nation's mind than how he lived. His truncated life remains an unfinished book and hence a temptation to writers who would complete it as they wish it had been written. This month, let it suffice to say what Stephen Spender did in "The Truly Great" (1932):

> Born of the sun, they travelled a short while toward the sun.
> And left the vivid air signed with their honour.

VIETNAM: SQUANDERED VALOR

October 18, 2018

WASHINGTON—Early in his Marine Corps career, which he concluded as a four-star general, Walt Boomer was decorated for valor in Vietnam. He distilled into three words the lesson of that debacle: "Tell the truth." Max Hastings, an eminent British journalist and historian, has done that in a book that is a painful but perhaps inoculating re-immersion in what Americans would prefer to forget.

Vietnam: An Epic Tragedy, 1945–1975 is a product of Hastings's prodigious research and his aptitude for pungent judgments. It is an unsparing look, by a warm friend of America, at the mountain of mendacities, political and military, that accumulated as the nation learned the truth of the philosopher Michael Oakeshott's axiom: "To try to do something which is inherently impossible is always a corrupting enterprise."

Vietnam remains an American sorrow of squandered valor, but it was vastly more a tragedy for the Vietnamese, 2 million to 3 million of whom died during the thirty years' war—around forty for every American who died during the ten years of intense U.S. futility. U.S. statesmen and commanders, Hastings writes, lied too much to the nation and the world but most calamitously to themselves.

In 1955, Hastings writes, Secretary of State John Foster Dulles sent a cable to Saigon authorizing the removal of South Vietnam's Prime Minister Ngo Dinh Diem, "much as he might have ordered the sacking of an unsatisfactory parlor maid." Six hours later, Dulles changed his mind, so Diem lived until he was murdered in the 1963 coup authorized by John Kennedy. Hastings's tangy writing tells us that as the coup approached, a U.S. operative arrived at the South Vietnamese army's headquarters "carrying a .357 revolver and $40,000 in cash, which he deemed the appropriate fashion accessories for an afternoon's work overthrowing a government."

"Old Ho [Chi Minh] can't turn that down," said Lyndon Johnson of his offer to buy North Vietnam out of the war with $1 billion for a Mekong River dam. America's president fit part of Graham Greene's description of the title character in the novel set in Saigon, *The Quiet American*: "I never knew a man who had better motives for all the trouble he caused" and who was "impregnably armored by his good intentions and his ignorance." Except Johnson's intentions were often self-serving.

In 1964, he unnecessarily sacrificed truth and, as an eventual result, young men to achieve a forty-four-state landslide, which was won three months after confusions compounded by lies produced the Tonkin Gulf Resolution's limitless authorization for war-making. Eight years later, Richard Nixon twisted military strategy, diplomacy, and the truth for domestic political advantage—while cruising to a forty-nine-state romp.

Soldiers and Marines died because their M16 rifles were given to malfunctioning in combat. The manufacturer's response was what Hastings calls "a barrage of lies," with which the Army was complicit.

Almost every Hastings page contains riveting facts, such as these about the French, whose Indochina miseries preceded America's: "While they abolished the old custom of condemning adulteresses to be trampled to death by elephants…opium consumption soared after the colonial power opened a Saigon refinery."

Eddie Adams's Pulitzer Prize–winning photograph of Saigon's police chief shooting a Viet Cong in the head during the 1968 Tet Offensive seemed to validate some Americans' sympathies for the enemy. Hastings casts a cold eye, noting that the Viet Cong was in civilian clothes and had just cut the throats of a South Vietnamese officer, his wife, their six children, and the officer's eighty-year-old mother.

Hastings's detailed reports of battles—a few famous ones; others unremembered except by participants on both sides, some of whom Hastings tracked down—are as successful as printed words can be in achieving his aim of answering the question "What was the war *like?*" "This," says Hastings, "was a 'Groundhog Day' conflict, in which contests for a portion of elephant grass, jungle, or rice paddy were repeated not merely month after month, but year upon year." America's inevitable failure there might, however, with Hastings's help, prevent America from having a "Groundhog Day" foreign policy.

A history book can be a historic act if, by modifying a nation's understanding of its past, it alters future behavior. Obviously Vietnam itself was insufficiently instructive. On page 752, the book's concluding words are General Boomer's: "It bothers me that we didn't learn a lot. If we had, we would not have invaded Iraq." Sometimes, contrary to Marx, history repeats itself, first as tragedy, then not as farce but as tragedy again.

NOT AN ILLNESS, A VACCINE

September 17, 2017

WASHINGTON—Many Americans' moral vanity is expressed nowadays in their rage to disparage. They are incapable of measured judgments about past politics—about flawed historical figures who were forced by cascading circumstances to make difficult decisions on the basis of imperfect information. So, the nation now needs an example of how to calmly assess episodes fraught with passion and sorrow. An example arrives Sunday night.

For ten nights on PBS, Ken Burns and Lynn Novick's *The Vietnam War*, ten years in the making and eighteen hours in length, tells the story of a war "begun in good faith by decent people, out of fateful misunderstandings," and "prolonged because it seemed easier to muddle through than admit that it had been caused by tragic decisions" during five presidencies. The combat films are extraordinary; the recollections and reflections of combatants and others on both sides are even more so, featuring photos of them then and interviews with many of them now.

A 1951 photo shows a congressman named John Kennedy dining in Saigon. There is an interview with Le Quan Cong, who became a guerilla fighter in 1951, at age twelve. Viewers will meet Madame Le Minh Khue, who was sixteen when she joined the "Youth Shock Brigade for National Salvation": "I love Hemingway. I learned from *For Whom the Bell Tolls*. Like the resourcefulness of the man who destroys the bridge. I saw how he coped with war, and I learned from that character." As did another combatant who loves that novel, John McCain.

Eleven years after his Saigon dinner, President Kennedy said, "We have not sent combat troops in the generally understood sense of the word." Obliqueness and evasions greased the slide into a ground war of attrition. Kennedy, his successor (who said, "Foreigners are not like the folks I'm used to"), and their advisers were determined not to make the Munich mistake of confronting an enemy tardily. Tapes of Lyndon Johnson's telephone conversations with advisers are haunting and horrifying. To national security adviser McGeorge Bundy: "What the hell am I ordering [those kids] out there for?"

In 1966 alone, eighteen large-scale U.S. offensives left more than 3 million South Vietnamese—approximately one-fifth of the country's population—homeless. Just on the Laos portion of the Ho Chi Minh Trail, more tons of bombs—3 million tons—were dropped than fell on Germany and Japan during World War II. By body counts, America was winning. As an Army adviser says in episode four, "If you can't count what's important, you make what you can count important."

Vincent Okamoto earned in Vietnam the Army's second-highest honor, the Distinguished Service Cross. He recalls the platoon he led:

> Nineteen-, 20-year-old high school dropouts…they looked upon military service as like the weather: you had to go in, and you'd do it. But to see these kids, who had the least to gain, there wasn't anything to look forward to.…And yet, their infinite patience, their loyalty to each other, their courage under fire.…You would ask yourself, "How does America produce young men like this?"

Or like Okamoto. He was born during World War II in Arizona, in a Japanese-American internment camp. Karl Marlantes, a Rhodes Scholar from Yale who voluntarily left Oxford for Marine service in Vietnam, recalls a fellow lieutenant radioing to battalion headquarters over twenty kilometers away the fact that he had spotted a convoy of trucks. The battalion commander replied that this was impossible because intelligence operatives reported no trucks near there. In a Texas drawl the lieutenant replied: "Be advised. I am where I am and you are where you are. Where I am, I see goddamned trucks."

Weary of hearing the prudence that was so painfully learned in Indochina derided as the "Vietnam syndrome," Marlantes says (in his *Wall Street Journal* review of Mark Bowden's book *Hue 1968*): "If by Vietnam syndrome we mean the belief that the U.S. should never again engage in (a) military interventions in foreign civil wars without clear objectives and a clear exit strategy, (b) 'nation building' in countries about whose history and culture we are ignorant, and (c) sacrificing our children when our lives, way of life, or 'government of, by, and for the people' are not directly threatened, then we should never get over Vietnam syndrome. It's not an illness; it's a vaccination." The Burns-Novick masterpiece is, in Marlantes's words about Bowden's book, "a powerful booster shot."

HAUNTED BY HUE

August 3, 2017

> One day [Marine Theodore Wallace] saw an officer casually aim
> his rifle and try to shoot a Vietnamese boy in the distance.
> "Sir, what are you doing?" he'd asked.
> "He's probably supplying the [North Vietnamese Army]," the
> officer said. "What's he doing out here anyway?"
> "It's his country!" said Wallace.
> —Mark Bowden, *Hue 1968: A Turning Point of the American
> War in Vietnam*

WASHINGTON—As Vietnam's 1968 Tet holiday approached, General William Westmoreland, commander of U.S. forces there, cabled the Joint Chiefs in Washington that he had a plan. He would serenade, perhaps into dissolution, the communist forces that he was certain would concentrate on attacking U.S. forces based at Khe Sanh near the demilitarized zone:

> The Vietnamese youth is quite sentimentally disposed toward his family, and Tet is a traditional time for intimate family gatherings. The Vietnamese PSY War [Psychological Warfare] people have recently written a highly sentimental Tet song which is recorded. The Vietnamese say it is a tear-jerker to the extent that they do not want it played to their troops during Tet for fear their desertion rate will skyrocket. This is one of the records we will play to the North Vietnamese soldiers in the Khe Sanh-Con Thien areas during Tet.

This surreal nugget is from Mark Bowden's magnificent and meticulous history, which tells, with excruciating detail, a story that is both inspiring and infuriating. His subtitle is an understatement. As the epicenter of North Vietnam's Tet offensive throughout South Vietnam, the swift capture of Hue, the country's third-largest city, by communist forces—and of the twenty-four days of ferocious fighting that expelled them—became a hinge of American history. A month later, President Lyndon Johnson announced he would not seek re-election in an America where opposition to the war and trust in the government were moving inversely.

After the battle's first day, January 31, Westmoreland told Washington that the enemy had about 500 men in Hue's Citadel. "He was," Bowden writes, "off by a factor of 20." So it went with U.S. intelligence. A few months earlier, Walt Rostow, Johnson's national security adviser, had told a Hue-bound reporter on "deep background" that the war was essentially already won because a crop called "IR8 rice" was going to stymie the communists' revolution with a green revolution. Rostow's theory was slain by this fact: The Vietnamese disliked the taste of IR8 rice.

The communists arriving in Hue immediately began advancing the revolution by purging "enemies of the people" in what quickly became an orgy of violent score-settling. While Westmoreland remained fixated on Khe Sanh—"Never," writes Bowden, "had a general so effectively willed away the facts"—a secret U.S. planning group met in Okinawa the day after the offensive began to consider a plan, code-named Fractured Jaw, involving tactical nuclear weapons. Westmoreland said these were not needed "in the present situation."

Bowden's interviews, almost half a century on, with those who fought, on both sides, have produced unexampled descriptions of small-unit combat. The communists' many months of large-scale infiltration and preparation were matched by their military skills. "To a man," Bowden writes, "the American veterans I interviewed told me they had faced a disciplined, highly motivated, skilled and determined enemy. To characterize them otherwise is to diminish the accomplishment of those who drove them out of Hue." In June 1968, Westmoreland was relieved of his command.

What Bowden calls "one of the great shots in the annals of combat photography" is of a U.S. tank in Hue draped with dead and wounded

Marines. None were identified. Until, more than four decades later, Bowden found that the eighteen-year-old with a hole in his chest, who looked "dead, or nearly so," was Alvin Bert Grantham from Mobile, Alabama, whose story Bowden tells.

During house-to-house fighting, Marine Eden Jimenez was clearing rooms—tossing in grenades, then spraying the room with bullets—in one of which he found a tall wardrobe that he had riddled. In it was a mortally wounded woman holding a rifle and a baby. Bowden writes: "When he was an old man, living in Odessa, Texas, he still wondered almost every day about that woman and child....Who was she? How would he have felt if he had killed the baby, too?"

Hue, like the war that pivoted there, continues to haunt some elderly men who live among us. And the war's legacy lives in Americans' diminished trust in government. Since 1968, trust has not risen to pre-Vietnam levels.

APOLLO 11: A CAP TOSSED OVER THE WALL

July 18, 2019

WASHINGTON—Thirty months after setting the goal of sending a mission 239,000 miles to the moon, and returning safely, President John Kennedy cited a story the Irish author Frank O'Connor told about his boyhood. Facing the challenge of a high wall, O'Connor and his playmates tossed their caps over it. Said Kennedy, "They had no choice but to follow them. This nation has tossed its cap over the wall of space." Kennedy said this on November 21, 1963, in San Antonio. The next day: Dallas.

To understand America's euphoria about the moon landing fifty years ago, remember fifty-one years ago: 1968 was one of America's worst years—the Tet Offensive in Vietnam, Martin Luther King Jr. and Robert Kennedy assassinated, urban riots. President Kennedy's May 25, 1961, vow to reach the moon before 1970 came forty-three days after Soviet cosmonaut Yuri Gagarin became the first person to enter outer space and orbit the Earth, and thirty-eight days after the Bay of Pigs debacle. When Kennedy audaciously pointed to the moon, America had only sent a single astronaut on a fifteen-minute suborbital flight.

Kennedy's goal was reckless, and exhilarating leadership. Given existing knowledge and technologies, it was impossible. But Kennedy said the space program would "serve to organize and measure the best of our energies and skills." It did. The thrilling story of collaborative science and individual daring is told well in HBO's twelve-part *From the Earth to the Moon*, and PBS's three-part *Chasing the Moon*, and in the companion volume with that title, by Robert Stone and Alan Andres, who write:

> The American effort to get to the moon was the largest peacetime government initiative in the nation's history. At its peak in the mid-1960s, nearly 2% of the American workforce was engaged in the effort to some degree. It employed more than 400,000 individuals, most of them working for 20,000 different private companies and 200 universities.

The "space race" began as a Cold War competition, military and political. Even before *Sputnik*, the first orbiting satellite, jolted Americans' complacency in 1957 (ten days after President Dwight Eisenhower sent paratroopers to Little Rock's Central High School), national security was at stake in the race for rockets with ever-greater thrusts to deliver thermonuclear warheads with ever-greater accuracy.

By 1969, however, the Soviet Union was out of the race to the moon, a capitulation that anticipated the Soviets' expiring gasp, two decades later, when confronted by the technological challenge of Ronald Reagan's Strategic Defense Initiative. By mid-1967, a majority of Americans no longer thought a moon landing was worth the expense.

But it triggered a final flaring of postwar confidence and pride. "The Eagle has landed" came as defiant last words of affirmation, at the end of a decade that, Stone and Andres note, had begun with harbingers of a coming culture of dark irony and satire: Joseph Heller's novel *Catch-22* (1961) and Stanley Kubrick's film *Dr. Strangelove* (1964).

Photos of Earth taken from the moon were said to herald a global sense of humanity's common destiny. Osama bin Laden was twelve in 1969.

Stone and Andres say *Apollo 11* was hurled upward by engines burning "15 tons of liquid oxygen and kerosene per second, producing energy equal to the combined power of 85 Hoover Dams." People spoke jauntily of "the conquest of space." Well.

The universe, 99.9 (and at least fifty-eight other nines) percent of which is already outside Earth's atmosphere, is expanding (into we know not what) at forty-six miles per second per megaparsec. (One megaparsec is approximately 3.26 million light years.) Astronomers are studying light that has taken perhaps 12 billion years to reach their instruments. This cooling cinder called Earth, spinning in the darkness at the back of beyond, is a minor speck of residue from the Big Bang, which lasted less than a billionth of a trillionth of a trillionth of a second 13.8 billion years ago. The estimated number of stars—they come and go—is 100 followed by twenty-two zeros. The visible universe (which is hardly all of it) contains more than 150 billion galaxies, each with billions of stars. But if there were only three bees in America, the air would be more crowded with bees than space is with stars. The distances, and the violently unheavenly conditions in "the heavens," tell us that our devices will roam our immediate cosmic neighborhood, but in spite of *Apollo 11*'s still-dazzling achievement, we are not really going anywhere.

THE THUNDERCLAP OF OCEAN VENTURE '81

August 12, 2018

WASHINGTON—Scholars have already debated for decades, and will debate for centuries, the role U.S. policies—military, diplomatic, economic—played in bringing the Cold War to endgame and the Soviet

Union to extinction. One milestone was Ronald Reagan's 1983 Strategic Defense Initiative proposal, a technological challenge that could not be met by a Soviet economy already buckling under the combined weight of military spending and socialism's ignorance. But before SDI there was Ocean Venture '81, initiated by Reagan as president-elect.

The protracted strategy, of which this enormous operation—fifteen nations' navies, 250 ships, more than 1,000 aircraft—was a harbinger, came to be referred to by some Soviets as the "Lehman strategy." In *Oceans Ventured: Winning the Cold War at Sea*, John Lehman, a Navy aviator who was secretary of the Navy during Reagan's first six years, explains the Navy's role in the "forward strategy" that implemented Reagan's Cold War policy. Reagan explained the policy when asked about it in 1977: "We win and they lose, what do you think of that?"

Among Reagan's early actions—in addition to reinstating the MX missile and B-1 bomber programs that President Carter had suspended—was to increase by 11 percent Carter's fiscal 1981 Navy budget, and increasing by 15 percent the fiscal 1982 request. By 1980, there was rough nuclear parity, and the Soviets, with 280 divisions, had superiority of land forces. Reagan campaigned on building the U.S. Navy to 600 ships and using it for purposes beyond merely keeping sea lanes open to deliver supplies for land forces.

Those purposes included signaling U.S. confidence and ambition— what Lehman calls a "combat-credible forward naval presence"—in order to ratchet up psychological pressure on Soviet leaders. So, in the autumn of Reagan's first year, Ocean Venture '81 surged U.S. naval power into what the Soviet Union had considered its maritime domain, especially the Norwegian and Barents Seas. (And eventually under the Arctic ice pack, where the Soviets had hoped to hide nuclear ballistic missile submarines.) By dispersing Ocean Venture '81 ships when Soviet satellites were overhead, the arrival of a large flotilla in northern waters was an unnerving surprise for Moscow.

This "transformative" operation, Lehman writes, "came as a thunder-clap to the Soviets, who had never seen such a NATO exercise on their northern doorstep…In preceding years," he says, "during the hopeful pursuit of detente and arms control by Presidents Ford and Carter, such robust NATO activity would have been unthinkable, as provocative to the Soviets." Provocation was a risk worth running, but a real risk:

"The Soviets were particularly fearful of being attacked under cover of a forward U.S. exercise. Why? Because their own doctrine was to use military exercises to mask surprise invasions," as with Poland in 1981. Soviet doctrine's "central concept was a high-speed offensive launched [against NATO] under the cover of military exercises in East Germany and Czechoslovakia."

Lehman says that in 1986, with Mikhail Gorbachev inching crabwise toward acknowledging the Soviet Union's terminal sclerosis, "the most delicate period of the Reagan naval strategy began." Reagan would continue to deploy and demonstrate the multiplying American military proficiencies, but would avoid a triumphalism that might provoke an anti-Gorbachev coup by the humiliated Soviet military.

By the end of 1986, with the Soviets having learned that they could not interfere with U.S. aircraft carriers operating in Norwegian fjords, the Soviet general staff told Gorbachev that they could not defend the nation's northern sector without tripling spending on naval and air forces there. Thus did the Cold War end because Reagan rejected the stale orthodoxy that the East-West military balance was solely about conventional land forces in central Europe, so NATO's sea power advantage was of secondary importance.

Today's naval problems posed by a rising China, particularly in the South China Sea, are unlike the problem of hastening the Soviet decline. Today's U.S. ships are more capable than ever, but too few for comfort, as Lehman's reader will realize when they consider what only the Navy can do.

In the movie *A Few Good Men*, a furious Colonel Nathan Jessup (Jack Nicholson) exclaimed to his courtroom tormentors—Navy officers— words that are actually true regarding almost all civilians in this age of complex professional military establishments configured for myriad and rapidly evolving threats: "You have no idea how to defend a nation." Lehman's book is a rare window on that world, and a validation of the axiom that if you want peace, prepare for war.

"THIS IS GOING TO BE DIFFICULT"

March 11, 2018

"The war is over."
—Secretary of Defense Donald Rumsfeld in Afghanistan
(April 2002)

"I believe victory is closer than ever before."
—Vice President Mike Pence in Afghanistan (December 2017)

WASHINGTON—With metronomic regularity, every thousand days or so, Americans should give some thought to the longest war in their nation's history. The war in Afghanistan, which is becoming one of the longest in world history, reaches its six-thousandth day on Monday, when it will have ground on for substantially more than four times longer than U.S. involvement in World War II from Pearl Harbor to V-J Day (1,346 days).

America went to war in Afghanistan because that not-really-governed nation was the safe haven from which al-Qaeda planned the 9/11 attacks. It was not mission creep but mission gallop that turned the intervention into a war against the Taliban who had provided, or at least not prevented, the safe haven. So, the United States was on a mission opposed by a supposed ally next door—Pakistan, which through Directorate S of its intelligence service has supported the Taliban.

This fascinating, if dispiriting, story is told in Steve Coll's new book *Directorate S: The CIA and America's Secret Wars in Afghanistan and Pakistan*. There cannot be many secrets about this subject that are not in Coll's almost 700 pages.

He reports when General Stanley McChrystal went to Afghanistan in May 2002, "A senior Army officer in Washington told him, 'Don't build [Bondsteels],' referring to the NATO base in [Kosovo] that Rumsfeld saw as a symbol of peacekeeping mission creep. The officer warned McChrystal against 'anything here that looks permanent....We are not staying long.' As McChrystal took the lay of the land, 'I felt like we were high-school students who had wandered into a Mafia-owned bar.'" It has been a learning experience. After blowing up tunnels, some almost as long as a football field, that were thought to be created by and for terrorists, U.S. officials learned that they were an ancient irrigation system.

A decade ago, seven years after the war began on October 7, 2001, then–Secretary of Defense Robert Gates said the U.S. objective was the creation of a strong central government. When he was asked if Afghanistan had ever had one, he answered without hesitation: "No." Which is still true.

Years have passed since the time when, years into the war, U.S. military and civilian officials heatedly debated "counterinsurgency" as contrasted with "counterterrorism," distinctions that now seem less than crucial. Coll says of military commanders rotating in and out of Afghanistan annually, "The commanders starting a rotation would say, 'This is going to be difficult.' Six months later, they'd say, 'We might be turning a corner.' At the end of their rotation, they would say, 'We have achieved irreversible momentum.' Then the next command group coming in would pronounce, 'This is going to be difficult...'" The earnestness and valor that Americans have brought to Afghanistan are as heartbreaking as they are admirable.

For seventy-three years, U.S. troops have been on the Rhine, where their presence helped win the Cold War and now serves vital U.S. interests as Vladimir Putin ignites Cold War 2.0. Significant numbers of U.S. troops have been in South Korea for sixty-eight years, and few people are foolish enough to doubt the usefulness of this deployment, or to think that it will or should end soon. It is conceivable, and conceivably desirable, that U.S. forces will be in Afghanistan, lending intelligence, logistical, and even lethal support to that nation's military and security forces for another 1,000, perhaps 6,000, days.

It would, however, be helpful to have an explanation of U.S. interests and objectives beyond vice presidential boilerplate about how "We will see it through to the end." And (to U.S. troops) how "the road before you is promising." And how the president has "unleashed the full range of American military might." And how "reality and facts and a relentless pursuit of victory will guide us." And how U.S. forces have "crushed the enemy in the field" (or at least "put the Taliban on the defensive") in "this fight for freedom in Afghanistan," where Bagram Airfield is "a beacon of freedom." If the U.S. objective is freedom there rather than security here, or if the theory is that the latter somehow depends on the former, the administration should clearly say so and defend those propositions, or liquidate this undertaking that has, so far, cost about $1 trillion and 2,200 American lives.

HOME TO HENRY WRIGHT'S FARM

September 1, 2013

> "The saviors come not home tonight: Themselves they could not save."
> —Lines from A. E. Housman, scribbled in a soldier's diary

WASHINGTON—On October 27, 1947, thousands of caskets were unloaded from a ship in New York. The bodies of soldiers from the European theater, writes Rick Atkinson, "then traveled by rail in a great diaspora across the republic for burial in their hometowns." Three young men, killed between the Battle of the Bulge in December 1944 and April 1945 in Germany two weeks before the war in Europe ended, were destined for Henry Wright's Missouri farm:

> Gray and stooped, the elder Wright watched as the caskets were carried into the rustic bedroom where each boy had been born. Neighbors kept vigil overnight, carpeting the floor with roses, and in the morning they bore the brothers to Hilltop Cemetery for burial side by side side beneath an iron sky.

Atkinson's *The Guns at Last Light*, the completion of his trilogy on the liberation of Western Europe, is history written at the level of literature. If, as a U.S. infantryman wrote, "No war is really over until the last veteran is dead," the war has not ended: About 400 World War II veterans, almost half a battalion, are dying each day. Spend the shank end of summer with Atkinson's tribute to all who served and suffered.

Western Europe was, Atkinson stresses, just one cauldron: "The Red Army suffered more combat deaths at Stalingrad alone than the U.S. armed forces did in the entire war." But "for magnitude and unalloyed violence, the battle in the Ardennes"—the Battle of the Bulge—"was unlike any seen before in American history." The 600,000 Americans who fought in the Ardennes were four times the number of Union and Confederate soldiers at Gettysburg.

Atkinson's story is propelled by vivid descriptions and delicious details. Britain before D-Day "was steeped in heavy smells, of old smoke and cheap coal and fatigue." General Lucian Truscott "possessed what one staff officer called a 'predatory' face, with protruding gray eyes and gapped incisors set in a jut jaw built to scowl." Field Marshall Bernard Montgomery chaffed under General Dwight Eisenhower's command: "Subordination held little appeal for a solipsist." Soldiers visited Picasso in his Paris studio where Hemingway, who ghostwrote love letters for some soldiers, "had left behind a box of grenades." Churchill, whose thoughts encompassed millennia past and future, ordered German rocket sites on the French side of the English Channel destroyed so the French could not use them "if they fall out of temper with us." Some of the 6 billion propaganda leaflets dropped over Germany drifted as far as Italy. Jewish soldiers in the chaos of the Bulge hammered out the "H"—for "Hebrew"—on their dog tags. In a German iron pit, U.S. soldiers found crates labeled "Aachen Cathedral" containing "a silver bust of Charlemagne embedded with a fragment of the emperor's skull." These words were on a fortification in France: "Austin White, Chicago, Ill., 1918. Austin White, Chicago, Ill., 1945. This is the last time I want to write my name here." In December 1944, the president's blood pressure was 260 over 150, and on an April day in 1945 American newspapers published the daily casualty list with next of kin, including this:

"Army-Navy Dead: ROOSEVELT, Franklin D., commander-in-chief; wife, Mrs. Anna Eleanor Roosevelt, the White House."

Atkinson's narrative glows with the poetic prose of the heartbroken—letters penned by people caught up in what he calls "the scarlet calamity." After Conrad Nutting died when his P-51 crashed, his pregnant wife wrote: "It will be my cross, my curse, and my joy forever, that in my mind you shall always be vibrantly alive." An American war correspondent listened in a cemetery as a French girl read a letter from a mother to her son: "My dearest and unfortunate son, on June 16, 1944, like a lamb you died and left me alone without hope... Your last words to me were, 'Mother, like the wind I came and like the wind I shall go.'"

Such reservoirs of eloquence were drawn from the depths of human dignity that survived the scalding obscenity of the war Atkinson describes unsparingly. The Battle of Agincourt (1415) is remembered less for its consequences than for what Shakespeare made of it in *Henry V*. World War II's reverberations will roll down the centuries in its geopolitical consequences, and in the literature it elicited in letters and in histories like Atkinson's trilogy.

LOOKING BACKWARD THROUGH ROSE-TINTED GLASSES

January 18, 2018

WASHINGTON—Is there anything more depressing than a cheerful liberal? The question is prompted by one such, historian David Goldfield, who has written a large-hearted book explaining that America's problems would yield to government's deft ameliorating touch if Americans would just rekindle their enthusiasm for it.

Goldfield's new book, *The Gifted Generation: When Government Was Good*, notes that in 1964 nearly 80 percent of Americans said they trusted Washington all or most of the time; today, about 20 percent do.

Goldfield does not explain why trust in government waned as government's confidence waxed. The question contains its answer.

He rightly celebrates the 1944 GI Bill of Rights, but misses what distinguished it from many subsequent social programs. It was intended as a prophylactic measure against unemployment and political extremism among millions demobilized from the military. It worked. Veterans overwhelmed campuses; Goldfield says that some in California resided in fuselages of half-built airplanes. Eligibility for the bill's benefits was contingent upon having performed military service. The bill used liberal means—subsidies for veterans' education and homebuying—to achieve conservative results: Rather than merely maintaining people as permanent wards of government, it created an educated, property-owning middle class equipped for self-reliant striving.

In contrast, much of the Great Society's liberalism sought to demoralize policies, deeming repressive those policies that promoted worthy behavior. This liberalism's political base was in government's caring professions that served "clients" in populations disorganized by behaviors involving sex and substance abuse. Surely this goes far toward explaining what Goldfield's narrative leaves inexplicable:

Postwar America's political process chose Harry Truman and then Dwight Eisenhower to preserve the post–New Deal status quo. And then it chose Lyndon Johnson over Barry Goldwater, who was (rightly) viewed as hostile to the New Deal's legacy. But just sixteen years later, the electorate, whose prior preferences Goldfield approves, made an emphatic choice that he considers a sudden eruption of dark impulses that hitherto were dormant. Goldfield does not distinguish, as Ronald Reagan did, between New Deal liberalism—of which the GI Bill was a culmination—and liberalism's subsequent swerve in another direction. And he has no answer as to why the electorate, so receptive for so long to hyperactive government, by 1980 was not.

Goldfield flecks his narrative with fascinating facts: Not until 1943 did the government remove the racial classification "Hebrew" from immigration forms. Cornell University's president promised to prevent Jewish enrollment from making the school "unpleasant for first-class Gentile students." When Jonas Salk, who would invent the polio vaccine, applied for a fellowship, one of his recommenders wrote, "Dr. Salk is a member of the Jewish race but has, I believe, a very great capacity to get on with people." That we cringe is a better metric of social progress than is government spending on social programs.

Goldfield's grasp of contemporary America can be gauged by his regret that the income tax, under which the top 10 percent of earners pay more than 70 percent of the tax and the bottom 50 percent pay 3 percent, is not "genuinely progressive." He idealizes government as an "umpire," a disinterested arbiter ensuring fair play. Has no liberal stumbled upon public choice theory, which demystifies politics, puncturing sentimentality about politicians and government officials being more nobly and unselfishly motivated than lesser mortals? Has no liberal noticed that no government is ever neutral in society's allocation of wealth and opportunity? And that the bigger government becomes, the more it is manipulated by those who are sufficiently confident, articulate, and sophisticated to understand government's complexities, and wealthy enough to hire skillful agents to navigate those complexities on their behalf? This is why big government is invariably regressive, transferring wealth upward.

During his long look backward through rose-tinted glasses, Goldfield, a Brooklyn native, pines for the days he remembers, or thinks he does, when his borough was defined by its devotion to the Dodgers (who decamped to Los Angeles in 1958). Such nostalgia is refuted by information: There still are seemingly millions of moist-eyed, aging members of the Brooklyn diaspora who claim to have spent every day of every summer of their halcyon youths in Ebbets Field (capacity 31,902). Actually, in the team's greatest season, 1955, when it won its only World Series, attendance averaged 13,423, worse than the worst 2017 team average (Tampa Bay's 15,670). The past—including government's salad days, when it said it could create "model cities" and other wonders, and people believed it—was often less romantic in fact than it is in memory.

POLITICS AND POLICIES

CRISES AND THE COLLECTIVIST TEMPTATION

April 5, 2020

WASHINGTON—Today's pandemic has simultaneously inflicted the isolation of "social distancing" and the social solidarity of shared anxiety. In tandem, these have exacerbated a tendency that was already infecting America's body politic before the virus insinuated itself into many bodies and every consciousness.

It is the recurring longing for escape from individualism, with its burden of personal responsibility. It includes a concomitant desire for immersive politics, whereby people infuse their lives with synthetic meaning by enlisting in mass movements or collective efforts. These usually derive their unity from a clear and present danger or, when that is lacking, from national, ethnic, racial, or class resentments (e.g., Donald Trump's and Bernie Sanders's not-so-very-different populisms of those who feel victimized).

Not all recoils against individualism are progressive, but progressivism always encourages such recoils. After World War I's solidarity, which had been enforced by public bullying and minatory government, a progressive philosopher, Mary Follett, hoped that in peacetime America would abandon the idea of "the particularist individual" and natural rights belonging thereto, the better to emancipate government from limits.

Until a taste of the real thing arrived with the coronavirus, there was, in societies perhaps bored by their comforts, a hunger for apocalypse. A great threat can infuse excitement into bourgeois dullness and can justify a flight into exciting collective undertakings. Hence the thrill many people recently derived from being excoriated by a Swedish teenager for abusing the planet. Earth's supposedly mortal peril late in this century, still over the horizon, suddenly seems a comparatively manageable menace for a world that, when it will need mitigation measures, will be at least five times wealthier than it was in 2000.

Political leaders frequently declare war, or its "moral equivalent," on this or that (cancer, drugs, poverty, climate change, etc.) because they justify muscular measures. In his first inaugural address, Franklin Roosevelt said that in order for him "to wage a war against the emergency" of the Depression, "we must move as a trained and loyal army" wielding "broad executive power" that should be "as great as the power that would be given to me if we were in fact invaded by a foreign foe." This was understandable, given the severity of pains and the public's panic. Never mind that the result—unconstrained government meddlesomeness—probably prolonged the twelve-year Depression, until rearmament ended it.

Today's pandemic is an even more valid justification for sweeping exercises of executive powers by governors wielding states' police powers. Governors know that to the axiom "to govern is to choose" there should be added seven words: "always on the basis of imperfect information." What is not justified are attempts to use today's real emergency as an excuse to rewrite the nation's social contract in order to accustom Americans to life suited to a permanent emergency.

Progressives' flirtation with the preposterous Green New Deal (the end of beef and of airplanes, etc.) is so revealing because it envisions federal micromanagement of the economy and individual choices *forever*. Consider also the somewhat successful attempt by the House Democratic caucus to lard the current economic rescue legislation with innumerable extraneous extensions of federal power over society. This illustrates progressivism's eager embrace of temporary crises as hammers to pound Americans into the permanent solidarity that socialism promises—until it produces permanent cynicism and bitterness about the inevitably political allocation of wealth and opportunity.

Inconveniently for progressives, every war must end, no crisis is forever, and individualism—the American idea: the pursuit of happiness as each defines it—reemerges through fissures in the solidarity produced by transient crises. The British, too, understand. In Muriel Spark's 1963 novel *The Girls of Slender Means*, members of a women's club go to Buckingham Palace to celebrate V-E Day, relishing "the huge organic murmur of the crowd" in this culmination of wartime solidarity. "The next day everyone began to consider where they personally stood in the new order of things." Yes, *personally*. After wartime's necessary collective exertions, a solidarity that had been obligatory during danger was undesirable as normality.

After World War II, A. J. Liebling, a war correspondent for the *New Yorker*, wrote that "you can feel [war's] pull on men's memories at the maudlin reunions of war divisions. They mourn for their dead, but also for war." Understandably so. Their nostalgia is for a temporary solidarity—aka regimentation—that was crowned by the glory of victory. But nostalgia for a time when society was fused by the heat of war or some other crisis is not a permanent basis for a free and open society.

THE ANNOUNCEMENT OF A PRESIDENTIAL CANDIDACY YOU WILL *NEVER* HEAR

May 25, 2014

WASHINGTON—All modern presidents of both parties have been too much with us. Talking incessantly, they have put politics unhealthily at the center of America's consciousness. Promising promiscuously, they have exaggerated government's proper scope and actual competence, making the public perpetually disappointed and surly. Inflating executive power, they have severed it from constitutional constraints. So, sensible voters might embrace someone who announced his 2016 candidacy this way:

"I am ambling—running suggests unseemly ardor—for president. It is axiomatic that anyone who nowadays will do what is necessary in order to become president thereby reveals character traits, including delusions of adequacy and obsessive compulsive disorder, that should disqualify him or her from proximity to powers concentrated in the executive branch. Therefore, my campaign will initially consist of driving around the Obnoxiously Entitled Four—Iowa, New Hampshire, South Carolina, and Nevada—trying to interest their 3.8 percent of America's population in a minimalist president.

"Candidates are constantly asked, 'Where will you take the country?' My answer is: 'Nowhere.' The country is not a parcel to be 'taken' anywhere. It is the spontaneous order of 316 million people making billions of daily decisions, cooperatively contracting together, moving the country in gloriously unplanned directions.

"To another inane question, 'How will you create jobs?' my answer will be: 'I won't.' Other than by doing whatever the chief executive can to reduce the regulatory state's impediments to industriousness. I will administer no major economic regulations—those with $100 million economic impacts—that Congress has not voted on. Legislators should be explicitly complicit in burdens they mandate.

"Congress, defined by the Constitution's Article I, is properly the first, the *initiating* branch of government. So, I will veto no bill merely because I disagree with the policy it implements. I will wield the veto power only on constitutional grounds—when Congress legislates beyond its constitutionally enumerated powers, correctly construed, as they have not been since the New Deal. So I expect to cast more vetoes than the 2,564 cast by all previous presidents.

"My judicial nominees will seek to narrow Congress's use of its power to regulate commerce as an excuse for minutely regulating Americans' lives. My nominees will broaden the judicial recognition of Americans' 'privileges or immunities,' the rights of national citizenship mentioned in the Fourteenth Amendment, and the unenumerated rights referred to by the Ninth.

"In a radio address to the nation, President Franklin Roosevelt urged Americans to tell him their troubles. Please do *not* tell me yours. Tell them to your spouse, friends, clergy—not to a politician who is far away, who doesn't know you, and whose job description does not include Empathizer in Chief. 'I feel your pain,' Bill Clinton vowed. I won't insult your intelligence by similarly pretending to feel yours.

"A congenial society is one in which most people most of the time, and all politicians almost all of the time, say, when asked about almost everything: 'This is none of my business.' If as president I am asked what I think about the death of a rock star, or the imbecilic opinions of rich blowhards who own professional sports teams, I will say: 'Americans should have no interest in my thoughts about such things, if I had any.' I will try not to come to the attention of any television camera more than once a week, and only that often if I am convinced that I can speak without violating what will be my administration's motto: 'Don't speak unless you can improve the silence.'

"I will not ruin any more American evenings with televised State of the Union addresses. I will mail my thoughts on that subject to Congress 'from time to time,' as the Constitution directs. This was good enough for Jefferson and every subsequent president until Woodrow Wilson, the first president who believed, as progressives do, that the nation cannot function without constant presidential tutoring and hectoring.

"This country has waged many wars since it last actually declared war, on June 5, 1942, against Bulgaria, Romania, and Hungary. If it is necessary to use military force, I shall, if exigencies permit, give Congress the pleasure of collaboration.

"Finally, there have been forty-four presidencies before the one I moderately aspire to administer, and there will be many more than forty-four after it. Mine will be a success if, a century hence, Americans remember me as dimly as they remember Grover Cleveland, the last Democratic president with proper understanding of this office's place in our constitutional order."

THE AWFUL STATE OF THE STATE OF THE UNION ADDRESS

March 12, 2010

WASHINGTON—The increasingly puerile spectacle of presidential State of the Union addresses is indicative of the state of the union, and is unnecessary: The Constitution requires only that the president "shall from time to time give to the Congress information of the state of the union." But a reaction may be brewing against these embarrassing events. Speaking in Alabama, Chief Justice John Roberts said "to the extent that" this occasion "has degenerated into a political pep rally," he is "not sure why we're there." He was referring to Supreme Court justices. But why is *anyone* there?

Roberts was responding to a question concerning the kerfuffle about Barack Obama's January address, wherein Obama criticized— and flagrantly mischaracterized—a recent Supreme Court decision that loosened limits on political speech. The decision neither overturned "a century of law" nor conferred an entitlement on foreign corporations to finance U.S. candidates. Nevertheless, the Democratic donkeys arrayed in front of Obama leapt onto their hind legs and brayed in unison, while the six justices who were present sat silently. Justice Sam Alito, in an act of *lese majeste*, appeared to mutter "not true" about Obama's untruths.

When Republican presidents deliver these addresses, Republican legislators, too, lurch up and down like puppets on strings. And Congress wonders why it is considered infantile.

Most of the blame for the State of the Union silliness, as for so much else, goes to the Root of Much Mischief, aka Woodrow Wilson. But a president whose middle name was Wilson made matters worse.

George Washington delivered his report on the state of the union in person, as did John Adams. But the third president, Thomas Jefferson, put his thoughts in writing and dispatched them to Congress. Such presidential reticence is impossible to imagine in the Age of Obama, but Jefferson disliked the sound of his voice and considered it monarchical for the executive to stand above the legislature and lecture it.

In 1913, however, Wilson, whose guiding principle was that the world could not hear too much from him, delivered his report in person. He thought the Founders had foolishly saddled the nation with a Constitution of checks and balances that made government sluggish or paralytic. Hence charismatic presidential leadership was needed to arouse public opinion that could compel Congress to bow to the president's will. The Founders thought statesmanship should restrain public opinion. Wilson's watery Caesarism preached that presidents should spur that dangerous stallion. He just *knew* he could control it. He learned otherwise when trying to ratify the Versailles Treaty.

George Washington considered Congress "the first wheel of the government, a wheel which communicates motion to all the rest." Wilson thought the presidency is the only office able to, or even entitled to, impart movement to the government.

Many conservatives were congressional supremacists until Ronald Wilson Reagan arrived possessing the rhetorical skills requisite for a Wilsonian presidency. His unfortunate filigree on the dramaturgy of State of the Union addresses was to begin the practice of stocking the House gallery with ordinary but exemplary people whose presence touches the public's erogenous zones.

The prolixity that is the defining characteristic of modern presidents blurs the distinction between campaigning and governing, and positions the presidency at the center of the nation's consciousness. This gives presidents delusions of omnipotence, and makes Americans susceptible to perpetual disappointment and political dyspepsia.

We could take one small step toward restoring institutional equilibrium by thinking as Jefferson did about State of the Union addresses. Justice Antonin Scalia has stopped going to them because justices "sit there like bumps on a log" in the midst of the partisan posturing—the political pep rally that Roberts described. Sis boom bah humbug.

Next year, Roberts and the rest of the justices should stay away from the president's address. So should the uniformed military, who are out of place in a setting of competitive political grandstanding. For that matter, the 535 legislators should boycott these undignified events. They would, if there were that many congressional grown-ups averse to being props in the childishness of popping up from their seats to cheer, or remaining sullenly seated in semi-pouts, as the politics of the moment dictates.

In the unlikely event that Obama or any other loquacious modern president has any thoughts about the State of the Union that he does not pour forth in the torrential course of his relentless rhetoric, he can mail those thoughts to Congress. The Postal Service needs the business.

HOW NOT TO SELECT PRESIDENTIAL CANDIDATES

March 24, 2013

WASHINGTON—Because of the grotesquely swollen place the presidency now occupies in the nation's governance and consciousness, we are never not preoccupied with presidential campaigning. The Constitution's Framers would be appalled.

The nation reveres the Framers, but long ago abandoned the presidential selection process they considered so important that they made it one of the four national institutions created by the Constitution. Hence the significance of the Republican National Committee's suggested reforms for the 2016 process.

University of Virginia professor James Ceaser says the four national institutions the Framers created were Congress, the Supreme Court, the presidency, and the presidential selection system based on the Electoral College. The fourth, wherein the selection of candidates and election of a president by each state's electors occurred simultaneously—they were the same deliberation—soon disappeared.

Since the emergence of the party system in the 1790s, and the ratification of the Twelfth Amendment in 1804, candidates have been selected by several different processes. First by their party's congressional caucuses; then by nominating conventions controlled by the party's organizations; then by conventions influenced by primaries and caucuses (Vice President Hubert Humphrey won the 1968 Democratic nomination without entering any primaries); and, since 1972, entirely by primaries and caucuses that have made conventions nullities.

Now, responding to the fact that the 2012 nomination process was ruinously protracted, the RNC suggests reforms that might, like many improvements, make matters worse. This is because of a prior "improvement"—campaign finance reform.

The RNC suggests a shorter nominating season with fewer debates—none earlier than September 1, 2015. The twenty debates in 2012 were actually one fewer than in 2008. But in 2000 there were thirteen. In 1988, seven. In 1980, just six. The May 5, 2011, debate was eight months before the Iowa caucuses. In 1980, the first was sixteen days before Iowa voted.

The RNC report does not challenge the role of Iowa, New Hampshire, South Carolina, and Nevada in beginning the delegate selection. Perhaps it is not worth the trouble to challenge these states' anachronistic entitlement; like all entitlements, it is fiercely defended by the beneficiaries. But a reform process that begins by accepting this crucial component of the status quo substantially limits possibilities. By the time these four states have had their say, the field of candidates often has been considerably—and excessively—winnowed, and the outcome is, if not settled, given a trajectory that is difficult to alter.

Supporters of Senator Rand Paul, or of any other candidate thoroughly unenthralled by the policies and procedures that have resulted in Republicans losing the popular vote in five of the last six presidential elections, are understandably suspicious of any proposed changes that might tilt the nomination process against the least known and less lavishly funded candidates. They are especially apt to squint disapprovingly at the RNC's suggestion of regional primaries.

The party, however, must balance two imperatives. One is the need to enlarge the number of voters participating in the process. Hence the suggestion that primaries should replace all nominating caucuses and conventions—events where ideologically motivated activists and insurgent candidates can more easily predominate.

The party's second imperative is to preserve opportunities for less-known and financially challenged candidates to break through. This is where government restrictions on campaign contributions restrict the range of candidates from which voters can choose.

Existing restrictions on large contributions to candidates are commonly called "post-Watergate" reforms. This is more accurate as a matter of chronology than causality. Democrats began advocating contribution as well as spending limits years before Watergate concluded in 1974. They were appalled that large contributions from a few wealthy liberals made possible Eugene McCarthy's 1968 anti-war insurgency against President Lyndon Johnson, and propelled George McGovern's doomed nomination in 1972.

Suppose political contributing were deregulated, which would deregulate political speech, the dissemination of which is the principal use of campaign contributions. This would make it easier to design a more compressed nominating process, with a reduced role for the first four states, which also would allow marginal candidates a financial opportunity to fight their way into the top tier of candidates.

Anyway, tinkering with the party's political process is no substitute for improving the party's political substance. No nominating process featuring an array of candidates as weak and eccentric as the Republicans' 2012 field would have produced a much better result. So the party must begin whatever 2016 process it devises by fielding better candidates, which should not be so difficult.

SOCIALISM: A CLASSIFICATION THAT NO LONGER CLASSIFIES

February 17, 2019

"From each according to his ability, to each according to his needs!"

—Karl Marx

WASHINGTON—Norman Thomas was not easily discouraged. Running for president in 1932, three years into the shattering, terrifying Depression, which seemed to many to be a systemic crisis of capitalism, Thomas, who had been the Socialist Party's candidate in 1928 and would be in 1936, 1940, 1944, and 1948, received, as this column previously noted, fewer votes (884,885) than Eugene Debs had won (913,693) as the party's candidate in 1920, when, thanks to the wartime hysteria President Woodrow Wilson had fomented, Debs was in jail.

In 1962, Michael Harrington, a founder of the Democratic Socialists of America (it succumbed to a familiar phenomenon: Two American socialists equals three factions), published *The Other America*. It supposedly kindled President John Kennedy's interest in poverty, which had not escaped his attention while campaigning in West Virginia's primary. Harrington, like "democratic socialist" Senator Bernie Sanders today, thought socialism should be advanced through the Democratic Party.

Today, socialism has new, angrier advocates. Speaking well of it gives the speaker the frisson of being naughty and the fun of provoking Republicans like those whose hosannas rattled the rafters when the president vowed that America would never become socialist. Socialism is, however, more frequently praised than defined because it has become a classification that no longer classifies. So, a president who promiscuously wields government power to influence the allocation of capital (e.g., bossing around Carrier even before he was inaugurated; using protectionism to pick industrial winners and losers) can preen as capitalism's defender against socialists who, like the Bolsheviks, would storm America's Winter Palace if America had one.

Time was, socialism meant thorough collectivism: state ownership of the means of production (including arable land), distribution, and exchange. When this did not go swimmingly where it was first tried, Lenin said (in 1922) that socialism meant government ownership of the economy's "commanding heights"—big entities. After many subsequent dilutions, today's watery conceptions of socialism amount to this: Almost everyone will be nice to almost everyone, using money taken from a few. This means having government distribute, according to its conception of equity, the wealth produced by capitalism. This conception is shaped by muscular factions: the elderly, government employees unions, the steel industry, the sugar growers, and so on and on and on. Some wealth is distributed to the poor; most goes to the "neglected" middle class. Some neglect: The political class talks of little else.

Two-thirds of the federal budget (and 14 percent of GDP) goes to transfer payments, mostly to the non-poor. The U.S. economy's health care sector (about 18 percent of the economy) is larger than the economies of all but three nations and is permeated by government money and mandates. *Before* the Affordable Care Act was enacted, forty cents of every health care dollar was government's forty cents. The sturdy yeomanry who till America's soil? Last year's 529-page Agriculture Improvement Act will be administered by the Agriculture Department, which has about one employee for every twenty American farms.

Socialists favor a steeply progressive income tax, as did those who created today's: The top 1 percent pay 40 percent of taxes; the bottom 50 percent pay only 3 percent; 50 percent of households pay either no income tax or 10 percent or less of their income. Law professor Richard Epstein notes that in the last thirty-five years the fraction of total taxes paid by the lower 90 percent has shrunk from more than 50 percent to about 35 percent.

In his volume in the *Oxford History of the United States* (*The Republic for Which It Stands*, covering 1865–1896) Stanford's Richard White says that John Bates Clark, the leading economist of that era, said "true socialism" is "economic republicanism," which meant more cooperation and less individualism. Others saw socialism as "a system of social ethics." All was vagueness.

Today's angrier socialists rail, with specificity and some justification, against today's "rigged" system of government in the service of the strong. But as the Hoover Institution's John H. Cochrane (aka the Grumpy Economist) says, "If the central problem is rent-seeking, abuse of the power of the state, to deliver economic goods to the wealthy and politically powerful, how in the world is *more government* the answer?"

The "boldness" of today's explicit and implicit socialists—taxing the "rich"—is a perennial temptation of democracy: inciting the majority to attack an unpopular minority. This is socialism now: From each faction according to its vulnerability, to each faction according to its ability to confiscate.

AMERICAN SOCIALISTS: HALF RIGHT

July 8, 2018

> Polly: He's a socialist but he doesn't like people.
> Brian: Nor do I, much.
> Polly: You're a conservative. You don't have to.
> —From *Getting On*, by Alan Bennett

WASHINGTON—This, one of the pleasures of being a conservative, is not for Alexandria Ocasio-Cortez, twenty-eight. She recently won the Democratic nomination—effectively, election—in a Bronx and Queens congressional district, running as a "democratic socialist." In response to her, progressives and conservatives are experiencing different excitements.

The left relishes the socialist label as a rejection of squishy centrism—a naughty, daring rejection of timidity: *Aux barricades, citoyens!* The right enjoys a tingle of delicious fear: We *told* you that the alternative to us is the dark night of socialism.

At the risk of spoiling the fun—the left's anticipation of the sunny uplands of social justice; the right's frisson of foreboding—consider two questions: What is socialism? And what might a socialist American government do?

In its nineteenth-century infancy, socialist theory was at least admirable in its clarity: It meant state ownership of the means of production (including arable land), distribution, and exchange. Until, of course, the state "withers away" (Friedrich Engels's phrase), when a classless, and hence harmonious, society can dispense with government.

After World War II, Britain's Labour Party diluted socialist doctrine to mean state ownership of the economy's "commanding heights" (Lenin's phrase from 1922)—heavy industry (e.g., steel), mining, railroads, telecommunications, etc. Since then, in Britain and elsewhere, further dilution has produced socialism as comprehensive economic regulation by the administrative state (obviating the need for nationalization of economic sectors) and government energetically redistributing wealth. So, if America had a socialist government today, what would it be like?

Socialism favors the thorough permeation of economic life by "social" (aka political) considerations, so it embraces protectionism—government telling consumers what they can buy, in what quantities, and at what prices. (A socialist American government might even set quotas and prices for foreign washing machines.)

Socialism favors maximizing government's role supplementing, even largely supplanting, the market—voluntary private transactions—in the allocation of wealth by implementing redistributionist programs. (Today America's sky is dark with dollars flying hither and yon at government's direction: Transfer payments distribute 14 percent of GDP, two-thirds of the federal budget, up from a little more than one-quarter in 1960. In the half-century 1963–2013, transfer payments were the fastest growing category of personal income. By 2010, American governments were transferring $2.2 trillion in government money, goods, and services.)

Socialism favors vigorous government interventions in the allocation of capital, directing it to uses that farsighted government knows, and the slow-witted market does not realize, constitute the wave of the future. So, an American socialist government might tell, say, Carrier Corporation and Harley-Davidson that the government knows better than they do where they should invest shareholders' assets.

Socialism requires—actually, socialism *is*—industrial policy, whereby government picks winners and losers in conformity with the government's vision of how the future ought to be rationally planned. What could go wrong? (Imagine, weirdly, a president practicing compassionate socialism by ordering his energy secretary to prop up yesterday's coal industry against the market menace of fracking—cheap oil and natural gas.)

Socialism, which fancies itself applied social science, requires a bureaucracy of largely autonomous experts unconstrained by a marginalized—ideally, a paralyzed—Congress. So, an American socialist government would rule less by laws than by regulations written in administrative agencies staffed by experts insulated from meddling by elected legislators.

(Utah Senator Mike Lee's office displays two piles of paper. One, a few inches high, contains the laws Congress passed in a recent year. The other, about eight feet tall, contains regulations churned out that year by the administrative state's agencies.)

Socialism favors vast scope for ad hoc executive actions unbound by constraining laws that stifle executive nimbleness and creativity. (For example, an aggrieved president telling, say, Harley-Davidson: "I've"— first-person singular pronoun—"done so much for you.")

Today's American socialists say that our government has become the handmaiden of rapacious factions and entrenched elites, and that there should be much more government. They are half right. To be fair, they also say that after America gets "on the right side of history" (an updated version of after "the last king is strangled with the entrails of the last priest"), government will be truly disinterested, manipulated by no rent-seeking factions, serving only justice. That is, government will be altogether different than it is, or ever has been. Seriously.

ANTI-CAPITALIST CONSERVATIVES VERSUS PROGRESSIVES: THE NARCISSISM OF SMALL DIFFERENCES

August 11, 2019

WASHINGTON—Regimes, however intellectually disreputable, rarely are unable to attract intellectuals eager to rationalize the regimes' behavior. America's current administration has "national conservatives." They advocate unprecedented expansion of government in order to purge America of excessive respect for market forces, and to affirm robust confidence in government as a social engineer allocating wealth and opportunity. They call themselves conservatives, perhaps because they loathe progressives, although they seem not to remember why.

The Manhattan Institute's Oren Cass advocates "industrial policy"— what other socialists call "economic planning"—because "market economies do not automatically allocate resources well across sectors." So government, he says, must create the proper "composition" of the economy by rescuing "vital sectors" from "underinvestment." By allocating resources "well," Cass does *not* mean efficiently—to their most economically productive uses. He especially means subsidizing manufacturing, which he says is the "primary" form of production because innovation and manufacturing production are not easily "disaggregated."

Manufacturing jobs, Cass's preoccupation, are, however, only 8 percent of U.S. employment. Furthermore, he admits that as government, i.e., politics, permeates the economy on manufacturing's behalf, "regulatory capture," other forms of corruption, and "market distortions will emerge." *Emerge*? Using government to create market distortions is national conservatism's agenda.

The national conservatives' pinup du jour is Fox News's Tucker Carlson, who, like the president he reveres, is a talented entertainer. Carlson says that what Senator Elizabeth Warren, D-Massachusetts, calls "economic patriotism" sounds like "Donald Trump at his best." Carlson approves how Warren excoriates U.S. companies' excessive "loyalty" to shareholders. She wants the government to "act aggressively" and "intervene in markets" in order to stop "abandoning loyal American workers and hollowing out American cities." Carlson darkly warns that this "pure old-fashioned economics" offends zealots "controlled by the banks."

He adds: "The main threat to your ability to live your life as you choose does not come from government anymore, but it comes from the private sector." Well. If living "as you choose" means living free from the friction of circumstances, the "threat" is large indeed. It is reality—the fact that individuals are situated in times and places not altogether of their choosing or making. National conservatives promise government can rectify this wrong.

Their agenda is much more ambitious than President Nixon's 1971 imposition of wage and price controls, which were *temporary* fiascos. Their agenda is even more ambitious than the New Deal's cartelization of industries, which had the temporary (and unachieved) purpose of curing unemployment. What national conservatives propose is government fine-tuning the economy's composition and making sure resources are "well" distributed, as the government (i.e., the political class) decides, *forever*.

What socialists are so fond of saying, national conservatives are now saying: *This* time will be different. It never is, because government's economic planning always involves the fatal conceit that government can aggregate, and act on, information more intelligently and nimbly than markets can.

National conservatives preen as defenders of the dignity of the rural and small-town—mostly white and non–college educated—working class. However, these defenders nullify the members' dignity by discounting their agency. National conservatives regard the objects of their compassion as inert victims, who are as passive as brown paper parcels, awaiting government rescue from circumstances. In contrast, there was dignity in the Joad family (of John Steinbeck's *The Grapes of Wrath*), who, when the Depression and Dust Bowl battered Oklahoma, went west seeking work.

Right-wing anticapitalism has a long pedigree as a largely aristocratic regret, symbolized by railroads—the noise, the soot, the lower orders not staying where they belong—that despoiled the Edenic tranquility of Europe's landed aristocracy. The aristocrats were not wrong in seeing their supremacy going up in the smoke from industrialism's smokestacks: Market forces powered by mass preferences do not defer to inherited status.

Although the national conservatives' anticapitalism purports to be populist, it would further empower the administrative state's faux aristocracy of administrators who would decide which communities and economic sectors should receive "well"-allocated resources. Furthermore, national conservatism is paternalistic populism. This might seem oxymoronic, but so did "Elizabeth Warren conservatives" until national conservatives emerged as such. The paternalists say to today's Joads: Stay put. We know what is best for you and will give it to you through government.

As national conservatives apply intellectual patinas to the president's mutable preferences, they continue their molten denunciations of progressives—hysteria about a "Flight 93 election" (the Republic's last chance!) and similar nonsense. Heat, however, neither disguises nor dignifies their narcissism of small differences.

BETTER NEVER MEANS BETTER FOR EVERYONE

December 8, 2019

WASHINGTON—Trying to give intellectual coherence to the visceral impulses that produced today's president, Senator Marco Rubio, R-Florida, is joining anticapitalist conservatives. Those who reject this characterization are unaware of how their skepticism about markets propels them to an imprudent leap of faith.

In a recent Washington speech, Rubio said America has "neglected the rights of workers to share in the benefits they create for their employer." Careless language—workers are not sharing America's bounty?—serves Rubio's economic determinism, which postulates a recent economic cause for complex and decades-long social changes. Economic "negligence" has, he asserts, "weakened families and eroded communities," diminished churchgoing and PTA participation, and increased substance abuse. If only the explanation of, say, family disintegration—a social disaster since the 1960s, before economic globalization—were monocausal.

Rubio deplores "financial flows detached from real production," flows bypassing the "real economy." But if not to "real"—an uninformative adjective—production, where are financial resources flowing, and why? And what expertise does a career politician bring to disparaging decisions of professionals trained to connect capital with productive opportunities?

Rubio's concern is not economic but philosophic: The efficient allocation of scarce resources—i.e., all resources—should be subordinated to communitarian concerns, including "the obligation of businesses to reinvest in America." The flow of Rubio's rhetoric is unimpeded by data—his 3,725-word speech contains almost none—perhaps because data do not demonstrate the neglect he asserts. If he thinks the $147 billion invested in research and development in 2018 by the 190 large corporations represented on the Business Roundtable (half as much as was distributed in dividends to the corporations' owners, the shareholders) is insufficient, by what metric does he determine this? His regret that since 1980 the financial sector's share of corporate profits has increased from about 10 percent to 30 percent reflects a desire, both reactionary and romantic, to restore and preserve, like a fly in amber, the imperfectly remembered economy of mid-twentieth-century America.

Twelve times Rubio celebrates, or laments the loss of, "dignified work," yet he never suggests the adjective's meaning. What work does he deem undignified? Does "dignified" denote a certain ratio of mind to muscle? If so, Rubio should compare the work of the relatively few who operate today's modern steel mills with the unpleasant, dangerous labor of the many who once toiled in dark, satanic mills containing open hearth furnaces. Fortunately, their jobs have been eliminated by technology-driven productivity.

Rubio substitutes for data a torrent of overheated rhetoric about America's "economic implosion," its "disordered economy" (whatever that might mean) that has created only "pockets of prosperity" because the economy is "rigged" (a verb and adjective also favored by Elizabeth Warren and Donald Trump). Rubio's limp solution to the American carnage he depicts is "common-good capitalism": discouraging corporations' buy-backs of their shares, immediate expensing of investments, reforming the Small Business Administration, which he says is financing "lifeless corporate conglomerates." Lifeless?

He says, perfunctorily and discordantly, "The idea that government can impose a balance between the obligations and rights of the private sector and working Americans has never worked." Yet he endorses "public policies," aka government, to "drive investments in key industries"—government picking winners; hence losers, too—because "pure" market principles are not "aligned" with the national interest.

So, *this* time what he says has never worked is going to work. Talk about faith-based policy. Public choice theory could teach him realism about the sociology of government: The theory dispels the romantic notion that governments are run by people more omniscient and nobly motivated—less interested in personal aggrandizement—than private-sector actors.

Rubio serves in a legislature whose constant resort to funding the government with continuing resolutions testifies to its incompetence concerning even its most elemental function: budgeting. Yet he expects this government to wisely define the "common good" and deftly allocate wealth and opportunities accordingly.

Abandoning actual conservatism's realism about the difficult trade-offs involved in policymaking, today's right-wing anticapitalists seem to seek a stagnant social equilibrium: No portion of society should become better off if in the process another portion would become worse off. About this, at least, the Commander in Margaret Atwood's *The Handmaid's Tale* was wiser: "Better never means better for everyone...It always means worse, for some."

Finally, when the sociologist Émile Durkheim (1858–1917) diagnosed "collective sadness" resulting from social isolation in the society—a "dust of individuals"—of his day, he partly blamed government's domination of society, to the detriment of the local, intermediary institutions Rubio wants to strengthen but actually would threaten.

THE EXTRAVAGANT FAITH OF MARKET SKEPTICS

January 9, 2020

WASHINGTON—The sails of Senator Josh Hawley's political skiff are filled with winds gusting from the right. They come from conservatives who think that an array of—perhaps most of—America's social injuries, from addiction to loneliness, have been inflicted by America's economy. Individualism, tendentiously defined, is the Missouri Republican's named target. Inevitably, however, the culprit becomes capitalism, which is what individual freedom *is* in a market society's spontaneous order.

In a November speech to like-minded social conservatives of the American Principles Project, Hawley said: "We live in a troubled age." Not pausing to identify a prior untroubled age, he elaborated: "Across age groups and regions, across races and income, the decline of community is undeniable. But it is not accidental." Well.

Time was, Marxists' characteristic rhetorical trope was "it is no accident" that this or that happened. As economic determinists, they believed that *everything* is explained by iron laws of economic development. They insisted that culture is downstream from economics and is decisively shaped by economic forces.

"It is not accidental," Hawley asserts, that there is "an epidemic of personal loneliness and isolation—driven by the loss of community." This is a consequence of being told "that to be truly free is to be without the constricting ties of family and place, without the demands of faith and tradition." Oh? By whom have we supposedly been sold this caricature of individualism?

Hawley says, "We've been told that liberty means release, separation." Actually, the intellectual pedigree of America's public philosophy traces to John Locke, who rejected Thomas Hobbes's view that man is naturally "solitary." Locke stressed that limited government is possible and desirable because human beings' natural sociability enables them to thrive together without ceding vast power to government.

Hawley, however, says, "It's no coincidence that the breakdown in community and the rise of oligarchy have happened together. They are both the products of a worldview." The culprit is "the Promethean ideal." In the twentieth century, Hawley says, this "ideal taught that the individual self exists apart from all social ties and relations. Our family, our religious society, our neighborhood and town—these communities don't constitute one's identity, because who one truly is exists separate from all of them."

William F. Buckley once described a friendly intellectual adversary as a pyromaniac in a field of straw men. Through the smoke of burning straw one can see in Hawley's social diagnosis the belief, held by many progressives and an increasing number of conservatives, that individualism, as expressed in and enabled by capitalism, is making Americans neither better off nor better.

"The statistics tell us," Hawley says, "that we are living in a new age of inequality." Actually, the statistics are complicated, shaped by assumptions about what is relevant, and can tell strikingly different stories.

Hawley calls it "unjust that the global economy" works "for so few." Actually, for a few billion people. Globally, 42 percent of the world's population lived in extreme poverty in 1981; by 2015, just 10 percent did. In America, the *Economist* reports, after adjusting for taxes and government transfer payments, since 2000 the share of national income of the top 1 percent "has been volatile around a flat trend" and perhaps has changed little since 1960. Among the poor, falling marriage rates, which have causes more complex than economics, indicate household incomes declining but not individuals' incomes. Furthermore, statistics often do not reflect the portion of corporate profits that flow to the middle class through pension funds: "In 1960 retirement accounts owned just 4% of American shares; by 2015 the figure was 50%." And the *Economist* also says:

If you argue that [household] income has shrunk you also have to claim that four decades' worth of innovation in goods and services, from mobile phones and video streaming to cholesterol-lowering statins, have not improved middle-earners' lives. That is simply not credible.

Hawley asserts, without demonstrating, a broad "collapse of community" across America, and blames this, without explaining the causation, on "market worship," without identifying the irrational worshipers. His logic is opaque but his destination is clear: Because markets do not properly allocate wealth and opportunity, much of their role must be supplanted by government.

Confidence in markets and confidence in government often vary inversely. Today, progressives assert a severely limited efficiency of markets in allocating resources for the public good, and they proclaim government's duty and ability to improve upon it. Increasingly, "Market Skeptic Republicans" (a Pew Research Center category) agree. They are selectively skeptical, having extravagant faith—in government.

NIKKI HALEY AGAINST
"HYPHENATED CAPITALISM"

March 8, 2020

> Hyphenated capitalism is no capitalism at all. The better name
> for it is socialism lite.
>
> —Nikki Haley

WASHINGTON—A sound heard recently on Pennsylvania Avenue
was a gauntlet being thrown down by a woman spoiling for a fight. Nikki
Haley went on offense in defense of America's economic system, which
she correctly says is inextricably woven into the nation's system of liberty.
Some Democratic presidential aspirants and a portion of the public have
been flirting with socialism, and some conspicuous Republicans might
as well be while they are promoting "hyphenated capitalism."

Speaking in a manner bracingly unusual in this city, Haley minced
no words: "The American system is capitalism." Although "the Founders
never used the word, they gave us capitalism in all but the name,"
because capitalism is "another word for freedom. And it springs from
America's most cherished ideals." The Founders understood something
the Supreme Court has forgotten for eight decades: Economic freedom
is, like freedom of speech and free exercise of religion, a fundamental
right. Capitalism has "lifted up more people, unlocked more progress,
and unleashed more prosperity" than any other system, yet "many
people avoid saying that word, including some conservatives and business leaders."

Haley said the Business Roundtable, which represents major corporations, wants companies to "focus not on business, but on some vague
notion of helping 'stakeholders,'" meaning customers, employees, and
communities. "This," Haley said astringently, "is puzzling." Companies
that do not serve their customers, reward their workers, and serve their

communities will fail—unless abusive or incompetent companies are saved by misguided government policies. Such business-government entanglement breeds cronyism, self-dealing, and bailouts from taxpayers.

"Some conservatives," Haley said, "have turned against the market system. They tell us America needs a…different kind of capitalism. A hyphenated capitalism. Yet while these critics keep the word capitalism, they lose its meaning. They want to give government more power to make more decisions for businesses and workers. They differ from the socialists only in degree."

She did not need to specify Florida Republican Senator Marco Rubio's aspiration for "common-good capitalism," or Missouri Republican Senator Josh Hawley's even vaguer capitalism that does not encourage "Pelagianism" and the "Promethean self." Really. Such conservatives inevitably advocate, in effect, government "industrial policy," socialism's essential ingredient.

"Only in a prosperous country like America," Haley said, "can people be so flippant about capitalism and so naive about socialism." She has stood on the Simon Bolivar Bridge connecting Venezuela and Colombia:

I watched thousands of Venezuelans go by. Entire families walking in the blazing heat for hours to get to Colombia where they would have the only meal they would eat that day. The average Venezuelan lost 24 pounds in 2017 alone. Four million have fled their homeland.…it was the richest country in Latin America when it was capitalist. It also had free and fair elections. Now Venezuelans are digging in trash cans and killing zoo animals for food.

The daughter of Indian immigrants, Haley was ambassador to the United Nations in the feisty manner of Daniel Patrick Moynihan and Jeane Kirkpatrick. Before that she was a resoundingly successful two-term governor of South Carolina. And before that she was a businesswoman in Bamberg, South Carolina (population then: 2,500). If a businesswoman can be twelve.

Haley's mother did what so many immigrants do: She started a business, a retail clothing and gift store. There came a time when her bookkeeper, who was leaving without having found a replacement, asked what she could do. Haley remembers:

> I happened to be walking past at that exact moment. My mom grabbed my arm and said, "Train her. She can do it." By the time I was 13 I was doing taxes, keeping the ledger, and balancing the expenses and bank account. It wasn't until I got to college that I realized that wasn't normal.

Normal is overrated. Haley is not.

The $20 billion in new capital investment she attracted to South Carolina as governor included five international tire companies, and Mercedes, Volvo, and BMW plants. The world's largest BMW plant is one reason why South Carolina builds more cars for export than any other state. Haley is one reason South Carolina has changed more, and more for the better, than any state in the previous fifty years.

Haley spoke at the Hudson Institute, which is at 1201 Pennsylvania Ave. It is about 900 yards from 1600. Anyone's path to that place is long and circuitous, but one way to begin is by picking a worthy fight.

DATA CONFOUNDS THE CASSANDRA CAUCUS

March 15, 2020

WASHINGTON—Today's bipartisan Cassandra caucus includes Democratic Senators Bernie Sanders ("our standard of living has fallen") and Elizabeth Warren ("the rich get richer while everyone else falls behind") and Republican Senators Marco Rubio ("we have been left with an economy and a society no one is happy with") and Josh Hawley ("over the last several decades, inflation-adjusted wages for the working class have barely budged"). The caucus says America's economy is primarily producing disappointment, even misery. This narrative is largely false, yet can be self-fulfilling.

Fortunately, Michael Strain's just-published *The American Dream Is Not Dead (But Populism Could Kill It)* is an inoculation against politically motivated misinformation. Strain, of the American Enterprise Institute, acknowledges that many towns damaged by automation and globalization are struggling, "But most towns are not former manufacturing towns." Since September 2010, the last month with a net job loss, the economy has added an average of about 200,000 jobs per month, and today there are more job openings than unemployed workers, which is one reason wage growth is accelerating and already is over 3 percent. For the bottom 10 percent of earners, weekly earnings have grown 20 percent over the past four years. The unemployment rate for workers without even high-school diplomas is further below its long-term average than is the rate for college-educated workers.

Hawley says 70 percent of Americans—those with neither family wealth nor four-year college degrees—"haven't seen a real wage increase in thirty years." Wages for typical workers, Strain says, have risen 34 percent over the past three decades. Using the personal consumption expenditures (PCE) price index as a more accurate measure of inflation than the consumer price index (CPI), wages increased by 21 percent between 1973 and 2018, and 34 percent in thirty years. In this period, Strain says, wages for the tenth percentile have increased 36 percent, for the twentieth percentile 34 percent, for the thirtieth percentile 29 percent. The picture is brighter still when the focus is broadened beyond wages to include, for example, employer-provided health care, which is untaxed compensation.

The Congressional Budget Office calculates "income after taxes and [government] transfers," which is income available to save and spend. Since 1990 it has increased 44 percent for the median household, for the bottom 20 percent it has increased 66 percent. Furthermore, Strain says, the gap between rich and poor "has stopped growing and might even be declining."

The argument that the typical household's and individual's quality of life has not improved for decades, says Strain, "borders on the absurd."

Leave aside the vast but difficult-to-quantify product quality improvements (e.g., cell phones before and after smartphones; automobiles in 1990 and 2020). Between 1983 and 2016, the median net worth for a family increased from approximately $52,000 to $97,300.

It is true, Strain says, that "employment in middle-skill, middle-wage occupations has been shrinking" as robots have replaced some manufacturing workers, ATMs have replaced bank tellers, software has replaced bookkeepers. Yes, between 1967 and 2018 the portion of households in the middle fell from 54 percent to 42 percent—but the share of low-income households (earning less than $35,000, measured in constant dollars) also fell from 36 percent to 28 percent, and the share of households earning over $100,000 has tripled, from 10 percent to 30 percent.

Upward mobility remains real. About seven out every one hundred Americans raised in the bottom 20 percent reach the top 20 percent. Seventy-three percent of Americans in their forties have higher (inflation-adjusted) family incomes than their parents had, including those raised in the second quintile of income distribution—the principal target constituency for populists left and right. Two-thirds of children raised in the bottom quintile rise above it in their prime earning years. And more than 60 percent of the children raised in the top quintile do not remain there.

Strain says "the populist message of economic and social despair" causes diminished expectations: When vociferous members of both parties say Americans are helpless victims of a system rigged by elites, this enervating message dims aspirations and reduces effort in an increasingly risk-averse nation that already is showing reduced restlessness and geographic mobility.

Intellectual trends—including the idea that human agency and personal responsibility are radically attenuated in complex societies—have produced a curdled politics emphasizing victimhood and resentments. These sour preoccupations make people susceptible to the infantilizing temptation of tantrum populism that demands the benefits of economic dynamism with none of its inevitable frictions and dislocations.

It is unfortunate that the Cassandra caucus might prosper politically by misdescribing America's economic prosperity. It is unforgiveable that the misdescription might be self-fulfilling.

WORSE CAN BE BETTER

October 27, 2019

WASHINGTON—There are political moments, and this might be one, in which worse is better. Moments, that is, when a society's per capita quantity of conspicuous stupidity is so high and public manners are so low that a critical mass of people are jolted into saying "enough, already." Looking on the bright side, as he wisely is disinclined to do, Jonathan Rauch thinks such a moment might be arriving.

Writing in *National Affairs* ("Rethinking Polarization"), Rauch, a Brookings Institution senior fellow, postulates a vast emptiness at the core of the politics that has engulfed us: "What if, to some significant extent, the increase in partisanship is not really *about* anything?" What if rival tribalisms are largely untethered from ideologies?

This is plausible. The angriest conservatives, or at least people brandishing this label, show no interest in what was, until recently, conservatism's substance—limited government, balanced budgets, free trade, curbs in executive power, entitlement reform, collective security. Conservatives' anger is eerily unrelated to the comprehensive apostasy from what was, three years ago, conservatism's catechism.

Of course, this catechism had long been (in Daniel Patrick Moynihan's formulation) avowed but not constraining: The conservative party did not allow professed beliefs to influence its behavior. So, on the right, a politics of passions unrelated to policy flooded into the vacuum of convictions unrelated to behavior.

Rauch's thesis is that increased polarization has little to do with ideas and much to do with hostile feelings—"negative partisanship"—about others. "It's not so much that we like our own party," Rauch surmises, "as that we detest the other." The left, like the right, has no plausible, meaning implementable, plan for solving pressing problems, from immigration to $1 trillion deficits at full employment. So, despising President Trump, who makes this easy, is a substitute for a politics of substance.

Group solidarity based on shared detestations is fun, and because fun can trigger dopamine bursts in the brain, it can be addictive. Rauch:

"One of the most important characteristics of this 'new' form of polarization is that there is nothing new about it. Tribalism has been the prevalent mode of social organization for all but approximately the most recent 2% of years that humans have lived on the planet." The decline of civic organizations has people searching for connectedness. "The declining hold of organized religion...[has] displaced apocalyptic and redemptive impulses into politics, where they don't belong." Economic stagnation among the less educated provides opportunities for demagogues on the left (despising a never-popular minority: the wealthy) as well as the right.

Rauch says "humans were designed for life in small, homogeneous groups where change was slow and choices were few." If he is correct, both left and right, like scorpions in a bottle, are in diametrically opposed but symbiotic reactions against modernity—against an open society "founded on compromise, toleration, and impersonal rules and institutions." Hence, "in education, elite universities frequently encourage students to burrow into their tribal identities rather than transcend them. In media, new technologies enable and monetize outrage and extremism."

All this began before Trump slouched onto the political stage, and because of his electoral success he already has emulators among his despisers. Consider Massachusetts Senator Elizabeth Warren's grotesque—and classically demagogic—ascription of blame to unpopular others for everyone else's personal complaints—which she says government can remedy: "You've got things that are broken in your life? I'll tell you exactly why. It's because giant corporations, billionaires have seized our government."

All demagogues begin by rejecting Samuel Johnson's wisdom: "How small, of all that human hearts endure, that part which laws or kings can cause or cure." Warren is a millimeter away from Trump's "I alone can fix it," where the antecedent of the pronoun "it" is: *everything*.

Rauch believes that although political parties are instruments of partisan mobilization, it is their weakness that feeds today's polarization by smoothing the way for demagogues. Time was, the parties vetted candidates, "screening out incompetents, sociopaths, and those with no interest in governing." Now, "the more parties weaken as institutions whose members are united by loyalty to their organization, the more they strengthen as tribes whose members are united by hostility to their enemy." As loyalty to parties' organizations and doctrines is supplanted by parties as hostility-based tribes, polarization supplies solidarity in an era of empty politics.

Rauch hopes that America's current public awfulness might "end up strengthening liberal norms and institutions by scaring us, at last, into defending them." Isn't it pretty to think so?

LEAR RAGING ON HIS TWITTER-HEATH

June 2, 2020

WASHINGTON—This unraveling presidency began with the Crybaby-in-Chief banging his spoon on his highchair tray to protest a photograph—a *photograph*—showing that his inauguration crowd the day before had been smaller than the one four years previous. Since then, this weak person's idea of a strong person, this chest-pounding advertisement of his own gnawing insecurities, this low-rent Lear raging on his Twitter-heath has proven that the phrase malignant buffoon is not an oxymoron.

Presidents, exploiting modern communications technologies and abetted *today* by journalists preening as the "resistance"—like members of the French Resistance, 1940–1944, minus the bravery—can set the tone of American society, which is regrettably soft wax on which presidents leave their marks. The president's provocations—his coarsening of public discourse that lowers the threshold for acting out by people as mentally crippled as he—do not excuse the violent few. They must be punished. He must be removed.

Social causation is difficult to demonstrate, particularly between one person's words and other persons' deeds. However: The person voters hired in 2016 to "take care that the laws be faithfully executed" stood on July 28, 2017, in front of uniformed police and urged them "please don't be too nice" when handling suspected offenders. His hope was fulfilled for eight minutes and forty-six seconds on Minneapolis pavement.

What Daniel Patrick Moynihan termed "defining deviancy down" now defines American politics. In 2016, voters were presented an unprecedentedly unpalatable choice: Never had both major parties offered nominees with higher disapproval than approval numbers. Voters chose what they wagered would be the lesser blight. Now, however, they have watched him govern for forty months, and more than 40 percent—slightly less than the percentage that voted for him—approve of his sordid conduct.

Presidents seeking reelection bask in chants of "Four more years!" This year, however, most Americans—perhaps because they are, as the president predicted, weary from all the winning—might flinch: Four more years of *this*? The taste of ashes, metaphorical and now literal, dampens enthusiasm.

The nation's downward spiral into acrimony and sporadic anarchy has had many causes much larger than the small man who is the great exacerbator of them. Most of the causes predate his presidency, and most will survive its January terminus. The measures necessary for restoration of national equilibrium are many and will be protracted far beyond his removal. One such measure must be the removal of those in Congress who, unlike the sycophantic mediocrities who cosset him in the White House, will not disappear "magically," as Eric Trump said the coronavirus would. Voters must dispatch his congressional enablers, especially the senators who still gambol around his ankles with a canine hunger for petting.

In life's unforgiving arithmetic, we are the sum of our choices. Congressional Republicans have made theirs for more than 1,200 days. We cannot know all the measures necessary to restore the nation's domestic health and international standing, but we know the first step: Senate Republicans must be routed, as condign punishment for their Vichyite collaboration, leaving the Republican remnant to wonder—was it sensible to sacrifice dignity, such as it ever was, and to shed principles, if convictions so easily jettisoned could be dignified as principles, for…what? Praying people should pray, and all others should hope: May I never crave *anything* as much as these people crave membership in the world's most risible deliberative body.

A political party's primary function is to bestow its imprimatur on candidates, thereby proclaiming: This is who we are. In 2016, the Republican Party gave its principal nomination to a vulgarian and then toiled to elect him. And to stock Congress with invertebrates whose unswerving abjectness has enabled his institutional vandalism, who have voiced no serious objections to his Niagara of lies, and whom T. S. Eliot anticipated:

We are the hollow men…
Our dried voices, when
We whisper together
Are quiet and meaningless
As wind in dry grass
or rats' feet over broken glass…

Those who think our unhinged president's recent mania about a murder two decades ago that never happened represents his moral nadir have missed the lesson of his life: There is no such thing as rock bottom. So, assume that the worst is yet to come. Which implicates national security: Abroad, anti-Americanism sleeps lightly when it sleeps at all, and it is wide awake as decent people judge our nation's health by the character of those to whom power is entrusted. Watching, too, are indecent people in Beijing and Moscow.

"BAUMOL'S DISEASE" IS THE PUBLIC SECTOR'S HEALTH

May 18, 2017

WASHINGTON—Although William J. Baumol, who recently died at ninety-five, was not widely known beyond the ranks of economists, all Americans are living with, and policy makers are struggling with, "Baumol's disease." It is one reason brisk economic growth is becoming more elusive as it becomes more urgent. And it is a disease particularly pertinent to the increasingly fraught health care debate.

Born in the Bronx, Baumol spent his teaching career at Princeton and NYU but remained an aficionado of New York opera, and when in 1962 the Metropolitan Opera's orchestra went on strike, Baumol sought an explanation for the Met's regularly recurring labor troubles. He postulated "cost disease" afflicting labor-intensive service industries: Productivity will often increase not at all, or much slower, in some sectors—e.g., nursing, teaching, the performing arts—than in the overall economy. Decades later, Senator Daniel Patrick Moynihan, who in 1962 was a young aide to Labor Secretary Arthur Goldberg as he arbitrated the orchestra dispute, explained Baumol's disease this way:

> The number of players, the number of instruments, the amount of time it took to "produce" a Mozart quartet in the 18th century will not have changed one whit two centuries later. To play the "Minute Waltz" in 50 seconds leaves something to be desired. True of first violinists, kindergarten teachers, beat cops, sculptors, and so through a great repertoire of occupations.

Goldberg's 1962 encounter with Baumol's disease in the Met's orchestra initiated thinking that led in 1965 to the National Endowment for the Arts (and, on the Great Society principle of no conceivable claimant left behind, the National Endowment for the Humanities). This elicited

99

Moynihan's corollary to Baumol's theory: "Activities with Baumol's disease migrate to the public sector."

Moynihan, thinking that it will be "the undoing of modern government" if there is too much migration, worried especially about health care. In 1993, at a health care hearing before the Senate Finance Committee, Chairman Moynihan received blank looks when he asked three medical deans what they could do about Baumol's disease.

So Moynihan elaborated: "Montefiore Hospital was founded in New York City in the 1880s. At that time, how long did it take for a professor of medicine to make his morning rounds, and how many interns would he take along with him?"

Dean: "Oh, about an hour; say twelve interns."

Moynihan: "And today?"

Dean: "Got it!"

Perhaps technological advances will somewhat increase the productivity of teachers (e.g., online learning) and doctors (e.g., diagnostic advances using the human genome) as they have of policing (e.g., more efficient deployments of personnel). But there are limits. And a Mozart quartet must raise prices and donations or become dependent on government.

As a Democrat, Moynihan worried that the "stagnant services" would become identified with government, as would his party, while the Republican Party would be increasingly identified with a private sector becoming ever more dynamic relative to the public sector. Actually, however, the current health care policy morass suggests this: Disregarding, as the public seems wisely inclined to do, Republicans' rhetorical flights, the two parties are about equally identified with government, and equally expected to use it to nurture public contentment with labor-intensive service industries.

Such industries might become increasingly important and problematic. In an appreciation of Baumol's work, the *Economist* noted this possible implication of Baumol's disease in a world of increasing automation:

As machines become better at doing things, the human role in generating faster productivity growth will converge towards zero. At that point, so long as society expects everyone to work, all spending in the economy will go towards services for which it is crucial that productivity *not* grow, in order to provide jobs for everyone. Society could seemingly be both characterized by technological abundance and paralyzed by cost disease.

Happily, predicted horrors have a way of not happening, because projected trends become disrupted by unforeseen developments. It is, however, not prudent to count on what cannot be anticipated.

John Maynard Keynes lamented that the "encroachment of ideas" in public policy usually is gradual because politicians and government officials are rarely influenced by new ideas after age thirty, so they apply to current events ideas that "are not likely to be the newest." Today, however, increased productivity is increasingly imperative as an aging workforce retires into the expensive embrace of the entitlement state. So, Baumol's disease is a now-old idea that should be on policy makers' minds.

DEFINING EFFICIENCY DOWN

June 11, 2017

WASHINGTON—Sensing that his Scottish enemies had blundered at the Battle of Dunbar in 1650, Oliver Cromwell said, "The Lord hath delivered them into our hands." Philip K. Howard, were he the exulting type, could rejoice that some of his adversaries have taken a stand on indefensible terrain. Because the inaccurately named Center for American Progress has chosen to defend the impediments that government places in its own path regarding public works, it has done Howard the favor of rekindling interest in something he wrote in 2015.

A mild-mannered Manhattan lawyer of unfailing gentility and civility, Howard is no fire-breathing Cromwell. Rather, he is a combination of Candide and Sisyphus, his patient optimism undiminished by redundant evidence that government resists commonsensical legal and regulatory reforms of the sort he pushes up the mountain of bureaucracy when not serving as senior counsel at the white shoe law firm of Covington & Burling.

In September 2015, Howard, founder and chair of the reform advocacy group Common Good, published a paper "Two Years Not Ten Years: Redesigning Infrastructure Approvals." In it, he argued that time is money, and that America is wasting enormous amounts of both with an infrastructure approval system that is an "accident of legal accretion over the past 50 years":

> America could modernize its infrastructure, at half the cost, while dramatically enhancing environmental benefits, with a two-year approval process. Our analysis shows that a six-year delay in starting construction on public projects costs the nation over $3.7 trillion, including the costs of prolonged inefficiencies and unnecessary pollution. This is more than double the $1.7 trillion needed through the end of this decade to modernize America's infrastructure.

The nation that built the Empire State Building in 410 days during the Depression and the Pentagon in sixteen months during wartime recently took nine years just for the permitting of a San Diego desalination plant. Five years and 20,000 pages of environmental assessments and permitting and regulatory materials were consumed before beginning to raise the roadway on New Jersey's Bayonne Bridge, a project with, as Howard says, "virtually no environmental impact (it uses existing foundations and right-of-way)." Fourteen years were devoted to the environmental review for dredging the Port of Savannah, which has been an ongoing process for almost thirty years. While faux environmentalists litigate against modernizing America's electrical grid, transmission lines waste 6 percent of the electricity they transmit, which equals 16 percent of 2015 coal power generation and is equal to the output of 200 average-size coal-burning power plants. In 2011, shippers using the inland waterway system of canals, dams, and locks endured delays amounting to twenty-five years. In 2012, the Treasury

Department estimated that traffic congestion wasted 1.9 billion gallons of gasoline annually. Diverting freight to trucks because of insufficient railway capacity quadruples fuel consumption. And so on, and on.

Twenty months after Howard published his article, the CAP's response shows how far we have defined efficiency down: It celebrates the fact that federal environmental statements average only 4.6 years. Actually, that would be bad enough if such reviews were all or even most of the problem. Actually, there are other kinds of reviews and other layers of government involved, as with the Bayonne Bridge—forty-seven permits from nineteen federal, state, and local agencies.

The CAP says that "the principal restraint facing state and local governments contemplating megaprojects is money, not environmental review." But, again, this ignores myriad other time-consuming reviews and the costs, in both construction and social inefficiencies, driven by lost time.

Today's governance is illuminated by presidential epiphanies (e.g., "Nobody knew that health care could be so complicated"). Barack Obama had one concerning infrastructure: "There's no such thing as shovel-ready projects." This is partly because, as Stanford political scientist Francis Fukuyama says, America has become a "vetocracy" in which intense, well-organized factions litigate projects into stasis.

Intelligent people of goodwill can dispute, as the CAP rejoinder does, Howard's cost-benefit calculations. But the CAP partakes of the hyperbole normal in today's environmental policy debates: It includes Howard among "hardcore opponents of environmental review" who "consider federal laws that protect the environment fundamentally illegitimate." Even the title of the CAP's response to Howard's arguments for more pertinent and efficacious environmental reviews is meretricious: "Debunking the False Claims of Environmental Review Opponents."

Opponents? Including Howard? Hardly. David Burge, who tweets as @iowahawkblog, satirizes this slapdash style of progressive argumentation:

"To help poor children, I am going to launch flaming accordions into the Grand Canyon."

"That's stupid."
"WHY DO YOU HATE POOR CHILDREN?"

AMERICA, DATED BY "RULE STUPOR"

January 11, 2009

WASHINGTON—Called to a Florida school that could not cope, police led the disorderly student away in handcuffs, all forty pounds of her five-year-old self. In a Solomonic compromise, schools in Broward County, Florida, banned running at recess. Long Beach, New Jersey, removed signs warning swimmers about riptides, although the oblivious tides continued. The warning label on a five-inch fishing lure with a three-pronged hook says, "Harmful if swallowed"; the label on a letter opener says, "Safety goggles recommended."

No official at the Florida school would put a restraining arm around the misbehaving child lest he or she be sued, as a young member of Teach for America was, for $20 million (the school settled for $90,000), because the teacher put a hand on the back of a turbulent seventh-grader to direct him to leave the classroom. Another teacher's career was ruined by accusations arising from her having positioned a child's fingers on a flute. A 2004 survey reported that 78 percent of middle and high school teachers have been subjected to legal threats from students bristling with rights. Students, sensing the anxiety that seizes schools when law intrudes into incidental relations, challenge teachers' authority.

Someone hurt while running at recess might sue the school district for inadequate supervision of the runner, as Broward County knows: It settled 189 playground lawsuits in five years. In Indiana, a boy did what boys do: He went down a slide head first—and broke his femur. The school district was sued for inadequate supervision. Because of fears of such liabilities, all over America playgrounds have been stripped of the equipment that made them fun. So now in front of televisions and computer terminals sit millions of obese children, casualties of what Manhattan attorney and author Philip K. Howard calls "a bubble wrap approach to child rearing" produced by the "cult of safety." Long Beach removed the warning signs because it is safer to say nothing: Reckless swimmers injured by the tides might sue, claiming that the signs were not sufficiently large or shrill or numerous, or something. Only a public outcry got the signs restored.

Defensive, and ludicrous, warning labels multiply because aggressiveness proliferates. Lawsuits express the theory that anyone should be able to sue to assert that *someone* is culpable for even an idiotic action by the plaintiff, such as swallowing a fishing lure.

A predictable byproduct of this theory is brazen cynicism, encouraged by what Howard calls trial lawyers "congregating at the intersection of human tragedy and human greed." So:

A volunteer for a Catholic charity in Milwaukee ran a red light and seriously injured another person. Because the volunteer did not have deep pockets, the injured person sued the archdiocese—successfully, for $17 million.

The thread connecting such lunacies is a fear permeating American life. It is, alas, a sensible fear arising from America's increasingly perverse legal culture that is the subject of what surely will be 2009's most needed book on public affairs—Howard's *Life Without Lawyers: Liberating Americans from Too Much Law.*

A nation in which the proportion of lawyers in the workforce almost doubled between 1970 and 2000 has become ludicrously dense with laws. Now legal self-consciousness is stifling the exercise of judgment. Today's entitlement culture inculcates the idea that everyone is entitled to a life without danger, disappointment, or aggravation. Any disagreement or annoyance can be aggressively "framed in the language of legal deprivation."

Law is essential to, but can stifle, freedom. Today, Howard writes, "Americans increasingly go through the day looking over their shoulders instead of where they want to go." The land of the free and the home of the brave has become "a legal minefield" through which we timidly tiptoe lest we trigger a legal claim. What should be routine daily choices and interactions are fraught with legal risk.

Time was, rights were defensive. They were to prevent government from doing things to you. Today, rights increasingly are offensive weapons wielded to inflict demands on other people, using state power for private aggrandizement. The multiplication of rights, each lacking limiting principles, multiplies nonnegotiable conflicts conducted with the inherent extremism of rights rhetoric, on the assumption, Howard says, "that society will somehow achieve equilibrium if it placates whomever is complaining."

But in such a society, dazed by what Howard calls "rule stupor" and victimized by litigious "victims," the incentives are for intensified complaining. Read Howard's book, and weep for the death of common sense.

LARRY SUMMERS'S EPIPHANY

November 27, 2016

WASHINGTON—History has a sly sense of humor. It caused an epiphany regarding infrastructure projects—roads, harbors, airports, etc.—to occur on a bridge over Boston's Charles River, hard by Harvard Yard, where rarely is heard a discouraging word about government.

Last spring, Larry Summers, former treasury secretary and Harvard president, was mired in congealed traffic on the bridge, which is being repaired, and he suddenly understood "American sclerosis." Repairing the bridge, which was built in eleven months in 1912, will take about five years. The problem, he concluded in a blog post, is "a gaggle of regulators and veto players"—Massachusetts's government, contractors, environmental agencies, the historical commission, etc.—"each with the power to block or to delay, and each with their own parochial concerns." Summers' sunburst of understanding continued:

I'm a progressive, but it seems plausible to wonder if government can build a nation abroad, fight social decay, run schools, mandate the design of cars, run health insurance exchanges or set proper sexual harassment policies on college campuses, if it can't even fix a 232-foot bridge competently. Waiting in traffic over the Anderson Bridge, I've empathized with the two-thirds of Americans who distrust government…We seem to be caught in a dismal cycle of low expectations, poor results and shared cynicism.

There is a trope for these times: "I'm a progressive, but…." Barack Obama should have understood this in 2009 when he serenely promised "shovel-ready projects," the scarcity of which was one reason his stimulus barely stimulated.

After seeing reconstruction of Manhattan's West Side Highway take thirty-five years (construction of the George Washington Bridge took thirty-nine months), Senator Daniel Patrick Moynihan despaired that whereas America once celebrated people who built things, it now honors those who block building.

Today's long lag between the conception and execution of infrastructure projects is one reason they are dubious as countercyclical economic stimulants, and as jobs programs for the unemployed. The economist Milton Friedman said that once, while he was taken to see a canal that was being dug, he expressed astonishment that there was no heavy earth-moving machinery, only men with shovels. A government official said that was because the project was a jobs program. Well, then, Friedman replied, shouldn't they use spoons rather than shovels?

New Deal public works gave the nation splendidly useful engineering marvels, including the Golden Gate Bridge and the Hoover Dam. It did not, however, significantly reduce unemployment, which never came below 14 percent until prewar military spending began.

Both presidential candidates endorsed huge increases in infrastructure spending, so we are about to relearn that bipartisanship, whatever its many merits, usually means a recklessly open spending spigot. Will there be wasteful projects? Indeed, boondoggles are transaction costs of democracy. As is the inclination to direct infrastructure spending to stagnant regions, where it is unlikely to stimulate growth, rather than to regions where economic dynamism is putting pressure on, and being dampened by, inadequate infrastructure.

Besides, the economic bang from every infrastructure buck is biggest in a society that is starting from a low base, as America did in the first half of the nineteenth century. Princeton historian James M. McPherson in *Battle Cry of Freedom* noted that before 1815—before all-weather macadamized roads—the only efficient means of moving goods long distances was sailing ships and down-river floats. "The cost of transporting a ton of goods 30 miles inland from an American port equaled the cost of carrying the same goods across the Atlantic." So, "America's transatlantic trade exceeded internal commerce" and "the economy grew little if any faster than population."

Then came the Erie Canal and the frenzied funding of emulative projects, many of which failed, but the successes redeemed the rest. Next came railroads, and soon Americans regarded infrastructure—then called "internal improvements"—as emblems of national greatness. When the Marquis de Lafayette toured America in 1824, a couple of years before the fiftieth anniversary of the Revolution, his New York banquet table groaned beneath the weight of a seventy-five-foot model of the Erie Canal, which opened in 1825.

Americans hoped that commerce, ignited by infrastructure, would weld the nation's sections, defusing the danger of disunion. Actually, this would require a railroad lawyer from Illinois.

THE NATIONAL ENDOWMENT FOR THE ARTS' ADAPTIVE EVOLUTION

March 16, 2017

WASHINGTON—Although the National Endowment for the Arts' 2016 cost of $148 million was less than one-hundredth of 1 percent of the federal budget, attempting to abolish the NEA is a fight worth having, never mind the certain futility of the fight.

Let's pretend, counterfactually, that the NEA no longer funds the sort of rubbish that once immersed it in the culture wars, e.g., "Piss Christ" (a photo depicting a crucifix immersed in a jar of the artist's urine) and "Genital Wallpaper" (don't ask). What, however, is art? We subsidize soybean production, but at least we can say what soybeans are. Are NEA enthusiasts serene about government stipulating, as it must, art's public purposes that justify public funding? Or do they insist that public funds should be expended for no defined public purpose?

Government breeds advocacy groups that lobby it to do what it wants to do anyway—expand what it is doing. The myriad entities with financial interests in preserving the NEA cloyingly call themselves the "arts community," a clever branding that other grasping factions should emulate, e.g., the "military-industrial community." The "arts community" has its pitter-patter down pat. The rhetorical cotton candy—sugary, jargon-clotted arts gush—asserts that the arts nurture "civically valuable dispositions" and a sense of "community and connectedness." And, of course, "diversity" and "self-esteem." Americans supposedly suffer from a scarcity of both.

The NEA was created in 1965 as a filigree on the Great Society. In 1995, Republicans won control of the House of Representatives and said the NEA was a frill the federal government should be shorn of. Twenty-two years later, it survives, having mastered adaptive evolution, government-style: It defines art democratically and circularly. Art is anything done by anyone calling himself or herself an artist, and an artist is anyone who produces art. An NEA report issued under Bill Clinton said "art includes the expressive behaviors of ordinary people," including "dinner-table arrangements" and "piecrust designs." As Walt Whitman neglected to say, "I hear America singing and everyone's singing is above average." Populist pandering is nothing new in Washington. Neither is this utilitarian calculus: Policies are good that provide the greatest self-esteem for the greatest number.

David Marcus, artistic director of a Brooklyn-based theater project and senior contributor to The Federalist, says the NEA produces "perverse market incentives" that explain why many arts institutions "are failing badly at reaching new audiences, and losing ground":

> Many theater companies, even the country's most "successful," get barely 50 percent of their revenue from ticket sales. Much of the rest comes from tax-deductible donations and direct government grants. This means that the real way to succeed as an arts organization is not to create a product that attracts new audiences, but to create a product that pleases those who dole out the free cash. The industry received more free money than it did a decade ago, and has fewer attendees.

Furthermore, the NEA's effects are regressive, funding programs that are, as Paul Ryan's House Budget Committee said, "generally enjoyed by people of higher income levels, making them a wealth transfer from poorer to wealthier." A frequently cited study purporting to prove otherwise was meretricious: It stressed income levels of ZIP codes where NEA-funded *institutions* are, inferring that institutions *located* in low-income areas are serving low-income people.

Defense contractors spread weapons systems' subcontracts across the nation like butter across toast; fifty states and perhaps all 435 congressional districts get NEA funds. And here is another reason for the immortality of government programs: If a program is a major expense, its spending generates so many dependent clients that legislators flinch from eliminating or even substantially trimming it. And if a program is, like the NEA, a minor expense, legislators wonder: Why take the trouble, and experience the pain (the NEA's affluent clients fluently articulate their grievances and sense of entitlement), for a trivial gain?

Americans' voluntary contributions to arts organizations ("arts/culture/humanities" institutions reaped $17 billion in 2015) dwarf the NEA's subventions, which would be replaced if those who actually use the organizations—many of them supported by state and local government arts councils—are as enthusiastic about them as they claim to be. The idea that the arts will wither away if the NEA goes away is risible. Distilled to its essence, the argument for the NEA is: Art is a Good

Thing, therefore a government subsidy for it is a Good Deed. To appreciate the non sequitur, substitute "macaroni and cheese" for "art."

IGNORANCE OF THE LAW IS . . . INEVITABLE

April 9, 2015

WASHINGTON—What began as a trickle has become a stream that could become a cleansing torrent. Criticisms of the overcriminalization of American life might catalyze an appreciation of the toll the administrative state is taking on the criminal justice system, and liberty generally.

In 2007, professor Tim Wu of Columbia Law School recounted a game played by some prosecutors. One would name a famous person—"say, Mother Teresa or John Lennon"—and other prosecutors would try to imagine "a plausible crime for which to indict him or her," usually a felony plucked from "the incredibly broad yet obscure crimes that populate the U.S. Code like a kind of jurisprudential minefield." Did the person make "false pretenses on the high seas"? Is he guilty of "injuring a mailbag"?

In 2009, Harvey Silverglate's book *Three Felonies a Day* demonstrated how almost any American could be unwittingly guilty of various crimes between breakfast and bedtime. Silverglate, a defense lawyer and civil libertarian, demonstrated the dangers posed by the intersection of prosecutorial ingenuity with the expansion of the regulatory state.

In 2013, Glenn Harlan Reynolds, University of Tennessee law professor and creator of Instapundit, published in the *Columbia Law Review* "Ham Sandwich Nation: Due Process When Everything is a Crime." Given the axiom that a competent prosecutor can persuade a grand jury to indict a ham sandwich, and given the proliferation of criminal statutes and regulations backed by criminal penalties, what becomes of the *mens rea* principle that people deserve criminal punishment only if they engage in conduct that is inherently wrong or that they know to be illegal?

Now comes "Rethinking Presumed Knowledge of the Law in the Regulatory Age" (*Tennessee Law Review*) by Michael Cottone, a federal judicial clerk. Cottone warns that as the *mens rea* requirement withers when the quantity and complexity of laws increase, the doctrine of *ignorantia legis neminem excusat*—ignorance of the law does not excuse—becomes problematic. The regulatory state is rendering unrealistic the presumption that a responsible citizen should be presumed to have knowledge of the law.

There are an estimated 4,500 federal criminal statutes—and innumerable regulations backed by criminal penalties that include incarceration. Even if none of these were arcane, which many are, their sheer number would mean that Americans would not have clear notice of what behavior is proscribed or prescribed. The presumption of knowledge of the law is refuted by the mere fact that estimates of the number of federal statutes vary by hundreds. If you are sent to prison for excavating arrowheads on federal land without a permit, your cellmate might have accidentally driven his snowmobile onto land protected by the Wilderness Act.

Regulatory crimes, Cottone observes, often are not patently discordant with our culture as are murder, rape, and robbery. Rather than implicating fundamental moral values, many regulatory offenses derive their moral significance, such as it is, from their relation to the promotion of some governmental goal.

The presumption of knowledge of the law is, Cottone argues, useful as an incentive for citizens to become informed of their legal duties. Complete elimination of the presumption would be a perverse incentive to remain in an ignorance that might immunize a person from culpability. But "there can be no moral obligation to do something impossible, such as know every criminal law," let alone all the even more numerous— perhaps tens of thousands—regulations with criminal sanctions. The morality of law, Cottone argues, requires laws to be, among other things, publicized, understandable, and not subject to constant changes. Otherwise everyone would have to be a talented lawyer, "a result hardly feasible or even desirable."

Overcriminalization, says Professor Reynolds, deepens the dangers of "a dynamic in which those charged with crimes have a lot at risk, while those doing the charging have very little 'skin in the game.'" With a vast menu of crimes from which to choose, prosecutors can "overcharge" a target, presenting him or her with the choice between capitulation-through-plea-bargain or a trial with a potentially severe sentence.

Given the principle—which itself should be reconsidered—of prosecutorial immunity, we have a criminal justice system with too many opportunities for generating defendants, too few inhibitions on prosecutors, and ongoing corrosion of the rule and morality of law. Congress, the ultimate cause of all this, has work to undo.

THE CATHOLIC CRIME WAVE

March 14, 2019

PHILADELPHIA—"Horseplay," a term used to denote child rape, is, says Pennsylvania Attorney General Josh Shapiro, part of a sinister glossary of euphemisms by which the Catholic Church's bureaucracy obfuscates in documents the church's "pattern of abuse" and conspiracy of silence "that goes all the way to the Vatican." "Benevolent bishops" are those who allow predatory priests, shuffled from other dioceses, to continue as priests.

The fuse for the national explosion of fury about sexual abuse by Catholic clergy was lit in Boston—the excellent 2015 movie *Spotlight* recounts the *Boston Globe*'s victory over the stonewalling Catholic hierarchy in 2001–2002. But the still-reverberating detonation occurred last August in a Pittsburgh grand jury's report on the sexual abuse by approximately 300 priests of at least 1,000 victims in six Pennsylvania dioceses.

Seven months later, the nationwide stonewalling and cover-up continue by the church that, Shapiro says, has resisted discovery "every step of the way." And "bishops are still involved." The church fought his office's jurisdiction, and fought the release of the report with its sickening details of, for example, giggling priests photographing and fondling boys, and "whips, violence and sadism."

Shapiro says that his being Jewish has not adversely affected public perceptions of his office's scrutiny of the church. This might be because of credible reports about a boy being raped and then forced into a confessional to confess *his* sin. Or a boy having his mouth washed out with holy water after oral sex.

The church's crime wave is global. A French cardinal is convicted of concealing decades of sexual abuse by a priest in his jurisdiction; the *Washington Post* reports how clerical pedophiles "preyed on the most isolated and submissive children," at an institute for the deaf in Argentina. Scrutiny of Latin America, from which today's pope came, will be interesting.

In America, the acid drizzle of stomach-turning revelations might become a deluge now that forty-five states' attorneys general have contacted Shapiro about possible investigations in their states. It is highly unlikely that the abuses and conspiracies of silence about them are confined to Pennsylvania. Asked if this might be, cumulatively, the worst crime in American history, Shapiro says: Perhaps, considering the power of the guilty institution, the scale and prolonged nature of the crime, and the "sophisticated criminal cover-up." He speaks of charging the guilty— when possible; many predatory priests have died, and statutes of limitations shield others—"the way you would typically charge the mob."

An issue that used to bedevil Western nations—negotiating the border between the powers of civil authorities and the church's prerogatives of self-governance—has been settled in favor of the former. So, when other states' attorneys general consult with him, Shapiro says "do not trust the church" about voluntarily surrendering archives. The U.S. Justice Department has put dioceses on notice about preserving records concerning such things as the shuffling of predatory priests to benevolent bishops.

In November, a much-anticipated meeting of American bishops in Baltimore concerning sexual abuse was neutered by the Vatican, and the pope's February meeting on the subject produced nothing reassuring.

In America, the unfolding story—Shapiro says this is "only the third or fourth inning"—will involve legislating. Pennsylvania might open "a civil window" for suing the church, a measure fiercely resisted by the insurance industry that has sold liability policies to dioceses.

"The Faith is Europe and Europe is the Faith," said the Catholic writer Hilaire Belloc in 1920, a statement wisely construed by Georgetown University professor emeritus James V. Schall, SJ: "Europe is where Old Testament, New Testament, and Greek and Roman traditions melded.... Catholic origins united [Europe] under common assumptions about what life, liberty, God, man, and cosmos were about." It is therefore momentous that the church is in perhaps the worst self-inflicted and self-prolonged crisis since the Reformation.

Many common locutions—e.g., "Catholic Italy" and "Catholic Ireland"—no longer denote anything real. In the United States, the most religious modern nation, Catholics are leaving their religious affiliation at a higher rate than any other Christian sect. In December, Illinois's attorney general said the church in that state concealed the names of all but 185 of the 690 priests accused of sexual abuses. The former archbishop in the nation's capital, Cardinal Donald Wuerl, came to Washington from Pittsburgh. The church's leaders, says Shapiro, "have shown over decades, centuries really, a focus on protecting the power of their institution."

In a homily last September, the pope discerned something Satanic in the sexual-abuse scandal. He meant, however, that "the Great Accuser," aka Satan, was attacking the pope's bishops.

BOOTLEGGERS AND BAPTISTS, TOGETHER YET AGAIN

April 23, 2015

WASHINGTON—Smoking, said King James I in 1604, is "loathsome to the eye, hateful to the nose, harmful to the brain, dangerous to the lungs." Three years later he planted a colony in Jamestown. Its tobacco enhanced the royal treasury until Virginia produced a bumper crop of revolutionaries, including the tobacco farmer George Washington.

King James might have been less censorious about "vaping," which almost certainly is less harmful than inhaling chemicals produced by the combustion of tobacco. Users of e-cigarettes inhale vapors from electronic sticks containing a liquid with nicotine, which is addictive and perhaps particularly unhealthy for adolescent brains. Between 2013 and 2014 the use of e-cigarettes by middle- and high-school students tripled, and now exceeds that cohort's use of traditional cigarettes.

E-cigarettes, sometimes flavored to tempt the immature ("Unicorn Puke," "Stoned Smurf," "German Chocolate Beefcake") might be "gateway drugs," leading to tobacco cigarettes. Currently, however, e-cigarettes often are substitutes for them. So, prepare for regulations combining high-mindedness and low cunning.

E-cigarettes raise public health issues, but also illustrate the unhealthy process by which public policy often is made. They illustrate a familiar phenomenon, the cooperation between "bootleggers and Baptists," meaning merchants and moralists—those motivated by profits and those motivated by social improvement.

In 1983, Bruce Yandle, then a Clemson University economist who now is at George Mason University's Mercatus Center, had an epiphany: Regulations often come from a counterintuitive convergence of pressures from two groups, the earnestness of one providing cover for the other's avarice. In his example, Baptists wanted laws closing liquor stores on Sundays to promote piety, and bootleggers wanted such laws to create an unserved market.

Today, New York has the highest state cigarette tax ($4.35 per pack—plus a $1.50 New York City tax) and North Carolina has the sixth-lowest (45 cents), so naturally Interstate-95 is a corridor for smuggled cigarettes, which in 2013 were nearly 60 percent of New York's cigarette market. Proclaiming morality while practicing cupidity, states have tried to hit the sweet spot of cigarette taxes—high enough to maximize revenue without excessively discouraging smoking.

States addicted to tobacco taxes need a large and renewable supply of smokers, so they wince whenever an e-cigarette displaces a traditional cigarette. As Yandle and three colleagues explain in the current issue of *Regulation* quarterly, state governments are now bootleggers masquerading as Baptists, and many are in a bind.

In 1998, acting on the dubious proposition that smoking costs governments substantial sums (actually, cigarettes are one of the most heavily taxed consumer products, and one in three smokers dies prematurely, before fully collecting government medical, pension, and nursing home entitlements), the tobacco companies agreed to pay forty-six states $206 billion through 2025. Some states, impatient to spend their windfall, securitized the future revenue in tobacco bonds. Now, as vaping supplants some smoking, there is a new cadre of bootleggers—the holders of tobacco bonds. They are supposed to be paid from a revenue stream from smokers (disproportionately low-income and low-information people), so they will urge regulations that discourage e-cigarettes. Or that bring e-cigarettes under the 1998 agreement, perhaps by declaring them "tobacco products" because the nicotine can come from tobacco.

In exchange for the big cigarette companies' payments, the 1998 agreement gave them tobacco marketing restrictions, which they welcomed. The restrictions impede the entrance of new competitors into the field, and hinder smaller companies from using cigarette advertising for its primary purpose, which is not to create new smokers but to capture a larger market share of existing smokers.

E-cigarettes can expect similar bootlegging regulations, couched in moralistic cadences. Also, manufacturers of nicotine replacement therapies (e.g., nicotine patches and gum) will be bootleggers seeking regulations that will discourage people from thinking e-cigarettes are a relatively safe way to enjoy nicotine.

Yandle's "bootleggers and Baptists" hypothesis is given many illustrations, from environmental regulations to Obamacare, in a new book of that title, co-authored with his economist grandson, Adam Smith. Yandle's hypothesis expands "public choice" theory, which demystifies and deromanticizes government by applying economic analysis—how incentives influence behavior—to politicians and bureaucrats. It rebuts the fiction that such officials are more disinterested than actors in the private sector. Yandle does the same thing regarding many of those who seek regulations.

Life would be sweeter if people would forgo the pleasures of inhaling smoke and vapors that do not improve the air, which is plentiful and untaxed. And government would be better if more people were clear-eyed about how Baptists and bootleggers collaborate.

OVERCRIMINALIZATION KILLED ERIC GARNER

December 10, 2014

WASHINGTON—By history's frequently brutal dialectic, the good that we call progress often comes spasmodically, in lurches propelled by tragedies caused by callousness, folly, or ignorance. With the grand jury's as yet inexplicable and probably inexcusable refusal to find criminal culpability in Eric Garner's death on a Staten Island sidewalk, the nation might have experienced sufficient affronts to its sense of decency. It might at long last be ready to stare into the abyss of its criminal justice system.

It will stare back, balefully. Furthermore, the radiating ripples from the nation's overdue reconsideration of present practices may reach beyond matters of crime and punishment, to basic truths about governance.

Garner died at the dangerous intersection of something wise, known as "broken windows" policing, and something worse than foolish: decades of overcriminalization. The policing applies the wisdom that when signs of disorder, such as broken windows, proliferate and persist, there is a general diminution of restraint and good comportment. So, because minor infractions are, cumulatively, not minor, police should not be lackadaisical about offenses such as jumping over subway turnstiles.

Overcriminalization has become a national plague. And when more and more behaviors are criminalized, there are more and more occasions for police, who embody the state's monopoly on legitimate violence, and who fully participate in humanity's flaws, to make mistakes.

Harvey Silverglate, a civil liberties attorney, titled his 2009 book *Three Felonies a Day* to indicate how easily we can fall afoul of America's metastasizing body of criminal laws. Professor Douglas Husak of Rutgers University says that approximately 70 percent of American adults have, usually unwittingly, committed a crime for which they could be imprisoned. In his 2008 book, *Overcriminalization: The Limits of the Criminal Law*, Husak says that more than half of the 3,000 *federal* crimes—itself a dismaying number—are found not in the Federal Criminal Code but in numerous other statutes. And, by one estimate, at least 300,000 federal regulations can be enforced by agencies wielding criminal punishments. Citing Husak, Professor Stephen L. Carter of the Yale Law School, like a hammer driving a nail head flush to a board, forcefully underscores the moral of this story:

Society needs laws; therefore it needs law enforcement. But "over-criminalization matters" because "making an offense criminal also means that the police will go armed to enforce it." The job of the police "is to carry out the legislative will." But today's political system takes "bizarre delight in creating new crimes" for enforcement. And "every act of enforcement includes the possibility of violence."

Carter continues: "It's unlikely that the New York Legislature, in creating the crime of selling untaxed cigarettes, imagined that anyone would die for violating it. But a wise legislator would give the matter some thought before creating a crime. Officials who fail to take into account the obvious fact that the laws they're so eager to pass will be enforced at the point of a gun cannot fairly be described as public servants."

Garner lived in part by illegally selling single cigarettes untaxed by New York jurisdictions. He lived in a progressive state and city that, being ravenous for revenues and determined to save smokers from themselves, have raised to $5.85 the combined taxes on a pack of cigarettes. To the surprise of no sentient being, this has created a black market in cigarettes that are bought in states that tax them much less. Garner died in a state that has a Cigarette Strike Force.

He lived and died in a country with 5 percent of the world's population but 25 percent of its prisoners. In 2012, one of every 108 adults was behind bars, many in federal prisons containing about 40 percent more inmates than they were designed to hold.

Most of today's 2.2 million prisoners will be coming back to their neighborhoods, and few of them will have been improved by the experience of incarceration. This will be true even if they did not experience the often deranging use of prolonged solitary confinement, which violates the Eighth Amendment's ban on "cruel and unusual punishments" and is, to put things plainly, torture.

The scandal of mass incarceration is partly produced by the frivolity of the political class, which uses the multiplication of criminal offenses as a form of moral exhibitionism. This, like Eric Garner's death, is a pebble in the mountain of evidence that American government is increasingly characterized by an ugly and sometimes lethal irresponsibility.

DRUG POLICY AND THE "BALLOON EFFECT"

April 5, 2012

WASHINGTON—The human nervous system interacts in pleasing and addictive ways with certain molecules derived from some plants, which is why humans may have developed beer before they developed bread. Psychoactive—consciousness-altering—and addictive drugs are natural, a fact that should immunize policy makers against extravagant hopes as they cope with America's drug problem, which is convulsing some nations to our south.

The costs—human, financial, and social—of combating (most) drugs are prompting calls for decriminalization or legalization. America should, however, learn from the psychoactive drug used by a majority of American adults—alcohol.

Mark Kleiman of UCLA, a policy analyst, was recently discussing drug policy with someone who said he had no experience with illegal drugs, not even marijuana, because he is of "the gin generation." Ah, said Kleiman, gin: "A much more dangerous drug." Twenty percent of all American prisoners—500,000 people—are incarcerated for dealing illegal drugs, but alcohol causes as much as half of America's criminal violence and vehicular fatalities.

Drinking alcohol had been a widely exercised private right for millennia when America tried to prohibit it. As a public health measure, Prohibition "worked": Alcohol-related illnesses declined dramatically. As the monetary cost of drinking tripled, deaths from cirrhosis of the liver declined by a third. This improvement was, however, paid for in the coin of rampant criminality and disrespect for law.

Prohibition resembled what is today called decriminalization: It did not make drinking illegal; it criminalized the making, importing, transporting, or selling of alcohol. Drinking remained legal, so oceans of alcoholic beverages were made, imported, transported, and sold.

Another legal drug, nicotine, kills more people than do alcohol and all illegal drugs—combined. For decades, government has aggressively publicized the health risks of smoking and made it unfashionable, stigmatized, expensive, and inconvenient. Yet 20 percent of every rising American generation becomes addicted to nicotine.

So, suppose cocaine or heroin were legalized and marketed as cigarettes and alcohol are. And suppose the level of addiction were to replicate the 7 percent of adults suffering from alcohol abuse or dependency. That would be a public health disaster. As the late James Q. Wilson said, nicotine shortens life, cocaine debases it.

Still, because the costs of prohibition—interdiction, mass incarceration, etc.—are staggeringly high, some people say, "Let's just try legalization for a while." Society is not, however, like a controlled laboratory; in society, experiments that produce disappointing or unexpected results cannot be tidily reversed.

Legalized marijuana could be produced for much less than a tenth of its current price as an illegal commodity. Legalization of cocaine and heroin would cut their prices, too; they would sell for a tiny percentage of their current prices. And using high excise taxes to maintain cocaine and heroin prices at current levels would produce widespread tax evasion—and an illegal market.

Furthermore, legalization would mean drugs of reliable quality would be conveniently available from clean stores for customers not risking the stigma of breaking the law in furtive transactions with unsavory people. So there is *no* reason to think today's levels of addiction are anywhere near the levels that would be reached under legalization.

Regarding the interdicting of drug shipments, capturing "kingpin" distributors and incarcerating dealers, consider data from the book *Drugs and Drug Policy: What Everyone Needs to Know* by Kleiman, Jonathan Caulkins, and Angela Hawken. Almost all heroin comes from poppies grown on 4 percent of the arable land of one country—Afghanistan. Four South American countries—Colombia, Ecuador, Peru, and Bolivia—produce more than 90 percent of the world's cocaine. But attempts to decrease production in source countries produce the "balloon effect." Squeeze a balloon in one spot, it bulges in another. Suppress production of poppies or coca leaves here, production moves there. The $8 billion Plan Colombia was a melancholy success, reducing coca production there 65 percent, while production increased 40 percent in Peru and doubled in Bolivia.

In the 1980s, when "cocaine cowboys" made Miami lawless, the U.S. government created the South Florida Task Force to interdict cocaine shipped from Central and South America by small planes and cigarette boats. This interdiction was so successful the cartels opened new delivery routes. Tranquility in Miami was purchased at the price of mayhem in Mexico.

America spends twenty times more on drug control than all the world's poppy and coca growers earn. A subsequent column will suggest a more economic approach to the "natural" problem of drugs.

RETHINKING THE DRUG CONTROL TRIAD

April 12, 2012

WASHINGTON—Amelioration of today's drug problem requires Americans to understand the significance of the 80/20 ratio. Twenty percent of American drinkers consume 80 percent of the alcohol sold here. The same 80-20 split obtains among users of illicit drugs.

About 3 million people—less than 1 percent of America's population—consume 80 percent of illegal hard drugs. Drug trafficking organizations can be most efficiently injured by changing the behavior of the 20 percent of heavy users, and we are learning how to do so. Reducing consumption by the 80 percent of casual users will not substantially reduce the northward flow of drugs or the southward flow of money.

Consider current policy concerning the only addictive intoxicant currently available as a consumer good—alcohol. America's alcohol industry, which is as dependent on the 20 percent of heavy drinkers as they are on alcohol, markets its products aggressively, and effectively. Because marketing can drive consumption, America's distillers, brewers, and vintners spend $6 billion on advertising and promoting their products. Americans' experience with marketing's power inclines them to favor prohibition and enforcement over legalization and marketing of drugs.

But this choice has consequences: More Americans are imprisoned for drug offenses or drug-related probation and parole violations than for property crimes. And although America spends five times more jailing drug dealers than it did thirty years ago, the prices of cocaine and heroin are 80 percent to 90 percent lower than thirty years ago.

In *Drugs and Drug Policy: What Everyone Needs to Know*, policy analysts Mark Kleiman, Jonathan Caulkins, and Angela Hawken argue that imprisoning low-ranking, street-corner dealers is pointless: A $200 transaction can cost society $100,000 for a three-year sentence. And imprisoning large numbers of dealers produces an army of people who, emerging from prison with blighted employment prospects, can only deal drugs. Which is why, although a few years ago Washington, D.C., dealers earned an average of $30 an hour, today they earn less than the federal minimum wage ($7.25).

Dealers, aka "pushers," have almost nothing to do with initiating drug use by future addicts; almost every user starts when given drugs by a friend, sibling, or acquaintance. There is a staggering disparity between the trivial sums earned by dealers who connect the cartels to the cartels' customers and the huge sums trying to slow the flow of drugs to those street-level dealers. Kleiman, Caulkins, and Hawken say that in developed nations, cocaine sells for about $3,000 per ounce— almost twice the price of gold. And the supply of cocaine, unlike that of gold, can be cheaply and quickly expanded. But in the countries where cocaine and heroin are produced, they sell for about 1 percent of their retail price in America. If cocaine were legalized, a $2,000 kilogram could be FedExed from Colombia for less than $50 and sold profitably in America for a small markup from its price in Colombia, and a $5 rock of crack might cost 25 cents. Criminalization drives the cost of the smuggled kilogram in America up to $20,000. But then it retails for more than $100,000.

People used to believe enforcement could raise prices but doubted that higher prices would decrease consumption. Now they know consumption declines as prices rise but wonder whether enforcement can substantially affect prices.

They urge rethinking the drug-control triad of enforcement, prevention, and treatment because we have been much too optimistic about all three.

And cartels have oceans of money for corrupting enforcement because drugs are so cheap to produce and easy to renew. So it is not unreasonable to consider modifying a policy that gives hundreds of billions of dollars a year to violent organized crime.

Marijuana probably provides less than 25 percent of the cartels' revenues. Legalizing it would take perhaps $10 billion from some bad and violent people, but the cartels would still make much more money from cocaine, heroin, and methamphetamines than they would lose from marijuana legalization.

Sixteen states and the District of Columbia have legalized "medical marijuana," a messy, mendacious semi-legalization that breeds cynicism regarding law. In 1990, 24 percent of Americans supported full legalization. Today, 50 percent do. In 2010, in California, where one-eighth of Americans live, 46 percent of voters supported legalization, and some opponents were marijuana growers who like the profits they make from prohibition of their product.

Would the public health problems resulting from legalization be a price worth paying for injuring the cartels and reducing the costs of enforcement? We probably are going to find out.

INJUSTICES IN THE CRIMINAL JUSTICE SYSTEM

October 25, 2015

WASHINGTON—The Republican Party, like Sisyphus, is again putting its shoulder to a boulder, hoping to make modest but significant changes in the Electoral College arithmetic by winning perhaps 12 percent of the African-American vote. To this end, they need to hone a rhetoric of skepticism about, and an agenda for reform of, the criminal justice system. They can draw on the thinking of a federal appellate judge nominated by Ronald Reagan.

In an article that has stirred considerable discussion since it appeared this past summer in the *Georgetown Law Journal*, Alex Kozinski of the U.S. Court of Appeals for the Ninth Circuit provides facts and judgments that should disturb everyone, but especially African Americans, whose encounters with the criminal justice system are dismayingly frequent and frequently dismaying.

Eyewitness testimony is, Kozinski says, "highly unreliable, especially where the witness and the perpetrator are of different races." Mistaken eyewitnesses figured in 34 percent of wrongful convictions in the database of the National Registry of Exonerations. Fingerprint evidence, too, has "a significant error rate," as do spectrographic voice identification (error rates up to 63 percent) and handwriting identification (error rates average 40 percent). Many defendants have spent years in prison "based on evidence by arson experts who were later shown to be little better than witch doctors." DNA evidence is reliable when properly handled, but is only as good as are the fallible testing labs.

"Much of what we do in the courtroom relies," Kozinski writes, "on human memory." But the more we learn about the way memories are "recorded, stored and retrieved," the less confidence we can have that memories are undistorted and unembellished by the mind or external influences. And courts rarely allow expert testimony on memory.

The idea that at least confessions are reliable because "innocent people never confess" is refuted by the indisputable fact that they do "with surprising regularity." They do for reasons ranging from a desire to end harsh interrogations, to emotional and financial exhaustion, and to coercive charging of multiple offenses made possible by the over-criminalization of life.

Kozinski says we know "very little" about how juries decide cases. "Do they assume that the presumption [of innocence] remains in place until it is overcome by persuasive evidence or do they believe it disappears as soon as any actual evidence is presented?" Do they actually distinguish between a "preponderance" of evidence, "clear and convincing" evidence, and evidence "beyond a reasonable doubt"? Research demonstrates that the person—the prosecutor—making a first assertion has a substantial advantage over those who subsequently deny it. In the courtroom, juries first hear from prosecutors.

Prosecutions are preceded by police investigations. Police, says Kozinski, have "vast discretion" about, among many other things, which leads to pursue and witnesses to interview. They also have opportunities "to manufacture or destroy evidence, influence witnesses, extract confessions" and otherwise "stack the deck against people they think should be convicted." A woman spent twenty-three years on death row because of an oral confession she supposedly made during a twenty-minute interrogation by a detective who Kozinski says was later shown "to be a serial liar." The conviction of a man who spent thirty-nine years in prison was based "entirely" on the eyewitness testimony of a twelve-year-old who saw the crime from a distance, failed to identify the man in a lineup, and was fed information by the police.

Kozinski suggests many reforms, including recording all interrogations of suspects, strictly limiting uses of jailhouse informants, allowing jurors to take notes and ask questions during the trial, and repealing three felony statutes a day for three years. He cites "disturbing indications that a non-trivial number of prosecutors—and sometimes entire prosecutorial offices—engage in misconduct." Because a conscientious FBI agent revealed that Justice Department prosecutors concealed exculpatory evidence, we know that Alaska's Republican Senator Ted Stevens was wrongly convicted of corruption. Kozinski, who recommends establishing independent prosecutorial integrity units, thinks the Justice Department's unit "seems to view its mission as cleaning up the reputation of prosecutors who have gotten themselves into trouble." Kozinski favors abrogating absolute prosecutorial immunity.

Finally, he advocates careful study of exonerations, of which there have been 1,576 since 1989. And for every one "there may be dozens who are innocent but cannot prove it." If the error rate is 1 percent, 22,000 innocent people are in prison. If the rate is 5 percent, the number is 110,000. Whatever the number, it almost certainly is disproportionately African American.

COERCIVE PLEA BARGAINING IS A NATIONAL EMBARRASSMENT

May 21, 2020

WASHINGTON—Michael Flynn, who was President Trump's national security adviser for twenty-four days and who has been entangled in the criminal-justice system for forty months, pleaded guilty of lying to FBI agents and now recants that plea. We shall return to Flynn below, but first consider Habeeb Audu, who is resisting extradition from Britain to the United States, where he is charged with various financial crimes.

The Cato Institute's Clark Neily was asked by Audu's lawyers to write, in accordance with British extradition practices, a Declaration— an "expert report"—about the risk that Audu would not have a meaningful right to a fair U.S. trial. Neily, a member of the American Bar Association's Plea Bargaining Task Force and head of its subcommittee on impermissibly coercive plea bargains and plea practices, concludes that extradition would "guarantee" Audu's subjection to a process that "routinely" coerces through plea bargaining. So Audu probably would experience "intolerable pressure designed to induce a waiver of his fundamental right to a fair trial."

Plea bargaining is, Neily argues "pervasive and coercive" partly because of today's "trial penalty"—the difference between the sentences offered to those who plead guilty and the much more severe sentences typically imposed after a trial. This penalty discourages exercising a constitutional right. A defendant in a computer hacking case, Neily says, committed suicide during plea bargaining in which prosecutors said he could avoid a trial conviction and sentence of up to thirty-five years by pleading guilty and accepting a six-month sentence.

The pressure prosecutors can exert—piling on ("stacking") criminal charges to expose defendants to extreme sentences; pretrial detention, nearly always in squalid confines; threatening to indict family members— can cause innocent people to plead guilty in order to avoid risking protracted incarceration for themselves and loved ones. Such pressures effectively transfer sentencing power from judges to prosecutors. How exactly are these pressures morally preferable to those that used to be administered by truncheons in the back of police stations?

These are reasons why of the nearly 80,000 defendants in federal criminal cases in fiscal 2018, just 2 percent went to trial and 90 percent pleaded guilty. In 2018, 94.7 percent of criminal convictions were obtained through plea bargains in the Southern District of New York, which is seeking Audu's extradition.

Prosecutors have discovered that almost any defendant can be persuaded to plead guilty, given sufficient inducements. This discovery has been partly a response to the fact that the overcriminalization of life, and particularly Congress's indefensible multiplication of federal crimes, means that otherwise the court system would, in Justice Antonin Scalia's words, "grind to a halt."

There is, Neily says, "abundant, undisputed evidence" of innocent defendants pleading guilty. Of the 367 convicts exonerated by DNA analysis to date, 11 percent had pleaded guilty. Various studies have concluded that between 1.6 percent and 8 percent of defendants who plead guilty would not have been convicted in a trial. The lowest estimate would mean that in 2009 there were more than 1,250 innocent people incarcerated in the federal system alone, and many multiples of that number in state systems.

Responding to Neily's Declaration, the Justice Department complacently asserts that U.S. law guarantees fair trials: Coercive plea bargains are forbidden, therefore they do not occur, so innocent people do not plead guilty. Move along, nothing to see here.

The DOJ should consult Jed S. Rakoff. In a 2014 essay, "Why Innocent People Plead Guilty," he wrote that since the last third of the previous century, a fair trial—an adversarial process, conducted in public before a neutral judge and a jury of the defendant's peers—has become "all a mirage." Rakoff is a senior judge on the U.S. District Court for the Southern District of New York.

Now, about Flynn. Perhaps he lied in an interview with FBI agents. We must, however, take their word for this, because, in accordance with an archaic and self-serving practice, the agents did not record the interview. They wrote their unverifiable version. This, although all FBI agents carry recording capabilities in their smartphones. After prosecutors threatened to indict his son, who was his business partner (remember the axiom: "A prosecutor can get a grand jury to indict a ham sandwich"), a coerced and impoverished Flynn, facing many millions in legal bills, and later selling his suburban Washington house, pleaded guilty. President Donald Trump pardoned Michael Flynn.

Perhaps Flynn now regrets leading "Lock her up!" chants at the Republican National Convention. All Americans should regret the need for

Neily's many proposed reforms, including a DOJ Office of Plea Integrity to scrutinize coercive plea bargaining, a national embarrassment.

HOW THE RIGHT TO A TRIAL IS NULLIFIED

December 26, 2013

WASHINGTON—Federal Judge John Gleeson of the Eastern District of New York says documents called "statements of reasons" are an optional way for a judge to express "views that might be of interest." The one he issued two months ago is still reverberating.

It expresses his dismay that although his vocation is the administration of justice, his function frequently is the infliction of injustice. The policy of mandatory minimum sentences for drug offenses has empowered the government to effectively nullify the constitutional right to a trial. As Lulzim Kupa learned.

Born to Albanian immigrants, he was convicted in 1999 and 2007 of distributing marijuana. Released from prison in 2010, he again engaged in trafficking, this time with enough cocaine to earn him charges involving a sentence of ten years to life. On March 5, 2013, prosecutors offered this: In exchange for a guilty plea, he would effectively be sentenced within the range of 110 to 137 months—but the offer would expire the next day. Kupa rejected the offer, so on March 15 prosecutors filed a "prior felony information," aka an 851 notice, citing the two marijuana convictions. So, ten days after saying a sentence of perhaps less than eight years (assuming good time credits) would be appropriate, prosecutors were threatening a sentence of life without parole. This gave him no incentive to plead guilty.

Then, however, they immediately proposed another plea agreement involving about nine years' imprisonment. Given a day to decide, he acted too slowly, so prosecutors again increased the recommended sentence. Finally, Kupa caved: "I want to plead guilty, Your Honor, before things get worse." If, after the 851 notice, he had insisted on a trial and been found guilty, he would have died in prison for a nonviolent drug offense. He is thirty-seven.

Tyquan Midyett, a high-school dropout from a broken home and foster care, began using marijuana at fourteen. He was twenty-six when arrested for selling less than four ounces of crack. Because this was his second offense, the best he could do pleading guilty was a ten-year sentence. When he hesitated, the government gave him a date to agree or it would file an 851 notice, which would double the mandatory minimum to twenty years. He went to trial, was convicted, and is serving 240 months for an offense that, without the escalating coercions aimed at a guilty plea, would have received a sentence of 46–57 months.

In 2008, an 851 notice was filed against Charles Doutre, based on two prior convictions for distribution of fifty dollars' worth of drugs and simple possession of drugs. The judge who was required to sentence him to life in prison said, "I've imposed a life sentence six times, and it was for a murder each time." Doutre is thirty-two.

Eleven years ago, Dennis Capps, thirty-nine, a methamphetamine addict, pled guilty to two instances of trafficking involving a quantity of drugs he could hold in his hand. He conquered his addiction for a long time, then relapsed, and in this year was convicted of another drug offense. Because he insisted on a trial, the government filed an 851 notice. He was convicted, and is serving life without parole.

Kenneth Harvey was twenty-four in 1989 when he committed a crack cocaine offense. He had two prior offenses that qualified as felony drug convictions even though they were not deemed serious enough for imprisonment. They, however, enabled the government to make an 851 filing. He will die in prison. Harvey is forty-eight.

Thousands of prisoners are serving life without parole for nonviolent crimes. Gleeson, who is neither naive nor sentimental (as a prosecutor, he sent mobster John Gotti to die in a supermax prison), knows that most defendants who plead guilty are guilty. He is, however, dismayed at the use of the threat of mandatory minimums as "sledgehammers" to extort guilty pleas, effectively vitiating the right to a trial. Ninety-seven percent of federal convictions are without trials, sparing the government the burden of proving guilt beyond a reasonable doubt. Mere probable cause, and the meager presentation required for a grand jury indictment, suffices. "Judging is removed," Gleeson says, "prosecutors become sentencers." And when threats of draconian sentences compel guilty pleas, "some innocent people will plead guilty."

Barack Obama, Attorney General Eric Holder, and Senators Pat Leahy, D-Vermont, and Rand Paul, R-Kentucky, are questioning the regime of mandatory minimum sentences, including recidivism enhancements, that began with the Anti-Drug Abuse Act of 1986. Meanwhile, the human and financial costs of mass incarceration mount.

DISENFRANCHISING FELONS: WHY?

April 8, 2018

JACKSONVILLE, Fla.—The bumpy path of Desmond Meade's life meandered to its current interesting point. He is a graduate of Florida International University law school but cannot vote in his home state because his path went through prison: He committed nonviolent felonies concerning drugs and other matters during the ten years when he was essentially homeless. And Florida is one of eleven states that effectively disqualify felons permanently.

Meade is one of 1.6 million disenfranchised Florida felons—more people than voted in twenty-two states in 2016. He is one of the 20 percent of African-American Floridians disenfranchised. The state has a low threshold for felonious acts: Someone who gets into a bar fight, or steals property worth $300—approximately two pairs of Air Jordans—or even drives without a license for a third time can be disenfranchised for life. There is a cumbersome, protracted process whereby an individual, after waiting five to seven years (it depends on the felony) can begin a trek that can consume ten years and culminates with politicians and their appointees deciding who can vote.

Meade heads the Florida Rights Restoration Coalition, which gathered more than a million signatures to get the state Supreme Court to approve, and local supervisors of elections to verify, the ballot initiative that voters will decide on November 6. Meade's basic argument on behalf of what he calls "returning citizens" like him is: "I challenge people to say that they never want to be forgiven for anything they've done." Persons convicted of murder or felony sexual offense would not be eligible for enfranchisement.

Intelligent and informed people of good will can strenuously disagree about the wisdom of policies that have produced mass incarceration. What is, however, indisputable is that this phenomenon creates an enormous problem of facilitating the re-entry into society of released prisoners who were not improved by the experience of incarceration and who face discouraging impediments to employment and other facets of social normality. In fourteen states and the District of Columbia, released felons automatically recover their civil rights.

Recidivism among Florida's released felons has been approximately 30 percent for the five years from 2011 to 2015. Of the 1,952 persons whose civil rights were restored, five committed new offenses, a recidivism rate of 0.4 percent. This sample is skewed by self-selection—overrepresentation of those who had the financial resources and tenacity to navigate the complex restoration process that each year serves a few hundred of the 1.6 million. Still, the recidivism numbers are suggestive.

What compelling government interest is served by felon disenfranchisement? Enhanced public safety? How? Is it to fine-tune the quality of the electorate? This is not a legitimate government objective for elected officials to pursue. A felony conviction is an indelible stain: What intelligent purpose is served by reminding felons, who really do not require reminding, of their past, and by advertising it to their community? The rule of law requires punishments, but it is not served by punishments that never end and that perpetuate a social stigma and a sense of never fully re-entering the community.

Meade, like one-third of the 4.7 million current citizens nationwide who have re-entered society from prison but cannot vote, is an African American. More than one in 13 African Americans nationally are similarly disenfranchised, as are one in five of Florida's African-American adults. Because African Americans overwhelmingly vote Democratic, ending the disenfranchisement of felons could become yet another debate swamped by partisanship, particularly in Florida, the largest swing state, where close elections are common: Republican Governor Rick Scott's margins of victory in 2010 and 2014 were 1.2 and 1.1 percent, respectively. And remember the 537 Florida votes that made George W. Bush president.

Last week, Scott's administration challenged a federal judge's order that the state adopt a rights-restoration procedure that is less arbitrary and dilatory. A Quinnipiac poll shows that 67 percent of Floridians favor and only 27 percent oppose enfranchisement of felons. These numbers might provoke Republicans, who control both houses of the legislature, to try to siphon away support for the restoration referendum by passing a law that somewhat mitigates the severity of the current policy. Such a law would be presented for the signature of the governor, who is trying to unseat three-term Democratic senator Bill Nelson.

Again, who is comfortable with elected politicians winnowing the electorate? When the voting results from around the nation are reported on the evening of November 6, some actual winners might include 1.6 million Floridians who were not allowed to cast ballots.

—

Desmond Meade's organization got the ballot initiative passed. The Florida Republican-controlled legislature tried to minimize its effect by requiring former felons to pay various fees—even the cost of a public defender—before voting.

HUMAN RECLAMATION THROUGH BRICKLAYING

February 2, 2020

PITTSBURGH—In the 1940s, Steve Shelton's grandfather dressed up—white shirt, tie, fedora—to take the streetcar to the steel mill where he would change into work clothes, and would shower before dressing up to return home. "There was," Shelton says, "such dignity in the trades back then."

There still is at the Trade Institute of Pittsburgh (TIP) that Shelton launched. There, in what used to be a Westinghouse Electric factory, some men, many in their thirties looking for their first legal jobs, and a few women learn to wield trowels and mortar, thereby deriving from bricklaying (and welding, carpentry, and painting) a dignity they did not feel when they grew up on this city's meanest streets, or when, for 85 percent of them, their incarcerations ended.

Shelton, fifty-nine, was twelve when he first was taken to a construction site. "I just wanted to build stuff," so after enjoying two things in high school (wood shop, metal shop), serving in the Navy, and working in the trades, he started a business "out of the trunk of my car." Eventually, however, he wondered: "Where are all the young guys?" He saw: "Everyone was being pushed to college." He thought: "Having guys fifty-five or sixty years old on top of scaffolding, laying bricks, is not sustainable."

He knew there were guys like him "who want to work with their hands." Many were coming out of jail. Shelton talked with churches and civic organizations, and eventually the local Mellon (banking) and Heinz (ketchup, etc.) foundations. One thing led to another, and to this: The abandoned factory—deindustrialization has upsides—has a floor covered with bricks, cinder blocks, tubs of mortar, and people trying to get the hang of building things, and get on the bottom rung of the ladder of upward mobility.

Things were made in the factory in the 1920s when Pittsburgh, then America's ninth most populous city (in 1920 it was just ahead of Los Angeles) made the nation's steel ligaments. In 2020, builders are made in the factory. Pittsburgh, now sixty-sixth in population, has put aside smokestacks and remade itself around technology and health care. It has, however, a construction boom—partly a result of Pennsylvania's fracking—and a shortage of workers for the building trades.

Shelton's $1.4 million annual budget, from private and public sources, enables him and his staff "to take someone from nothing to a living wage in ten weeks." Cameron Meadows, TIP's assistant masonry instructor, served ten years for shooting someone in a bar fight, long before TIP changed his life. Shelton notes that when his human reclamation program prevents someone from spending sixty years in prison, costing Pennsylvania $50,000 a year, "I've saved taxpayers three million bucks."

One in thirty-eight American adults is incarcerated, on probation, or on parole. Many former inmates return to communities where they had barely been connected to its constitutive units—families, schools, and civic, religious, and commercial institutions. Reintegration—acquiring residences, driver's licenses, bus passes, bank accounts, health care, child care, employment—can be bewildering, demoralizing, and exhausting. Some of TIP's trainees are "couch surfing"—moving from one residence to another, night by night. All receive financial counseling. And there are driving lessons in the factory's parking lot.

But every morning at eight a.m.—not 8:01, because, Shelton says, in construction time is money—the trainees sit in the "gratitude circle." There, each says something for which he or she is thankful. They all can mention this: ten weeks—340 hours—of free training. And a job on the horizon, sometimes a union job at $22.58 an hour.

To a person from a fractured family, a job says: Someone objectively values you—enough to pay you to spend eight hours a day adding value to a project. To a person fresh from prison, a job says: You are a welcomed, functioning part of the society that decided it had to put you in a cage for a while. To a person whose education conferred only rudimentary skills, a job says: You have risen from among the unskilled to the rank of craftsman.

An expert bricklayer's virtuosity with a trowel and mortar—Shelton's is magical—as he or she manipulates bricks with motions so fluid that the bricks seem weightless, has the elegance that characterizes all craftsmanship. The recidivism rate among formerly incarcerated Pennsylvanians is around 43 percent. The rate among Shelton's former trainees is 9 percent.

It is an old saying that the devil fills idle hands. But not hands holding trowels.

SING SING: "NOT A LANDFILL BUT A RECYCLING CENTER"

June 15, 2017

OSSINING, N.Y.—Sparkling in the sunlight that inspired nineteenth-century romantic painters of the Hudson River School, Sing Sing prison's razor wire, through which inmates can see the flowing river, is almost pretty. Almost. Rain or shine, however, a fog of regret permeates any maximum-security prison. But thirty-seven men—almost all minorities; mostly African Americans—recently received celebratory attention. It was their commencement—attended by Harry Belafonte, ninety, and the singer Usher—as freshly minted college graduates. Their lives after prison will not soon, if ever, commence, but when they do these men will have unusual momentum for success.

Most of the 2.3 million people now incarcerated in America will return to their communities, and few will have been improved by their experiences inside. It is said that a convict's successful re-entry into society begins the day he enters a correctional facility, as prison administrators prefer to call their institutions. But the criminal justice system is failing to accomplish lasting correction: More than half of released prisoners are arrested again in the first year, more than two-thirds within three years, more than three-quarters within five years.

The odds are dramatically better for the thirty-seven men here who received bachelor of behavioral science degrees or associate's degrees conferred by Mercy College from nearby Dobbs Ferry. Graduates from Sing Sing's Hudson Link for Higher Education in Prison program have a 1 percent recidivism rate.

This is partly a function of self-selection: There is a long waiting list for admission to the program, and those admitted pay ten dollars tuition per semester, funded by their prison wages of eighteen cents an hour. Some have not been in school for twenty years. All are motivated.

Sixty-one percent of America's inmates have fewer than eight years of education. An often insuperable impediment to post-prison success is the scarcity of jobs for formerly incarcerated people whose years since their truncated schooling have been barren of the attention and instruction that could give them the manners and skills necessary for life after institutionalization. However, 95 percent of Hudson Link graduates have jobs within six months of their release. One just received a graduate degree from Columbia University; another just began postgraduate study there.

Thirty miles downriver, a significant number of New York City social workers are formerly incarcerated people who know the temptations of, and the tolls taken by, bad choices. That phrase, "bad choices," is spoken often by those inmates who, by affirming their agency—their capacity to freely choose their behavior—are halfway home.

Hudson Link's executive director, Sean Pica, is an ebullient forty-year-old who, convicted of manslaughter at sixteen, was incarcerated for half of his first thirty-two years. He was close to earning a degree while in prison when, in 1994, Congress, in a punitive act, banned Pell Grants for inmates. So Hudson Link, a nonprofit, was created with the support of donors like Doris Buffett, whose brother Warren has attended a commencement here. Hudson Link now operates in six New York prisons with eight college partners.

The Sing Sing Class of 2017's valedictorian, deftly quoting Franz Kafka ("There are some things one can only achieve by a deliberate leap in the opposite direction"), William James, and Frederick Douglass, said to his classmates, "We are better than we were but not the best that we can be." Most inmates in the Hudson Link program are acquainted with Langston Hughes's 1951 poem "Harlem":

What happens to a dream deferred?
Does it dry up
Like a raisin in the sun?

The poem concludes:

Maybe it just sags
like a heavy load
Or does it explode?

The load of thirty-seven pasts that were strewn with explosions was lightened for this year's graduates as they flipped tassels from the right to the left sides of their mortarboards. To the strains of Elgar's "Pomp and Circumstance," they marched as college graduates in their academic gowns to join their families for lunch, as an inmate on the kitchen staff called out, "You've not had chicken until you've had chicken at Sing Sing." It did not disappoint.

Film festivals' awards have been showered on *Zero Percent*, a movie about Hudson Link, in which a Sing Sing inmate, speaking to and for a prior year's graduating class, says that the program's purpose is to make sure prison is "not a landfill but a recycling center." Many such men have done terrible things, but it would be terrible to ignore the capacity some have for regeneration.

JUSTICE. MORE OR LESS. SOMETIMES.

ARISTOTLE AND THE BIKINI-CLAD BARISTAS

October 5, 2017

SEATTLE—Amazon, which has made this city the epicenter of a retailing revolution, is not the Northwest's only commercial disrupter. In the nearby city of Everett, Liberty Ziska and some other bikini baristas, giving new meaning to coffee as a stimulant, have provoked the City Council to pass, unanimously, ordinances requiring baristas to be less nearly naked when they work. The baristas, in turn, have hired a lawyer and made an argument that is germane to current disputes about freedom of speech. Their argument, they might be surprised to learn, is Aristotelian. Sort of.

Everett has not succumbed to Pecksniffian Comstockery: The police chief and city attorney allege that bikini barista stands attract a clientele that sometimes behaves badly, and that some of the baristas do, too. The city reports "a proliferation of crimes of a sexual nature occurring at bikini barista stands," which it primly suggests has something to do with "the minimalistic nature of the clothing worn by baristas." Seattle's ABC affiliate reports that "in 2014, the owner of Java Juggs pleaded guilty to running a brothel out of several stands." Henceforth the baristas must wear at least shorts and tank tops. The new dress code cannot be faulted for vagueness. Indeed, it has notable specificity (it mentions the "bottom one-half of the anal cleft" and is even more detailed about breasts) that has the baristas incensed about the examinations and anatomical measurements that law enforcement might require.

What makes this a matter of more than mere ribaldry is that the baristas have unlimbered heavy constitutional artillery. They fire it in ways pertinent to the manner in which freedom of speech is debated and defended—or not—where it is most important and most besieged: on campuses. The baristas say:

The ordinances banning bikinis violate the First Amendment because they are "content-based and viewpoint-based restrictions" that "impermissibly burden and chill" their freedom to "convey their messages of female empowerment, positive body image" and other things. Their bikinis are "a branding message" communicating "approachability and friendliness." The ordinances regulate only speech "common and fundamental" at bikini barista stands, targeting them "because Everett does not agree with their message" and restricting "channels of communication." Ziska says that if clothing covers the tattoos on her legs, arms, wrists, back, neck, and hips she cannot have such interesting conversations with customers. Brittany Giazzi and Leah Humphrey argue similarly about their piercings and scars, respectively.

Never mind the baristas' further barrage of allegations in their everything-but-the-kitchen-sink complaint—e.g., that the ordinances are "an equal-protection violation" because they target women ("a protected class") and do not burden men. Instead, note how strenuously, even imaginatively, Ziska and her co-workers strain to argue teleologically.

In recent lectures at Georgetown and American universities in Washington, Greg Weiner, an Assumption College political philosopher and frequent contributor to the Library of Law & Liberty website, urged participants in the campus arguments to reason as Aristotle did. That is, to be less deontological (rights-based in their advocacy) and more teleological (ends-based). To argue deontologically is to treat speech as an autonomous good, regardless of its moral or social purpose, if it has one. To argue teleologically is to stress why—for what purpose—we should value speech.

Aristotle—here he was not the baristas' ally—defined human beings as *language*-using creatures, which makes the expressive value of tattoos, piercings, body parts, etc., less than fundamental. The Supreme Court's First Amendment jurisprudence, Weiner notes, has generally accorded the most robust protection to *speech*, and speech that is political, broadly defined—concerned with securing the goods of self-government. The *fundamental* purpose (telos), although not the only purpose, of the right to free speech is to protect a panoply of other rights.

So, the First Amendment rightly protects not just speech but "expression," and a free society should give generous protection even to expressions that serve no public purpose, but just make the expressing persons happy. But speech about the pursuit of truth, justice, and other important public matters—the sort of speech central to academic institutions—merits more rigorous protection than the baristas' right to display, among much else, their tattoos, piercings, and scars.

Everett should have some latitude to balance other public goods against the expressive pleasure and even commercial advantages that Liberty Ziska and her colleagues derive from sartorial minimalism. Universities should protect almost absolute freedom for arguments about politics, classically and properly defined broadly as the subject of how we should live.

—

In July 2019 an Aristotelian federal appeals court splashed cold water on the baristas' First Amendment argument.

THE RECURRING EVIL OF THE "ONE DROP" RULE

September 3, 2015

"It is a sordid business, this divvying us up by race."
—Chief Justice John Roberts

WASHINGTON—Sordid, always. And sometimes lethal, as some Native American children could attest, were they not, like Declan Stewart and Laurynn Whiteshield, dead. They were victims of the Indian Child Welfare Act (ICWA), which as construed and applied demonstrates how identity politics can leave a trail of broken bodies and broken hearts.

The 1978 act's advocates say it is not about race but about the rights of sovereign tribes, as though that distinction is meaningful. The act empowers tribes to abort adoption proceedings, or even take children from foster homes, solely because the children have even a minuscule quantum of American Indian blood. Although, remember, this act is supposedly not about race.

The most recent case to reach the U.S. Supreme Court concerned a child who was 1.2 percent Cherokee. The Goldwater Institute, the Phoenix think tank whose litigators are challenging ICWA's constitutionality, says "her nearest full-blooded Indian ancestor lived in the time of George Washington's father."

Children's welfare, which is paramount under all fifty states' laws, is sacrificed to abstractions like tribal "integrity" or "coherence." The Goldwater litigators say that guidelines from the U.S. Bureau of Indian Affairs tell courts that in determining foster care or adoption, "Placement in an Indian home is presumed to be in the child's best interest." ICWA forbids blocking placement in an Indian home because of poverty, substance abuse, or "nonconforming social behavior."

ICWA was passed to prevent a real abuse, the taking of Indian children from their homes without justifiable cause. But by protecting tribal sovereignty without stipulating the primary importance of protecting the best interests of the children, the rights of the tribes have essentially erased those of the children and the parents who wish to adopt them.

Declan Stewart was five when he was beaten to death by his mother's live-in boyfriend. Declan had been removed from her by Oklahoma state officials in 2006, after his skull had been fractured and he received severe bruising between his testicles and rectum. But when the Cherokee Nation objected to his removal, Oklahoma, knowing how ICWA favors tribal rights, relented. Declan was murdered a month after being returned to his mother.

From age nine months until she was almost three, Laurynn Whiteshield and her twin sister were in the foster care of Jeanine Kersey-Russell, a Methodist minister in Bismarck, North Dakota. But when she tried to terminate the twins' parents' rights in order to adopt them, the Spirit Lake Sioux tribe invoked ICWA, and the children were sent to the reservation and the custody of their grandfather. Thirty-seven days later, Laurynn died after being thrown down an embankment by her grandfather's wife, who had a record of neglecting, endangering, and abusing her own children. Laurynn's sister was returned to Kersey-Russell.

Laura and Pete Lupo of Lynden, Washington, raised Elle, who was less than 2 percent Cherokee and who came to them at age fourteen months from a mother who was a drug addict and a father who was in prison. When Elle was three, her uncle objected to the Lupos adopting her, and she was given to him.

By treating children, however attenuated or imaginary their Indian ancestry, as little trophies for tribal power, ICWA discourages adoptions by parents who see only children, not pawns of identity politics. The Goldwater Institute hopes to establish the right of Indian children to be treated as all other children are, rather than as subordinate to tribal rights. "Is it one drop of blood that triggers all these extraordinary rights?" asked Chief Justice Roberts during oral arguments in a case involving ICWA. Indeed.

The most pernicious idea ever in general circulation in the United States is the "one-drop rule," according to which persons whose ancestry includes any black or Indian admixture are assigned a black or Indian identity. In final adoption hearings in Arizona, a judge asks, "Does this child contain any Native American blood?" It is revolting that judicial proceedings in America can turn on questions about group rights deriving from "blood."

It has been a protracted, serpentine path from *Plessy v. Ferguson* (1896) and "separate but equal" to today's racial preferences. The nation still is stained by the sordid business of assigning group identities and rights. This is discordant with the inherent individualism of the nation's foundational natural rights tradition, which is incompatible with ICWA. It should be overturned or revised before more bodies and hearts are broken.

"JUDICIAL ENGAGEMENT" AGAINST THE ADMINISTRATIVE STATE

April 22, 2018

WASHINGTON—Last week, one week after the first anniversary of Neil Gorsuch's ascension to the Supreme Court, he delivered an opinion that was excellent as it pertained to the case at issue and momentous in its implications pertaining to the institutional tangle known as the administrative state. If he can persuade his fellow court conservatives to see why they were mistaken in disagreeing with him, and if he can persuade his liberal colleagues to follow the logic of their decision with which he concurred, the judiciary will begin restoring constitutional equilibrium. It will limit Congress's imprecise legislating that requires excessive unguided improvising by all those involved in seeing that the laws are "faithfully" executed.

In 1992, when James Dimaya, a Philippine citizen, was thirteen, he became a lawful permanent resident of the United States, where, unfortunately, his behavior has been less than lawful: In 2007 and 2009, he was convicted of residential burglary. The Department of Homeland Security says he should be deported because he committed a "crime of violence," hence covered by a portion of immigration law that, after listing specific crimes (rape, murder, etc.), adds a catchall category of crimes involving "a substantial risk that physical force against the person or property of another may be used in the course of committing the offense." How are judges supposed to apply this?

Writing for the majority in a 5–4 decision—and joined by Ruth Bader Ginsburg, Stephen Breyer, and Sonia Sotomayor (with Gorsuch concurring in the judgment and much of the opinion)—Elena Kagan wrote: The law's category, a "crime of violence," is so indeterminate ("fuzzy," she said) that deporting Dimaya under it would violate the Constitution's "due process of law" guarantee. Vague laws beget two evils that are related: They do not give citizens reasonably clear notice of what behavior is proscribed or prescribed. And they give—actually, require of—judges and law enforcement officials excessive discretion in improvising a fuzzy law's meaning. In agreeing with this (and disagreeing with John Roberts, Anthony Kennedy, Clarence Thomas, and Samuel Alito), Gorsuch wrote:

Vague laws "invite the exercise of arbitrary power" by "leaving the people in the dark about what the law demands and allowing prosecutors and courts to make it up." The lack of "precise and sufficient certainty" (criteria stipulated by the English jurist William Blackstone, whose writings influenced the Constitution's Framers) invites "more unpredictability and arbitrariness" than is constitutional. Furthermore, the crux of America's constitutional architecture, the separation of powers, is implicated. All legislative power is vested in Congress. The judicial power, Gorsuch wrote, "does not license judges to craft new laws" but only to discern and follow an existing law's prescribed course. With the fuzzy "crime of violence" category, Congress abdicated its "responsibilities for setting the standards of the criminal law." So, allowing vague laws would allow Congress "to hand off the job of lawmaking." Hence such laws not only illegitimately transfer power to police and prosecutors but also would "leave it all to a judicial hunch."

The principle Gorsuch enunciates here regarding one provision of immigration law is a scythe sharp enough to slice through many practices of the administrative state, which translates often vague congressional sentiments into binding rules, a practice indistinguishable from legislating. Gorsuch's principle is also pertinent to something pernicious concerning which he has hitherto expressed wholesome skepticism: "Chevron deference."

This is the policy (named for the 1984 case in which the Supreme Court propounded it) whereby courts are required to defer to administrative agencies' interpretations of "ambiguous" laws when the interpretations are "reasonable." Gorsuch has criticized this emancipation of the administrative state from judicial supervision as "a judge-made doctrine for the abdication of judicial duty." It also is an incentive for slovenly lawmaking by a Congress too lazy or risk-averse to be precise in making policy choices, and so lacking in institutional pride that it complacently sloughs off its Article I powers onto Article II entities. Gorsuch wants Article III courts to circumscribe this disreputable behavior.

Gorsuch represents the growing ascendency of one kind of conservative jurisprudence, "judicial engagement," over another kind, "judicial deference." Many conservatives have embraced populism where it least belongs, in judicial reasoning. They have advocated broad judicial deference to decisions because they emanate from majoritarian institutions and processes. Progressives favor such deference because it liberates executive power from congressional direction or judicial supervision. Gorsuch, a thinking person's conservative, declines to be complicit in this, which raises this question: When has a progressive justice provided the fifth vote joining four conservative colleagues?

LEGAL LOGIC VERSUS JUDICIAL LABELS

June 18, 2020

> "[T]he limits of the drafters' imagination supply no reason to ignore the law's demands."
>
> Justice Neil M. Gorsuch on Monday

WASHINGTON—Monday illustrated the limited usefulness of the political labels that often are carelessly bandied: The four Supreme Court justices called liberals (Ruth Bader Ginsburg, Stephen G. Breyer, Elena Kagan, and Sonia Sotomayor) joined two called conservatives (John G. Roberts Jr. and Neil M. Gorsuch) in this ruling: In the 1964 Civil Rights Act, Congress did something it was unaware of doing.

The majority opinion and two dissents featured conflicting conceptions of "textualism" in construing statutes. The decision affirmed this: A majoritarian institution, Congress, is not, by its action *or inaction*, decisive in determining the meaning of legislation, or the scope of rights.

In 1964, in the first of its two noblest acts (the other: the 1965 Voting Rights Act), Congress banned discrimination "because of" race, color, religion, national origin, or sex. For forty-five years Congress has intermittently rejected attempts to amend the 1964 act to ban discrimination because of "sexual orientation" and what is now termed "gender identity." Supporters of these attempts implicitly accepted that such discrimination was not encompassed by the ban on discrimination because of sex.

On Monday, however, Gorsuch, writing for the majority, said that neither Congress's refusal for forty-five years nor its state of mind fifty-six years ago are dispositive. He said that "only the written word is the law," and the meaning of a law's words should be determined without reference to the authors' intentions regarding possible future applications. Without, that is, considering whether those who wrote it anticipated future results of applying the law's principles to practices they did not consider:

"An employer who fires an individual for being homosexual or transgender fires that person for traits or actions"—e.g., a man dating a man, a woman marrying a woman—"it would not have questioned in members of a different sex. Sex plays a necessary and undisguisable role in the decision."

Regarding Monday's three cases (concerning gay and transgender employees), Gorsuch conceded that "homosexuality and transgender status are distinct concepts from sex," and that since 1964 applications of the ban on discrimination because of sex have "likely" been beyond what many in Congress expected. Gorsuch's point was: The text, meaning the word "sex," not the 1964 Congress's imagining of future applications of the ban down the decades, must be controlling in 2020.

Joined in dissent by Clarence Thomas, Samuel A. Alito Jr. dismissed Gorsuch's opinion as spurious textualism: "[W]hat it actually represents is...the theory that courts should 'update' old statutes so that they better reflect the current values of society." The question about banning sexual discrimination is only "*whether Congress did that in 1964*" (Alito's italics).

Alito's alternate textualism holds that a statute's words mean what they meant to those who used them when writing the statute. Gorsuch's textualism says that Monday's majority was properly controlled by the meaning, then as now, of Congress's 1964 words. "The ordinary public meaning" (Gorsuch's phrasing) of those words, were, he grants, *intended* to ban only discrimination against women, not sexual orientation. But the words' meanings have not been changed by society's subsequent attitudinal changes. Rather, the unchanged meaning of the 1964 language entails the conclusion that the court's majority reached Monday about the nature of actions (e.g., employers firing gay, lesbian, or transgender employees) that, although not on Congress's mind in 1964, are today necessarily recognized as actions taken "because of sex."

Brett M. Kavanaugh's separate dissent emphasized the separation of powers: "[T]his case boils down to one fundamental question: Who decides?" He said the majority has "expanded" the 1964 act, effectively amending it, which is the dual responsibility of Congress presenting statutory changes to the president.

Again, the majority's response is: Congress did decide, without knowing it, in 1964. What Kavanaugh calls expansion of the act is merely following the logic *of the act's language*, even though this has led to places those who wrote the language did not anticipate. The 1964 language has an unchanged internal logic, regardless of the words' contemporary salience that was unforeseen by the words' authors.

So, Monday's decision was logical, not paradoxical. Congress's 1964 language implied—intended, really—outcomes Congress did not contemplate. Now, about labels:

Is Gorsuch's reasoning unconservative because it affirms broader protection to rights than the 1964 congressional majorities understood to be latent in the logic of their language? Or are Gorsuch's conservative critics reasoning backward from a policy outcome of which they disapprove, thereby embracing the result-oriented jurisprudence they usually associate with judicial liberalism?

PUBLIC SECTOR UNIONS: FDR WAS RIGHT

February 25, 2018

WASHINGTON—Overturning mistaken decisions is an occasional duty of the Supreme Court, whose noblest achievement was the protracted, piecemeal repudiation, with *Brown v. Board of Education* (1954) and subsequent decisions, of its 1896 ruling that segregated "separate but equal" public facilities were constitutional. This Monday, the court will hear oral arguments that probably will presage another overdue correction.

The issue is: Are Mark Janus's First Amendment rights of freedom of speech and association (which entails the freedom not to associate) violated when government requires him, an employee, to pay "fair share" or "agency" fees to a private entity, a labor union, to which government has given exclusive power to represent him, although he chooses not to be a member? Janus argues that an exclusive representative "is indistinguishable from a government-appointed lobbyist." The fees are usually significantly more than half of—sometimes up to 100 percent of—union dues.

In its 1977 *Abood* decision, the court upheld such exactions. But the ruling contained the seeds of its coming—by this June—reversal, because it acknowledged this: "There can be no quarrel with the truism that, because public employee unions attempt to influence governmental policymaking, their activities...may be properly termed political." And in a concurring opinion, Justice Lewis Powell noted that "the ultimate objective of a union in the public sector, like that of a political party, is to influence public decision-making." So *Abood* made compulsory political contributions constitutional.

For forty-one years, the court has advanced the slow-motion undoing of *Abood* with decisions subjecting various instances of compelled speech to strict scrutiny. For example, in 1983 it held that "speech on public issues occupies the 'highest rung of the hierarchy of First Amendment values.'" In 2014, the court said it is a "bedrock principle that, except perhaps in the rarest of circumstances, no person in this country may be compelled to subsidize speech by a third party that he or she does not wish to support."

Abood ignored the inherently political nature of bargaining by government employees' unions. In America's twenty-seven right-to-work states, employees cannot be forced to join a union as a condition of employment. In the other twenty-three, including Janus's Illinois, workers must join a union or pay fees. The supposed constitutionality of this compelled speech rests on the fiction that these fees pay only the costs of collective bargaining, from which the fee payers benefit.

In private-sector collective bargaining, management and labor negotiate about how to distribute companies' profits. No comparably adversarial process exists in the public sector. There government, which acquires its "profits" (revenues) from a third party—taxpayers—"negotiates" with unions that have an interest in government doing what it wants to do anyway: expand. Because government is both employer and policymaker, collective bargaining by the union is inherently political advocacy and indistinguishable from lobbying. Hence in 2012 the court acknowledged that compulsory fees are "compelled speech and association" implicating on First Amendment rights. President Franklin Roosevelt was right: "The process of collective bargaining, as usually understood, cannot be transplanted into the public service."

Although organized labor's portion of the private-sector workforce has plummeted from around 35 percent in 1953 to 6.5 percent today, it now organizes about one-third of local, state, and national government workers. Organized labor now is primarily governments organized as interest groups.

Union officials' salaries and benefits are the biggest expense of the union that Janus is forced to finance (the American Federation of State, County, and Municipal Employees). It is facially implausible that most of what these officials do is devoted exclusively to collective bargaining and is hermetically sealed from AFSCME's aggressive promotion of its broad political agenda. Besides, money is fungible: Money extracted from reluctant nonmembers can fund activities that otherwise would have been paid for with money that now can be devoted to other political causes.

And AFSCME's approximately 3,400 local unions calculate their own supposed "collective bargaining" allocations. So each enjoys vast discretion in deciding which of its expenditures are germane to collective bargaining, and therefore what their nonmembers owe to the union.

Many Democrats are, or say they are, distraught about "big money" and there being "too much" money in political campaigns. They will, however, be seriously distraught if help arrives by June with Janus winning. This will stop the coerced flow of money to government workers' unions, which in the 2016 election cycle spent $63.9 million on politics, 90 percent supporting Democratic candidates and causes.

THE COURT'S CORRECT CORRECTION

July 1, 2018

WASHINGTON—The Supreme Court is especially admirable when correcting especially deplorable prior decisions, as with the 1954 school desegregation decision rejecting a 1896 decision's "separate but equal" doctrine. It did so again last Wednesday, overturning a forty-one-year-old precedent inimical to the First Amendment.

Shortly before the court made this predictable ruling, a *Wall Street Journal* headline revealed why it was necessary. The headline said: "Unions Court Own Members Ahead of Ruling." Anticipating defeat, government-employee unions had begun resorting to persuasion—imagine that—in the hope of retaining members and convincing nonmembers to continue making payments to the unions that the court says can no longer be obligatory.

In 1977, the court upheld, 6–3, the constitutionality of compelling government employees who exercise their right not to join a union to pay "fair share" or "agency" fees. These, which the union determines, supposedly cover only the costs of collective bargaining from which non-members benefit. But the payments usually are much more than half of, and sometimes equal to, dues that members pay.

The majority opinion in 1977 admitted something that was too obvious to deny and so constitutionality problematic that a future challenge was inevitable. That majority said: "There can be no quarrel with the truism that, because public employee unions attempt to influence government policymaking, their activities…may be properly termed political." And one justice, concurring with the majority, said "the ultimate objective of a union in the public sector, *like that of a political party*, is to influence public decision-making." (Emphasis added.)

Actually, *everything* public-sector unions do is political. Therefore, the 1977 decision made compulsory political contributions constitutional. Which made the court queasy.

By 2014, it was affirming the principle that doomed the 1977 decision and foretold Wednesday's: It is a "bedrock principle that, except perhaps in the rarest of circumstances, no person in this country may be compelled to subsidize speech by a third party that he or she does not wish to support." Which is what the court now says regarding compulsory financial support of government-employee unions. Yet Justice Elena Kagan, in her uncharacteristically strident dissent, said:

> There is no sugarcoating today's opinion. The majority overthrows a decision entrenched in this nation's law—and in its economic life—for over 40 years. As a result, it prevents the American people, acting through their state and local officials, from making important choices about workplace governance. And it does so by weaponizing the First Amendment, in a way that unleashes judges, now and in the future, to intervene in economic and regulatory policy.

How does Kagan err? Let us count the ways.

The 1977 decision was no more entrenched than the 1896 "separate but equal" decision was for fifty-eight years. The First Amendment exists to prevent the people's representatives from making certain kinds of choices ("Congress shall make no law…"). Wednesday's decision was not about "workplace governance" or "economic and regulatory policy." It was about coerced speech. And about denial of another First Amendment guarantee, freedom of association, which includes the freedom not to associate, through coerced financial support, with uncongenial political organizations. And judges are supposed to be unleashed to wield the First Amendment as a weapon against officials perpetrating such abuses.

Wednesday's 5–4 decision accords with President Franklin Roosevelt's judgment that "the process of collective bargaining, as usually understood, cannot be transplanted into the public service." In private-sector bargaining, unions contest management concerning the distribution of companies' profits. In the public sector, government gets its revenues from a third party—taxpayers. Because a majority of organized labor's members are government employees, the labor movement is mostly not horny-handed sons of toil. It increasingly is government organized as an interest group that pressures government to do what it has a metabolic urge to do anyway: grow.

The deadliest dagger in Wednesday's decision was the stipulation that nonmembers' fees cannot be automatically deducted from their wages—nonmembers must affirmatively consent to deductions. So, public-sector unions must *persuade* people. No wonder they are panicking.

There is no sugarcoating today's reality. Public-sector unions are conveyor belts that move a portion of government employees' salaries—some of the amount paid in union dues—into political campaigns, almost always Democrats', to elect the people with whom the unions "negotiate" for taxpayers' money. Progressives who are theatrically distraught about there being "too much money in politics" are now theatrically distraught that the court has ended coercing contributions that have flowed to progressive candidates.

SOCIAL SCIENCES, BRAIN SCIENCE, AND THE EIGHTH AMENDMENT

April 22, 2012

WASHINGTON—In the summer of 1787, just ninety-four years after the Salem witch trials, as paragons of the Enlightenment such as James Madison, George Washington, and Benjamin Franklin deliberated in the Constitutional Convention in Philadelphia, a mob pelted and otherwise tormented to death a woman accused of being a witch. Prosecution of alleged witches, writes historian Edmund Morgan, had ceased in the colonies long before the English statute criminalizing witchcraft was repealed in 1736. Some popular sentiment, however, lagged.

Today, 221 years after the Bill of Rights was added to the Constitution, the Supreme Court is again pondering the Eighth Amendment's proscription of "cruel and unusual punishments." The case illustrates the complexity of construing some constitutional language in changing contexts of social science and brain science.

Evan Miller, whose five suicide attempts surely had something to do with his having suffered domestic abuse, was complicit in a brutal murder and in 2006 was sentenced to life in an Alabama prison without the possibility of parole. Kuntrell Jackson was involved in a video store robbery during which an accomplice fatally shot the store clerk. In 2003, Jackson was sentenced to life in an Arkansas prison without the possibility of parole. Miller and Jackson were fourteen when they committed their crimes. Both were tried as adults before judges who had no discretion to impose any other sentence. Such mandatory sentences preclude judges weighing a consideration of Eighth Amendment jurisprudence— proportionality.

Before its June 26 recess, the Supreme Court will decide whether sentencing children to die in prison is cruel. It certainly is unusual: Although 2,300 current prisoners have been sentenced to life without parole for crimes committed as juveniles (age seventeen or younger), just seventy-nine prisoners in eighteen states are serving sentences of life without parole for crimes committed when they were thirteen or fourteen.

The court must consider not only what is society's sense of cruelty, but also how that sense *should* be shaped by what some new technologies reveal about adolescent brain biology. Shakespeare's shepherd in *The Winter's Tale* did not need to see brain scans in order to wish that "there were no age between ten and three-and-twenty, or that youth would sleep out the rest; for there is nothing in the between but getting wenches with child, wronging the ancientry, stealing, fighting."

And with age-related laws restricting the right to drink, drive, marry, serve on juries, etc., all American states have long acknowledged adolescents' developmental shortcomings. Neuroscience, however, now helps explain *why* aspects of adolescents' brains make young people susceptible to impulsive behavior, and to failing to anticipate and understand the consequences of it.

Without opening the floodgates to "excuse abuse," the Supreme Court has accommodated what science teaches. In 2005, the court proscribed imposing the death penalty on someone who committed a murder as a juvenile, arguing that "the susceptibility of juveniles to immature and irresponsible behavior" can diminish the reprehensible nature of their crimes. In 2010, the court proscribed sentences of life without parole for juveniles convicted of a crime other than homicide, arguing that such sentences improperly deny juvenile offenders "a chance to demonstrate growth and maturity."

In both cases, the sentences were judged cruel and unusual because they were disproportional to actual culpability. Increasingly, the criminal justice system acknowledges the importance of scientific findings about adolescents' entangled neurological, physiological, and psychological developments. Such findings condition how we read some constitutional language.

In 1958, the court said: "The (Eighth) Amendment must draw its meaning from the evolving standards of decency that mark the progress of a maturing society." Justice Antonin Scalia has warned: "A society that adopts a bill of rights is skeptical that 'evolving standards of decency' always 'mark progress,' and that societies always 'mature,' as opposed to rot." But even the "originalist" Scalia, although disposed to construe the Constitution's terms as they were understood when ratified, would today proscribe some late eighteenth-century punishments, such as public lashing and branding.

Denying juveniles even a *chance* for parole defeats the penal objective of rehabilitation. It deprives prisoners of the incentive to reform themselves. Some prisons withhold education, counseling, and other rehabilitation programs from prisoners ineligible for parole. Denying these to adolescents in a period of life crucial to social and psychological growth stunts what the court in 2005 called the prisoner's "potential to attain a mature understanding of his own humanity." Which seems, in a word—actually, three words—"cruel and unusual."

———

In June 2012 the Supreme Court held that it is unconstitutional to impose on people under age eighteen sentences of life in prison without the possibility of parole.

"DEPRAVITY" AND THE EIGHTH AMENDMENT

November 11, 2018

WASHINGTON—In the previous fifty years, the state of Mississippi has validated Lord Tennyson's belief that "men may rise on stepping-stones of their dead selves to higher things." Now the state has asked the U.S. Supreme Court for twenty more days to provide the court with a defense of the proposition that a state court was sufficiently serious in ruling that Joey Chandler is so depraved that he could never undergo a regeneration comparable to what Mississippi has managed.

In 2003, Chandler, then seventeen and seeking money to support his pregnant girlfriend, tried selling marijuana. When his supply was stolen from his car, he believed the thief was his cousin Emmitt, nineteen.

Chandler fatally shot Emmitt and fled the scene, but later that night he surrendered to authorities. Convicted of murder, Chandler was sentenced to life imprisonment without possibility of parole.

Parents who have raised sons understand that civilization's primary task is to civilize adolescent males, a task that is difficult for many reasons, some of which neuroscience explains. The part of the brain that stimulates anger and aggression is larger in males than in females (for evolutionary, meaning adaptive, reasons). And the part that restrains anger is smaller in males. The Supreme Court has noted that adolescent brain anatomy can cause "transient rashness, proclivity for risk, and inability to assess consequences," thereby diminishing "moral culpability" and, more important, enhancing "the prospect that, as the years go by," offenders' "deficiencies will be reformed." Hence "a lifetime in prison is a disproportionate sentence for all but the rarest of children, those whose crimes reflect 'irreparable corruption.'"

Now, there is spirited disagreement among thoughtful people concerning whether such disproportion constitutes a violation of the Constitution's Eighth Amendment proscription of "cruel and unusual punishments." There is disagreement concerning whether the Eighth Amendment as originally understood by those who wrote and ratified it was intended to forbid only certain methods of punishment or to assign to courts the task of enunciating standards of proportionality in sentencing. There is disagreement about what the modern court has done in incrementally circumscribing states' discretion in punishing juveniles: It has held that the Eighth Amendment forbids capital punishment for children under eighteen. And that it forbids life imprisonment without parole for juveniles convicted of non-homicide offenses. And that it forbids—this is the issue in Chandler's case—mandatory life imprisonment without possibility of parole for juvenile homicide offenders unless they have demonstrated "such irretrievable depravity that rehabilitation is impossible."

Never mind that it is difficult to imagine how a sentencing court could determine that a juvenile has manifested such depravity. Clearly, however, the Mississippi court that heard Chandler's argument for resentencing in light of Supreme Court rulings about sentencing juveniles did not seriously attempt this difficult task.

While incarcerated, Chandler has not been a discipline problem. He has earned a GED and completed college-level coursework in Bible studies. He has earned certificates in construction trade skills and made substantial progress toward a certificate in automotive repair. Nevertheless, the resentencing court's almost flippant reasons for reaffirming Chandler's sentence to die in prison included the following:

"Nothing in the record" suggested that Chandler "suffered from a lack of maturity" when he shot his cousin. (Science demonstrates a physiological basis of varying maturities of male adolescents.) The seventeen-year-old Chandler was "very mature" because he planned his crime. (His prompt surrender suggests more bewilderment than planning.) He was mature because he came from a nuclear family. (How does a family's attribute prove the existence of a different attribute in a family member?) He was mature because seventeen-year-olds are allowed to get driver's and pilot's licenses, and abortions, and because he fathered a child, and because in World War II a seventeen-year-old won a Medal of Honor.

Really. And the court simply ignored the evidence of Chandler's efforts at rehabilitation.

Fifty years ago, many Americans thought Mississippi itself exemplified irretrievable depravity. Today the state has more—not more relative to population, *more*—African Americans in elective offices than any other state. Culturally and economically, Mississippi is a vibrant participant in the American mainstream. The state's self-rehabilitation was not impossible.

In 2053, the fiftieth anniversary of Joey Chandler's crime, he will be sixty-seven, if he lives that long. Today, the Supreme Court should hear Chandler's case in order to provide standards requiring sentencing courts to be serious when making an extraordinarily serious judgment about someone's "irretrievable depravity."

—

In January 2019 the Supreme Court denied Chandler's petition asking the court to review his case.

WHEN VERNON MADISON WAS NOT "COMPETENT TO BE EXECUTED"

September 30, 2018

WASHINGTON—Without being aware of it, Vernon Madison might become a footnote in constitutional law because he is barely aware of anything. For more than thirty years, Alabama, with a tenacity that deserves a better cause, has been trying to execute him for the crime he certainly committed, the 1985 murder of a police officer. Twice the state convicted him unconstitutionally (first excluding African Americans from the jury, then insinuating inadmissible evidence into the record). In a third trial the judge, who during his time on the bench overrode more life sentences (six) than any other Alabama judge, disregarded the jury's recommended sentence of life imprisonment and imposed the death penalty.

The mills of justice grind especially slowly regarding capital punishment, which courts have enveloped in labyrinthine legal protocols. As the mills have ground on, life has ground Madison, sixty-eight, down to wreckage. After multiple serious strokes, he has vascular dementia, an irreversible and progressive degenerative disease. He also is legally blind, his speech is slurred, he has Type 2 diabetes and chronic hypertension, he cannot walk unassisted, he has dead brain tissue and urinary incontinence.

And he no longer remembers the crime that put him on death row for most of his adult life. This is why on Tuesday the Supreme Court will hear oral arguments about the constitutionality of executing him.

His counsel of record, Bryan A. Stevenson, head of the Equal Justice Initiative in Montgomery, Alabama, says that it was undisputed in the penalty phase of Madison's third trial that he already "suffered from a mental illness marked by paranoid delusions." Stevenson says that Madison, who has been mentally ill since adolescence and who over the years had been prescribed "numerous psychotropic medications," cannot remember "numerous events" of the past thirty years, including "events from the offense to his arrest or to his trial," and cannot remember the name of the police officer he shot.

The mere phrasing of the matter at issue—whether Madison is "competent to be executed"—induces moral vertigo. A unanimous three-judge panel of the Eleventh U.S. Circuit Court of Appeals held that Madison lacks the requisite competence because he lacks understanding of the connection between his crime and his execution. The question before the Supreme Court is whether executing Madison would violate the Eighth Amendment's proscription of "cruel and unusual punishments."

The court has said that "we may seriously question the retributive value of executing a person who has no comprehension of why he has been singled out and stripped of his fundamental right to life." For many people, the death penalty for especially heinous crimes satisfies a sense of moral symmetry. Retribution—society's cathartic expression of a proportional response to attacks on its norms—is not, however, the only justification offered for capital punishment. Deterrence is another. But by now this power is vanishingly small because imposition of the death penalty is so sporadic and glacial. Because the process of getting from sentencing to execution is so protracted, currently averaging fifteen years, senescent persons on the nation's death rows are going to be problems as long as there is capital punishment.

Madison's case compels us to focus on the death penalty in its granular reality: Assisting someone who is non-ambulatory, and bewildered because he is (in Stevenson's phrase) "memory-disordered," to be strapped down so an executioner can try to find a vein—often a problem with the elderly— to receive a lethal injection. Capital punishment is withering away because the process of litigating the administration of it is so expensive, and hence disproportionate to any demonstrable enhancement of public safety, but also because of a healthy squeamishness that speaks well of us.

Sixty years ago, Chief Justice Earl Warren wrote that the Eighth Amendment—particularly the idea of what counts as "cruel" punishments—"must draw its meaning from the evolving standards of decency that mark the progress of a maturing society." Concerning which, two caveats are apposite: "evolving" is not a synonym for "improving," and a society can become, as America arguably is becoming, infantilized as it "matures." That said, it certainly is true that standards of decency do evolve, and that America's have improved astonishingly since 1958: Think about segregated lunch counters, and much else.

Conservatives have their own standards, including this one: The state—government—already is altogether too full of itself, and investing it with the power to inflict death on anyone exacerbates its sense of majesty and delusions of adequacy.

—

In February 2019 the Supreme Court ruled in favor of Madison.

WILL IT BE 1972 FOREVER? THE HIGH COURT'S MISPLACED MODESTY

July 13, 2009

WASHINGTON—The question to which the Supreme Court recently gave a mistaken answer was: Has the revolution in race relations since enactment of the 1965 Voting Rights Act rendered the act's Section 5 anachronistic and hence unconstitutional as a no-longer defensible encroachment on the rights of the affected jurisdictions? The court's 8–1 ruling to preserve Section 5 is a reminder how misguided are conservatives' indiscriminate denunciations of "judicial activism."

Clarence Thomas, the court's only black justice, and arguably its most conservative, cast the only vote to strike down Section 5. He did so because of social changes made vivid by the election of the first black president.

Because a number of states and some jurisdictions in others had been ingenious in devising tactics to suppress voting by blacks, the 1965 act required them to seek permission—"preclearance"—from the Justice Department for even minor changes in voting procedures, such as locating polling places. The act's "bailout" provision, which ostensibly provides a process by which jurisdictions can seek to end federal supervision, is extremely burdensome: Since 1982, only seventeen of the more than 12,000 political subdivisions subject to the preclearance requirement have been allowed to bail out.

In 1965, the preclearance requirements were authorized for just five years. But they have been extended four times, most recently in 2006 for *twenty-five years*. By 2031, when Congress probably will extend it again, Barack Obama will be collecting Social Security.

The latest electoral data used to justify the 2006 extension was from 1972. Then gasoline cost thirty-six cents a gallon, the Dow's high was 1036, the most-watched television program was *All in the Family*, and the winner of the Academy Award for best picture was *The Godfather*.

In 2006, an Austin, Texas, utility district, which did not even exist until 1987, went to court seeking relief from preclearance. The court held that the bailout provision was unavailable to the district because it does not register its own voters. The district appealed, arguing that no such restriction on bailouts is in the Voting Rights Act, and that if it is, the preclearance requirement is unconstitutional.

The district's lawyer acknowledged that if the court supported the district's right to seek a bailout, then the court "need not" settle the constitutional point. So John Roberts and seven colleagues said there was no point "rushing" to decide whether events have rendered Section 5 unconstitutional. Doing so would have infuriated persons attached to that provision not as a still-needed protection but as a symbol of heroic days long gone.

Roberts acknowledged that in some states covered by the preclearance requirements, "blacks now register and vote at higher rates than whites." He noted that Section 5, which "imposes current burdens and must be justified by current needs," entails substantial "federalism costs." And he quoted Alexander Hamilton on the court's duty to resist "legislative encroachments."

But because declaring an act of Congress unconstitutional is the court's "gravest and most delicate duty" (Oliver Wendell Holmes), and because the court has hitherto noted that Congress, too, takes an oath to uphold the Constitution, Roberts held that the court normally should (in words from a 1984 ruling) "not decide a constitutional question if there is some other ground upon which to dispose of the case." So, said Roberts, it was sufficient to hold that the Texas district could have recourse to Section 5's bailout provision.

Thomas, however, believes that the "doctrine of constitutional avoidance" was inappropriate in this case. The fact that the court has declared the Texas district eligible to seek a bailout neither guarantees relief from a burden that has lost its rationale nor addresses Section 5's now patent unconstitutionality. Allowing its continuance in the absence of the emergency that long ago justified it seriously damages the nation's constitutional structure: "State autonomy with respect to the machinery of self-government defines the states as sovereign entities rather than mere provincial outposts subject to every dictate of a central governing authority."

The Fifteenth Amendment guarantees the right to vote and grants Congress the power to enforce the right with "appropriate" legislation. Thomas argued that Section 5 is now inappropriate: "Punishment for long past sins is not a legitimate basis for imposing a forward-looking preventative measure that has already served its purpose."

Thomas, refusing deference to a branch of government that has not done its duty, said: "The burden remains with Congress to prove that the extreme circumstances warranting Section 5's enactment persist today." His position constitutes the sort of judicial activism on which constitutional government depends—a determination to enforce institutional boundaries on the political branches that have a perennial itch to overstep them.

PHILADELPHIA'S "ROOM 101"

December 25, 2016

"The thing that is in Room 101 is the worst thing in the world.... The worst thing in the world varies from individual to individual."
—George Orwell, *1984*

PHILADELPHIA—For Christos and Markela Sourovelis, for whom the worst thing was losing their home, "Room 101" was Courtroom 478 in City Hall. This "courtroom's" name is Orwellian: There was neither judge nor jury in it. There the city government enriched itself—more than $64 million in a recent eleven-year span—by disregarding due process requirements in order to seize and sell the property of people who have not been accused, never mind convicted, of a crime.

The Sourovelises' son, who lived at home, was arrested for selling a small amount of drugs away from home. Soon there was a knock on their door by police who said, "We're here to take your house" and "You're going to be living on the street" and "We do this every day." The Sourovelises' doors were locked with screws and their utilities were cut off. They had paid off the mortgage on their $350,000 home, making it a tempting target for policing for profit.

Nationwide, proceeds from sales of seized property (homes, cars, etc.) go to the seizers. And under a federal program, state and local law enforcement can partner with federal authorities in forfeiture and reap up to 80 percent of the proceeds. This is called—more Orwellian newspeak—"equitable sharing."

No crime had been committed in the Sourovelises' house, but the title of the case against them was the *Commonwealth of Pennsylvania v. 12011 Ferndale St.* Somehow, a crime had been committed *by* the house. In civil forfeiture, it suffices that property is *suspected* of having been involved in a crime. Once seized, the property's owners bear the burden of proving their property's innocence. "Sentence first—verdict afterwards," says the queen in "Alice in Wonderland."

In Courtroom 478, the prosecutors usually assured people seeking to reclaim their property that they would not need lawyers. The prosecutors practiced semi-extortion, suggesting how people could regain limited control of their property: They could sell it and give half the proceeds to the city. The "hearings" in Courtroom 478 were often protracted over months, and missing even one hearing could result in instant forfeiture.

The Sourovelises were allowed to return to their house only after waiving their rights to statutory or constitutional defenses in a future forfeiture action. Such action was forestalled when their case came to the attention of the Institute for Justice (IJ), public interest litigators who never received the "You can't fight city hall" memo. It disentangled the Sourovelises from the forfeiture machine, shut down Courtroom 478, and now is seeking a court ruling to tether this machine to constitutional standards.

There might somewhere be a second prominent American who endorses today's civil forfeiture practices, but one such person is "very unhappy" with criticisms of it. At a 2015 Senate Judiciary Committee hearing on forfeiture abuses, one senator said "taking and seizing and forfeiting, through a government judicial process, illegal gains from criminal enterprises is not wrong," and neither is law enforcement enriching itself from this. In the manner of the man for whom he soon will work, this senator asserted an unverifiable number: "95 percent" of forfeitures involve people who have "done nothing in their lives but sell dope." This senator said it should not be more difficult for "government to take money from a drug dealer than it is for a businessperson to defend themselves in a lawsuit." In seizing property suspected of involvement in a crime, government "should not have a burden of proof higher than in a normal civil case."

IJ's Robert Everett Johnson notes that this senator missed a few salient points: In civil forfeiture there usually is no proper "judicial process." There is no way of knowing how many forfeitures involve criminals because the government takes property without even charging anyone with a crime. The government's vast prosecutorial resources are one reason it properly bears the burden of proving criminal culpability "beyond a reasonable doubt." A sued businessperson does not have assets taken until he or she has lost in a trial, whereas civil forfeiture takes property without a trial, and the property owner must wage a protracted, complex, and expensive fight to get it returned. The Senate Judiciary Committee might want to discuss all this when considering the nominee to be the next attorney general, Alabama Senator Jeff Sessions.

"WHAT COUNTRY ARE WE IN?"

May 20, 2012

TEWKSBURY, Mass.—Russ Caswell, sixty-eight, is bewildered: "What country are we in?" He and his wife, Pat, are ensnared in a Kafkaesque nightmare unfolding in Orwellian language.

This town's police department is conniving with the federal government to circumvent Massachusetts law—which is less permissive than federal law—in order to seize his livelihood and retirement asset. In the lawsuit titled *United States of America v. 434 Main Street, Tewksbury, Massachusetts* the government is suing an inanimate object, the motel Caswell's father built in 1955. The U.S. Department of Justice intends to seize it, sell it for perhaps $1.5 million, and give up to 80 percent of that to the Tewksbury Police Department, whose budget is just $5.5 million. The Caswells have not been charged with, let alone convicted of, a crime. They are being persecuted by two governments eager to profit from what is antiseptically called the "equitable sharing" of the fruits of civil forfeiture, a process of government enrichment that often is indistinguishable from robbery.

The Merrimack River Valley near the New Hampshire border has had more downs than ups since the nineteenth century, when the nearby towns of Lowell and Lawrence were centers of America's textile industry. In the 1960s the area briefly enjoyed a high-tech boom. Caswell's "budget" motel, too, has seen better days, as when the touring Annette Funicello and the Mouseketeers checked in. In its sixth decade the motel hosts tourists, some workers on extended stays, and some elderly people who call it home. The fifty-six rooms rent for $56 a night or $285 a week.

Since 1994, about thirty motel customers have been arrested on drug dealing charges. Even if those police figures are accurate—the police have a substantial monetary incentive to exaggerate—these thirty episodes involved less than five one-hundredths of 1 percent of the 125,000 rooms Caswell has rented over those more than 6,700 days. Yet this is the government's excuse for impoverishing the Caswells by seizing this property, which is their only significant source of income and all of their retirement security.

The government says the rooms were used to "facilitate" a crime. It does not say the Caswells knew or even that they were supposed to know what was going on in all their rooms all the time. Civil forfeiture law treats citizens worse than criminals, requiring them to prove their innocence—to prove they did everything possible to prevent those rare crimes from occurring in a few of those rooms. What counts as possible remains vague. The Caswells voluntarily installed security cameras, they photocopy customers' identifications and record their license plates, and turn the information over to the police, who have never asked the Caswells to do more.

The Caswells are represented by the Institute for Justice, a libertarian public-interest law firm. IJ explains that civil forfeiture is a proceeding in which property is said to have acted wrongly. This was useful long ago against pirates, who might be out of reach but whose ill-gotten gains could be seized. The Caswells, however, are not pirates.

Rather, they are victims of two piratical governments that, IJ argues, are violating the U.S. Constitution twice. They are violating the Eighth Amendment, which has been construed to forbid "excessive fines" that deprive individuals of their livelihoods. And the federal "equitable sharing" program violates the Tenth Amendment by vitiating state law, thereby enabling Congress to compel the states to adopt Congress's policies where states possess a reserved power and primary authority— in the definition and enforcement of the criminal law.

A federal drug agent operating in this region roots around in public records in search of targets—property with at least $50,000 equity. Caswell thinks that if his motel "had a big mortgage, this would not be happening."

"Equitable sharing"—the consensual splitting of ill-gotten loot by the looters—reeks of the moral hazard that exists in situations in which incentives are for perverse behavior. To see where this leads, read IJ's scalding report "Policing for Profit: The Abuse of Civil Asset Forfeiture" (http://ow.ly/aYME1), a sickening litany of law enforcement agencies padding their budgets and financing boondoggles by, for example, smelling, or imagining to smell, or pretending to smell, marijuana in cars they covet.

None of this is surprising to Madisonians, which all sensible Americans are. James Madison warned (in Federalist 48) that government power "is of an encroaching nature." If unresisted, it produces iniquitous sharing of other people's property.

—

In January 2013 a federal judge in Boston ruled in Caswell's favor, dismissing the forfeiture action against his motel and stating that the government had engaged in "gross exaggeration" about the evidence.

DO FISH PERFORM PEDICURES?

September 25, 2011

PHOENIX—Cindy Vong is a tiny woman with a problem as big as the government that is causing it. She wants to provide a service that will enable customers "to brighten up their days." Having fish nibble your feet may not be your idea of fun, but lots of people around the world enjoy it, and so did some Arizonans until their bossy government butted in, in the service of a cartel. Herewith a story that illustrates how governments that will not mind their own business impede the flourishing of businesses.

Vong, forty-seven, left Vietnam in 1982 and, after stops in Indonesia, Thailand, Taiwan, and Hong Kong, settled in San Francisco for twenty years, before coming to Phoenix to open a nail salon with a difference. Her salon offered thirty-dollar fish therapy, wherein small fish from China nibble dead skin from people's feet. Arizona's Board of Cosmetology decided the fish were performing pedicures, and because all pedicure instruments must be sterilized and fish cannot be, the therapy must be discontinued. Vong lost her more than $50,000 investment in fish tanks and other equipment, and some customers. Three of her employees lost their jobs.

The plucky litigators at the Goldwater Institute are representing Vong in arguing that the Constitution protects the individual's right to earn a living free from unreasonable regulations. In a 1932 case (overturning an Oklahoma law requiring a new ice company to prove a "public need" for it), the U.S. Supreme Court said the law's tendency was to "foster monopoly in the hands of existing establishments." The court also said:

> The principle is imbedded in our constitutional system that there are certain essentials of liberty with which the state is not entitled to dispense...The theory of experimentation in censorship (is) not permitted to interfere with the fundamental doctrine of the freedom of the press. The opportunity to apply one's labor and skill in an ordinary occupation with proper regard for all reasonable regulations is no less entitled to protection.

Unfortunately, soon after 1932, New Deal progressivism washed over the courts, which became derelict regarding their duty to protect economic liberty. Courts deferred to governments eager to experiment with economic micromanagement. Inevitably, this became regulation in the service of existing interests. And regulatory agencies often succumbed to "regulatory capture," whereby regulated businesses and professions dominate regulatory bodies. Arizona's Board of Cosmetology consists mostly of professional cosmetologists.

In the Cato Institute's journal *Regulation*, Timothy Sandefur of the conservative Pacific Legal Foundation examines how "certificate of necessity" (CON) laws stifle opportunity and competition. For example, Michael Munie of St. Louis has a federal license for his moving business to operate across state lines, but when he tried to expand his business to operate throughout Missouri he discovered that state law requires him to somehow prove in advance that there is a "public need" for his business outside St. Louis.

Who, Sandefur wonders, could have *proved* twenty years ago that Americans would support a nationwide chain of coffee shops called Starbucks? And in 1985, experts at Coca-Cola thought they knew the public wanted New Coke.

CON laws began with early twentieth-century progressives who, like their ideological descendants today, thought that resources should be allocated not by markets but by clever, disinterested experts—themselves.

As Sandefur says, the toll on opportunity is obvious: "Requiring an unknown dreamer, with no political connections, reputation with consumers, or allies among local business magnates to persuade a government board to let him open a new business can often be a prohibitive cost."

Such laws often are explicitly biased against new businesses. In Illinois, someone wanting to open a car dealership must get a certificate from the Motor Vehicle Review Board, and if any existing dealer objects, the board must consider, among other things, "the effect of an additional franchise…upon the existing" dealers and "the permanency of the investment of the objecting motor vehicle dealer."

When in March Florida's legislature considered a bill to end licensing requirements for twenty professions, including interior design, the interior design cartel, eager to restrict entry into the profession, got a professor of interior design to ask legislators: "Do you know the color schemes that affect your salivation, your autonomic nervous system?" A Tampa interior designer warned: "What you're basically doing is contributing to 88,000 deaths every year."

Fatal color schemes? Who knew. This overwrought designer should calm down, perhaps by having some fish nibble her feet.

—

Vong's case swam upstream through the judicial system, reaching the U.S. Supreme Court, which in April 2015 rejected her appeal for relief from the Board of Cosmetology's pettifoggery.

"SHUT UP!": NORTH CAROLINA EXPLAINED

September 27, 2012

RALEIGH, N.C.—North Carolina is giving Steve Cooksey some choices. He can stop speaking. Or he can get a PhD in nutrition, or a medical degree, or a bachelor's degree in nutrition and then pass an examination after completing a 900-hour clinical internship. Or he can skip this onerous credentialing, keep speaking, and risk prosecution.

He has chosen instead to get a lawyer. His case, argued by the libertarians at the Institute for Justice, will clarify the First Amendment's relevance to an ancient human behavior and a modern technology.

Four years ago, Cooksey was a walking—actually, barely walking—collection of health risks. He was obese, lethargic, asthmatic, chronically ill, and pre-diabetic. The diet advice he was getting from medical and other sources was, he decided, radically wrong. Rather than eat a high-carbohydrate, low-fat diet, he adopted what he and other enthusiasts call a Paleolithic diet, eating as primitive humans did—e.g., beef, pork, chicken, leafy green vegetables. Cooksey lost seventy-five pounds and the need for drugs and insulin. And, being a modern Paleo, he became a blogger, communicating his dietary opinions.

When a busybody notified North Carolina's Board of Dietetics/Nutrition that Cooksey was opining about which foods were and were not beneficial, the board launched a three-month investigation of his Internet writings and his dialogues with people who read and responded to them. The board sent him copies of his writings, with red pen markings of such disapproved postings as: "I do suggest that your friend eat as I do and exercise the best they can."

"If," the board sternly said, "people are writing you with diabetic specific questions and you are responding, you are no longer just providing information—you are counseling—you need a license to provide this service." This had the intended effect of chilling his speech;

his self-censorship stopped his blog. By saying his bloggings will be subject to continuous review, North Carolina hopes to silence him in perpetuity.

IJ's Jeff Rowes notes that Cooksey's speech "involves no sensitive relationship (as in psychological counseling), no uniquely vulnerable listeners (as in potential legal clients forced to make snap decisions), and no plausible presumption that the listeners are unable to exercise independent judgment." That presumption is, however, the animating principle of modern regulatory government. North Carolina is uninterested in the fact that Cooksey's advice is unpaid, freely solicited, and outside any context of a professional-client relationship. The state simply asserts that Cooksey's audience is "a uniquely vulnerable population," which is how paternalistic government views everybody all the time.

Were Cooksey blogging for profit to sell beef and other Paleolithic food, he would be free to advise anyone to improve their health by buying his wares. So his case raises two questions: Is an individual's uncompensated advice, when volunteered to other individuals who seek and value it, constitutionally protected? And does the Internet—cost-free dissemination of speech to spontaneous, self-generated audiences—render many traditional forms of licensing obsolete?

Two principles are colliding. One is that when government regulates speech based on its content, judicial "strict scrutiny" of the regulation requires government to bear the burden of demonstrating a "compelling" need for "narrowly tailored" speech restrictions. The second is that when government regulates occupations in ways that restrict entry to them, excluded citizens bear an enormous burden of demonstrating that there is *no* reasonable basis for the regulation.

Since the New Deal, courts have applied the extremely permissive "rational basis" test: If legislatures articulate almost *any* reasons for regulating, courts will defer to them. This has given a patina of high principle to the judiciary's dereliction of its duty to prevent individuals' liberty from being sacrificed to groups' rent-seeking. Laws like the one silencing Cooksey are primarily rent-seeking. They are written to enhance the prestige and prosperity of a profession by restricting competition that would result from easy entry into it, or from provision of alternatives to its services.

People, being opinionated mammals, have been dispensing advice to one another since the advent of language, and have been foisting dietary opinions since cavemen weighed the relative benefits of eating woolly mammoths or saber-toothed tigers. So IJ has two questions for North Carolina and for the judicial system:

Did Ann Landers and Dear Abby conduct fifty-year crime sprees by offering unlicensed psychological advice? Is personal advice as constitutionally unprotected as child pornography? If so, since a 2010 Supreme Court opinion, it is less protected expression than videos of animals being tortured.

—

In February 2016 the North Carolina Board of Dietetics/Nutrition adopted new guidelines permitting people to give ordinary diet advice without getting the government's permission.

⸺

A CAKE AND "ANIMUS" IN COLORADO

December 3, 2017

WASHINGTON—The conversation about a cake lasted less than a minute but will long reverberate in constitutional law. On Tuesday, the Supreme Court is scheduled to hear sixty minutes of speech about when, if at all, making a cake counts as constitutionally protected speech and, if so, what the implications are for the Colorado Civil Rights Commission's contention that Jack Phillips violated the state's law against sexual-orientation discrimination.

Phillips, sixty-one, is a devout Christian and proprietor of Masterpiece Cakeshop in Lakewood, Colorado, where he works as—his description—a cake artist. Charlie Craig and David Mullins entered his shop to order a cake to celebrate their wedding. Phillips said that although he would gladly make cakes for gay people for birthdays or other celebrations, he disapproves of same-sex marriage on religious grounds, and so does not make cakes for such celebrations. (He also refuses, for religious reasons, to make Halloween cakes.) To be compelled to do so would, he says, violate his constitutional right to speak freely. This, he says, includes the right not to be compelled to contribute his expressive cake artistry to a ceremony or occasion celebrating ideas or practices he does not condone. Well.

The First Amendment speaks of speech; its presence in a political document establishes its core purpose as the protection of speech intended for public persuasion. The amendment has, however, been rightly construed broadly to protect many expressive *activities*. Many, but there must be limits.

Phillips was neither asked nor required to attend, let alone participate in, the wedding. Same-sex marriage was not yet legal in Colorado, so Craig and Mullins were to be married in Massachusetts. The cake was for a subsequent reception in Denver. But even if the cake were to have been consumed at a wedding, Phillips's creation of the cake before the ceremony would not have constituted participation in any meaningful sense.

Six decades ago, the civil rights movement gained momentum through heroic acts of civil disobedience by African Americans whose sit-ins at lunch counters, and other challenges to segregation in commerce, produced the "public accommodations" section of the 1964 Civil Rights Act. It established the principle that those who open their doors for business must serve all who enter. That principle would become quite porous were it suspended whenever someone claimed his or her conduct was speech expressing an idea, and therefore created a constitutional exemption from a valid and neutral law of general applicability.

Photography is inherently a creative, expressive art, so photographers have a strong case against compulsory documentation of ceremonies at which they must be present. Less clearly but plausibly, florists can claim aesthetic expression in floral arrangements, but their work is done before wedding ceremonies occur. Chauffeurs facilitate ceremonies, but First Amendment jurisprudence would become incoherent if it protected unwilling chauffeurs from their supposedly expressive participation in ceremonies to which they deliver actual participants.

It is difficult to formulate a limiting principle that draws a bright line distinguishing essentially expressive conduct from conduct with incidental or negligible expressive possibilities. Nevertheless, it can be easy to identify *some* things that clearly are on one side of the line or the other. So, regarding Phillips's creations:

A cake can be a medium for creativity; hence, in some not-too-expansive sense, it can be food for thought. However, it certainly, and primarily, is food. And the creator's involvement with it ends when he sends it away to those who consume it. Phillips ought to lose this case. But Craig and Mullins, who sought his punishment, have behaved abominably.

To make his vocation compatible with his convictions and Colorado law Phillips has stopped making wedding cakes, which was his principal pleasure and 40 percent of his business. He now has only four employees, down from ten. Craig and Mullins, who have caused him serious financial loss and emotional distress, might be feeling virtuous for having done so. But siccing the government on him was nasty.

Denver has many bakers who, not having Phillips's scruples, would have unhesitatingly supplied the cake they desired. So, it was not necessary for Craig's and Mullins' satisfaction as consumers to submit Phillips to government coercion. Evidently, however, it was necessary for their satisfaction as asserters of their rights as a same-sex couple.

Phillips's obedience to his religious convictions neither expressed animus toward them nor injured them nor seriously inconvenienced them. Their side's sweeping victory in the struggle over gay rights has been decisive, and now less bullying and more magnanimity from the victors would be seemly.

A VICTORY (ONLY) FOR THE BAKER

June 7, 2018

WASHINGTON—"Loose lips sink ships" was a World War II slogan warning Americans against inadvertently disclosing important secrets, such as troop ships' sailing schedules. On Monday, the Supreme Court showed that loose lips can sink cases.

In Colorado in 2012, a Christian baker declined the request of a same-sex couple to decorate a cake for a reception celebrating their marriage in Massachusetts. The baker said that compelling him to put his expressive activity of cake artistry in the service of an act his faith condemns—and that was not legal in Colorado—would violate his First Amendment right to free speech, which includes the freedom not to speak, and to the free exercise of religion (which also is his basis for refusing to make Halloween cakes).

Rather than find, as would not have been burdensome, bakers with no objections to their request, the couple abandoned what once was the live-and-let-live spirit of the gay rights movement. In the truculent spirit of this era, they sicced the Colorado Civil Rights Commission on the baker. It said he violated the state's law against sexual-orientation discrimination.

On Monday, the court held 7–2 for the baker, *but only for him*. Writing for the court, Justice Anthony Kennedy (with Chief Justice John Roberts and Justices Clarence Thomas, Stephen Breyer, Samuel Alito, Elena Kagan, and Neil Gorsuch joining in the judgment) concluded that the Civil Rights Commission manifested animus regarding the baker's religious beliefs. For example, a notably obtuse member said that "despicable" rhetoric about freedom of religion had been used to justify slavery and the Holocaust.

The nation remains resolutely committed to the public accommodations section of the 1964 Civil Rights Act, which Colorado law anticipated in an 1885 law: If you open your doors for business, you must serve all who enter. Furthermore, it is maddeningly problematic to begin carving out exemptions from obedience to laws of general applicability that are neutral regarding religion. Wedding planners, photographers, flower arrangers, even chauffeurs who have religious objections to same-sex weddings can claim, with varying degrees of plausibility, that their activities are "expressive" and therefore their varying degrees of "participation" in religious events implicate the two First Amendment provisions the baker invoked.

In this case, the court prudently avoided trying to promulgate a limiting principle that would distinguish essentially expressive conduct from that with merely negligible or incidental expressive elements. But because the principle remains unformulated, other cases will come to the court lacking the sort of convenient escape hatch that the court found in the commission's loose lips. Looking down the road, Kennedy on Monday warned that "there are no doubt innumerable goods and services that no one could argue implicate the First Amendment."

First Amendment protections of freedom of speech are now more comprehensively attacked than ever before. The Alien and Sedition Acts of the 1790s (which were allowed to expire), the abuses of the post–World War I "Red Scare," and the McCarthyism of the early 1950s arose from temporary public fevers, and ended when the fevers broke. Today's attacks, emanating from authoritarian intellectuals, will not be as transitory as a mere political mood because they are theoretical: They argue that free speech is a chimera—speech often is a mere manifestation of an individual's retrograde socialization, aka "false consciousness," hence it is not morally serious and does not merit protection. Or they argue that free speech is only contingently important—it should be "balanced" against superior claims, such as community harmony or listeners' serenity.

Because attacks on freedom of speech are today ubiquitous and aggressive, its defenders understandably, but sometimes more reflexively than reflectively, support any claim that this freedom is importantly implicated, however tangentially, in this or that dispute. A danger in the cake case was that victory for the baker would make First Amendment law incoherent, even absurd: Expressive activities merit some constitutional protection, but not everything expressive is as important as speech, which America's foundational political document protects because speech communicates ideas for public persuasion.

Friends of the First Amendment should not be impatient for the court to embark on drawing ever-finer distinctions about which commercial transactions, by which kinds of believers, involving which kinds of ceremonies, implicate the Constitution's free speech and free exercise guarantees. Taking religious advice, the court on Monday acted on the principle that "sufficient unto the day is the evil thereof," which means: Cope with today's ample troubles and cope with tomorrow's when they arrive, as surely they will.

SUPREME COURT TO THE PRICKLY PLAINTIFFS OF GREECE, NEW YORK: LIGHTEN UP

May 8, 2014

WASHINGTON—After the marshal on Monday spoke the traditional "God save the United States and this honorable court," the Supreme Court ruled that the upstate New York town of Greece does not violate the First Amendment's prohibition of "establishment of religion" by opening its board of supervisors' meetings with a prayer. This ruling would not scandalize James Madison and other members of the First Congress, which drafted and sent to the states for ratification the First Amendment and the rest of the Bill of Rights. The Congress did this *after* hiring a chaplain.

Three decades have passed since the court last ruled on the matter of prayers during government meetings. In 1983, the court held:

The opening of sessions of legislative and other deliberative public bodies with prayer is deeply embedded in the history and tradition of this country. From colonial times through the founding of the Republic and ever since, the practice of legislative prayer has coexisted with the principles of disestablishment and religious freedom.

Since then, however, many Americans have become more irritable and litigious, and less neighborly. Also, there are many more nonbelievers. And the court has made Establishment Clause jurisprudence more labyrinthine with nuances such as the "endorsement test": What government behavior touching religion would a reasonable observer see as endorsing—or disapproving—a particular religion or religiosity generally?

Until 1999, Greece's board usually opened its meetings with a moment of silence. Since then, it has invited local clergy, most of whom are Christians, to deliver prayers, most of which have had Christian content. The court has never held that legislative prayer must be nonsectarian. But the two plaintiffs against Greece argued that the predominance of Christian voices (there were others—Jewish, Baha'i, and a Wiccan priestess who prayed to Athena and Apollo, rather fitting for a town named Greece) constituted establishment of Christianity as the town's religion. A lower court agreed.

On Monday, the Supreme Court split 5–4 in reversing that court. The majority held that ceremonial prayer—an encouragement to gravity and sobriety—is not harmful to the plaintiffs, who felt somehow coerced when present at public prayers, and who said such prayers are necessarily divisive. The court should have told them: If you feel coerced, you are flimsy people, and it is a choice—an unattractive one—to feel divided from your neighbors by their affection for brief and mild occasional expressions of religiosity.

The court prudently avoided the potentially endless task of adumbrating criteria by which local governments, acting as piety police, could finely calibrate a constitutionally acceptable quantity of devoutness in public prayers, or could draw a bright line between acknowledging and worshiping a divinity. So, the court can expect to hear again from militantly aggravated secularists.

Taking offense has become America's national pastime; being theatrically offended supposedly signifies the exquisitely refined moral delicacy of people who feel entitled to pass through life without encountering ideas or practices that annoy them. As the number of nonbelievers grows—about 20 percent of Americans are religiously unaffiliated, as are one-third of adults under thirty—so does the itch to litigate believers into submission to secular sensibilities.

America would be a more congenial place if it had more amiable atheists who say, as one such did, that "it does me no injury for my neighbor to say there are 20 gods, or no god. It neither picks my pocket nor breaks my leg." Some will say Jefferson was a deist, not an atheist. Atheism, however, simply involves having no theism, and deism—belief that a celestial Clockmaker wound up the universe and set it ticking—is too watery a theism to count. Any religion worthy of the name explains, enjoins, and consoles; undemanding deism merely explains, and does this minimally. Deism purports to explain the universe; so does the Big Bang theory, which is not a religion.

Still, Jefferson made statesmanlike accommodations of the public's strong preference for religious observances. As president, he attended Christian services conducted in the House of Representatives. They also were conducted in the Supreme Court chamber and the Treasury building. Jefferson attended a service in the House two days after praising (in an 1802 letter) "a wall of separation between church and state."

Jefferson was no slouch when it came to asserting rights. But Greece's prickly plaintiffs, having taken their town to court, might now ponder his example of relaxed, friendly respect for practices cherished by others and harmless to him.

CRANKY SECULARISTS HAVE THEIR CROSS TO BEAR

February 24, 2019

WASHINGTON—For decades the Supreme Court has entangled itself in Establishment Clause decisions that have been, in the words of *Alice in Wonderland*, curiouser and curiouser. On Wednesday, it can leaven with clarity the confusion it has sown.

The First Amendment's first words say, "Congress shall make no law respecting an establishment of religion." The court conducts its business after a chant that includes "God save the United States and this honorable court" and both houses of Congress have taxpayer-paid chaplains who pray for divine guidance. The court has, however, held that any policy or practice by a public entity that touches religion, however marginally, violates the Establishment Clause unless (a) it has a secular purpose and (b) its primary effect neither advances nor inhibits religion and (c) it does not foster excessive government entanglement with religion. In 1983, the court held, rudely but prudently, that Nebraska's legislature could continue being prayed over by its paid chaplain, thereby implying that the chaplain negligibly advanced religion. (The First Congress hired a chaplain, but James Madison, principal progenitor of the First Amendment, later said tersely that this "was not with my approbation.")

The court has refereed controversies involving, among many other things, the permissible quantity of religious symbols in Christmas displays on public property, where and what kind of displays of the Ten Commandments are constitutional, and what cannot be said to "solemnize" a high school football game in Texas, where football hardly needs solemnity infusions. The court has held that books but not maps can be provided by public funds to parochial schools, causing the late Senator Daniel Patrick Moynihan to wonder: What about atlases, which are books of maps?

Come Wednesday, the court will worry about a war memorial 4.8 miles away in Bladensburg, Maryland. In 1925, the Peace Cross, privately built on land given by the town to an American Legion post, was dedicated to forty-nine local men killed in World War I, when crosses marked most overseas graves of U.S. dead, regardless of their religious affiliations. Time passed, the population grew, a local government commission acquired the land, which is now in a traffic roundabout. A commemoration event occurs there each Veterans Day. There is no record that a religious event has ever been held at the cross in ninety-four years.

But a few cranky, persnickety, hairsplitting secularists say, with religious zeal, that the cross is now on public land so the Establishment Clause is violated. A district court affirmed the obvious: Honoring the war dead is a secular purpose. But a divided three-judge circuit court panel reversed. Engaging in something akin to Jesuitical casuistry, two judges said a cross must everywhere and always be a primarily symbol of Jesus's death, and because government provides maintenance for the plot in the roundabout, this cross excessively entangles government with religion.

In 1984, the court added an "endorsement" consideration: Would a commonsensical observer of a government display that includes a symbol with religious overtones—an observer knowing how the display came about—think the government is using it to "endorse" religion? In 1989 the court sidled even closer to wisdom, with a "coercion" criterion. Rather than ignite tens of thousands of skirmishes aimed at scrubbing all visual religious references to religion from this nation's public spaces (including the names of Corpus Christi, Texas, and Las Cruces, New Mexico), let's say this: Religion is not "established" when a passive monument on government property in no way coerces reasonable, informed passersby to believe, practice, or support religion.

It was for reasons of traffic safety that the government in 1961 acquired the ground on which the Bladensburg cross sits. If, fifty-eight years later, a few people in this age of hair-trigger rage choose to be offended by a long-standing monument reflecting the nation's culture and traditions, those people, not the First Amendment, need help. The court should so rule when, sometime before this term ends in June, it announces its decision in this case, as the nine justices sit beneath a frieze that includes a symbol of religion: Moses with the Ten Commandments.

Bladensburg last had the nation's attention because of the shambolic events of August 24, 1814. President James Madison fled from there, where feeble American resistance enabled British soldiers to proceed to torch the president's house and the Capitol. At Wednesday's oral argument, the court, sitting across the street from the Capitol, can begin to tidy up its Establishment Clause jurisprudence that Justice Clarence Thomas correctly says is "in shambles."

—

In June 2019 the Supreme Court held that the Bladensburg cross did not constitute the establishment of religion.

RESUSCITATING THE RIGHTS OF
NATIONAL CITIZENSHIP

February 28, 2019

WASHINGTON—There have been many memorable—and eventually consequential—Supreme Court dissents that affirmed principles that, in time, commanded a court majority. It is, however, rare that a justice's opinion *concurring* in a *unanimous* ruling is more intellectually scintillating and potentially portentous than the ruling itself. This happened last week, when the court dealt with an Indiana civil forfeiture case in which a man's $42,000 Land Rover was seized by the state as part of his punishment for a drug offense (selling $225 of drugs to undercover police officers) for which the maximum fine is $10,000.

In an excellent decision, the court held that the Constitution's Eighth Amendment ban on "excessive fines" applies to states. The court has explicitly applied ("incorporated") most of the Bill of Rights' protections, piecemeal, against states' actions. The court's standard has been that a particular protection must be "deeply rooted" in the nation's history and "fundamental to our scheme of ordered liberty." The court said that the Eighth Amendment's proscription of excessive fines should be incorporated, as the amendment's other two proscriptions ("excessive bail" and "cruel and unusual punishments") have been. Writing for the court, Ruth Bader Ginsburg said that such fines violate the Fourteenth Amendment's guarantee that people shall not be deprived of life, liberty, or property without "due process of law."

The court has long relied on the doctrine of "substantive due process"—*due* process produces nonarbitrary outcomes—to protect rights. This reliance came about because, in an 1873 decision, the court effectively nullified a more straightforward—and capacious—guarantee. Ratified in 1868, the Fourteenth Amendment's protection of Americans' "privileges or immunities" was written during the Southern suppression of the economic liberties and other rights of freed slaves. The clause was intended to protect the full panoply of national rights. But just five years later, the court construed the clause so narrowly (as protecting a few "national" rights, such as access to navigable waterways and federal subtreasuries) as to nullify it.

Last week, Justice Clarence Thomas again argued for righting this wrong. He said that the phrase "substantive due process" is "oxymoronic," and that the court, struggling to extract substance from process, has engaged in a process without a discernible principle—distinguishing "fundamental" rights meriting protection from undeserving lesser rights. This distinction has no basis in the Constitution's text or structure, and leaves the court free to improvise new rights and ignore others. Thomas demonstrates that the ban on excessive fines has a long pedigree, before and since the American Founding, which should place it among Americans' privileges or immunities.

What else would a revived Privileges or Immunities Clause protect? Certainly economic liberty, including the right to earn a living unburdened by unreasonable occupational licensure laws. There would be ample additional scope for the protection of rights by courts guided by the clause's premise, which is: American government's primary task is the protection of rights, aka privileges or immunities, which, as the Ninth Amendment stipulates, are not exhaustively enumerated in the first eight amendments.

In a one-paragraph concurrence, Justice Neil Gorsuch almost endorsed Thomas's argument: "[T]he appropriate vehicle for incorporation may well be the Fourteenth Amendment's Privileges or Immunities Clause, rather than, as this court has long assumed, the Due Process Clause." Gorsuch cited Yale law professor Akhil Amar's book *The Bill of Rights*, in which Amar notes that if those who wrote and ratified the clause merely meant to apply against the states the Bill of Rights, they could, and presumably would, have said so. Hence it is reasonable to think that, properly construed, the clause denotes a richer menu of rights, encompassing those in Anglo-American legal traditions and state constitutions, and not ignoring the Ninth Amendment: "The enumeration in the Constitution, of certain rights, shall not be construed to deny or disparage others retained by the people."

Thomas, who correctly regards *stare decisis*—the principle of deciding cases by adhering to precedents—as less than sacramental, has for many years been 20 percent of a potential court majority for resuscitating the Privileges or Immunities Clause. With Gorsuch, who last week suggested that the privileges or immunities of U.S. citizens "include, *at minimum*, the individual rights enumerated in the Bill of Rights" (emphasis added), there would be 40 percent of such a majority. America might be moving closer to a more robust role for an engaged judiciary in protecting a more spacious conception of the rights attached to national citizenship.

KOREMATSU V. UNITED STATES, REPUDIATED

April 25, 2013

WASHINGTON—Two of the three most infamous Supreme Court decisions were erased by events. The Civil War and postwar constitutional amendments effectively overturned *Dred Scott v. Sandford* (1857), which held that blacks could never have rights that whites must respect. *Plessy v. Ferguson* (1896), which upheld legally enforced segregation, was undone by court decisions and legislation.

Korematsu v. United States (1944), which affirmed the president's wartime power to sweep Americans of disfavored racial groups into concentration camps, elicited a 1988 congressional apology. Now Peter Irons, founder of the Earl Warren Bill of Rights Project at the University of California, San Diego, is campaigning for a Supreme Court "repudiation" of the *Korematsu* decision and other Japanese internment rulings. A repudiation would be unprecedented, but an essay that Irons is circulating among constitutional law professors whose support he seeks is timely reading in today's context of anti-constitutional presidencies, particularly regarding war powers.

On February 19, 1942, President Franklin Roosevelt authorized the military to "prescribe military areas...from which any or all persons may be excluded." So 110,000 Americans of Japanese ancestry, two-thirds of them born here, were sent to camps in desolate Western locations. Supposedly, this was a precaution against espionage and sabotage. Actually, it rested entirely on the racial animus of General John DeWitt, head of the Western Defense Command.

Using government records, Irons demonstrates that because senior officials, including Solicitor General Charles Fahy, committed "numerous and knowing acts of governmental misconduct," the court based its decision on "records and arguments that were fabricated and fraudulent." Officials altered and destroyed evidence that would have revealed the racist motives for the internments. And to preserve the pretext of a "military necessity" for the concentration camps, officials suppressed reports on the lack of evidence of disloyalty or espionage by Japanese Americans.

The 1943 "Final Report" on Japanese "evacuation," prepared under DeWitt's direction and signed by him, said a Japanese invasion was probable, that "racial characteristics" of Japanese Americans predisposed them to assist the invasion, and that is was "impossible" to distinguish loyal from disloyal Japanese-American citizens, if there were any: "The Japanese race is an enemy race and while many second- and third-generation Japanese born on United States soil, possessed of United States citizenship, have become 'Americanized,' the racial strains are undiluted."

When War Department officials objected to such assertions and demanded revisions, DeWitt ordered all copies and records of the original report destroyed, but one copy escaped DeWitt's cover-up. The court, however, never saw it, remaining unaware of the racist basis of the theory of internment's "military necessity."

Also kept from the court was a report, prepared for the Chief of Naval Operations and made available to DeWitt, estimating potentially disloyal Japanese as just 3 percent of the Japanese-American population, and declaring that these were "already fairly well known to naval intelligence" and could be quickly apprehended, if necessary. The suppressed reports' conclusion: "The entire Japanese problem has been magnified out of its true proportion, largely because of the physical characteristics of the people (and) should be handled on the basis of the *individual...* and *not* on a racial basis."

Fahy ignored an assistant attorney general's warning that not advising the court of this report would constitute "suppression of evidence." Furthermore, DeWitt justified internment because "the interception of unauthorized radio communications" emanating from along the coast "conclusively" accounted for Japanese submarine attacks on U.S. ships. The FBI, however, reported "no information" of "any espionage activity ashore or... illicit shore-to-ship signaling." The Federal Communications Commission investigated "hundreds" of reports of suspicious radio communications but found nothing to confirm DeWitt's accusations. Yet Fahy in his oral argument assured the court he could guarantee the veracity of "every line, every word, and every syllable" of DeWitt's report, and that "no person in any responsible position has ever taken a contrary position."

The *Korematsu* decision reflected perennial dangers: panic, and excessive deference, judicial and other, to presidents or others who would suspend constitutional protections in the name of wartime exigencies. It is less important that the decision be repudiated than that it be remembered.

Especially by those currently clamoring, since Boston, for an American citizen—arrested in America, and concerning whom there is no evidence of a connection with al-Qaeda, the Taliban, or other terror network— to be detained by the military as an "enemy combatant." The *Korematsu* case is a reminder that waiving constitutional rights is rarely necessary and rarely ends well.

—

In June 2018 the Supreme Court formally repudiated the then seventy- four-year-old Korematsu *ruling.*

THE COURT AND THE POLITICS OF POLITICS

March 24, 2019

WASHINGTON—If an adjective creates a redundancy, does preceding it with two other adjectives give the Supreme Court a reason to venture where it has never gone before? Come Tuesday, the court will hear oral arguments urging it to referee gerrymandering in the drawing of congressional districts. The justices should, like Ulysses, listen to this siren song but bind themselves from obeying it.

The arguments will concern two cases: one from Maryland, where Republicans are aggrieved, another from North Carolina, where Democrats are unhappy. The practice the court will consider is (adjective one) "*partisan* gerrymandering." This modifier, however, does not modify; there is no other kind of gerrymandering, which is always partisan.

Tuesday's issue is whether the court should attempt something for which it has neither an aptitude nor any constitutional warrant—concocting criteria for deciding when (adjective two) *excessive* partisan gerrymandering becomes (adjective three) *unconstitutional*.

Gerrymandering is generally as surreptitious as a brass band and is, always and everywhere, as political as lemonade is lemony. It is the drawing of district lines by faction A for the purpose of disadvantaging faction B. This practice is older than the republic: Pennsylvanians and North Carolinians were engaging in it in the first half of the eighteenth century, about a century before it acquired its name. (In 1812, Massachusetts Democratic-Republicans, serving Governor Elbridge Gerry, drew a district shaped like a salamander.)

Until 1962, the court stayed away from the inherently political process of the drawing of district lines by legislatures organized along partisan lines because the Constitution is unambiguous: "The times, places and manner of holding elections for senators and representatives, shall be prescribed in each state by the legislature thereof." There are enough open-textured terms in the Constitution ("establishment" of religion, "unreasonable" searches, "cruel" punishments, etc.) to rescue the Supreme Court from ennui. The Elections Clause just quoted contains no such terms. (Although four years ago five misguided justices said "legislature" can mean a commission vested with redistricting power taken away by referendum from a state legislature.)

Furthermore, the political realists who framed the Constitution, and who understood the pervasiveness of partisanship, added the following to the Elections Clause quoted above: Congress may "at any time by law make or alter such regulations" as the states might write regarding congressional elections. So, the Constitution is explicit: Congress, not the judiciary, is the federal remedy for alleged defects in the drawing of congressional districts. The political branches of the state and federal governments are assigned to deal with the inherently value-laden politics of drawing district lines.

In 1872, ninety-two years before the court found a constitutional requirement (equal protection of the laws) for "one person, one vote," Congress had said that districts must contain "as nearly as practicable an equal number of inhabitants." This stipulation was strictly enforced after 1964, when the court enunciated the simple and neutral principle of numerically equal districts.

There can, however, be nothing simple or neutral about what opponents of gerrymandering want to inveigle the court into trying to devise. These include criteria for measuring unconstitutional excesses in the common practices of "cracking" (dispersing one party's voters across districts dominated by the other party) and "packing" (one party concentrating the other party's voters into supermajorities in a few districts). And the political science professoriate stands ready to tutor the court about "wasted votes" resulting from "efficiency gaps."

Today, people who are unhappy about North Carolina's gerrymandering argue (as a lower court did) that "the Constitution does not *authorize* state redistricting bodies to engage in...partisan gerrymandering." (Emphasis added.) Now, *there* is a perverse doctrine: Everything is forbidden that the Constitution does not explicitly authorize.

Those who are eager to sink the judiciary waist-deep into the politics of politics resort to blunderbuss arguments. For example, they say they have suffered justiciable injury because gerrymandering "dilutes" their votes and infringes their First Amendment rights—even though everyone everywhere remains free to associate with his or her party of choice, and campaign and vote for any candidate.

The Constitution is silent regarding limits on state legislatures' partisan redistricting practices and is explicit regarding Congress's exclusive power to modify these practices. If the court nevertheless assigns a portion of this power to itself, its condign punishment, inflicted after each decennial census, will be avalanches of litigation arising from partisan unhappiness about states' redistricting plans. And no matter how the court decides each case, its reputation as a nonpolitical institution will be steadily tarnished.

—

In June 2019 the Supreme Court ruled, 5–4, that there is no legal standard for identifying unconstitutional gerrymandering, so state legislatures or Congress, not federal courts, must reform the drawing of election districts.

LITIGATING THROUGH A FOG OF EUPHEMISMS

June 30, 2009

WASHINGTON—Although New Haven's firefighters deservedly won in the Supreme Court, it is deeply depressing that they won narrowly— 5–4. The egregious behavior by that city's government, in a context of racial rabble-rousing, did not seem legally suspect to even one of the court's four liberals, whose harmony seemed to reflect result-oriented rather than law-driven reasoning.

The undisputed facts are that in 2003 the city gave promotion exams to 118 firemen, 27 of them black. The tests were prepared by a firm specializing in employment exams and were validated, as federal law requires, by independent experts. When none of the African Americans did well enough to qualify for the available promotions, a black minister allied with the seven-term mayor warned of a dire "political ramification" if the city promoted from the list of persons (including one Hispanic) that the exams identified as qualified. The city decided that no one would be promoted, calling this a race-neutral outcome because no group was disadvantaged more than any other.

The city's idea of equal treatment—denying promotions equally to those deemed and those not deemed qualified—was particularly galling to Frank Ricci, who had prepared for the exams by quitting his second job, buying the more than $1,000 worth of books the city recommended, paying to have them read onto audiotapes—he is dyslexic—and taking practice tests and interviews. His efforts earned him the sixth-highest score.

He and others denied promotions for which their exam scores made them eligible sued, charging violations of the Constitution's guarantee of equal protection of the laws and of the 1964 Civil Rights Act. The city argued that if it had made promotions based on the test results, it would have been vulnerable under the 1964 act to being sued for adopting a practice that had a "disparate impact" on minorities. On Monday, the court's conservatives (Anthony Kennedy writing for the majority, joined by John Roberts, Antonin Scalia, Clarence Thomas, and Samuel Alito) held:

The rights of Ricci et al. under the 1964 act were violated. The city's fear of a disparate impact litigation was not unfounded, but that did not justify the race-based response to the exam results because New Haven did not have "a strong basis in evidence" to believe it would be held liable. There is such evidence only if the exams "were not job related and consistent with business necessity, or if there existed an equally valid, less discriminatory alternative" that would have served the city's needs but that it refused to adopt.

"*All* the evidence *demonstrates* that the city rejected the test results because the higher scoring candidates were white." The city's criticisms of the exam "are *blatantly contradicted* by the record." And "the city *turned a blind eye* to evidence supporting the exams' validity" (emphases added).

Ruth Bader Ginsburg, joined in dissent by John Paul Stevens, David Souter, and Stephen Breyer, rejected the majority's conclusions root and branch. She cited a federal report from the early 1970s about discrimination in hiring firefighters, disputed even the "business necessity" of the exams' 60/40 written/oral ratio, and defended the integrity of New Haven's decision-making—rejecting Alito's concurrence, which dwelt on the rancid racial politics of the Reverend Boise Kimber. Alito concluded that "no reasonable jury" could find that the city possessed a "substantial basis in evidence to find the tests inadequate."

Scalia, concurring separately, said Monday's ruling "merely postpones the evil day" on which the court must decide "whether, or to what extent," existing disparate-impact law conflicts with the Fourteenth Amendment guarantee of equal protection of the law. Conceding that "the question is not an easy one," Scalia said: The federal government is prohibited from discriminating on the basis of race, so surely "it is also prohibited from enacting laws mandating that third parties"—e.g., a city government—"discriminate on the basis of race." Scalia added:

> Would a private employer not be guilty of unlawful discrimination if he refrained from establishing a racial hiring quota but intentionally designed his hiring practices to achieve the same end? Surely he would. Intentional discrimination is still occurring, just one step up the chain.

The nation shall slog on, litigating through a fog of euphemisms and blurry categories (e.g., "race-conscious" actions that somehow are not racial discrimination because they "remedy" discrimination that no one has intended). This is the predictable price of failing to simply insist that government cannot take cognizance of race.

EXCURSIONS INTO SCIENCE

MAPPING THE UNIVERSE BETWEEN OUR EARS

August 25, 2013

PRINCETON, N.J.—Fifty years from now, when Malia and Sasha are grandmothers, their father's presidency might seem most consequential because of a small sum—$100 million—for studying something small. "As humans," Barack Obama said when announcing the initiative to study the brain, "we can identify galaxies light-years away…but we still haven't unlocked the mystery of the three pounds of matter that sits between our ears."

Actually, understanding the brain will be a resounding success without unlocking the essential mystery, which is: How does matter become conscious of itself? Or should we say, how does it become—or acquire—consciousness? Just trying to describe this subject takes scientists onto intellectual terrain long occupied by philosophers. Those whose field is the philosophy of mind will learn from scientists such as Princeton's David Tank, a participant in the BRAIN Initiative, which aims at understanding how brain regions and cells work together, moment to moment, throughout our lives.

If, as is said, a physicist is an atom's way of knowing about atoms, then a neuroscientist like Tank is a brain cell's way of knowing about brain cells. Each of us has about 100 billion of those, each of which communicates with an average of 10,000 other nerve cells. The goal of neuroscientists is to discover how these neural conversations give rise to a thought, a memory, or a decision. And to understand how the brain functions, from which we may understand disorders such as autism, schizophrenia, and epilepsy.

Biological causes have been determined for only about 3 percent of the disorders listed in the *Diagnostic and Statistical Manual of Mental Disorders*. With "mapping," scientists may at last establish connections between neurotransmitters and particular mental disorders. This might influence how pharmaceutical companies direct their research. And treatments of post-traumatic stress disorders might benefit from learning how the mind erases disturbing memories.

Understanding the brain is, Tank says, different from the Human Genome Project. The latter simply sequenced, and made straightforward extrapolations, concerning a well-defined group of 3.1 billion "letters" that comprise the "alphabet" that determines the growth of a human being from a single cell to a complex human being. We are learning *what* each letter does, if not yet *how*. In the case of the brain, "mapping" is not just trying to ascertain what particular parts of the brain do in response to external events, but how the brain parts engage in "conversation" with each other, and how they can change over time.

Much brain activity—much thinking—is not, Tank notes, the result of external stimuli. So, is the brain conversing with—acting upon—itself? This internal conversation is at the core of who—and what—we are.

New technologies enable scientists to watch the brain in action, monitoring neural activity as it thinks. Even a decades-old technology, functional magnetic resonance imaging (fMRI) reveals, Tank says, "what parts of the brain are active in particular computations and behaviors."

In fifty years, fMRI images will seem as crude as Magellan's maps. We will understand thought processes with instantaneous cellular resolution, and hence the essence of what brains do, and what derails them.

Development of the transistor, progenitor of the Digital Age, required only advances in materials science. There is, Tank says, "no comparable base of knowledge for the brain" because there is no mechanistic understanding of how the brain works. Pharmacology is groping for therapeutic effects because drugs target particular receptors, the workings of which are not understood. To the brain, small pills can be sledgehammers. Understanding brain dynamics will enable ever more precise chemical and other interventions.

If we had to *think* about combing our hair or making toast, we would never get out of the house in the morning. Habits enable us to function because neurons are "conversing" with networks involving thousands of other cells. But ethicists—and courts, and poets—will be warily watching what is learned about the neural basis of choices, habits, love, and other important things.

Do we *have* bodies or *are* we bodies? What will become of the field of psychology as explorations of brain anatomy advances our understanding of how brain architecture influences, or even determines, behavior? "The devil made me do it" is no longer an exculpation. But what about "My brain circuitry made me do it"? Someday debates about free will may be resolved by understanding that we are responsible for our actions because we have "ownership" of three especially intricate pounds of matter.

MEDICALIZING CHARACTER FLAWS

February 28, 2010

WASHINGTON—Novelist Peter De Vries died seventeen years ago but his discernment of this country's cultural foibles still amazes. In a 1983 novel, he spotted the tendency of America's therapeutic culture to medicalize character flaws: "Once terms like identity doubts and midlife crisis become current," De Vries wrote, "the reported cases of them increase by leaps and bounds." And: "Rapid-fire means of communication have brought psychic dilapidation within the reach of the most provincial backwaters, so that large metropolitan centers and educated circles need no longer consider it their exclusive property, nor preen themselves on their special malaises."

Life is about to imitate De Vries's literature, again. The fourth edition of the *Diagnostic and Statistical Manual of Mental Disorders* (DSM), psychiatry's encyclopedia of supposed mental "disorders," is being revised. The sixteen years since the last revision evidently were prolific in producing new afflictions. The revision may aggravate the confusion of moral categories.

Today's DSM defines "oppositional defiant disorder" as a pattern of "negativistic, defiant, disobedient and hostile behavior toward authority figures." Symptoms include "often loses temper," "often deliberately annoys people" or "is often touchy." DSM omits this symptom: "is a teenager."

This DSM defines as "personality disorders" attributes that once were considered character flaws. "Antisocial personality disorder" is "a pervasive pattern of disregard for...the rights of others...callous, cynical...an inflated and arrogant self-appraisal." "Histrionic personality disorder" is "excessive emotionality and attention-seeking." "Narcissistic personality disorder" involves "grandiosity, need for admiration...boastful and pretentious." And so on.

If every character blemish or emotional turbulence is a "disorder" akin to a physical disability, legal accommodations are mandatory. Under federal law, "disabilities" include any "mental impairment that substantially limits one or more major life activities"; "mental impairments" include "emotional or mental illness." So there might be a legal entitlement to be a jerk. (See above, "antisocial personality disorder.")

The revised DSM reportedly may include "binge eating disorder" and "hypersexual disorder" ("a great deal of time" devoted to "sexual fantasies and urges" and "planning for and engaging in sexual behavior"). Concerning children, there might be "temper dysregulation disorder with dysphoria."

This last categorization illustrates the serious stakes in the categorization of behaviors. Extremely irritable or aggressive children are frequently diagnosed as bipolar and treated with powerful antipsychotic drugs. This can be a damaging mistake if behavioral modification treatment can mitigate the problem.

Another danger is that childhood eccentricities, sometimes inextricable from creativity, might be labeled "disorders" to be "cured." If seven-year-old Mozart tried composing his concertos today, he might be diagnosed with attention-deficit hyperactivity disorder and medicated into barren normality.

Furthermore, intellectual chaos can result from medicalizing the assessment of character. Today's therapeutic ethos, which celebrates curing and disparages judging, expresses the liberal disposition to assume that crime and other problematic behaviors reflect social or biological causation. While this absolves the individual of responsibility, it also strips the individual of personhood, and moral dignity.

James Q. Wilson, America's pre-eminent social scientist, has noted how "abuse excuse" threatens the legal system and society's moral equilibrium. Writing in *National Affairs* quarterly ("The Future of Blame"), Wilson notes that genetics and neuroscience seem to suggest that self-control is more attenuated—perhaps to the vanishing point—than our legal and ethical traditions assume.

The part of the brain that stimulates anger and aggression is larger in men than in women, and the part that restrains anger is smaller in men than in women. "Men," Wilson writes, "by no choice of their own, are far more prone to violence and far less capable of self-restraint than women." That does not, however, absolve violent men of blame. As Wilson says, biology and environment interact. And the social environment includes moral assumptions, sometimes codified in law, concerning expectations about our duty to desire what we *ought* to desire.

It is scientifically sensible to say that all behavior is *in some sense* caused. But a society that thinks scientific determinism renders personal responsibility a chimera must consider it absurd not only to condemn depravity but also to praise nobility. Such moral derangement can flow from exaggerated notions of what science teaches, or can teach, about the biological and environmental roots of behavior.

Or—revisers of the DSM, please note—confusion can flow from the notion that normality is always obvious and normative, meaning preferable. And the notion that deviations from it should be considered "disorders" to be "cured" rather than stigmatized as offenses against valid moral norms.

A TELESCOPE AS HISTORY TEACHER

October 4, 2015

BALTIMORE—Twinkling stars are pretty but, for astronomers, problematic. Twinkles are caused by the interference of Earth's atmosphere with light radiating throughout the breathtakingly beautiful and unimaginably violent universe. In 1990, however, the Hubble telescope went into orbit 370 miles above Earth, beyond the atmospheric filter, peering perhaps 12 billion years into the past, almost to the Big Bang of 13.7 billion years ago.

It has seen interesting things, including HD 189733b, a planet about 63 light-years (370 trillion miles) away, where winds exceed 4,000 miles per hour and it rains molten glass. As Hubble nears the end of its life, its much more capable successor, the James Webb Space Telescope, named after a former NASA administrator, is being developed at Johns Hopkins University.

The campus has several history departments. Some study humanity's achievements during its existence, which has been barely a blink in cosmic time. Other historians—the scientists and engineers of the Space Telescope Science Institute—study the origins of *everything* in order to understand humanity's origins. In 2018, Webb will be situated 940,000 miles from Earth, orbiting the sun in tandem with Earth, to continue investigating our place in the universe.

Our wee solar system is an infinitesimally small smudge among uncountable billions of galaxies, each with uncountable billions of stars. Our Milky Way galaxy, where we live, probably has 40 billion planets approximately Earth's size. Looking at the sky through a drinking straw, the spot you see contains 10,000 galaxies. Yet the cosmos is not crowded: If there were just three bees in America, the air would be more congested with bees than space is with stars. Matter, however, is not all that matters.

America's manned moon expeditions ended in 1972, but modern cosmology began with the 1965 discovery that the universe is permeated with background radiation. This, like everything else, is a residue of the Big Bang that, in a hundredth of a billionth of a trillionth of a trillionth of a second, set stuff—some of it now congealed into galaxies—flying apart. The recipe for our biophilic (friendly to life) planet was cooked in the universe's first one-hundredth of a second, at a temperature of a hundred thousand million degrees Celsius. Einstein's theory that space is curved by gravity requires a nonstatic universe, expanding or contracting. With a light-gathering mirror seven times larger than Hubble's, and operating in temperatures of minus 388 degrees Fahrenheit, Webb will gather extraordinarily faint light that has been traveling for billions of years since the Big Bang. With Webb looking back in time to a few hundred million years after the explosion, scientists will analyze light for clues concerning the earliest formation of stars, planets, galaxies, and us.

Hubble, which is the size of a school bus, supplies data for more than one-fifth of all scholarly astronomy papers. Webb, which will be the size of a tennis court, will advance knowledge about this stupendous improbability: How did material complexity, then single-cell life, then animals and consciousness emerge from chaos?

Webb will not shed light on two interesting questions: How many universes are there? Is everything the result of a meaningless cosmic sneeze or of an intentional First Cause? Webb will, however, express our species' dignity as curious creatures.

Since Copernicus's great impertinence—displacing Earth and its passengers from the center of the universe—we have learned that "center" is senseless in an expanding universe that has no edge and where space and time are warped. Our solar system is not even the center of our galaxy. We know neither the conditions when, 4 billion years ago, Earth became home for life, nor the processes that ignited life. But half of the 200 billion stars just in our Milky Way have planetary systems, so a basic question of religion—Where did we come from?—leads to another: Are we—carbon- and water-based, oxygen-breathing creatures—alone?

Earth revolves around our expiring sun, which is scheduled to burn out in just 5 billion years. At about that time, our Milky Way will collide with the neighboring Andromeda galaxy. This is not apt to end well. Meanwhile, however, the scientist-historians here will try to tickle from the cosmos information for its own sake.

Space exploration began from Cold War imperatives, producing rocketry, intelligence satellites, and national prestige. Webb, which only America could make happen, does not contribute to the nation's defense, but, as its creators say with justifiable pride, it makes the nation all the more worth defending.

"TAKE A SUN AND PUT IT IN A BOX"

December 22, 2013

PRINCETON, N.J.—In a scientific complex on eighty-eight bucolic acres near here, some astonishingly talented people are advancing a decades-long project to create a sun on Earth. When—not if; when—decades hence they and collaborators around the world succeed, their achievement will be more transformative of human life than any prior scientific achievement.

The Princeton Plasma Physics Laboratory's (PPPL) focus—magnetic fusion research—began at the university in 1951. It was grounded in the earlier work of a European scientist then living in Princeton. Einstein's theory that mass could be converted into energy had been demonstrated six years earlier near Alamogordo, New Mexico, by fission—the splitting of atoms, which released the energy that held the atoms together. By the 1950s, however, attention was turning to an unimaginably more promising method of releasing energy from transforming matter—the way the sun does, by fusion.

Every second the sun produces a million times more energy than the world consumes in a year. But to "take a sun and put it in a box"—the description of one scientist here—requires developing the new field of plasma physics and solving the most difficult engineering problems in the history of science. The objective is to create conditions for the controlled release of huge amounts of energy from the fusion of two hydrogen isotopes, deuterium and tritium. Hydrogen is the most abundant element in the universe; Earth's water contains a virtually inexhaustible supply (10 million million tons) of deuterium, and tritium is "bred" in the fusion plant itself.

The sun is a huge sphere of plasma, which is a hot, electrically charged gas. The production and confinement of plasma in laboratories is now routine. The task now is to solve the problem of "net energy"—producing more electrical power than is required for the production of it.

Magnets produce a magnetic field sufficient to prevent particles heated beyond the sun's temperature—more than 100 million degrees Celsius—from hitting the walls of the containment vessel. Understanding plasma's behavior requires the assistance of Titan, one of the world's fastest computers, which is located at Oak Ridge National Laboratory in Tennessee and can perform more than 17 quadrillion—a million billion—calculations a second.

As in today's coal-fired power plants, the ultimate object is heat—to turn water into steam that drives generators. Fusion, however, produces no greenhouse gases, no long-lived nuclear waste, and no risk of the sort of runaway reaction that occurred at Fukushima. Fusion research here and elsewhere is supported by nations with half the world's population— China, India, Japan, Russia, South Korea, and the European Union. The current domestic spending pace would cost $2.5 billion over ten years—about one-thirtieth of what may be squandered in California on a nineteenth-century technology (a train). By one estimate, to bring about a working fusion reactor in twenty years would cost $30 billion— approximately the cost of one week of U.S. energy consumption.

Given the societal will, commercially feasible production of fusion energy is possible in the lifetimes of most people now living. The cost of operating the PPPL complex, which a century from now might be designated a historic site, is 0.01 percent of U.S. energy spending. PPPL's budget is a minuscule fraction of U.S. energy infrastructure investment (power plants, pipelines). Yet the laboratory, which once had a staff of 1,400, today has only 450.

The Apollo space program was much less technologically demanding and much more accessible to public understanding. It occurred in the context of U.S.–Soviet competition; it was directly relevant to national security (ballistic missiles; the coin of international prestige); it had a time frame for success—President Kennedy's pledge to go to the moon in the 1960s—that could hold the public's attention, and incremental progress (orbital flights) the public could comprehend.

Because the fusion energy program lacks such immediacy, transparency, and glamour, it poses a much more difficult test for the political process. Because of its large scale and long time horizon, the fusion project is a perfect example of a public good the private sector cannot pursue and the public sector should not slight. Most government revenues now feed the public's unslakable appetite for transfer payments. The challenge for today's political class is to moderate its subservience to this appetite sufficiently to enable the basic science that will earn tomorrow's gratitude.

THE PATHOLOGY OF CLIMATOLOGY

September 13, 2010

WASHINGTON—The cover of *The American Scholar* quarterly carries an impertinent assertion: The Earth doesn't care if you drive a hybrid. The essay inside is titled "What the Earth Knows." What it knows, according to Robert B. Laughlin, co-winner of the 1998 Nobel Prize in Physics, is this: What humans do to, and ostensibly for, the Earth does not matter in the long run, and the long run is what matters to the Earth. We must, Laughlin says, think about the Earth's past in terms of geologic time.

For example: The world's total precipitation in a year is about one meter—"the height of a golden retriever." About 200 meters—the height of the Hoover Dam—have fallen on Earth since the Industrial

Revolution. Since the Ice Age ended, enough rain has fallen to fill all the oceans four times; since the dinosaurs died, rainfall has been sufficient to fill the oceans 20,000 times. Yet the amount of water on Earth probably hasn't changed significantly over geologic time. Damaging this old Earth is, Laughlin says, "easier to imagine than it is to accomplish." There have been mass volcanic explosions, meteor impacts, "and all manner of other abuses greater than anything people could inflict, and it's still here. It's a survivor."

Laughlin acknowledges that "a lot of responsible people" are worried about atmospheric concentrations of carbon dioxide from burning fossil fuels. This has, he says, "the potential" to modify the weather by raising average temperatures several degrees Celsius and that governments have taken "significant, although ineffective," steps to slow the warming. "On the scales of time relevant to itself, the earth doesn't care about any of these governments or their legislation."

Buy a hybrid, turn off your air conditioner, unplug your refrigerator, yank your phone charger from the wall socket—such actions will "leave the end result exactly the same." Someday, all the fossil fuels that used to be in the ground will be burned. After that, in about a millennium, the Earth will dissolve most of the resulting carbon dioxide into the oceans. (The oceans have dissolved in them "40 times more carbon than the atmosphere contains, a total of 30 trillion tons, or 30 times the world's coal reserves.") The dissolving will leave the concentration in the atmosphere only slightly higher than today's. Then "over tens of millennia, or perhaps hundreds" the Earth will transfer the excess carbon dioxide into its rocks, "eventually returning levels in the sea and air to what they were before humans arrived on the scene." This will take an eternity as humans reckon, but a blink in geologic time.

It seems, Laughlin says, that "something, presumably a geologic regulatory process, fixed the world's carbon dioxide levels before humans arrived" with their SUVs and computers. Some scientists argue that "the photosynthetic machinery of plants seems optimized" to certain carbon dioxide levels. But "most models, even pessimistic ones," envision "a thousand-year carbon dioxide pulse followed by glacially slow decay back to the pre-civilization situation."

Laughlin believes that humans can "do damage persisting for geologic time" by "biodiversity loss"—extinctions that are, unlike carbon dioxide excesses, permanent. The Earth did not reverse the extinction of the dinosaurs. Today extinctions result mostly from human population pressures—habitat destruction, pesticides, etc.—but "slowing man-made extinctions in a meaningful way would require drastically reducing the world's human population." Which will not happen.

There is something like a pathology of climatology. To avoid mixing fact and speculation, earth scientists are, Laughlin says, "ultraconservative," meaning they focus on the present and the immediate future: "[They] go to extraordinary lengths to prove by means of measurement that the globe is warming now, the ocean is acidifying now, fossil fuel is being exhausted now, and so forth, even though these things are self-evident in geologic time."

Climate change over geologic time is, Laughlin says, something the Earth has done "on its own without asking anyone's permission or explaining itself." People can cause climate change, but major glacial episodes have occurred "at regular intervals of 100,000 years," always "a slow, steady cooling followed by abrupt warming back to conditions similar to today's."

Six million years ago the Mediterranean dried up. Ninety million years ago there were alligators in the Arctic. Three hundred million years ago Northern Europe was a desert, and coal formed in Antarctica. "One thing we know for sure," Laughlin says about these convulsions, "is that people weren't involved."

THE MWP, LIA, AND THE CLIMATE CHANGE DEBATE

January 8, 2015

WASHINGTON—We know, because they often say so, that those who think catastrophic global warming is probable and perhaps imminent are exemplary empiricists. They say those who disagree with them are "climate change deniers" disrespectful of science. Actually, however, something about which everyone can agree is that *of course* the climate is changing—it always is. And if climate Cassandras are as conscientious as they claim to be about weighing evidence, how do they accommodate historical evidence of enormously consequential episodes of climate change not produced by human activity? Before wagering vast wealth and curtailments of liberty on correcting the climate, two recent books should be considered.

In *The Third Horseman: A Story of Weather, War, and the Famine History Forgot*, William Rosen explains how Europe's "most widespread and destructive famine" was the result of "an almost incomprehensibly complicated mixture of climate, commerce, and conflict, four centuries in gestation." Early in that century, 10 percent of the population from the Atlantic to the Urals died, partly because of the effect of climate change on "the incredible amalgam of molecules that comprises a few inches of soil that produces the world's food."

In the Medieval Warm Period (MWP), from the end of the ninth century to the beginning of the fourteenth, the Northern Hemisphere was warmer than at any time in the last 8,000 years—for reasons concerning which there is no consensus. Warming increased the amount of arable land—there were vineyards in northern England—leading, Rosen says, to Europe's "first sustained population increase since the fall of the Roman Empire." The need for land on which to grow cereals drove deforestation. The MWP population explosion gave rise to towns, textile manufacturing, and new wealthy classes.

Then, near the end of the MWP, came the severe winters of 1309–1312, when polar bears could walk from Greenland to Iceland on pack ice. In 1315 there was rain for perhaps 155 consecutive days, washing away topsoil. Upwards of half the arable land in much of Europe was gone; cannibalism arrived as parents ate children. Corpses hanging from gallows were devoured.

Human behavior did not cause this climate change. Instead, climate warming caused behavioral change (10 million mouths to feed became 30 million). Then climate cooling caused social changes (rebelliousness and bellicosity) that amplified the consequences of climate, a pattern repeated four centuries later.

In *Global Crisis: War, Climate Change & Catastrophe in the Seventeenth Century*, Geoffrey Parker, a history professor at Ohio State, explains how a "fatal synergy" between climatological and political factors produced turmoil from Europe to China. What he calls "the placenta of the crisis" of that century included "the Little Ice Age" (LIA) between the 1640s and the 1690s. Unusual weather, protracted enough to qualify as a change in climate, correlated so strongly with political upheavals as to constitute causation.

Whatever caused the LIA—decreased sunspot activity and increased seismic activity were important factors—it caused, among other horrific things, "stunting" that, Parker says, "reduced the average height of those born in 1675, the 'year without a summer,' or during the years of cold and famine in the early 1690s, to only 63 inches: the lowest ever recorded."

In northerly latitudes, Parker says, each decline of 0.5 degrees Celsius in the mean summer temperature "decreases the number of days on which crops ripen by 10 percent, doubles the risk of a single harvest failure, and increases the risk of a double failure sixfold." For those farming at least 1,000 feet above sea level this temperature decline "increases the chance of two consecutive failures a hundredfold."

The flight from abandoned farms to cities produced "the urban graveyard effect," crises of disease, nutrition, water, sanitation, housing, fire, crime, abortion, infanticide, marriages forgone, and suicide. Given the ubiquity of desperation, it is not surprising that more wars took place during the seventeenth-century crisis "than in any other era before the Second World War."

By documenting the appalling consequences of two climate changes, Rosen and Parker validate wariness about behaviors that might cause changes. The last twelve of Parker's 712 pages of text deliver a scalding exhortation to be alarmed about what he considers preventable global warming. Neither book, however, supports those who believe human behavior is the sovereign or even primary disrupter of climate normality, whatever that might be. With the hands that today's climate Cassandras are not using to pat themselves on the back for their virtuous empiricism, they should pick up such books.

A NOTE ON VIOLINS AND CLIMATE CHANGE

The following was a response to the Wall Street Journal's *request for this author to identify an exemplary book of 2019.*

Might it be that Antonio Stradivari could create such magnificent violins because of the most momentous climate change in recorded history? This possibility is one of the intriguing delights in Philipp Blom's *Nature's Mutiny: How the Little Ice Age of the Long Seventeenth Century Transformed the West and Shaped the Present,* a book so replete with tantalizing uncertainties that it seems to have disconcerted its author. We do not know whether the cold produced trees with unusually dense structure that made possible unusually exquisite musical instruments. But then we do not know what caused such cold decades that France's Henry IV awakened with his beard frozen. We do know that these wintery years were not caused by carbon-based human activity. Mr. Blom dissects "the connections between climate and culture," showing how puzzled Europeans turned away from blaming (and burning) witches for bad weather and toward a scientific turn of mind to help them adapt. His concluding—and discordant—certitudes about today's climate change (and his tub-thumping disapproval of "the theology of the market" and other "neoliberal" sins) should not spoil his readers' enjoyment.

YOU ARE NOT A TEETERING CONTRAPTION

March 22, 2020

WASHINGTON—"Worrying," wrote Lewis Thomas, "is the most natural and spontaneous of all human functions." Thomas—physician, philosopher, essayist, administrator (dean of the Yale and New York University medical schools, head of Memorial Sloan Kettering Cancer Center)—thought we worry too much about our health, as though a human being is "a teetering, fallible contraption, always needing watching and patching, always on the verge of flapping to pieces."

So at this worrisome moment, fill your idle hands with Bill Bryson's 2019 book, *The Body: A Guide for Occupants.* It will fill your mind with reasons for believing that you are not flimsy, even though "we are just a collection of inert components." Including seven billion billion billion (7,000,000,000,000,000,000,000,000,000) atoms, not one of which cares a fig about you. In the time it took to read this far into this sentence, your busy body manufactured a million red blood cells that will surge through you every fifty seconds—150,000 times (a hundred or so miles) before, in about four months, they die and are replaced for the greater good, meaning: for you.

Bryson says it is estimated that every day between one and five of your cells turns cancerous and your immune system kills them: "A couple of dozen times a week, well over a thousand times a year, you get the most dreaded disease of our age, and each time your body saves you." What he calls "three billion years of evolutionary tweaks" have taught your body some neat tricks.

Viruses, Bryson says, "bide their time." A previously unknown one, found in Siberia in 2014 after having been confined in permafrost for 30,000 years, was injected into an amoeba and "sprang into action with the lustiness of youth." To stave off death from the coronavirus, we diligently scrub our largest organ, our skin, the surface of which, the epidermis, is…dead. Bryson says "all that makes you lovely is deceased. Where body meets air, we are all cadavers," shedding a million dead flakes an hour.

Just as well, considering that every square centimeter of your skin contains about 100,000 microbes, and about 200 species of microbes inhabit your skin. Some of the many trillions of living things that call your body home were studied in North Carolina State University's Belly Button Biodiversity Project, which swabbed the belly buttons of sixty randomly selected Americans and found 2,368 species of bacteria, 1,458 of which were previously unknown to science.

The three spongy pounds of mostly water, plus fat and protein, called the brain exists in darkness, yet it tells us everything we know about the world that it has never seen. "Just sitting quietly, doing nothing at all, your brain churns through more information in thirty seconds than the Hubble Space Telescope has processed in thirty years." A grain-of-sand-sized bit of cortex "could hold two thousand terabytes of information," enough to store every movie, or 1.2 billion copies of Bryson's book. Small wonder this 2 percent of body weight uses 20 percent of our energy.

The energy expended by the 200 million steps you will take in your lifetime comes from improved modern nutrition that explains why puberty, which began at sixteen or seventeen five centuries ago, now generally begins at eleven. Food, of which Americans consume unhealthy amounts (25 percent more calories than in 1970, when they already were not svelte), makes this nation simultaneously overfed and nutritionally deficient. Millennials scarf down avocado toast, oblivious of the fact that one avocado has, Bryson says, "five times as much saturated fat as a small bag of potato chips." He adds: "The amount of vegetables eaten by the average American between 2000 and 2010 dropped by thirty pounds," which is not alarming because America's most popular vegetable "by a very wide margin is the French fry."

The aforementioned brain does not always generate prudent choices, but it did rid the world of the most devastating disease, smallpox, which, Bryson reminds us, "infected nearly everyone who was exposed to it and killed about 30 percent of victims"—about half a billion in the twentieth century. This is one of many reasons why "if you are a seventy-year-old man in America today, you have only a 2 percent chance of dying in the next year. In 1940, that probability was reached at age fifty-six."

Globally, the approximately 160,000 people who will die today picked a good time to live. And it is highly probable that the ratio of human worrying about health, to actually worrisome conditions, will continue to enlarge.

THE CORONAVIRUS'S DISTURBING LESSON

March 19, 2020

WASHINGTON—Today's ill wind has blown in something good, a renewed interest in a neglected novel by a gifted writer. Albert Camus's *The Plague* (1947) was allegorical: Europe's political plague had been Nazism, which Camus had actively resisted in occupied Paris. But he had been born in French Algeria and surely knew of the 1849 cholera epidemic that ravaged the city of Oran, where *The Plague* is set.

At the novel's conclusion, as crowds celebrate the infestation's end, Camus's protagonist, Dr. Rieux, "remembered that such joy is always imperiled. He knew what those jubilant crowds did not know…that the plague bacillus never dies or disappears for good; that it can lie dormant for years and years in furniture and linen chests; that it bides its time in bedrooms, cellars, trunks, and bookshelves; and that perhaps the day would come when, for the bane and the enlightening of men, it would rouse up its rats again and send them forth to die in a happy city."

For Camus, "enlightening" was a double-edged word. Nature, red in tooth and claw, can be brutally didactic, as it was with the 1755 Lisbon earthquake. This was a chastening reminder, during the Enlightenment's high tide of confident aspiration, that nature always has something to say about what human beings always prematurely call "the conquest of nature."

Humanity, which is given to optimism and amnesia (the latter contributing to the former), was nudged toward theological skepticism by the felt contradiction between the fact of Lisbon and the theory that a benevolent God has ordained Earth as a commodious habitat in a congenial universe. But, then, four centuries before Lisbon, the Black Death plague had killed about a third of Europe's population. Besides, the idea that Earth is miraculously biophilic—*designed* to enable human life to thrive—disregards many inconveniences, from saber-toothed tigers, meteor strikes, and typhoons, to volcanoes, insect infestations, and multitudes of mutating viruses.

In 1900, about when medicine at last began to do more good than harm, 37 percent of all American deaths were from infectious diseases. Today the figure is 2 percent. By 1940 and the arrival of penicillin, medicine seemed on the verge of conquering infectious diseases, especially smallpox. No human achievement has done as much to lessen human suffering.

In the early 1950s, the Salk vaccine seemed to complete the conquest by banishing childhood polio, which fostered the misconception that pharmacological silver bullets are the key to large improvements in public health. This distracted attention from the staggering costs of lung cancer, coronary artery disease, AIDS, violence, substance abuses, Type 2 diabetes brought on by obesity, and other consequences of known-to-be-risky behaviors.

In *The Body: A Guide for Occupants* (2019), Bill Bryson notes a milestone in human history: 2011 was the first year in which more people died from noncommunicable diseases (e.g., heart failure, stroke, diabetes) than from all infectious diseases combined. "We live," Bryson writes, "in an age in which we are killed, more often than not, by lifestyle." The bacterium that caused the fourteenth century's Black Death was in the air, food, and water, so breathing, eating, and drinking were risky behaviors. Today, deaths from the coronavirus are not apt to match what Bryson calls "suicide by lifestyle," an epidemic that will continue long after the coronavirus has.

Three decades after Jonas Salk's good deed, AIDS shattered complacency about infectious disease epidemics being mere memories. AIDS, however, was largely a behaviorally caused epidemic based in the United States primarily in thirty or so urban neighborhoods. Changes in sexual behavior, and less sharing of needles by intravenous drug users, tamed the epidemic.

Modern medicine, and especially pharmacology, has brought Americans blessings beyond their grandparents' dreams. Nevertheless, a sour aroma of disappointment surrounds health care, which is the most important policy issue in a nation gripped by political, social, and actual hypochondria. An old axiom ("Eat sensibly, exercise diligently, die anyway") has become a new grievance: Medicine's limitations, made more conspicuous by medicine's successes, are disturbing reminders of the skull beneath the skin of life.

Because epidemics are silent and invisible during their incubation, and are swift and unpredictable in their trajectories, they could be devastating terror weapons—except that, as the coronavirus is vividly demonstrating, no intentional perpetrator could be confident of remaining immune. The connectedness of the modern world, thanks in part to the jet engine's democratization of intercontinental air travel, deters the weaponization of epidemics that the connectedness facilitates. For now, this must suffice as good news.

THINKING ECONOMICALLY

A PESSIMIST'S FATAL CONCEIT

March 27, 2016

WASHINGTON—Presidential campaigns incite both hypochondria and euphoria, portraying the present as grimmer than it is and the future as grander than it can be. As an antidote to both, read a rarity, an academic's thick book (762 pages) widely recognized as relevant to America's current discontents.

Robert Gordon's *The Rise and Fall of American Growth* argues that an unprecedented and unrepeatable "special century" of life-changing inventions has produced unrealistic expectations, so the future will disappoint: "The economic revolution of 1870 to 1970 was unique...No other era in human history, either before or since, combined so many elements in which the standard of living increased as quickly and in which the human condition was transformed so completely."

In many ways, the world of 1870 was more medieval than modern. Three necessities—food, clothing, shelter—absorbed almost all consumer spending. No household was wired for electricity. Flickering light came from candles and whale oil, manufacturing power from steam engines, water wheels, and horses. Urban horses produced mountains and rivers of waste. Window screens were rare, so insects commuted to and fro between animal and human waste outdoors and the dinner table. A typical North Carolina housewife in the 1880s carried water into her home eight to ten times daily, walking 148 miles a year to tote thirty-six tons of it. Few children were in school after age twelve.

But on October 10, 1879, Thomas Edison found a cotton filament for the incandescent light bulb. Ten weeks later in Germany, Karl Benz demonstrated the first workable internal combustion engine. In the 1880s, refrigerated rail cars began to banish "spring sickness," a result of winters without green vegetables. Adult stature increased as mechanical refrigeration and Clarence Birdseye's Birds Eye frozen foods improved nutrition. By 1940, households were networked—electrified, with clean water flowing in and waste flowing out, radio flowing in and telephonic communications flowing both ways. Today's dwellings, Gordon says, are much more like those of 1940 than 1940 dwellings were like those of 1900. No more lack of privacy for people living and bathing in the kitchen, the only room that was warm year-round. Since 1940, however, only air conditioning, television, and the Internet have dramatically changed everyday life, and these combined have not remotely matched the impact of pre-1940 changes.

Nineteenth-century medicine mostly made patients as comfortable as possible until nature healed or killed them. In 1878, yellow fever killed 10 percent of the Memphis population. But twentieth-century medicine moved quickly from the conquest of infectious diseases (the cause of 37 percent of deaths in 1900; 2 percent in 2009) to the management of chronic ailments of the elderly. There were 8,000 registered automobiles in 1900 but 26.8 million in 1930. Ford's Model T, introduced in 1908 at $950, sold in 1923 for $269.

Gordon says two calamities—the Depression and World War II—fueled the postwar boom: The Depression by speeding unionization (hence rising real wages and declining work hours), the war by high-pressure "productivity-enhancing learning" that, for example, manufactured a bomber an hour at Michigan's Willow Run plant.

But the classic modernization trek from rural conditions into sanitized urban life and the entry of women into the workforce were vast, unrepeatable advances. Today the inflation-adjusted median wage of American males is lower than in 1969, and median household income is lower than when this century began. If the growth rate since 1970 had matched that of 1920–1970, instead of being one-third of it, per capita GDP in 2014 would have been $97,300 instead of $50,600.

America's entitlement state is buckling beneath the pressure of an aging population retiring into Social Security and Medicare during chronically slow economic growth. Gordon doubts the "techno-optimists" who think exotic developments—robots, artificial intelligence, etc.—can match what such by-now-banal developments as electricity and the internal combustion engine accomplished. There is, however, no reason to expect that medical advances have been exhausted. And there are many reasons to believe that the rapid expansion of regulatory, redistributive government, which can be reformed, has contributed to—it certainly has coincided with—the onset of (relative) economic anemia.

The "fatal conceit" (Friedrich Hayek's term) is the optimistic delusion that planners can manage economic growth by substituting their expertise for the information generated by the billions of daily interactions of a complex market society. Gordon's stimulating book expresses a pessimist's fatal conceit, the belief that we know the future will be less creative than the "special century."

"CREATIVE DESTRUCTION": MORE THE FORMER THAN THE LATTER

March 22, 2012

In Retreat, Sears Set to Unload Stores
— *The Wall Street Journal*, February 24

WASHINGTON—Retreat need not mean surrender. Still…

In 1886, a shipment of twenty-five-dollar watches from a Chicago jeweler was rejected by the addressee in Redwood Falls, Minnesota. The jeweler offered to sell the undeliverable goods for twelve dollars apiece to a railroad station agent, who could then sell them to other agents, of whom there were more than 20,000. Which is what the agent, twenty-three-year-old Richard Warren Sears, did. Soon his watch business was booming, so he quit working on the railroad, moved to Minneapolis, then quickly to the nation's railroad hub, Chicago, where in 1887 he met Alvah Curtis Roebuck, a watchmaker and printer. Rural life and retailing were about to change.

As the late Daniel Boorstin explained in *The Americans: The Democratic Experience*, Sears and Roebuck were on a trail blazed by Aaron Montgomery Ward. After a few years as a dry goods salesman in the rural West, in 1872, the year after the Chicago fire, Ward, then twenty-nine, rented a twelve-by-fourteen-foot loft over a livery stable there and began a mail-order business. In two years his single price sheet became an eight-page booklet, then a seventy-two-page catalog, with woodcuts illustrating most items. The 240-page catalog for 1884 listed almost 10,000 items.

Hitherto, the goods most Americans bought—things they could not make for themselves—were items they could handle and examine, sold by people they knew. Now they were enticed to buy unseen goods from distant strangers. The name Sears, Roebuck and Company appeared in 1893, and the catalog was the company's shop window, store counter, and salesman. The Big Book—by 1894 the catalog had more than 500 pages—became second only to the Good Book in American life. By 1903, Sears had its own printing plant. There were 1 million copies of the 1904 spring catalog, 2 million the next year, and more than 3 million of the 1907 fall catalog. All this depended on government in the form of the post office's RFD—rural free delivery.

By the middle of the twentieth century, Sears Roebuck had come to town as the nation's largest retailer, with stores that defined many towns' downtowns. But in Bentonville, Arkansas, Sam Walton had an idea for bigger stores on the outskirts of towns. Sears has become a casualty of Walmart's retailing revolution. Today new mothers sign up at Amazon Mom for regular deliveries of diapers. This is a twenty-first-century permutation of an innovation in long-distance commerce that began in nineteenth-century Chicago.

Creative destruction continues in the digital age. After 244 years—it began publication five years before the 1773 Boston Tea Party—the *Encyclopedia Britannica* will henceforth be available only in digital form as it tries to catch up to reference websites such as Google and

Wikipedia. Another digital casualty forgot it was selling the preservation of memories, aka "Kodak moments," not film.

America now is divided between those who find this social churning unnerving and those who find it exhilarating. What Virginia Postrel postulated in 1998 in *The Future and Its Enemies: The Growing Conflict over Creativity, Enterprise, and Progress*—the best book for rescuing the country from a ruinous itch for tidiness—is even more true now. Today's primary political and cultural conflict is, Postrel says, between people, mislabeled "progressives," who crave social stasis, and those, paradoxically called conservatives, who welcome the perpetual churning of society by dynamism.

Stasists see Borders succumb to ebooks (and Amazon) and lament the passing of familiar things. Dynamists say: Relax, reading is thriving. In 2001, the iPod appeared and soon stores such as Tower Records disappeared. Who misses them?

Theodore Roosevelt, America's first progressive president, thought it was government's duty to "look ahead and plan out the right kind of civilization." TR looked ahead and saw a "timber famine" caused by railroads' ravenous appetites for crossties that rotted. He did not foresee creosote, which preserves crossties. Imagine all the things government planners cannot anticipate when, in their defining hubris, they try to impose their static dream of the "right kind" of future.

As long as America is itself, it will welcome the messy chaos that is not really disorder but rather what Postrel calls "an order that is unpredictable, spontaneous, and ever shifting, a pattern created by millions of uncoordinated, independent decisions." Professional coordinators, aka bureaucracies, are dismayed. Good.

THE ACCELERATED CHURNING

June 22, 2017

WASHINGTON—In 1859, when Manhattan still had many farms, near the Battery on the island's southern tip the Great American Tea Company was launched. It grew, and outgrew its name, becoming in 1870 the Great Atlantic & Pacific Tea Company, which in 1912 begat the first A&P Economy Store, a semi-modern grocery store.

By 1920, there were 4,500 such stores; by 1930, 15,000. In 1936, in Braddock, Pennsylvania, A&P opened a "supermarket." By the 1950s, A&P was, briefly, what Walmart now is, the nation's largest retailer, with a 75 percent share of America's grocery business. A&P was, however, about to learn that Karl Marx was right.

In *The Communist Manifesto*, Marx testified to capitalism's transformative power: "All that is solid melts into air." Sixty-eight years after he wrote that, in 1916, in Memphis, just as Henry Ford's Model T was making personal mobility a universal aspiration, and that aspiration was making suburbs practical and alluring, the first Piggly Wiggly opened.

This was the beginning of self-service grocery chains. Hitherto, shoppers handed their grocery lists to clerks, who plucked the goods from shelves. Soon shoppers were pushing carts along aisles lined with goods enticingly packaged to prompt impulse purchases.

A&P flourished when people went downtown to shop. As new suburbs spread, A&P's stores were old and distant. A&P filed for bankruptcy in 2015. By November 25, 2016, its last stores had closed.

Last week, the Kroger grocery chain's lowered earnings forecast caused a 19 percent drop in share prices, which had already declined 12 percent in 2017. This was *before* Amazon announced that it is buying the Whole Foods grocery chain—more than 460 stores in forty-two states, Canada, and Britain—for $13.7 billion, which is approximately how much Amazon's market capitalization increased after the Whole Foods announcement.

Whole Foods, like Kroger, had been experiencing difficulties from competitors and expanding consumer options. *The Wall Street Journal* reports: "Consumers are buying more of their groceries outside of traditional supermarkets. Online merchants, discounters and meal-kit delivery services are all grabbing market share."

Daniel Patrick Moynihan's Iron Law of Emulation—competitive branches of government adopt their rivals' techniques—applies to the private sector, too. Neil Irwin of the *New York Times* writes of Amazon: "The online retailer is on a collision course with Walmart to try to be the predominant seller of pretty much everything you buy. Each one is trying to become more like the other—Walmart by investing heavily in technology, Amazon by opening physical bookstores and now buying physical supermarkets." Something similar, says Irwin, is happening in "nearly every major industry," benefiting "the biggest and best-run organizations, to the detriment of upstarts and second-fiddle players."

In the accelerated churning of today's capitalism, changing tastes and expanding choices destroy some jobs and create others, with net gains in price and quality. But disruption is never restful, and America now faces a decision unique in its history: Is it tired—tired of the turmoil of creative destruction? If so, it had better be ready to do without creativity. And ready to stop being what it has always been: restless.

Americans just now are being plied with promises that the political class can, and is eager to, protect them from the need to make strenuous exertions to provide for themselves in an increasingly competitive world. If the nation really is ready to sag into a rocking chair, it can while away its days and ward off ennui by reading the poet Philip Larkin.

It seems, just now,
To be happening so very fast.

Those lines are from Larkin's 1972 poem "Going, Going," his melancholy, elegiac lament about the pace of what he considered despoiling change that was, he thought, erasing all that was familiar in his England. The first line of Larkin's final stanza is: "Most things are never meant."

This is a profound truth: The interacting processes that propel the world produce outcomes that no one intends. The fatal conceit—fatal to the fecundity of spontaneous order—is the belief that anyone, or any group of savants, is clever and farsighted enough to forecast the outcomes of complex systems. Who really wants to live in a society where outcomes are "meant," meaning planned and unsurprising?

In his poem, Larkin explained why he wrote it: He was feeling "age, simply." He was forty-nine.

Soon America will be 241. It is too young to flinch from the frictions—and the more than compensating blessings—of a fast-unfolding future.

THE GREAT ENRICHMENT, THE GREAT FLINCH, AND THE COMPLACENT CLASS

September 24, 2017

WASHINGTON—It was an epoch-defining decision to place in Westminster Abbey, among statues of monarchs, priests, and poets, a large one of James Watt, inventor of the separate-condenser steam engine. The statue's inscription says Watt ranks among the world's benefactors because he "increased the power of man." The economist and historian Deirdre McCloskey believes this honor, conferred in 1834, signified society's endorsement of the dignity of practical people who apply science for human betterment.

The Great Enrichment is McCloskey's term for what, in a sense, started with steam and has been, she believes, the most important human development since the invention of agriculture 10,000 years ago. The development is the explosion of economic growth that began around 1800 and has, especially since reaching China and India, lifted billions of people from poverty. Today, however, the Great Enrichment might be running out of steam in the United States, which for two centuries has given propulsive energy to it.

In 1800, McCloskey says, the world's economy was where Bangladesh's economy now is, with no expectation of change. Today, most of the jobs that existed just a century ago are gone. And we are delighted that this protracted disruption occurred. Now, however, the Great Enrichment is being superseded by the Great Flinch, a recoil against the frictions and uncertainties—the permanent revolution—of economic dynamism. If this continues, the consequences, from increased distributional conflicts to decreased social mobility, are going to be unpleasant.

Although America is said to be—and many Americans are—seething about economic grievances, Tyler Cowen thinks a bigger problem is complacency. In his latest book, *The Complacent Class: The Self-Defeating Quest for the American Dream*, Cowen, professor of almost everything (economics, law, literature) at George Mason University and co-author of the Marginal Revolution blog, argues that the complacent class, although a minority, is skillful at entrenching itself in ways detrimental to the majority.

For forty years, Cowen believes, "we have been building toward stasis," with a diminishing "sense of urgency." Americans and American businesses are, on average, older than ever. Interstate migration—a risk-taking investment in a hoped-for future—has been declining since the mid-1980s. Although there is much talk about job churning, the percentage of workers with five or more years on the job has increased in twenty years from forty-four to more than fifty. Declining labor mobility is partly the result of the domestic protectionism of occupational licensing. "In the 1950s," Cowen writes, "only about 5 percent of workers required a government-issued license to do their jobs, but by 2008, that figure had risen to about 29 percent."

There is "more pairing of like with like" (assortative mating, economically homogenous neighborhoods, segregation by educational status), and the nation is losing the capacity and will "to regenerate itself." In the nineteenth century and much of the twentieth century, travel speeds increased dramatically; since the 1970s, ground and air congestion has slowed travel. Fifty-two years ago, children's most common leisure activity was outdoor play; today, the average nine-year-old spends fifty hours a week staring at electronic screens. Today, Cowen notes, campuses are one of society's segments "where the complacent class exercises its strongest influences," doing so to preserve, like flies in amber, its status and consensus, thereby slowing what the economist Vilfredo Pareto called the "circulation of elites."

Most alarming is American democracy becoming a gerontocracy. The Steuerle-Roeper Fiscal Democracy Index measures how much of the allocation of government revenues is determined by current democratic processes and how much by prior decisions establishing permanent programs running on autopilot. The portion of the federal budget automatically spent by choices made years ago is approaching 90 percent. An aging population is devouring an increasing portion of national resources—federal revenues dispersed by the entitlement state to provide Social Security and Medicare to the elderly, the nation's past. This will worsen. Because government is more important to its elderly beneficiaries than to any other age cohort, a higher percentage of the elderly vote compared to any younger cohort.

For complacent Americans, a less dynamic, growth-oriented nation seems less like an alarming prospect than a soothing promise of restfulness. In a great testimonial to capitalism's power, *The Communist Manifesto*, Karl Marx wrote: "All fixed, fast-frozen relations, with their train of ancient and venerable prejudices and opinions, are swept away, all new-formed ones become antiquated before they can ossify. All that is solid melts into air." Complacent, because comfortable, Americans have had enough of that.

POPE FRANCIS'S FACT-FREE SANCTIMONY

September 20, 2015

WASHINGTON—Pope Francis embodies sanctity but comes trailing clouds of sanctimony. With a convert's indiscriminate zeal, he embraces ideas impeccably fashionable, demonstrably false, and deeply reactionary. They would devastate the poor on whose behalf he purports to speak—if his policy prescriptions were not as implausible as his social diagnoses are shrill.

Supporters of Francis have bought newspaper and broadcast advertisements to disseminate some of his woolly sentiments that have the intellectual tone of fortune cookies. One example: "People occasionally forgive, but nature never does." The Vatican's majesty does not disguise the vacuity of this. Is Francis intimating that environmental damage is irreversible? He neglects what technology has accomplished regarding London's air (see Page 1 of Dickens's *Bleak House*) and other matters.

And the Earth is becoming "an immense pile of filth"? Hyperbole is a predictable precursor of yet another UN Climate Change Conference—the twenty-first since 1995. Fortunately, rhetorical exhibitionism increases as its effectiveness diminishes. In his June encyclical and elsewhere, Francis lectures about our responsibilities, but neglects the duty to be as intelligent as one can be. This man who says "the Church does not presume to settle scientific questions" proceeds as though everything about which he declaims is settled, from imperiled plankton to air conditioning being among humanity's "harmful habits." The church that thought it was settled science that Galileo was heretical should be attentive to all evidence.

Francis deplores "compulsive consumption," a sin to which the 1.3 billion persons without even electricity can only aspire. He leaves the Vatican to jet around praising subsistence farming, a romance best enjoyed from 30,000 feet above the realities that such farmers yearn to escape.

The saint who is Francis's namesake supposedly lived in sweet harmony with nature. For most of mankind, however, nature has been, and remains, scarcity, disease, and natural—note the adjective—disasters. Our flourishing requires affordable, abundant energy for the production of everything from food to pharmaceuticals. Poverty has probably decreased more in the last two centuries than it has in the preceding three millennia because of industrialization powered by fossil fuels. Only economic growth has ever produced broad amelioration of poverty, and since growth began in the late eighteenth century, it has depended on such fuels.

Matt Ridley, author of *The Rational Optimist*, notes that coal supplanting wood fuel reversed deforestation, and "fertilizer manufactured with gas halved the amount of land needed to produce a given amount of food." The capitalist commerce that Francis disdains is the reason the portion of the planet's population living in "absolute poverty" ($1.25 a day) declined from 53 percent to 17 percent in three decades after 1981. Even in low-income countries, writes economist Indur Goklany, life expectancy increased from between twenty-five and thirty years in 1900 to sixty-two years today. Sixty-three percent of fibers are synthetic and derived from fossil fuels; of the rest, 79 percent come from cotton, which requires synthetic fertilizers and pesticides. "Synthetic fertilizers and pesticides derived from fossil fuels," he says, "are responsible for at least 60 percent of today's global food supply." Without fossil fuels, he says, global cropland would have to increase at least 150 percent— equal to the combined land areas of South America and the European Union—to meet current food demands.

Francis grew up around the rancid political culture of Peronist populism, the sterile redistributionism that has reduced his Argentina from the world's fourteenth highest per-capita GDP in 1900 to sixty-third today. Francis's agenda for the planet—"global regulatory norms"— would globalize Argentina's downward mobility.

As the world spurns his church's teachings about abortion, contraception, divorce, same-sex marriage, and other matters, Francis jauntily makes his church congruent with the secular religion of "sustainability." Because this is hostile to growth, it fits Francis's seeming sympathy for medieval stasis, when his church ruled the roost, economic growth was essentially nonexistent, and life expectancy was around thirty.

Francis's fact-free flamboyance reduces him to a shepherd whose selectively reverent flock, genuflecting only at green altars, is tiny relative to the publicity it receives from media otherwise disdainful of his church. Secular people with anti-Catholic agendas drain his prestige, a dwindling asset, into promotion of policies inimical to the most vulnerable people and unrelated to what once was the papacy's very different salvific mission.

He stands against modernity, rationality, science, and, ultimately, the spontaneous creativity of open societies in which people and their desires are not problems but precious resources. Americans cannot simultaneously honor him and celebrate their nation's premises.

PEAK NONSENSE ABOUT SCARCITIES

June 13, 2019

WASHINGTON—Randolph Bourne (1886–1918) said, "War is the health of the state." James Madison said, "War is in fact the true nurse of executive aggrandizement," and the executive almost *is* the American state, Congress now being more theatrical than actual. Advocates of an ever-larger state, remembering Franklin Roosevelt's first inaugural address (seeking "broad executive power to wage a war against the emergency, as great as the power that would be given to me if we were in fact invaded by a foreign foe"), declare "wars" on this and that (poverty, cancer, drugs, global warming, etc.).

Such declarations have become trite, but scarcities are recyclable excuses for expanding government: There are so many things that alarmists can be alarmed about possibly becoming scarce and therefore supposedly requiring government rationers. Because there is an inexhaustible, because renewable, supply of alarmists, Washington's libertarian Cato Institute has created the Simon Abundance Index to refute them.

Its name honors the late Julian Simon, an economist who won a famous bet with Paul Ehrlich, the Stanford hysteric whose 1968 book *The Population Bomb* predicted that "hundreds of millions of people" would starve to death in the 1970s as population growth swamped agriculture production. Simon's 1980 wager was that any five commodities *that Ehrlich would pick* would be cheaper in 1990. Ehrlich picked five metals. All were cheaper in 1990.

In 1972, in the extravagantly hyped and resoundingly refuted (by events) "Limits to Growth," MIT computer modelers foresaw civilization collapsing because of "nonrenewable resource depletion." The modelers extrapolated from the then-current use of nineteen commodities and projected the exhaustion, before 2012, of the supply of twelve—aluminum, copper, gold, lead, mercury, molybdenum, natural gas, oil, silver, tin, tungsten, and zinc. Forty years later, Bjorn Lomborg, the Danish academic and "skeptical environmentalist," noted this: Because of technological innovations replacing mercury in batteries, dental fillings, and thermometers, mercury consumption had plunged 98%, and its price 90%. Since 1970, when gold reserves were estimated at 10,980 tons, more than 81,000 tons had been mined and reserves were estimated at 51,000 tons. Since 1970, when known copper reserves were 280 million tons, about 400 million tons had been produced and reserves were estimated to be almost 700 million tons. Aluminum consumption had increased 16-fold since 1950 as the world consumed four times 1950's known reserves. Known reserves could sustain current consumption for 177 years. And so on.

"Peak oil" has been exasperatingly (to eco-pessimists) elusive. In 1914, the U.S. government said oil reserves would be exhausted by 1924. In 1939, it said the world's reserves would be gone in thirteen years. In 1951, after oil fueled a global war and the postwar boom, the government again said the world had thirteen years of proven reserves. By 1970, however, there were 612 billion barrels, and by 2006, after another 767 billion barrels had been pumped, there were estimated to be 1.2 trillion.

Along came fracking, which has illustrated one of Cato's points: Unforeseen technologies continually alter the relationship between population growth (which is beneficial: people are, as Simon said, "the ultimate resource") and resource availability. The Abundance Index emphasizes "time price" (the amount of time required to earn the price of items) and the price elasticity of population (PEP), which measures the "sensitivity of resource availability to population growth." Cato's Abundance Index, covering 50 commodities, finds that between 1980 and 2018:

The average time price of the commodities fell 72.3 percent. The time it took to earn enough to buy one unit in the basket of commodities in 1980 bought 3.62 units in 2018. The compounded growth rate of abundance means that the affordability of the basket of commodities doubles every 20.49 years. According to the PEP metric, since 1980 "every additional human being born on our planet appears to have made resources proportionately more plentiful for the rest of us."

Cato's Abundance Index (measured with global prices relative to average global GDP per capita per hour) indicates this: The growth of abundance is highly probable because the fecundity of the future is almost certain. But the rate of growth is unpredictable because of government's willingness to expedite rather than regulate change.

Many people who want to stampede a panicked public into expanding government's micromanagement of everything have forgotten Gregg Easterbrook's "Law of Doomsaying": Predict catastrophe no later than ten years hence but no sooner than five years away—soon enough to terrify people but distant enough that they will not remember that you were wrong.

THE NOT AT ALL DISMAL SCIENCE

March 26, 2015

WASHINGTON—Every day the Chinese go to work, Americans get a raise: Chinese workers, many earning each day about what Americans spend on a Starbucks latte, produce apparel, appliances, and other stuff cheaply, thereby enlarging Americans' disposable income. Americans similarly get a raise when they shop at the stores that made Sam Walton a billionaire.

The ranks of billionaires are constantly churned. Most of the persons on the original Forbes 400 list of richest Americans in 1982 were off the list in 2013. Mark Zuckerberg, Facebook's CEO, was not born until 1984. America needs more billionaires like him, Michael Dell, Bill Gates, Jeff Bezos, and Steve Jobs. With the iPod, iPhone, and iPad, unique products when introduced, Jobs's Apple created monopolies. But instead of raising their prices, Apple has cut them because "profits attract imitators and innovators." Which is one reason why monopolies come and go. When John D. Rockefeller began selling kerosene in 1870, he had approximately 4 percent of the market. By 1890, he had 85 percent. Did he use this market dominance to gouge consumers? Kerosene prices fell from thirty cents a gallon in 1869 to six cents in 1897. And in the process of being branded a menacing monopoly, Rockefeller's Standard Oil made gasoline so cheap that Ford found a mass market for Model T's.

Monopoly profits are social blessings when they "signal to the ambitious the wealth they can earn by entering previously unknown markets." So "when the wealth gap widens, the lifestyle gap *shrinks*." Hence, "income inequality in a capitalist system is truly beautiful" because "it provides the incentive for creative people to gamble on new ideas, and it turns luxuries into common goods." Since 2000, the price of a fifty-inch plasma TV has fallen from $20,000 to $550.

Henry Ford doubled his employees' basic wage in 1914, supposedly to enable them to buy Fords. Actually, he did it because in 1913 annual worker turnover was 370 percent. He *lowered* labor costs by reducing turnover and the expense of constantly training new hires.

All these thoughts are from John Tamny, a one-man antidote to economic obfuscation and mystification. Thomas Carlyle (1795–1881), who called economics "the dismal science," never read Tamny, a *Forbes* editor, editor of RealClearMarkets, and now author of the cheerful, mind-opening book, *Popular Economics: What the Rolling Stones, Downton Abbey, and LeBron James Can Teach You about Economics*.

In the early 1970s, when the Rolling Stones were coining money and Britain's top tax rate was 83 percent, Keith Richards, lead guitarist and social philosopher, said: "That's the same as being told to leave the country." The Stones decamped to France, leaving Britain, Tamny notes, to collect 83 percent of nothing.

Americans execrate "outsourcing," which supposedly involves sending "American jobs" overseas. Well. Nike employs forty times more manufacturing workers in Vietnam than in America, but could not afford as many American workers as it has without the efficiencies of outsourcing. Tamny cites Enrico Moretti, a Berkeley economist, who says that when Americans buy an iPhone online, it is shipped from China, and the only American who touches it is the UPS delivery person. Is it regrettable that Americans are not doing the assembly jobs for which Chinese are paid the "latte wage"?

Actually, Americans incessantly "outsource" here at home by, for example, having Iowans grow their corn and dentists take care of their teeth, jobs at which Iowans and dentists excel and the rest of us do not. LeBron James could be an adequate NFL tight end, but why subtract time from being a superb basketball player? The lesson, says Tamny, is that individuals—and nations—should do what they do better than others, and let others do other things.

Millions of jobs, he says, would be created if we banned computers, ATMs, and tractors. The mechanization of agriculture destroyed millions of jobs performed with hoes and scythes. Was Cyrus McCormick a curse?

The best way to (in Barack Obama's 2008 words to Joe the Plumber) "spread the wealth around," is, Tamny argues, "to leave it in the hands of the wealthy." Personal consumption absorbs a small portion of their money, and the remainder is not idle. It is invested by them, using the skill that earned it. Will it be more beneficially employed by the political class of a confiscatory government?

"Nothing," Tamny demonstrates, "is easier to understand than economics. It is everywhere you look." Readers of his book will subsequently look at things differently.

"WHERE IS THE PENCIL CZAR?"

September 14, 2008

WASHINGTON—Improbable as it might seem, perhaps the most important fact for a voter or politician to know is: No one can make a pencil. That truth is the essence of a novella that is, remarkably, both didactic and romantic. Even more remarkable, its author is an economist. If you read Russell Roberts's *The Price of Everything: A Parable of Possibility and Prosperity* you will see the world afresh—unless you already understand Friedrich Hayek's idea of spontaneous order.

Roberts, an economist at George Mason University and Stanford's Hoover Institution, sets his story in the Bay Area, where some Stanford students are indignant because a Big Box store doubled its prices after an earthquake. A student leader plans to protest Stanford's acceptance of a large gift from Big Box. The student's economics professor, Ruth, rather than attempting to dissuade him, begins leading him and his classmates to an understanding of prices, markets, and the marvel of social cooperation. Holding up a Dixon Ticonderoga No. 2, she says: "No one can make a pencil."

Nonsense, her students think—someone made that one. Not really, says Ruth. Loggers felled the cedar trees, truckers hauled them, manufacturers built the machines that cut the wood into five-sided portions to hold graphite mined in Sri Lanka, Mexico, China, and Brazil. Miners and smelters produced the aluminum that holds the rubber eraser, produced far away, as were the machines that stamp TICONDEROGA in green paint, made somewhere else, on the finished pencil.

Producing this simple, mundane device is, Ruth says, "an achievement on the order of a jazz quartet improvising a tune when the band members are in separate cities." An unimpressed student says, "So a lot of people work on a pencil. What's the big deal?" Ruth responds: Who commands the millions of people involved in making a pencil? Who is in charge? Where is the pencil czar?

Her point is that markets allow order to emerge without anyone imposing it. The "poetry of the possible" is that things are organized without an organizer. "The graphite miner in Sri Lanka doesn't realize he's cooperating with the cedar farmer in California to serve the pencil customer in Maine." The boss of the pencil factory does not boss very much: He does not decide the prices of the elements of his product— or of his product. No one decides. Everyone buying and selling things does so as prices steer resources hither and yon, harmonizing supplies and demands.

Goods and services, like languages, result from innumerable human actions—but not from any human design. "We," says Ruth, "create them with our actions, but not intentionally. They are tapestries we weave unknowingly." They are "emergent phenomena," the results of human action but not of human design.

When a student asks about the exploitation of housecleaners, Ruth responds that if they are exploited making between ten dollars—above the minimum wage—and twenty dollars an hour, why are they not exploited even more? The answer is that the market makes people pay maids more than the law requires because maids have alternatives.

But back to Big Box doubling prices after the earthquake. The indignant student, who had first gone to Home Depot for a flashlight, says it "didn't try to rip us off." It was, however, out of flashlights. Ruth suggests that the reason Big Box had flashlights was that its prices were high. If prices were left at regular levels, the people who would have got the flashlights would have been those who got to the store first. With the higher prices, "someone who had candles at home decided to do without the flashlight and left it there for you on the shelf." Neither Home Depot nor the student who was angry at Big Box had benefited from Home Depot's price restraint. Capitalism, Ruth reminds him, is a profit *and loss* system. Corfam—Du Pont's fake leather that made awful shoes in the 1960s— and the Edsel quickly vanished. But, Ruth notes, "the post office and ethanol subsidies and agricultural price supports and mediocre public schools live forever." They are insulated from market forces; they are created, in defiance of those forces, by government, which can disregard prices, which means disregarding the rational allocation of resources. To disrupt markets is to tamper with the unseen source of the harmony that is all around us.

The spontaneous emergence of social cooperation—the emergence of a system vastly more complex, responsive, and efficient than any government could organize—is not universally acknowledged or appreciated. It discomforts a certain political sensibility, the one that exaggerates the importance of government and the competence of the political class.

Government is important in establishing the legal framework for markets to function. The most competent political class allows markets to work wonders that government cannot replicate. Hayek, a 1974 Nobel laureate in economics, said, "The curious task of economics is to demonstrate to men how little they really know about what they imagine they can design." People, and especially political people, are rarely grateful to be taught their limits. *That* is why economics is called the dismal science.

SKIRMISHES IN THE CULTURE WAR

THE IDEOLOGICAL AX-GRINDING OF
THE 1619 PROJECT

May 7, 2020

WASHINGTON—Confidence in institutions declines when they imprudently enlarge their missions. Empty pews rebuke churches that subordinate pastoral to political concerns. Prestige flows away from universities that prefer indoctrination to instruction. And trust evaporates when journalistic entities embrace political projects. On Monday, however, the *New York Times*—technically, one of its writers—received a Pulitzer Prize for just such an embrace.

Last August, an entire *Times* Sunday magazine was devoted to the multi-author "1619 Project," whose proposition—subsequently developed in many other articles and multimedia content, and turned into a curriculum for schools—is that the nation's real founding was the arrival of twenty slaves in Virginia in 1619: The nation is *about* racism. Because the *Times* ignored today's most eminent relevant scholars—e.g., Brown University's Gordon Wood, Princeton's James McPherson and Sean Wilentz and Allen Guelzo, City University of New York's James Oakes, Columbia's Barbara Fields—the Project's hectoring tone and ideological ax-grinding are unsurprising. Herewith three examples of slovenliness, even meretriciousness, regarding facts:

To establish that the American Revolution was launched to protect slavery, the Project asserts that a November 1775 British offer of freedom to slaves fleeing to join the British army was decisive in the move to independence. But this offer was a *response* to the war that had been boiling since April's battles at Lexington and Concord and simmering

243

for a year before that, as detailed in Mary Beth Norton's just-published *1774: The Long Year of Revolution.*

Misdescribing an 1862 White House meeting with African-American leaders, the Project falsely says President Lincoln flatly "opposed black equality" and adamantly favored colonization of emancipated slaves. Actually, Lincoln had already decided on an Emancipation Proclamation with no imperative of colonization. In Lincoln's last speech, his openness to black enfranchisement infuriated a member of his audience: John Wilkes Booth.

The Project asserts that in the long struggle for freedom and civil rights, "for the most part" blacks fought "alone." This erases from history the important participation of whites, assiduously enlisted by, among others, Frederick Douglass and Martin Luther King Jr.

The Project's purpose is to displace the nation's actual 1776 Founding, thereby draining from America's story the moral majesty of the first modern nation's Enlightenment precepts proclaimed in the Declaration of Independence and implemented by the Constitution. Although monomaniacally focused on slavery, the Project completely misses the most salient point:

The phenomenon of slavery was millennia old in 1776, but as Gordon Wood says, "It's the American Revolution that makes [slavery] a problem for the world." Princeton's Sean Wilentz (see his 2018 book *No Property in Man*) correctly insists that what "originated in America" was "organized anti-slavery politics," and it did so because of those Enlightenment precepts in the Declaration's first two paragraphs.

The Constitution was written in 1787 for a nation conscious of its youth. It would grow under a federal government whose constituting document did not acknowledge "property in man," and instead acknowledged slaves as persons. This gave slavery no *national* validation. It left slavery solely a creature of state laws and therefore susceptible to the process that in fact occurred—the process of being regionally confined and put on a path to ultimate extinction. Secession was the South's desperate response when it recognized this impending outcome that the Constitution had facilitated.

The Constitution's tolerance of the slave trade until 1808, the fugitive slave clause, and the counting slaves as three-fifths of a person for political representation, were three hard-fought accommodations of slave states, accommodations that were the price of nationhood. However, the Founders' generation enacted the 1787 Northwest Ordinance, with its proscription of slavery in a vast swath of territory north of the Ohio River. This *preceded* the Constitution. And so widespread were antislavery convictions among the Founders and the Constitution's Framers, that Lincoln in his February 1860 Cooper Union speech cited them to shred Chief Justice Roger Taney's assertion, in the 1857 *Dred Scott* decision, that the Founding generation assumed that all blacks would be forever excluded from rights-bearing citizenship. Martin Luther King Jr., congruent with Frederick Douglass, built his movement on the premise, denied by "The 1619 Project," that the Constitution is properly read as an instrument for enabling fulfillment of the Declaration's egalitarian promise.

The ferocity of arguments among professors often is inversely proportional to the arguments' stakes. Not, however, those about "The 1619 Project," because, "Who controls the past controls the future: Who controls the present controls the past." Has this, the slogan of the party governing Oceania in George Orwell's *1984*, supplanted "All the news that's fit to print" as the *Times*'s credo?

"IS FOOD THE NEW SEX?"

February 26, 2009

WASHINGTON—Put down that cheeseburger and listen up: If food has become what sex was a generation ago—the intimidatingly intelligent Mary Eberstadt says it has—then a cheeseburger is akin to adultery, or worse. As eating has become highly charged with moral judgments, sex has become notably less so, and Eberstadt, a fellow at Stanford

University's Hoover Institution, thinks these trends involving two primal appetites are related.

In a *Policy Review* essay "Is Food the New Sex?"—it has a section titled "Broccoli, Pornography, and Kant"—she notes that for the first time ever, most people in advanced nations "are more or less free to have all the sex and food they want." One might think, she says, either that food and sex would both be pursued with an ardor heedless of consequences, or that both would be subjected to analogous codes constraining consumption. The opposite has happened—mindful eating and mindless sex.

Imagine, says Eberstadt, a thirty-year-old Betty in 1958, and her thirty-year-old granddaughter Jennifer today. Betty's kitchen is replete with things—red meat, dairy products, refined sugars, etc.—that nutritionists now instruct us to minimize. She serves meat from her freezer, accompanied by this and that from jars. If she serves anything "fresh," it would be a potato. If she thinks about food, she thinks only about what she enjoys, not what she, and everyone else, ought to eat.

Jennifer pays close attention to food, about which she has strong opinions. She eats neither red meat nor endangered fish, buys "organic" meat and produce, fresh fruits and vegetables, and has only ice in her freezer. These choices are, for her, matters of right and wrong. Regarding food, writes Eberstadt, Jennifer exemplifies Immanuel Kant's Categorical Imperative: She acts according to rules she thinks are universally valid and should be universally embraced.

Betty would be baffled by draping moral abstractions over food, a mere matter of personal taste. Regarding sex, however, she had her Categorical Imperative—the 1950s' encompassing sexual ethic that proscribed almost all sex outside of marriage. Jennifer is a Whole Foods Woman, an apostle of thoroughly thought-out eating. She bristles with judgments—moral as well as nutritional—about eating, but is essentially laissez-faire about sex.

In fifty years, Eberstadt writes, for many people "the moral poles of sex and food have been reversed." Today, there is, concerning food, "a level of metaphysical attentiveness" previously invested in sex; there are more "schismatic differences" about food than about (other) religions.

If food is the new sex, Eberstadt asks, "where does that leave sex?" She says it leaves much of sex dumbed-down—junk sex akin to junk food. It also leaves sexual attitudes poised for a reversal. Since Betty's era, abundant research has demonstrated that diet can have potent effects, beneficial or injurious. Now, says Eberstadt, an empirical record is being assembled about the societal costs of laissez-faire sex.

Eberstadt says two generations of "social science replete with studies, surveys and regression analyses galore" have produced clear findings: "The sexual revolution—meaning the widespread extension of sex outside of marriage and frequently outside commitment of any kind—has had negative effects on many people, chiefly the most vulnerable; and it has also had clear financial costs to society at large."

In 1965, the Moynihan Report sounded an alarm about 23.6 percent of African-American children born out of wedlock. Today the figure for the entire American population is 38.5 percent, and 70.7 percent for African Americans. To that, add AIDS and other sexually transmitted diseases, and the unquantifiable coarsening of the culture and devaluing of personal intimacy.

Today "the all-you-can-eat buffet" is stigmatized and the "sexual smorgasbord" is not. Eberstadt's surmise about a society "puritanical about food, and licentious about sex" is this: "The rules being drawn around food receive some force from the fact that people are uncomfortable with how far the sexual revolution has gone—and not knowing what to do about it, they turn for increasing consolation to mining morality out of what they eat."

Perhaps. Stigmas are compasses, pointing toward society's sense of its prerequisites for self-protection. Furthermore, as increasing numbers of people are led to a materialist understanding of life—who say not that "I have a body" but that "I am a body"—society becomes more obsessive about the body's maintenance. Alas, expiration is written into the leases we have on our bodies, so *bon appétit*.

ABOUT THAT SNAKE IN THE CENTER SEAT...

February 8, 2018

WASHINGTON—When next you shoehorn yourself into one of America's ever-shrinking airline seats, you might encounter a new wrinkle in the romance of air travel. You might be amused, or not, to discover a midsize—say, seven feet long—boa constrictor named Oscar coiled contentedly, or so you hope, in the seat next to you. Oscar is an "emotional-support animal." He belongs to the person in the seat on the other side of him, and he is a manifestation of a new item, or the metastasizing of an old item, on America's menu of rights. Fortunately, the federal government is on the case, so you can relax and enjoy the flight.

The rapid recent increase of emotional-support animals in airplane cabins is an unanticipated consequence of a federal law passed with the best of intentions, none of which pertained to Dexter the peacock, more about whom anon. In 2013, the Department of Housing and Urban Development told providers of public housing that the Americans with Disabilities Act of 1990 (ADA) mandates "reasonable accommodations" for persons who require "assistance animals."

The Air Carrier Access Act of 1986 allows access to animals trained to provide emotional support. Federal guidelines say airlines must allow even emotional-support animals that have a potential to "offend or annoy" passengers, but that airlines are allowed to—let us not sugarcoat this—*discriminate* against some "unusual" animals.

Yet a New York photographer and performance artist named, according to the Associated Press, Ventiko recently was denied the right to board her Newark-to-Los Angeles flight with her "emotional-support peacock," for whom Ventiko had bought a ticket. And there is a twenty-nine-year-old traveler who insists that she cannot "think about life without" Stormy, her emotional-support parakeet. So, if Oscar's owner says Oscar provides support, and the owner lawyers up...

In contemporary America, where whims swiftly become necessities en route to becoming government-guaranteed entitlements, it is difficult to draw lines. Besides, lines are discouraged lest someone (or some species?) be "stigmatized" by being "marginalized." The line JetBlue has drawn dehumanizes snakes. Yes, they are not technically human, but don't quibble. Anyway, soon enough there will be a lobby ("Rights for Reptiles"?), and lobbies are precursors to entitlements.

JetBlue is attempting to fly between the Scylla of passengers discomforted by a duck waddling down the aisle (even though it is wearing a diaper; this has happened more than once) and the Charybdis of animal advocates who are hypersensitive to speciesism, aka anti-pet fascism. JetBlue says that "unusual animals" such as "snakes, other reptiles, ferrets, rodents and spiders" are verboten, even as emotional-support animals. Southwest rather sternly says that passengers accompanied by emotional-support animals had better have papers from credentialed experts certifying "a mental or emotional disability recognized in the *Diagnostic and Statistical Manual of Mental Disorders*—Fourth Edition." But the DSM already accords the status of disability to almost every imaginable human trait or quirk and is eager to imagine new ones.

Delta experienced a nearly one-year doubling of what it delicately calls "incidents" (urinating, defecating, biting). "Farm poultry," hedgehogs, and creatures with tusks are unwelcome on Delta, which is going to be alert regarding the booming market for forged documents attesting to emotional neediness. The Association of Flight Attendants is pleased, perhaps because one of its members was asked to give a dog oxygen because the dog's owner said it was having a panic attack.

Now, let us, as the lawyers say, stipulate a few things. Quadrupeds, and no-peds like Oscar, have done a lot less damage to the world than have bipeds, and often are better mannered than many of today's human air travelers. Animals can be comforting to anyone and can be therapeutic to the lonely, the elderly with symptoms of senescence, and soldiers and others suffering post-traumatic stress disorder. Studies have purported to show that people living with pets derive myriad benefits, including lower cholesterol. A *Washington Post* report says "horses are used to treat sex addiction." Thank you, *Post*, for not elaborating.

But the proliferation of emotional-support animals suggests that a cult of personal fragility is becoming an aspect of the quest for the coveted status of victim. The cult is especially rampant in colleges and universities, which increasingly embrace the therapeutic mission of assuaging the anxieties of the emotionally brittle. There, puppies are deployed to help students cope with otherwise unbearable stresses, such as those caused by final exams or rumors of conservatism.

SANITIZING NAMES IS STEADY WORK

September 6, 2015

WASHINGTON—Autumn, season of mists and mellow fruitfulness, also is the time for the *Washington Post* and other sensitivity auditors to get back on—if they will pardon the expression—the warpath against the name of the Washington Redskins. The niceness police at the U.S. Patent and Trademark Office have won court approval of their decision that the team's name "may disparage" Native Americans. We have a new national passion for moral and historical hygiene, a determination to scrub away remembrances of unpleasant things, such as the name Oklahoma, which is a compound of two Choctaw words meaning "red" and "people."

Connecticut's state Democratic Party has leapt into the vanguard of this movement, vowing to sin no more: Never again will it have a Jefferson-Jackson Day dinner. Connecticut Democrats shall still dine to celebrate their party's pedigree but shall not sully the occasions by mentioning the names of two slave owners. Because Jefferson-Jackson Day dinners have long been liturgical events for Democrats nation-wide, now begins an entertaining scramble by states' parties—Georgia's, Missouri's, Iowa's, New Hampshire's, and Maine's already have taken penitential actions—to escape guilt by association with the third and seventh presidents.

The *Post* should join this campaign for sanitized names, thus purging the present of disquieting references to the past. The newspaper bears the name of the nation's capital, which is named for a slave owner who also was—trigger warning—a tobacco farmer. Washington, D.C., needs a new name. Perhaps Eleanor Roosevelt, D.C. She had nothing to do with her husband's World War II internment of 117,000 persons of Japanese descent, two-thirds of whom were native-born American citizens.

Hundreds of towns, counties, parks, schools, etc., are named for Washington. The name of Washington and Lee University is no mere micro-aggression, it is compounded hate speech: Robert E. Lee probably *saluted* the Confederate flag. Speaking of which: During the Senate debate on the 1964 Civil Rights Act, when Virginia's Willis Robertson waved a small Confederate flag on the Senate floor, Minnesota's Hubert Humphrey, liberal hero and architect of the legislation, called this flag a symbol of "bravery and courage and conviction." So, the University of Minnesota should seek a less tainted name for its Humphrey School of Public Affairs. Princeton University can make amends for its Woodrow Wilson School, named after the native Virginian who aggressively resegregated the federal workforce.

Jacksonville, Florida—a state where Andrew Jackson honed his skill at tormenting Native Americans; Jefferson City, Missouri; Madison, Wisconsin; and other places must be renamed for people more saintly. And speaking of saints:

Even secularists have feelings. And the Supreme Court says the First Amendment's proscription of the "establishment of religion" forbids nondenominational prayers at high school graduations. What, then, of the names of St. Louis, San Diego, San Antonio, and numerous other places named for religious figures. Including San Francisco, the Vatican, so to speak, of American liberalism. Let the renaming begin, perhaps for liberal saints: Gore City, Sharpton City. Tony Bennett can sing, "I left my heart in Pelosi City."

Conservatives do not have feelings, but they are truculent, so perhaps a better idea comes from Joseph Knippenberg, who is an American rarity—a professor with good sense and a sense of humor. He suggests that, in order to spare everyone discomfort, cities, buildings, and other things should be given names that are inoffensive because they have no meaning whatsoever. Give things perfectly vacuous names like those given to car models—Acura, Elantra, and Sentra.

Unfortunately, Knippenberg teaches at Atlanta's Oglethorpe University, which is named for James Oglethorpe, who founded the colony that became the slave state of Georgia. So, let us move on.

To Massachusetts and Minnesota, which should furl their flags. Massachusetts's flag shows a Native American holding a bow and arrow, a weapon that reinforces a hurtful stereotype of Native Americans as less than perfectly peaceful. A gimlet-eyed professor in Wisconsin has noticed that Minnesota's flag includes the state seal, which depicts two figures, a pioneer tilling a field and a Native American riding away—and carrying a spear. A weapon. Yikes. The farmer is white and industrious; the Native America is nomadic. So, Minnesota's seal communicates a subliminal slander, a coded message of white superiority. Who knew that Minnesotans, who have voted Democratic in ten consecutive presidential elections since 1972, are so insensitive?

This is liberalism's dilemma: There are so many things to be offended by, and so little time to agonize about each.

BAN "OKLAHOMA"?

June 29, 2014

WASHINGTON—Amanda Blackhorse, a Navajo who successfully moved a federal agency to withdraw trademark protections from the Washington Redskins because it considers the team's name derogatory, lives on a reservation where Navajos root for the Red Mesa High School Redskins. She opposes this name; the Native Americans who picked and retain it evidently do not.

The Patent and Trademark Office acted on a 1946 law banning trademarks that "may disparage" persons. "May" gives the agency latitude to disregard evidence regarding how many people actually feel disparaged, or feel that others should feel disparaged. Blackhorse speaks of "the majority of Native American people who have spoken out on this." This would seem implausible even if a 2004 poll had not found that 90 percent of Native Americans were not offended by the Redskins' name. A 2013 AP-GfK poll showed that 79 percent of Americans of all ethnicities opposed changing it, and just 18 percent of "nonwhite football fans" favored changing it.

The federal agency acted in the absence of general or Native American revulsion about "Redskins," and probably because of this absence. Are the Americans who are paying attention to this controversy comfortable with government saying, in effect, that if people are not offended, they should be, so government must decide what uses of language should be punished?

In today's regulatory state, agencies often do pretty much as they please, exercising discretion unconstrained by law.

George Washington University law professor Jonathan Turley notes that in 2004 the Federal Election Commission held that the anti–George W. Bush movie *Fahrenheit 9/11* did not need to be regulated as an "electioneering communication" but in 2008 held that the hostile *Hillary: The Movie* was such a communication. In the regulatory state, the rule of law is the rule that law barely limits regulators' discretion.

Although the death penalty clearly was not considered a "cruel and unusual" punishment when the Eighth Amendment proscription of such punishments was adopted, perhaps society's "evolving standards of decency" have brought this punishment under the proscription. Standards of decency do evolve: No sports team launched today would select the name "Redskins." Although Thomas Sowell is correct that "some people are in the business of being offended, just as Campbell is in the business of making soup," the fact that some people are professionally indignant does not mean offense may be given promiscuously to others.

The name "Redskins" is more problematic than, say, that of the Chicago Blackhawks or Cleveland Indians presumably because "Redskins" refers to skin pigmentation. People offended by this might be similarly distressed if they knew that "Oklahoma" is a compound of two Choctaw words meaning "red" and "people." Blackhorse, however, has two larger objections.

She says "someone" once told her that teams' mascots "are meant to be ridiculed," "to be toyed with," "to be pushed around and disrespected," and "have stuff thrown at them." She should supplement the opinion of that someone with information from persons more knowledgeable. But she considers "any team name that references Native Americans" an injurious "appropriation of our culture." Has an "appropriation" been committed by the University of Utah and Florida State University even though they have the approval of the respective tribes for their teams' nicknames, the Utes and Seminoles?

William Voegeli, a senior editor of the *Claremont Review of Books*, writes that the kerfuffle over an NFL team's name involves serious matters. They include comity in a diverse nation, civil discourse, and "not only how we make decisions, but how we decide what needs to be decided, and who will do the deciding."

Time was, Voegeli writes, a tolerant society was one with "a mutual nonaggression pact": If your beliefs and practices offend but do not otherwise affect me, I will not interfere with them if you will reciprocate regarding my beliefs and practices. Now, however, tolerance supposedly requires compulsory acknowledgment that certain people's beliefs and practices deserve, Voegeli says, "to be honored, respected, affirmed and validated" lest they suffer irreparable injury to their sense of worth. And it requires compelling conformity for the good of the compelled.

When two Oregon bakers chose, for religious reasons, not to provide a cake for a same-sex wedding, an Oregon government official explained why tolerance meant coercing the bakers: "The goal is to rehabilitate." Tolerance required declaring the bakers' beliefs and practices intolerable. We are going to discover whether a society can be congenial while its government is being coercive regarding wedding cakes and teams' names.

A RAISED EYEBROW ABOUT "REDSKINS"

October 16, 2014

WASHINGTON—Wretched excess by government can be beneficial if it startles people into wholesome disgust and deepened distrust, and prompts judicial rebukes that enlarge freedom. So let's hope the Federal Communications Commission embraces the formal petition inciting it to deny licenses to broadcasters who use the word "Redskins" when reporting on the Washington Redskins.

Using the FCC to break another private institution to the state's saddle for the satisfaction of a clamorous faction illustrates how the government's many tentacles give it many means of intimidating people who offend it. The U.S. Patent and Trademark Office, empowered to ban trademarks that "may" disparage persons, has already limited trademark protection of the Redskins' name.

The FCC petition argues that broadcasting during prime time of the word "Redskins" has "an adverse impact on impressionable young Indian as well as non-Indian children." (Today's sensitivity arbiters say the word "Indian" does, too, but never mind.) Furthermore, uttering "Redskins" is "akin to broadcasting obscenity" and pornography, is "hate speech" and an "ethnic slur" that "keep[s] alive the spirit of inhumanity, subjugation and genocide" and "may" cause violence against Native Americans. Besides, it is a "nuisance," defined as something "annoying."

Is the FCC empowered to protect an entitlement to a life without annoyances? What if the FCC is annoying? This is complicated.

Professor Eugene Volokh, who specializes in First Amendment law at UCLA's School of Law and supervises an invaluable website, The Volokh Conspiracy, thinks the petition refutes itself. It argues that "Redskins" is offensive because of the ideas and attitudes the word conveys. But when the Supreme Court upheld restrictions on the broadcasting of certain vulgarities (George Carlin's "seven dirty words"), it stressed that the mere fact that speech is offensive is not a sufficient reason for suppressing it. And although the court focused on the content of the words, it did not focus on the *political* content or on the speaker's opinion. "Indeed," Justice John Paul Stevens wrote, "if it is the speaker's opinion that gives offense, that consequence is a reason for according [an utterance] constitutional protection," because "the government must remain neutral in the marketplace of ideas."

Volokh adds: "The premise of the criticism of 'Redskins' is precisely that it embodies a racist, demeaning message about American Indians (whether or not this is intended by those who use it), and that it offends because of this racist meaning. It thus is the speaker's imputed opinion and supposed 'political content' of the word that gives offense."

Some say "Redskins" is merely an offensive epithet with a negligible ideological message. Volokh replies that the epithet is offensive to those who are offended "because of its allegedly racist ideology, and the call to suppress it stems precisely from the perception that it conveys this racist ideology." Anyway, the anti-"Redskins" petition is less legal reasoning than a form of bureaucratic bullying known as regulation by "raised eyebrow." The petition's author notes that the FCC sometimes indicates disapproval of this or that, thereby compelling broadcasters, worried about being put out of business, to practice self-censorship. So the petition seems designed to trigger this, thereby succeeding even if it fails—even if the FCC dismisses the petition.

If, however, the FCC under progressives today but conservatives tomorrow, can, in the petition's words, define and ban particular words as "nuisances" because they "annoy" a "substantial composite" of the population, what other words will appear on an ever-lengthening list?

Today many colleges and universities have "free speech zones"—wee spaces to which the First Amendment is confined. Such institutions are run by educators whose meager educations did not teach them that the amendment made America a free speech zone. Campuses are habitats for progressives, and the distilled essence of today's progressivism is the use of power to limit speech. The fact that censorship is progressivism's default position regarding so many things is evidence of progressives' pessimism about the ability of their agenda to advance under a regime of robust discussion. It also indicates the delight progressives derive from bossing people around and imposing a particular sensibility, in the name of diversity, of course.

The petition, which uses "R*dskins" (this typographical delicacy supposedly will help prevent pogroms against Native Americans), says the phrase "colored people," too, is "now considered derogatory." If so, some progressive has the awkward duty of notifying the NAACP that its name is "akin to" a disparagement, an obscenity, pornography, a racial slur, and hate speech. The language policeman's lot is not a happy one.

SLANTS, REDSKINS, AND OTHER INSENSITIVITIES

January 15, 2017

WASHINGTON—In 1929, Chief Justice William Howard Taft convinced Congress to finance construction of "a building of dignity and importance" for the Supreme Court. He could not have imagined what the court will ponder during oral arguments this Wednesday. The case concerns the name of an Asian-American rock band: the Slants. And surely Taft never read a friend-of-the-court brief as amusing as one filed in this case. It is titled "Brief of the Cato Institute and a Basket of Deplorable People and Organizations."

The U.S. Patent and Trademark Office is empowered, by the so-called "disparagement clause" of a 1946 law, to protect American sensitivities by denying trademark protection to "immoral, deceptive or scandalous" trademarks. These have included those that a substantial portion of a particular group perceive as disparaging that group—an ethnic, religious, national, or other cohort. The PTO has canceled the trademark registrations of entities named Mormon Whiskey, Abort the Republicans, Democrats Shouldn't Breed, Marriage Is For Fags, and many more.

The Cato/Deplorables brief urges compassionate libertarianism: "This Court should make the jobs of the employees at the…[PTO] much easier and put an end to the disparagement clause." Government officials cannot be trusted to "neutrally" identify speech that disparages. Besides, "disparaging speech has been central to political debate, cultural discourse, and personal identity" throughout American history. The brief notes that a donkey became the Democratic Party's symbol because someone called Andrew Jackson a "jackass" and he, whose default mode was defiance, put the creature on campaign posters. Entire American professions—e.g., newspaper columnists—exist in part to disparage.

Many rock bands pick names obviously intended to disparage or shock: Dead Kennedys, Dying Fetus, Sex Pistols, etc. Does the title of the best-selling book *Hillbilly Elegy* disparage a group? The Cato/Deplorables brief says: "One of this brief's authors is a cracker (as distinct from a hillbilly) who grew up near Atlanta, but he wrote this sentence, so we can get away with saying that." Then comes a footnote: "But he only moved to Atlanta when he was 10 and doesn't have a Southern accent—and modern Atlanta isn't really part of the South—so maybe we can't." Furthermore, the lead counsel on the brief "is a Russian-Jewish émigré who's now a dual U.S.-Canadian citizen. Can he make borscht-belt jokes about Canuck frostbacks even though the first time he went to shul was while clerking in Jackson, Mississippi?"

When the government registers a trademark, it is not endorsing or subsidizing a product. It should not be allowed to use its power to deny registration in order to discourage or punish the adoption of controversial expressions. By registering trademarks, government confers a benefit—a legal right—on those who hold them. Trademarks are speech. The disparagement clause empowers the PTO to deny a benefit because of the viewpoint of the speech. This is unconstitutional.

Trademarks are not commercial speech—essentially, advertising—which is accorded less robust protection than that given to other speech. Eugene Volokh, a UCLA law professor and one of the Slants' lawyers, correctly says the band's name is expressive speech. The Asian Americans of the Slants agree. They say they adopted this name "to take on these stereotypes that people have about us, like the slanted eyes, and own them."

The PTO applies the disparagement clause by assessing "what message the referenced group takes from the applicant's [trade]mark in the context of the applicant's use" and denies registration "only if the message received is a negative one." The PTO, which has denied trademark protection for the Slants, has given it to a band named N.W.A which stands for [a version of the N-word] Wit Attitudes.

The PTO's decisions are unpredictable because they depend on the agency speculating about what might be the feelings of others in hypothetical circumstances. This vague and arbitrarily enforced law, if such it can be called, chills speech by encouraging blandness.

The PTO last earned the nation's attention, if not its approbation, in 2014, when it denied protection to the name of the Washington Redskins, in spite of polls showing that 90 percent of Native Americans were not offended by the name and only 18 percent of "nonwhite football fans" favored changing it. Now the PTO sees a national problem in provocative, naughty, childish, or tasteless band names. By doing this the PTO encourages something of which there already is an annoying surfeit—the belief that speech should be regulated hither and yon in order to preserve the serenity of those Americans who are most easily upset.

WHAT IS THE MATTER WITH OREGON?

August 9, 2018

"The past is a foreign country; they do things differently there."
—L. P. Hartley

WASHINGTON—They do things differently in Portland, but not because it is a foreign country, although many Americans might wish it were: At this moment, it is one national embarrassment too many. Rather, the tumults in Portland, which is a petri dish of progressivism, perhaps reveal something about Oregon's political DNA. A century ago, the state was a bastion of reaction.

Recently in Portland, an "intersectional" feminist bookstore ("intersectionality" postulates that society's victims—basically, everyone but white males—suffer interlocking and overlapping victimizations), which appeared in the television series *Portlandia*, closed. It blamed its failure not on a scarcity of customers but on an excess of "capitalism," "white supremacy," and "patriarchy." (Presumably these made customers scarce.) Poor Portland progressives: So much to protest, so little time. However, right wingers spoiling for fights have done "antifa" (anti-fascist) Portlanders the favor of flocking to the city to provide a simulacrum of fascism, thereby assuaging progressives' Thirties Envy—nostalgia for the good old days of barricading Madrid against Franco's advancing forces.

In the twenties, however, Oregon was a national leader in a different flavor of nonsense, as historian Linda Gordon recounts in *The Second Coming of the KKK: The Ku Klux Klan of the 1920s and the American Political Tradition*. The Klan's revival began in 1915 with the romanticizing of it in the film *Birth of a Nation*, adapted from the novel *The Clansman* by Thomas Dixon. He was a John Hopkins University classmate and friend of Woodrow Wilson, who as president made the movie the first one shown in the White House. Wilson was enraptured: "It is like writing history with lightning. And my only regret is that it is all so terribly true."

The resuscitated Klan flourished nationwide as a vehicle of post–World War I populism. It addressed grievances about national identity—prewar immigration (too many Catholics and Jews) had diluted Anglo-Saxon purity—and disappointment with the recalcitrant world that had not been sufficiently improved by, or grateful for, U.S. involvement in the war.

Gordon, who grew up in Portland, says: "Starting in the mid-nineteenth century, and extending through the mid-twentieth century, Oregon was arguably the most racist place outside the southern states, possibly even of all the states." By the early 1920s, "Oregon shared with Indiana the distinction of having the highest per capita Klan membership" because the Klan's agenda "fit comfortably into the state's tradition."

In 1844, Oregon territory banned slavery—and required African Americans to leave. Prevented by federal law from expelling African Americans, Gordon says it became the only state to ban "any further blacks from entering, living, voting or owning property," a law "to be enforced by lashings for violators." The state offered free land, but only to whites. It imposed an annual tax on non-whites who remained. Oregon refused to ratify the post–Civil War Fourteenth and Fifteenth Amendments (not doing so until 1959 and 1973, respectively).

In 1920, Oregon's population was 0.006 percent Japanese (they came after the federal government banned Chinese immigration in 1882), 0.3 percent African American, 0.1 percent Jewish, and 8 percent Catholic. To make living difficult for Japanese, Gordon says, the state "banned immigrants from operating hospitality businesses." In 1923, only one state legislator voted against barring immigrants from owning or renting land. In advance of today's progressive hostility to private schools competing with government schools, Klan-dominated Oregon—it was primarily hostile to Catholic schools—banned all private schools. In 1925, in *Pierce v. Society of Sisters* (Governor Walter Pierce was a Democrat and, Gordon says, "an ardent Klan ally"), the U.S. Supreme Court unanimously struck down this law.

In a let-bygones-be-bygones spirit that Oregon progressives probably are too stern to embrace, let us assume that what Shakespeare said of individuals can be said of American states: "Use every man after his desert, and who shall 'scape whipping?" Today, Portland's generally irritable, often cranky, and sometimes violent progressivism suggests that William Faulkner's famous axiom—"The past is never dead. It's not even past"—needs this codicil: The bacillus of past stupidities lurks dormant but not dead in the social soil everywhere, ready to infect fresh fanaticisms when they come along, as they invariably do.

Perhaps the proportion of stupidity to intelligence in America is fairly constant over time, and today just seems especially soggy with stupidity because social media and mesmerized journalists give it such velocity. Isn't it pretty to think so?

GEORGE F. WILL

PROGRESSIVISM AT OREGON'S GAS PUMPS

January 14, 2018

WASHINGTON—Frank Lloyd Wright purportedly said, "Tip the world over on its side and everything loose will land in Los Angeles." Today, however, Oregon is the state with the strangest state of mind, which has something to do with it being impeccably progressive: In the series *Portlandia*, the mention of artisanal light bulbs might be satirical, but given today's gas-pumping controversy, perhaps not.

On January 1, by the grace of God—or of the government, which is pretty much the same thing to progressives—a sliver of a right was granted to Oregonians: Henceforth they can pump gas into their cars and trucks, all by themselves. But only in counties with populations of less than 40,000, evidently because this walk on the wild side is deemed to be prudent only in the hinterlands, where there is a scarcity of qualified technicians trained in the science of pumping. Still, 2018 will be the year of living dangerously in the state that was settled by people who trekked there on the Oregon Trail, through the territory of Native Americans hostile to Manifest Destiny.

Oregon is one of two states that ban self-service filling stations. The other is almost-as-deep-blue New Jersey. There the ban is straight-forward, no-damned-nonsense-about-anything-else protectionism: The point is to spare full-service gas stations from competing with self-service stations that, having lower labor costs, have lower prices.

Oregon's legislature offers seventeen reasons "it is in the public interest to maintain a prohibition on the self-service dispensing of Class 1 flammable liquids"—aka, gasoline, which you put in your car's "Class 1 flammable liquids tank." The first reason is: The dispensing of such liquids "by dispensers properly trained in appropriate safety procedures reduces fire hazards." This presumably refers to the many conflagrations regularly occurring at filling stations throughout the forty-eight states where 96 percent of Americans live lives jeopardized by state legislators who are negligent regarding their nanny-state duty to assume that their constituents are imbeciles.

Among Oregon's sixteen other reasons are: Service-station cashiers are often unable to "give undivided attention" to the rank amateurs dispensing flammable liquids. When purchasers of such liquids leave their vehicles they risk "crime," and "personal injury" from slick surfaces. ("Oregon's weather is uniquely adverse"; i.e., it rains there.) "Exposure to toxic fumes." Senior citizens or persons with disabilities might have to pay a higher cost at a full-service pump, which would be discriminatory. When people pump gas without the help of "trained and certified" specialists, no specialists peer under the hood to administer prophylactic maintenance, thereby "endangering both the customer and other motorists and resulting in unnecessary and costly repairs." Self-service "has contributed to diminishing the availability of automotive repair facilities at gasoline stations" without providing—note the adjective— "sustained" reduction in gas prices. Self-service causes unemployment. And "small children left unattended" by novice gas pumpers "creates a dangerous situation." So there.

Oregon's Solomonic decision—freedom to pump in rural counties; everywhere else, unthinkable—terrified some Oregonians: "No! Disabled, seniors, people with young children in the car need help. Not to mention getting out of your car with transients around and not feeling safe too. This is a very bad idea." "Not a good idea, there are lots of reason to have an attendant helping, one is they need a job too. Many people are not capable of knowing how to pump gas and the hazards of not doing it correctly. Besides I don't want to go to work smelling of gas."

The complainers drew complaints: "You put the gas in your car not shower in it princess." "If your only marketable job skill is being able to pump gas, by god, move to Oregon and you will have reached the promised land." "Pumped my own gas my whole life and now my hands have literally melted down to my wrists. I'm typing this with my tongue." These days, civic discourse is not for shrinking violets.

To be fair, when Oregonians flinch from a rendezvous with an unattended gas pump, progressive government has done its duty, as it understands this. It *wants* the governed to become used to having things done for them, as by "trained and certified" gas pumpers. Progressives are proud believers in providing experts—usually themselves—to help the rest of us cope with life. The only downside is that, as Alexis de Tocqueville anticipated, such government, by being the "shepherd" of the governed, can "take away from them entirely the trouble of thinking" and keep them "fixed irrevocably in childhood."

OREGON ENGINEERS ANOTHER EMBARRASSMENT

June 8, 2017

WASHINGTON—Beginning this week, Washington hopes that infrastructure, which is a product of civil engineering, will be much discussed. But if you find yourself in Oregon, keep your opinions to yourself, lest you get fined $500 for practicing engineering without a license. This happened to Mats Jarlstrom as a result of events that would be comic if they were not symptoms of something sinister.

Jarlstrom's troubles began when his wife got a $150 red-light camera ticket. He became interested in the timing of traffic lights and decided there was something wrong with the formula used in Oregon and elsewhere to time how long traffic lights stay yellow as they transition from green to red. He began thinking, Googling, corresponding, and—here he made his big mistake—talking about this subject. He has ignored repeated demands by the Oregon State Board of Examiners for Engineering and Land Surveying that he pipe down. So the board considers him to be, like Jesse James, Al Capone, and John Dillinger, a dangerous recidivist.

Not that it should matter, but Jarlstrom actually is an engineer. He has a degree in electrical engineering, served in a technical capacity in the Swedish air force, and worked for Sweden's Luxor Electronics before immigrating to the United States in 1992. He is, however, not licensed by Oregon to "practice engineering"—design skyscrapers, bridges, etc.—so, according to the board, he should not be allowed to talk about engineering, or even call himself an engineer. Only those the board licenses are admitted to the clerisy uniquely entitled to publicly discuss engineering.

After Jarlstrom emailed his traffic lights ideas to the board, it declared the emails illegal because in them he called himself an engineer. The board investigated him for twenty-two months and fined him $500 for expressing opinions without getting a professional-engineer license. This would have involved a six-hour examination ($225 fee), an eight-hour examination ($350 fee), an application to the board ($360 fee), and a demonstration of "education and experience" that usually requires a four-year apprenticeship.

The board has tried to bully others, too. It investigated and warned a political candidate about calling himself an engineer without being licensed by the board. (He has Cornell and MIT degrees in environmental and civil engineering, and membership in the American Society of Civil Engineers.) For the same reason, the board is in its twelfth month investigating a gubernatorial candidate who said "I'm an engineer" in a political ad. (He has a mechanical engineering degree from Purdue and was an engineer at Ford and Boeing.)

The Oregon board has until June 14 to answer the court complaint filed on Jarlstrom's behalf by the Institute for Justice, the nation's liberty law firm that a few years ago stopped North Carolina's Board of Dietetics/Nutrition from silencing a blogger who dispensed his opinions about various diets. Oregon's board will probably receive a judicial spanking for suppressing Jarlstrom's right to speak and, were he to try to earn income from his work on traffic lights, his freedom of occupational speech.

William Mellor and Dick M. Carpenter, the Institute for Justice's founding general counsel and director of strategic research, respectively, have recently published a book, *Bottleneckers*, about people like the officious nuisances on the Oregon board. The book defines a bottlenecker as "a person who advocates for the creation or perpetuation of government regulation, particularly an occupational license, to restrict entry into his or her occupation, thereby accruing an economic advantage without providing a benefit to consumers."

Gargantuan government, which becomes so by considering itself entitled to allocate wealth and opportunity, incites such rent-seeking. And given today's acceptance of increased regulation and censorship of speech, bottleneckers buttress their power (as incumbent politicians do with spending regulations that control the quantity of campaign speech) by making the exercise of a constitutional right contingent on government approval.

The Oregon board should remember Diane Hartley, who probably prevented a Manhattan calamity. In 1977, the fifty-nine-story Citicorp Center was built on Lexington Avenue. In 1978, Hartley, an undergraduate engineering student, concluded that the building could be toppled by strong winds that could be expected during the building's life. After her math was validated, emergency repairs were made.

If busybodies like those on Oregon's board had been wielding power in New York in 1978, Hartley would have been fined for "practicing"— that is, speaking her mind about—engineering without a license, and what then was the world's seventh-tallest building might have fallen, full of people, into congested Midtown.

THE 1960s ECHO: THE POLITICS OF RECIPROCAL RESENTMENT

February 19, 2017

WASHINGTON—In his seventy-two years, Judge J. Harvie Wilkinson III of the U.S. Court of Appeals for the Fourth Circuit, who was raised in segregated Richmond, Virginia, acknowledges that he has seen much change, often for the better, including advances in the 1960s. But in his elegant new memoir, *All Falling Faiths: Reflections on the Promise and Failure of the 1960s*, he explains why today's distemper was incubated in that "burnt and ravaged forest of a decade."

He arrived at Yale in September 1963, a year after John Kerry and a year before George W. Bush, "never dreaming that this great university would in many ways set the example of what education should not be." Everything on campus became politicized, a precursor to the saturation of the larger culture. America was careening toward today's contentiousness, as "those who rightly challenged the assumptions of others became slowly more indignant at any challenge to their own."

As the teaching of American history became "one extended exercise in self-flagellation," historical illiteracy grew, leading to today's "War on Names." Wilkinson's book arrives as Yale, plumbing new depths of shallowness, renames Calhoun College. Yale has chosen virtue-signaling rather than teaching. It should have helped students think about the complex assessments of complicated historical figures, such as the South Carolinian who was a profound political theorist, an anti-imperialist, an accomplished statesman, and a defender of slavery, a challenging compound of greatness and moral failure. Yale's past, as Wilkinson experienced it, was prologue: "Yale itself became less a place for original thought than an intellectual inferno policed for its allegiance to the prevailing alienation."

Disoriented by the Vietnam War, "Yale became a place of childlike clarity. I arrived at a university that asked questions; I left one that fastened a creed." We still live with this 1960s legacy—controversy has acquired a "razor's edge" and "venom and vehemence" have become fashionable.

Wilkinson's memoir also arrives as the nation braces for another battle over a Supreme Court nominee, perhaps illustrating Wilkinson's belief that another legacy of the 1960s is that "America's legal culture is also terribly divided." When he entered law school in 1968, the school's dean said: "Laws are the great riverbanks between which society flows." The law, the dean said, "verbalized aggression," taming it through an adversarial system that requires each party to listen to the other's argument.

For the Earl Warren Court, Wilkinson, who was nominated to the bench by Ronald Reagan, has warm words: It "opened the arteries of change, broadened the franchise, equalized access to schools and facilities, gave the common man the First Amendment, and donated to a society in turmoil its lasting gift of peaceful change."

In addition to being an ornament to the nation's judiciary, Wilkinson is a splendid anachronism, a gentleman raised by a father who "came to Saturday breakfast in his coat and tie" and who believed that "manners fortified man against his nature." Wilkinson was raised in 1950s affluence: Summers were "a long queue of black-tie galas," "luncheons in the day and debutante parties every evening." His world was "short on ambiguity" but not on absolutes, so he grew up "anchored, fortified by constancy."

When he went to prep school in New Jersey, his Southern accent caused a telephone operator to ask him to "speak English." He played soccer with Dick Pershing, the grandson of General John J. Pershing. Dick went to Vietnam and is buried in Arlington beside his grandfather.

But in the coarsening, embittering 1960s, Wilkinson writes, "more Americans annihilated fellow citizens in their consciousness than were slain on the field of any battle." In a harbinger of very recent events, "the shorthaired and hard-hatted sensed that class prejudice had simply been substituted for race hatred."

He locates the genesis of today's politics of reciprocal resentments in "the contempt with which the young elites of the Sixties dismissed the contributions of America's working classes." We have reached a point where "sub-cultures begin to predominate and the power of our unifying symbols fades. We become others to ourselves." The "insistent presentism" that became a permanent mentality in the 1960s cripples our ability to contemplate where we came from or can go. "Sometimes individuals lose, and societies gain," Wilkinson writes. "Maybe someone's loss of privilege is another's gain in dignity. Perhaps there is a selfishness in every song of lament." At this moment of pandemic vulgarity and childishness, his elegiac memoir is a precious reminder of what an adult voice sounds like.

THE "HOMETOWN-GYM-ON-A-FRIDAY-NIGHT" FEELING

October 14, 2018

WASHINGTON—If Senator Ben Sasse is right—he has not recently been wrong about anything important—the nation's most-discussed political problem is entangled with the least-understood public health problem. The political problem is furious partisanship. The public health problem is loneliness. Sasse's new book argues that Americans are richer, more informed, and "connected" than ever—and unhappier, more isolated, and less fulfilled.

In *Them: Why We Hate Each Other—and How to Heal*, Sasse's subject is "the evaporation of social capital"—the satisfactions of work and community. This reflects a perverse phenomenon: What has come to count as connectedness is displacing the real thing. And matters might quickly become dramatically worse.

Loneliness in "epidemic proportions" is producing a "loneliness literature" of sociological and medical findings about the effect of loneliness on individuals' brains and bodies, and on communities. Sasse says "there is a growing consensus" that loneliness—not obesity, cancer, or heart disease—is the nation's "number one health crisis." "Persistent loneliness" reduces average longevity more than twice as much as does heavy drinking and more than three times as much as obesity, which often is a consequence of loneliness. Research demonstrates that loneliness is as *physically* dangerous as smoking fifteen cigarettes a day and contributes to cognitive decline, including more rapid advance of Alzheimer's disease. Sasse says, "We're literally dying of despair," of the failure "to fill the hole millions of Americans feel in their lives."

Symptoms large and small are everywhere. Time was, Sasse notes, Americans "stocked their imaginations with the same things": In the 1950s, frequently 70 percent of television sets in use tuned in to *I Love Lucy*. Today, when 93 percent of Americans have access to more than 500 channels, the most-watched cable news program, *Hannity*, has about 1 percent of the U.S. population. In the last quarter of the twentieth century, the average number of times Americans entertained at home declined almost 50 percent. Americans are hyperconnected but disconnected, with "fewer non-virtual friends than at any point in decades." With the median American checking (according to a Pew survey) a smartphone every 4.3 minutes, and with nearly 40 percent of those eighteen to twenty-nine online almost every waking minute, we are "addicted to distraction" and "parched for genuine community." Social media, those "tendrils of resentment" that Sasse calls accelerants for political anger, create a nuance-free "outrage loop" for "professional rage-peddlers." And for people for whom enemies have the psychic value of giving life coherence.

Work, which Sasse calls "arguably the most fundamental anchor of human identity," is at the beginning of "a staggering level of cultural disruption" swifter and more radical than even America's transformation from a rural and agricultural to an urban and industrial nation. At that time, one response to social disruption was alcoholism, which begat Prohibition. Today, one reason the average American life span has declined for three consecutive years is that many more are dying of drug overdoses—one of the "diseases of despair"—*annually* than died during the entire Vietnam War. People "need to be needed," but McKinsey & Company analysts calculate that, globally, 50 percent of paid activities—jobs—could be automated by *currently demonstrated* technologies. America's largest job category is "driver" and, with self-driving vehicles coming, two-thirds of such jobs could disappear in a decade.

This future of accelerating flux exhilarates the educated and socially nimble. It frightens those who, their work identities erased and their communities atomized, are tempted not by what Sasse calls "healthy local tribes" but by political tribalism of grievances, or by chemical oblivion, or both. In today's bifurcated nation, 2016 was the tenth consecutive year when 40 percent of American children were born outside of marriage. America has "two almost entirely different cultures," exemplified by this: Under 10 percent of births to college-educated women are outside of marriage compared to almost 70 percent of births to women with high school diplomas or less.

Repairing America's physical infrastructure, although expensive, is conceptually simple, involving steel and concrete. The crumbling of America's *social* infrastructure presents a daunting challenge: We do not know how to develop what Sasse wants, "new habits of mind and heart...new practices of neighborliness." We do know that more government, which means more saturation of society with politics, is not a sufficient answer.

Sasse, a fifth-generation Nebraskan who dedicates his book to the Kiwanis and Rotary clubs and other little platoons of Fremont, Nebraska (population 26,000), wants to rekindle the "hometown-gym-on-a-Friday-night feeling." But Americans can't go home again to Fremont.

AN ENDANGERED SPECIES:
THE AMERICAN ADULT

May 28, 2017

WASHINGTON—When in the Senate chamber, Ben Sasse, a Nebraska Republican, sits by choice at the desk used by the late Daniel Patrick Moynihan. New York's scholar-senator would have recognized that Sasse has published a book of political philosophy in the form of a guide to parenting.

Moynihan understood that politics is downstream from culture, which flows through families. Sasse, a Yale history PhD whose well-furnished mind resembles Moynihan's, understands this:

America is a creedal nation made not by history's churning but by the decision of philosophic Founders. Modern America, with its enervating comforts—including cosseting parents—and present-minded education that produces cultural amnesia, must deliberately *make* its citizens. This requires constructing a menu of disciplines, rigors, and instructions conducive to the grit, self-reliance, and self-possession required for democratic citizenship.

Sasse's argument in *The Vanishing American Adult: Our Coming-of-Age Crisis and How to Rebuild a Culture of Self-Reliance* is not another scolding of the young. Rather, he regrets how the no-longer-young have crippled the rising generation with kindness, flinching from the truth that the good pain of hard physical work produces the "scar tissue of character."

Adolescents spending scores of hours a week on screen time with their devices acquire "a zombie-like passivity" that saps their "agency." This makes them susceptible to perpetual adolescence, and ill-suited to the velocity of life in an accelerating world of shorter job durations and the necessity of perpetual learning. In this world, Sasse warns, "college graduates will change not only jobs but industries an average of three times *by age thirty*."

Childhood obesity has increased 500 percent in five decades. For "the most medicated generation of youth in history," sales of ADHD drugs have increased 8 percent a year since 2010. Research shows that teenage texters exhibit addictive, sleep-depriving behaviors akin to those of habit-denying addictive gamblers. Teenagers clutching their devices "are spending nearly two-thirds of their waking hours with their eyes tied down and bodies stationary." Five million Americans, many of them low-skilled young men, play forty-five hours of video games per week.

In the long-running rivalry between the realist and romantic views of human nature, Sasse is firmly with the former. This aligns him against those who believe that schooling should be "a substitute for parents" as life's "defining formative institution." In the progressive view of education with which the philosopher John Dewey imbued America's primary and secondary schools, parents "with their supposedly petty interests in their children as individuals" are deemed retrograde influences, hindering schools' mission of making malleable young people outfitted with the proper "social consciousness." Schools should embrace the need of "controlling" students and "the influences by which they are controlled." Parents must be marginalized lest they interfere with education understood, as Sasse witheringly says, as "not primarily about helping individuals, but rather about molding the collective."

When America was founded, Sasse the historian reminds us, "nobody commuted to work. People worked where they lived." Before the "generational segregation" of modern life, children saw adults working and were expected to pitch in. The replacement of "the gritty parenting of early America" by "a more nurturing approach" coincided with the rise of mass schooling. In 1870, fewer than 2 percent of Americans had high school diplomas. An average of one new high school a day was built between 1890 and 1920, and by 1950, more than 75 percent of Americans were high school graduates.

Sasse, forty-five, a former university president, regrets neither nurturing nor mass education. He does regret the failure to supplement these softening experiences with rigors sought out for their toughening effects. With ancestral Nebraska memories of hard life on the high plains, Sasse thinks the generation coming of age "has begun life with far too few problems." He has tried to spare his daughters this disabling aspect of modern life. When his fourteen-year-old daughter Corrie spent a month at a cattle ranch, her texts included:

"Kids learned that artificial insemination works 60% of the time. Then the 'clean-up bull' gets called to duty."
"I've gone 4 days w/out a single 'electrifying experience' with a fence. I might not have electrocution in my future."
"We're also castrating bulls today."

America, Sasse says, needs to teach its children what life used to teach everyone, and what F. Scott Fitzgerald told his daughter: "Nothing any good isn't hard." What will be hard is the future of Americans who do not cultivate a toughness that goes against the grain of today's America.

THE PLIGHT OF PRINCETON WOMEN

March 22, 2015

WASHINGTON—The rate of dog ownership is rising ominously. How can a profusion of puppies be worrisome? A report from the Raymond James financial services firm concerning trends in the housing market explains: Increasing numbers of women "are adopting dogs for security and/or companionship," partly because of "the great education divide."

Since 1979, the report says, the number of women going to college has accelerated relative to male enrollments. By 2012, there were 2.8 million more women than men in college, and by 2020 this "enrollment gap" is projected to grow to 4.4 million as women account for 74 percent of enrollment growth.

In 2000, the adult populations of college-educated men and women were approximately equal. By 2013, there were 4.9 million more women twenty-five or older with college degrees than men in that age group. This means a shortage of suitable male partners for a growing cohort of young women, who are postponing family formation. The report says millions of female-led households are being established by women who, being focused on their careers, are delaying motherhood, partly because of a shortage of suitable partners. More about suitability anon.

"Increased 'competition' for college-educated males" might mean that college-educated bachelors will feel less incentive to become domesticated, further depressing family formation. And for the growing class of undereducated young men, there are increasingly bleak "employment, income and dating prospects." What is good news for dog breeders is bad news for the culture.

Two years ago, Susan Patton, a Princeton graduate and mother of two sons who attended Princeton, detonated multiple explosions in the culture wars when, in a letter to the *Daily Princetonian*, she told "the young women of Princeton" what "you really need to know that nobody is telling you." Which is that their future happiness will be "inextricably linked" to the men they marry, so they should "find a husband on campus" because "you will never again have this concentration of men who are worthy of you." She explains:

> Men regularly marry women who are younger, less intelligent, less educated. It's amazing how forgiving men can be about a woman's lack of erudition, if she is exceptionally pretty. Smart women can't (shouldn't) marry men who aren't at least their intellectual equal. As Princeton women, we have almost priced ourselves out of the market. Simply put, there is a very limited population of men who are as smart or smarter than we are....It will frustrate you to be with a man who just isn't as smart as you.

Patton's brassy indifference to delicacy served the serious purpose of riveting attention on what social scientists call "assortative mating." Plainly put, America has always aspired to be a meritocracy in which careers are open to talents, and status is earned rather than inherited. But the more merit matters to upward mobility, the more inequality becomes entrenched in a stratified society.

Those favored by genetics, and by family acculturation the acquired social capital (the habits and dispositions necessary for taking advantage of opportunities), tend to go to school and then to work together. And they marry one another, concentrating advantages in their children.

Hence today's interest in what is called "privilege theory," which takes a dark view of the old couplet, "All men are by nature equal, but differ greatly in the sequel." The theory leaps from the obvious to the dubious. Obviously some people are born with, and into, advantages, congenital and social. What is dubious is the conclusion that government has the capacity and duty to calibrate, redistribute, and equalize advantages.

Joy Pullmann, writing at The Federalist, a conservative website of which she is executive editor, notes something else obvious: This agenda is incompatible with freedom. Furthermore, although some individuals have advantages they did not earn, "very often someone else did earn them"—by, for example, nurturing children in a stable family. It is hardly an injustice—an invidious privilege—for nurturing parents to be able to confer on their children the advantages of conscientiousness. The ability to do so, says Pullmann, is a powerful motivation for noble behavior that, by enlarging society's stock of parental "hard work, self-control and sacrifice," produces "positive spillover effects for everyone else."

Enhancing equality of opportunity is increasingly urgent and increasingly difficult in an increasingly complex, information-intensive society. The delicate task is to do so without damaging freedom and the incentives for using freedom for individual striving, which is the privilege—actually, the natural right—that matters most.

ANTI-ELITISM AND THE "METEOROLOGIST FALLACY"

November 21, 2019

WASHINGTON—"Elitist" is the most wounding epithet in an epoch when millions of Americans, having the courage of their egalitarian convictions, have placed in the presidency someone innocent of any intellectual, moral, or other excellence that might remind them that some people have superior attributes. Elitism, more frequently deplored than defined, gets a sly examination in Joel Stein's *In Defense of Elitism: Why I'm Better Than You and You're Better than Someone Who Didn't Buy This Book.* This subversive romp pretends not to be the defense that it really is.

After the 2016 election, Stein sojourned in Roberts County, Texas, which had the nation's highest percentage (95.3 percent) of Trump voters and has several people named Rifle (the name Remington has become "too popular") and a dog trained to emit a pained whimper at the word "Hillary." But 33.2 percent of the residents have at least a bachelor's degree, which is around the national rate.

When a Roberts County judge asks Stein, who lives in Los Angeles, "Would you leave your child with anyone in a 10-block radius of your house?" Stein thinks his community is "virtual": "My friends appear on my phone far more often than on my doorstep." Roberts County people are especially "connected" to each other and relish this. They are, however, "a remote tribal island, untouched by the last 30 years." (Of the twenty-five states with the lowest percentage of passport holders, Donald Trump won twenty-four.) And they are increasingly "distanced from their country." ("Even when things are desperate," Stein writes, "people won't venture far: Less than a third as many unemployed men move across state lines than they did in the mid-1950s....White people who stayed in their hometown were 50% more likely to vote for Trump than whites who moved even two hours away.")

It is, Stein says, understandable that people "still living in the 1950s"—in Roberts County, a cutting-edge, curved ultra-HD television is used to watch *Gunsmoke*—often feel disoriented and resentful. It is, however, "dangerous for people in the 1950s to vote on how people in the 21st century should behave."

Back in Los Angeles, Stein worries that "our striving, global, diverse, loosely intertwined lifestyle is breaking the world into angry atoms." At a dinner party with anti-Trump resisters, "I have never been part of a more heated conversation in which everyone agrees." He is unenthralled with the elite milieu: "[The elite] are far more into impressing each other than into making money. The elite dream is not to own a yacht but to give a TED talk." Some of today's elites are plebian, prominent without being distinguished, something that worried Winston Churchill nine decades ago: "The leadership of the privileged has passed away; but it has not been succeeded by that of the eminent."

Today's anti-elitism reflects the not-always-mistaken belief that eminence, even when validated by achievement, often reflects transmitted family advantages. It does not, however, follow that elites have neither earned their eminence nor are socially beneficial.

Granted, expert economists did not anticipate the 2008–2009 financial crisis, but some of them prevented it from becoming Depression 2.0. Today's anti-elitism wields what Stein calls the Meteorologist Fallacy—because forecasts are sometimes wrong, meteorology is worthless:

Populists argue that banks can't be trusted because their mortgage derivatives collapsed in 2008. It's an argument that is tricky to refute unless you've ever dealt with a child. Their first method of challenging adults is to say that you were wrong this one time about that one obscure fact, so you're probably wrong about humans needing to go to sleep at night.

Elites are necessarily small groups that exercise disproportionate influence. In any modern, complex democracy, the question is not whether elites shall rule, but which elites shall, so the perennial political problem is to get popular consent to worthy elites. In their calmer moments, Americans do not idealize mediocrity cloaked with power. And they know that representative government means that "the people" do not decide issues, they decide who shall decide. Away from politics, which most people treat more passionately than seriously, they are serious about depending on credentialed elites: "Nice landing, pilot." "Who is the city's best thoracic surgeon?"

"History," said the sociologist Vilfredo Pareto (1848–1923), "is a graveyard of elites." Yes, but of everyone else, too. And elites have produced things—from vaccines to the globalized commerce that has reduced extreme poverty worldwide 70 percent since 1990—that have made lives better and longer before graveyards beckon.

THE PROBLEM WITH "PARENTAL DETERMINISM"

September 20, 2018

WASHINGTON—Police came to Kim Brooks's parents' door in suburban Richmond, Virginia, demanding that her mother say where her daughter was or be arrested for obstructing justice. So began a Kafkaesque two-year ordeal that plunged Brooks into reflections about current parenting practices. It also produced a book, *Small Animals: Parenthood in the Age of Fear*, that is a catalog of symptoms of America's descent into unfocused furiousness.

On a mild day, rushing to catch a plane home to Chicago, she darted into a Virginia Target to make a purchase, leaving her four-year-old son in the locked car with a window slightly open. After five minutes, during which the car was in her view near the store's door, she drove away. Before she boarded the plane to O'Hare, the police were in pursuit, summoned by a bystander who gave them Brooks's license plate number and an iPhone video of the boy in the car. The video was supposedly evidence of a crime, "contributing to the delinquency of a minor." A five-minute contribution.

Brooks's penitential acknowledgment of "a lapse in judgment" attested to her immersion in the prevalent weirdness about parenting. She is an anxious person. She medicates before flying, although she acknowledges how safe flying is compared with driving. She worries about "stranger danger," although she knows "the statistical near impossibility" of child abductions that, always rare, are rarer than ever. She knows that risk assessment is a basic test of rationality that she and so many other parents flunk. Today, well past her sentence of one hundred hours of community service and twenty hours of parenting instruction, Brooks, who calls herself "an uncritical consumer of anxiety," also knows the following:

Because of the belief in "parental determinism," mothers, especially, are susceptible to the fear that something seemingly minor that is done or left undone will impede Suzy's path to Princeton and Congress. On what Brooks calls "the landscape of competitive, intensive, hyper-controlling parenthood" there is "performance" parenting, the constant mentioning—which means shaming parents with different approaches—of Billy's myriad "enrichment" activities. Helicopter parents, who hover over their progeny all the way to college, subscribe to the belief—a neurosis, really—that "a child cannot be out of an adult's sight for one second." The practical implication is that parenthood is a middle-class entitlement; poor people need not apply. Helicopter parents are indignant—indignation is the default setting of millions of people for whom the personal is political—about "free-range" parents who allow their children to walk alone to, and play unsupervised in, a neighborhood park. No wonder children who have never had unstructured play and never had to negotiate their disputes with one another flinch in bewilderment from the open society of a well-run campus.

Brooks cites a psychologist who notes that technology has made it easier not just to monitor others with smartphone videos ("vigilante parent policing"), but also to critique and condemn others. And to distribute digital disapproval, reinforcing a supposed moral and intellectual hierarchy of mothers, wherein the best are the most cautious, most irrationally afraid, most risk-averse.

Brooks wonders how parenting became "a labyrinth of societal anxieties," a toxic compound of "competitiveness and insecurity," an arena of "chronic, gnawing perfectionism." Start here: Why did the noun "parent" become a verb? Brooks says that "observing the arc of parenting norms" since World War II suggests that within the last ten years we have "reached peak madness." If only.

Contemporary America is a bubbling cauldron of acidic judgmentalism, a stew of status anxieties, of preening about lifestyle fads, and of nasty habits learned from government: Brooks seems to understand that "the criminalization of parenthood" occurs "within the confines of an oppressive and infantilizing nanny state." The ever-metastasizing administrative state's rage to regulate bleeds into a pandemic urge to criminalize more and more of life, and to excoriate and shame those whose behaviors cannot (yet) be formally punished.

It is not unrelated that whenever a third-rate comedian or an adjunct professor of gender studies at a third-tier college says something politically idiotic or—which is much the same thing—culturally "insensitive," Internet hordes who are happy only when unhappy become ecstatically enraged: A brain map might show their pleasure receptors ablaze, as if stimulated by another controlling addiction, cocaine.

Parenting will become increasingly frenzied as does the national culture of which such parenting is symptomatic. Such parenting is a transmissible social disease: People often parent as they were parented.

FREE-RANGE PARENTING

May 10, 2015

WASHINGTON—Controversies about "free-range parenting" illuminate today's scarred cultural landscape. Neighbors summon police in response to parenting choices the neighbors disapprove. Government extends its incompetence with an ever-broader mission of "child protection." And these phenomena are related to campus hysteria about protecting infantilized undergraduates from various menaces, including uncongenial ideas.

The Meitivs live in suburban Montgomery County, Maryland, which is a bedroom for many Washington bureaucrats who make their living minding other people's business. The Meitivs, to encourage independence and self-reliance, let their ten- and six-year-old children walk home alone from a park about a mile from their home. For a second time, their children were picked up by police, this time three blocks from home. After confinement in a squad car for almost three hours, during which the police never called or allowed the children to call the Meitivs, the children were given to social workers who finally allowed the parents to reclaim their children at about eleven p.m. on a school night. The Meitivs' Kafkaesque experiences concluded with them accused of "unsubstantiated" neglect.

Today's saturating media tug children beyond childhood prematurely, but not to maturity. Children are cosseted by intensive parenting that encourages passivity and dependency, and stunts their abilities to improvise, adapt, and weigh risks. Mark Hemingway, writing at The Federalist, asks: "You know what it's called when kids make mistakes without adult supervision and have to wrestle with the resulting consequences? *Growing up.*"

Increased knowledge of early childhood development has produced increased belief in a "science" of child rearing. This has increased intolerance of parenting that deviates from norms that are as changeable as most intellectual fads.

"Intensive parenting" is becoming a government-enforced norm. Read "The day I left my son in the car" (Salon.com), Kim Brooks's essay on her ordeal after leaving her four-year-old in the car as she darted into a store for about five minutes.

Writing in the *Utah Law Review*, David Pimentel of Ohio Northern University notes that at a moment when "children have never been safer," government is abandoning deference to parents' discretion in child rearing. In 1925, the Supreme Court affirmed the right of parents "to direct the upbringing and education of children." Today, however, vague statutes that criminalize child "neglect" or "endangerment" undermine the social legitimacy of parental autonomy. And they ignore the reality that almost every decision a parent makes involves risks. Let your child ride a bike to school, or strap her into a car for the trip? Which child is more at risk, the sedentary one playing video games and risking obesity, or the one riding a bike? It is, Pimentel says, problematic for the legal system to enforce cultural expectations when expectations, partly shaped by media hysteria over rare dangers such as child abductions, are in constant flux.

Time was, colleges and universities acted *in loco parentis* to moderate undergraduates' comportment, particularly regarding sex and alcohol. Institutions have largely abandoned this, having decided that students are mature possessors of moral agency. But institutions have also decided that although undergraduates can cope with hormones and intoxicants, they must be protected from discomforting speech, which must be regulated by codes and confined to "free speech zones." Uncongenial ideas must be foreshadowed by "trigger warnings," lest students, who never were free-range children and now are as brittle as pretzels, crumble. Young people shaped by smothering parents come to college not really separated from their "helicopter parents." Such students come convinced that the world is properly devoted to guaranteeing their serenity, and that their fragility entitles them to protection from distressing thoughts.

As Penn State historian Gary Cross says, adolescence is being redefined to extend well into the twenties, and the "clustering of rites of passage" into adulthood—marriage, childbearing, permanent employment—"has largely disappeared." Writing in the *Chronicle of Higher Education*, Cross says that "delayed social adulthood" means that "in 2011, almost a fifth of men between 25 and 34 still lived with their parents," where many play video games: "The average player is 30 years old." The percentage of men in their early forties who have never married "has risen fourfold to 20 percent."

In the 1950s, Cross says, with Jack Kerouac and Hugh Hefner "the escape from male responsibility became a kind of subculture." Today, oldies radio and concerts by septuagenarian rockers nurture the cult of youth nostalgia among people who, wearing jeans, T-shirts, and sneakers all the way, have slouched from adolescence to Social Security without ever reaching maturity.

THE DAMAGE DONE BY TOO MUCH PARENTAL PRAISE

March 4, 2010

WASHINGTON—Memo to that Massachusetts school where children in physical education classes jump rope without using ropes: Get some ropes. And you—you are about 85 percent of all parents—who are constantly telling your children how intelligent they are: Do your children a favor and pipe down.

These are nuggets from *NurtureShock: New Thinking About Children* by Po Bronson and Ashley Merryman. It is another book to torment modern parents who are determined to bring to bear on their offspring the accumulated science of child-rearing. Modern parents want to nurture so skillfully that Mother Nature will gasp in admiration at the marvels their parenting produces from the soft clay of children.

Those Massachusetts children are jumping rope without ropes because of a self-esteem obsession. The assumption is that thinking highly of oneself is a prerequisite for high achievement. That is why some children's soccer teams stopped counting goals (think of the damaged psyches of children who rarely scored) and shower trophies on everyone. No child at that Massachusetts school suffers damaged self-esteem by tripping on the jump rope.

But the theory that praise, self-esteem, and accomplishment increase in tandem is false. Children incessantly praised for their intelligence (often by parents who are really praising themselves) often underrate the importance of effort. Children who open their lunchboxes and find mothers' handwritten notes telling them how amazingly bright they are tend to falter when they encounter academic difficulties. Also, Bronson and Merryman say that overpraised children are prone to cheating because they have not developed strategies for coping with failure.

"We put our children in high-pressure environments," Bronson and Merryman write, "seeking out the best schools we can find, then we use the constant praise to soften the intensity of those environments." But children excessively praised for their intelligence become risk averse in order to preserve their reputations. Instead, Bronson and Merryman say, praise effort ("I like how you keep trying"): It is a variable children can control.

They often cannot control cars. In 1999, a Johns Hopkins University study found some school districts that abolished driver's education courses experienced a 27 percent decrease in auto accidents among sixteen- and seventeen-year-olds. Odd.

Not really. Bronson and Merryman say driver's ed teaches the rules of the road and mechanics of driving, but teenagers are in fatal crashes at twice the rate of other drivers because of poor decisions, not poor skills. The wiring in the frontal lobe of the teenage brain is not fully formed. Driver's ed courses make getting a license easy, thereby increasing the supply of young drivers who actually have holes in their heads.

Their unfinished heads should spend more time on pillows. Only 5 percent of high school seniors get eight hours of sleep a night. Children get a hour less than they did thirty years ago, which subtracts IQ points and adds body weight.

Until age twenty-one, the circuitry of a child's brain is being completed. Bronson and Merryman report research on grade schoolers showing that "the performance gap caused by an hour's difference in sleep was bigger than the gap between a normal fourth-grader and a normal sixth-grader." In high school there is a steep decline in sleep hours, and a striking correlation of sleep and grades.

Tired children have trouble retaining learning "because neurons lose their plasticity, becoming incapable of forming the new synaptic connections necessary to encode a memory...The more you learned during the day, the more you need to sleep that night."

The school day starts too early because that is convenient for parents and teachers. Awakened at dawn, teenage brains are still releasing melatonin, which makes them sleepy. This is one reason why young adults are responsible for half the 100,000 annual "fall asleep" automobile crashes. When Edina, Minnesota, changed its high school start from 7:25 a.m. to 8:30 a.m., math and verbal SAT scores rose substantially.

Furthermore, sleep loss increases the hormone that stimulates hunger and decreases the one that suppresses appetite. Hence the correlation between less sleep and more obesity.

Bronson and Merryman slay a slew of myths. But perhaps the soundest advice for parents is: Lighten up. People have been raising children for approximately as long as there have been people. Only recently—about five minutes ago, relative to the long-running human comedy—have parents been driving themselves to distraction by taking too seriously the idea that "as the twig is bent the tree's inclined." Twigs are not limitlessly bendable; trees will be what they will be.

"ADVANTAGE HOARDING" IN COGNITIVELY STRATIFIED AMERICA

September 1, 2019

WASHINGTON—Nestled on the Front Range of the Rockies, the city of Crystal was a largely upper-middle-class paradise, chock full of health-conscious and socially conscious—meaning, of course, impeccably progressive—Coloradans. Then in slithered a serpent in the form of a proposal for a new school, to be called "Crystal Academy," for "accelerated and exceptional learners." Suddenly it was paradise lost.

This "deliciously repulsive" story (one reviewer's scrumptious description) with *Big Little Lies* overtones (the same reviewer) is told in Bruce Holsinger's compulsively readable new novel *The Gifted School*. It is perfect back-to-school reading, especially for parents of students in grades K–12. And it is wonderfully timely, arriving in the aftermath of Operation Varsity Blues—who knew the FBI could be droll?—which was the investigation into a very up-to-date crime wave, the scandalous goings-on among some wealthy parents who were determined to leave no ethical norm unbroken in their conniving to get their children into elite colleges and universities.

In Holsinger's book, school officials, speaking educationese, promise that as 100,000 children compete for 1,000 spots—the dreaded 1 percent rears its ugly head—there will be "a visionary, equitable, and inclusive admission process." Four mothers who have been friends forever, but might not be for long, begin becoming rivals in what they regard as a nearly zero-sum game, as they plot to game a process that looks alarmingly fair. Their children are embarked on a forced march to demonstrate that they are "gifted," a word "that slashed like a guillotine through other topics": "Advanced math, Chinese, martial arts, flute lessons with the principal player in the Colorado Symphony: by eighth grade Tessa had become a living, breathing benchmark, a proof of concept for the overinvested parenting they all practiced with varying degrees of obliviousness and guilt."

This is what Holsinger calls "advantage hoarding" and the "delicate ecology of privilege." Everything is hypercompetitive, even among Crystal's eleven-year-olds, from History Day at school to the travel soccer teams, which involve "a lot of mileage, a lot of Panera" in an Audi Q7 with a "Feel the Bern" bumper sticker, with "all the Patagonia parents huddled by the pitch, cheering on their spawn in socially appropriate ways."

When one father takes his toddlers to a playground and other parents ask about his children's ages, he subtracts a few months to make them seem developmentally remarkable, for the pleasure of seeing "that flicker of worry in the parents' eyes." And when rival children do not make the cut for the new school, schadenfreude drapes the Rockies like snowdrifts.

Because Crystal Academy is to be a magnet for students whose transcripts are clotted with AP (advanced placement) courses, it is definitionally elitist, and consequently an awkward fit for good (and affluent, and credentialed) progressives who are determined to lie and cheat in order to maximize the already considerable advantages of their family cultures. Students' submissions for a school's science fair become the parents' projects.

Soon, and inevitably, there is a movement against the new school: "We are a group of concerned parents strongly opposed to the creation of the new public magnet school for allegedly gifted students. We believe that gifted education should be democratic, egalitarian, and nonexclusive." Holsinger's "allegedly" is priceless in conjunction with the insistence on gifted education that eschews exclusivity and inequality. It is not easy being an affluent progressive and a scourge of privilege.

The parents in Holsinger's book insist that their corner-cutting, truth-shading, thumbs-on-the-scale maneuverings and brazen lies are, as people usually say, "all for the children." All, that is, except for the large dollop that is for the bragging rights of parents who have hitched their status anxieties to their children.

Now teaching English literature at the University of Virginia, Holsinger previously was at the University of Colorado, and he says Crystal is a "reimagined Boulder." He probably did not have to strain his imagination. He told the *Wall Street Journal* that you take "over-parented kids, over-invested parents, a cutthroat [college] selection process, and the rest kind of writes itself."

He has deftly written a satire that arrives when it is needed most—when it is difficult to distinguish from sociology. As America becomes more cognitively stratified, with rewards increasingly flowing to the well-educated (or expensively credentialed, which is *not* the same thing), the recent college admission scandal has become, Holsinger says, "one of the great cultural parables of our time." It is a parable about, in another Holsinger phrase, "privilege-hoarding," as American life uncomfortably imitates his art.

AWESOME CHILDREN AND DIFFICULT FOOD CHOICES IN GENTRIFIED BROOKLYN

September 14, 2017

WASHINGTON—Life is exhausting—and daily choices are unbearably burdensome—for some Americans who are so comfortably situated that they have the time and means to make themselves morally uncomfortable. They think constantly about what they believe are the global ripples, and hence the moral-cum-political ramifications, of their quotidian decisions. And they are making themselves nervous wrecks.

If your anthropological curiosity is aroused, venture to gentrifying Brooklyn, in the spirit of Margaret Mead going among the Samoans. It is not necessary to actually go to Brooklyn. You can observe Karen Kipple's agonies while she drives herself to distraction and her life into a ditch as the protagonist of Lucinda Rosenfeld's novel *Class*. It is a book with which to begin another school year. The drama swirls around two elementary schools that, because of the vagaries of neighborhood boundaries, are physically proximate but socially miles apart.

Karen works for a nonprofit—what else?—and has been "trying to write" an op-ed "for the past two years." Her daughter, Ruby, attends Constance C. Betts Elementary, which epitomizes Karen's fervent belief that "racially and economically integrated schools" are essential to "equal opportunity." Still, Karen is vaguely troubled because Ruby's class "completed the same study unit on [Martin Luther King Jr.] four years in a row. Ruby could even recite the date he'd married Coretta (June 18, 1953). At Betts, it sometimes seemed to Karen that every month was Black History Month—except when it was Latino History Month. In keeping with the new Common Core curriculum, Ruby had recently written an 'informative text,' as essays were now known, on Cesar Chavez's advocacy on behalf of Latino migrant workers."

"Over the past several weeks," Ruby's teacher tells a parents' meeting, "your *awesome* kids have been busy creating their own *amazing* community." The parents, however, are problems, including some white mothers, "new to the school and likely soon to depart it, who were constantly complaining about how the milk served in the cafeteria came from hormone-treated cows" rather than from "aseptic eight-ounce cartons of organic vanilla milk" suitable to wash down seaweed snacks.

Karen knows that "the outsize importance" that people like her place on food has "become a dividing line between the social classes, with the Earth Day-esque ideals of the 1960s having acquired snob appeal." Karen, who favors single-origin organic coffee from Burundi, takes Ruby to the artisanal ice cream shop with flavors such as maple fennel, and no corn syrup. When Ruby, pausing over her organic Applegate turkey sandwich on European rye, pronounces a classmate's lunch—white bread sandwich, Cheetos, grape soda—"disgusting," Karen frets that in her effort to simultaneously save "both the health of her daughter and that of the planet" she has produced "a hideous food snob."

Ruby became such at her mother's knee. Karen has one of her tsunamis of disapproval when another mother brings to a playdate chocolate-chip cookies with embedded Reese's Pieces. "Dark visions of polyunsaturated cooking oil" addled Karen's head. Her adherence to the "urban-farming movement"—evidently there is one—is strained by a restaurant offering "pan-seared locally sourced pigeon."

Reluctant to disadvantage her daughter because of her own progressivism, Karen lies about her residential address in order to sneak Ruby into a school that is less diverse than Betts but more financially flush, thanks to more affluent parents—the kind who arrange playdates by saying, "Have your nanny text our nanny." Karen is, however, a virtuoso of guilt, and to assuage hers she embezzles money from the new school and mails it to Betts. By the time her lies and stealing are revealed, she realizes that her "negativity was like a wisteria vine that, if left to its own devices, would creep into every last crevice of her conscience." So she returns Ruby to Betts, leaving behind the school where "the experimental puppeteering troupe Stringtheory is performing a kid-friendly version of *Schindler's List*."

Rosenfeld's novel is a glimpse of how arduous life is for progressives, bowed as they are beneath the crushing weight of every choice's immense social significance. Convinced that people, like the planet, are frightfully fragile—vulnerable to ingesting refined flour and countless other dangers—it's no wonder progressives want a caring government to superintend our lives. This is for our own good, so they are, in their meddlesome way, nice. They also are tuckered out by their incontinent conscientiousness, so take one to lunch, if you can think of something he or she will eat.

PECULIAR GOINGS-ON IN THE GROVES OF ACADEME

36,000 VALEDICTORIANS: "THEY CAN'T ALL GO TO BROWN."

March 27, 2011

WASHINGTON—For many families, *this* is March madness—the moment of high anxiety concerning higher education as many colleges announce their admittance decisions. It is the culmination of a protracted mating dance between selective institutions and anxious students. Part agony, part situation comedy, it has provoked Andrew Ferguson to write a laugh-until-your-ribs-squeak book—*Crazy U: One Dad's Crash Course in Getting His Kid into College.*

He begins in Greenwich, Connecticut—a hedge fund habitat—watching Katherine Cohen, an "independent college admissions counselor," market her $40,000 "platinum package" of strategies for bewitching Ivy League admissions officers. "Everyone in the room," writes Ferguson, "was on full alert, with that feral look of parental ambition. They swiveled their tail-gunning eyes toward Kat when she was introduced." Kat introduced them to terror:

> There are 36,000 high schools in this country. That means there are at least 36,000 valedictorians. They can't all go to Brown. You could take the "deny pile" of applications and make two more classes that were every bit as solid as the class that gets in.

Your son's gazillion extracurricular activities? Kat sniffs: "He's a serial joiner...just running up the score." He was "invited" to participate in a "leadership" program in Washington? Kat's lip curls: "The invitation

293

came in the mail, I guess. It said he was 'selected.' Do you know why he was selected? Your ZIP code. They knew you could pay."

Ferguson becomes one of the Kitchen People—parents who at parties cluster in kitchens where "in the reflected shimmer from the brushed-steel doors of the Sub-Zero, the subtle dance would begin." Squirming against the Viking oven, a mother is bursting—or wanting to burst—with pride over her child's SAT scores.

Her eyes plead, *Ask me what they were, just please please ask...*
"Oh?" I'd say.
"Her father was like, Oh, My, God." And from the eyes, silently: *Ask.*
"Mmm," I'd say.
"Of course, she's always been a smart kid."
"Mmm."
"Of course, she tests well in general. But scores like these...." Her pride bladder was terribly distended now, swelling in all directions, this painful unsatisfied need driving her nearly to the slate flooring.
"I mean when the email with the scores arrived, I just had to peek! And then when I did, I'm thinking, My God—this is *my* kid?"
At last she'd catch a sympathetic eye, and another parent would say, "They must have been really—"
"Twenty-four hundred! I'm like, Wow!"
And then she'd sip the Zin with a humble smile.

Ferguson goes on campus tours conducted by backward-walking students armed with Harry Potter references—the dining hall looks like Hogwarts, there are Quidditch matches, a sociology seminar explores "Voldemort and Differentiation in Imperialist Identities." Kat says that in his son's application essays he must "talk about his innermost thoughts." Ferguson shudders at this "compulsive self-exposure":

He's a seventeen-year-old boy! I wanted to tell her: Seventeen-year-old boys do not have innermost thoughts—and if they did, neither you nor I would want to know what they are.

This complicates writing the essays, which some people say should be liberally flecked with the word "diversity." Ferguson's son worries that his happy life is a handicap:

"Couldn't you guys get a divorce?"

"No," I said.

"It would give me something to write about. You can get back together once I'm done with the essays."

"Not going to happen."

"I wish I'd grown up in the inner city."

"No, you don't."

"I wish I'd become a drug addict."

"There's still time."

Ferguson's whimsy is, however, finite. He becomes serious—and seriously informative—concerning the spiraling costs of college:

It is, he says, nice to know there is $143 billion for student aid—but worrisome that $143 billion is needed. His history of the SAT confirms the assessment that it is "impossible to find a measure of academic achievement that is unrelated to family income." It has been well observed that America's least diverse classes are SAT prep classes.

Still, the college admission process occasions too much angst. America is thickly planted with 1,400 four-year institutions. Motivated, selective students can get a fine education at any of them—unmotivated, undiscerning students at none. Most students love the schools they attend.

And the admissions quest can have splendid moments. Last year, Wake Forest, a wonderful university with a stimulating application form, asked applicants what they would title their autobiographies. One, obviously a golfer, answered: "Mulligan." Wouldn't we all?

THE FIRST AMENDMENT AMENDED: FREEDOM *FROM* SPEECH

May 31, 2015

WASHINGTON—Commencement season brings a respite from the sinister childishness rampant on campuses. Attacks on freedom of speech come from the professoriate, that herd of independent minds, and from the ever-thickening layer of university administrators who keep busy constricting freedom in order to fine-tune campus atmospherics.

The attacks are childish because they infantilize students who flinch from the intellectual free-for-all of adult society. When Brown University's tranquility of conformity was threatened by a woman speaker who is skeptical about the "rape culture" on campuses, students planned a "safe space" for those who would be traumatized by exposure to skepticism. Judith Shulevitz, writing in the *New York Times*, reported that the space had "cookies, coloring books, bubbles, Play-Doh, calming music, pillows, blankets and a video of frolicking puppies."

The attack on free expression is sinister because it asserts that such freedom is not merely unwise but, in a sense, meaningless. Free speech is more comprehensively and aggressively embattled now than ever before in American history, largely because of two nineteenth-century ideas. One is that history—actually, History, a proper noun—has a mind of its own. The other is that most people do not really have minds of their own.

Progressives frequently disparage this or that person or idea as "on the wrong side of history." They regard history as an autonomous force with its own laws of unfolding development: Progress *is* wherever history goes. This belief entails disparagement of human agency—or at least that of most people, who do not understand history's implacable logic and hence do not get on history's "right side." Such people are crippled by "false consciousness." Fortunately, a saving clerisy, a vanguard composed of the understanding few, know where history is going and how to help it get there.

One way to help is by molding the minds of young people. The molders believe that the sociology of knowledge demonstrates that most people do not make up their minds, "society" does this. But progressive minds can be furnished for them by controlling the promptings from the social environment. This can be done by making campuses into hermetically sealed laboratories.

In *The Promise of American Life* (1909), progressivism's canonical text, Herbert Croly said, "The average American individual is morally and intellectually inadequate to a serious and consistent conception of his responsibilities as a democrat." National life should be "a school," with the government as the stern but caring principal: "The exigencies of such schooling frequently demand severe coercive measures, but what schooling does not?" "Unregenerate citizens" can be saved "many costly perversions, in case the official school-masters are wise, and the pupils neither truant nor insubordinate."

In *Kindly Inquisitors* (1993), Jonathan Rauch showed how attacks on the free market in speech undermine three pillars of American liberty. They subvert democracy, the culture of persuasion by which we decide who shall wield legitimate power. (Progressives advocate government regulation of the quantity, content, and timing of political campaign speech.) The attacks undermine capitalism—markets registering the freely expressed choices by which we allocate wealth. And the attacks undermine science, which is how we decide what is true. (Note progressives' insistence that the science about this or that is "settled.")

For decades, much academic ingenuity has been devoted to jurisprudential theorizing to evade the First Amendment's majestic simplicity about "no law...abridging the freedom of speech." We are urged to "balance" this freedom against competing, and putatively superior, considerations such as individual serenity, institutional tranquility, or social improvement.

On campuses, the right of free speech has been supplanted by an entitlement to what Greg Lukianoff of the Foundation for Individual Rights in Education calls a right to freedom from speech deemed uncongenial. This entitlement is buttressed by "trigger warnings" against spoken "micro-aggressions" that lacerate the delicate sensibilities of individuals who are encouraged to be exquisitely, paralyzingly sensitive.

Lukianoff says "sensitivity-based censorship" on campus reflects a broader and global phenomena. It is the demand for coercive measures to do for our mental lives what pharmacology has done for our bodies—the banishment or mitigation of many discomforts. In the social milieu fostered by today's entitlement state, expectations quickly generate entitlements. Students are taught to expect intellectual comfort, including the reinforcement of their beliefs, or at least those that conform to progressive orthodoxies imbibed and enforced on campuses. Until September, however, the culture of freedom will be safe from its cultured despisers.

THE FIRST AMENDMENT IN THE "FREE SPEECH GAZEBO"

December 2, 2012

WASHINGTON—In 2007, Keith John Sampson, a middle-aged student working his way through Indiana University-Purdue University Indianapolis as a janitor, was declared guilty of racial harassment. Without granting Sampson a hearing, the university administration—acting as prosecutor, judge, and jury—convicted him of "openly reading [a] book related to a historically and racially abhorrent subject."

"Openly." "Related to." Good grief.

The book, *Notre Dame vs. the Klan*, celebrated the 1924 defeat of the Ku Klux Klan in a fight with Notre Dame students. But some of Sampson's co-workers disliked the book's cover, which featured a black-and-white photograph of a Klan rally. Someone was offended, therefore someone else *must be* guilty of harassment.

This non sequitur reflects the right never to be annoyed, a new campus entitlement. Legions of administrators, who now outnumber full-time faculty, are kept busy making students mind their manners, with good manners understood as conformity to liberal politics.

Liberals are most concentrated and untrammeled on campuses, so look there for evidence of what, given the opportunity, they would do to America. Ample evidence is in "Unlearning Liberty: Campus Censorship and the End of American Debate" by Greg Lukianoff, thirty-eight, a graduate of Stanford Law School who describes himself as a liberal, pro-choice, pro-gay rights, lifelong Democrat who belongs to "the notoriously politically correct Park Slope Food Co-Op in Brooklyn" and has never voted for a Republican "nor do I plan to." But as president of the Foundation for Individual Rights in Education (FIRE) he knows that the most common justifications for liberal censorship are "sensitivity" about "diversity" and "multiculturalism," as academic liberals understand those things.

In recent years, a University of Oklahoma vice president has declared that no university resources, including email, could be used for "the forwarding of political humor/commentary." The College at Brockport in New York banned using the Internet to "annoy or otherwise inconvenience" anyone. Rhode Island College prohibited, among many other things, certain "attitudes." Texas Southern University's comprehensive proscriptions included "verbal harm" from damaging "assumptions" or "implications." Texas A&M promised "freedom from indignity of any type." Davidson banned "patronizing remarks." Drexel University forbade "inappropriately directed laughter." Western Michigan University banned "sexism," including "the perception" of a person "not as an individual, but as a member of a category based on sex." Banning "perceptions" must provide full employment for the burgeoning ranks of academic administrators.

Many campuses congratulate themselves on their broad-mindedness when they establish small "free speech zones" where political advocacy can be scheduled. At one point Texas Tech's 28,000 students had a "free speech gazebo" that was twenty feet wide. And you thought the First Amendment made America a free speech zone.

At Tufts, a conservative newspaper committed "harassment" by printing accurate quotations from the Quran and a verified fact about the status of women in Saudi Arabia. Lukianoff says Tufts may have been the first American institution "to find someone guilty of harassment for stating verifiable facts directed at no one in particular."

He documents how "orientation" programs for freshmen become propaganda to (in the words of one orthodoxy enforcer) "leave a mental footprint on their consciousness." Faculty, too, can face mandatory consciousness-raising.

In 2007, Donald Hindley, a politics professor at Brandeis, was found guilty of harassment because when teaching Latin American politics he explained the origin of the word "wetbacks," which refers to immigrants crossing the Rio Grande. Without a hearing, the university provost sent Hindley a letter stating that the university "will not tolerate inappropriate, racial and discriminatory conduct." The assistant provost was assigned to monitor Hindley's classes "to ensure that you do not engage in further violations of the nondiscrimination and harassment policy." Hindley was required to attend "anti-discrimination training."

Such coercion is a natural augmentation of censorship. Next comes mob rule. Last year, at the University of Wisconsin-Madison, the vice provost for diversity and climate—really; you can't make this stuff up—encouraged students to disrupt a news conference by a speaker opposed to racial preferences. They did, which the vice provost called "awesome." This is the climate on an especially liberal campus that celebrates "diversity" in everything but thought.

"What happens on campus," Lukianoff says, "doesn't stay on campus" because censorship has "downstream effects." He quotes a sociologist whose data he says demonstrate that "those with the highest levels of education have the *lowest* exposure to people with conflicting points of view." This encourages "the human tendency to live within our own echo chambers." Parents' tuition dollars and student indebtedness are paying for this. Good grief.

THE "SURVEILLANCE STATE" IN ANN ARBOR

May 20, 2018

WASHINGTON—On election night 2016, Mark Schlissel, the University of Michigan's president, addressed more than 1,000 students, declaring that the 90 percent of them who had favored the losing candidate had rejected "hate." He thereby effectively made those who disagreed with him and with the campus majority eligible to be targets of the university's "bias response teams." That his announced contempt for them made him a suitable target of the university's thought police is a thought that presumably occurred to no one, least of all him.

Now, however, this leader of a public institution is being sued for constitutional violations. So are some members of Michigan's archetypal administrative bloat—the ever-thickening layer of social-justice crusaders and orthodoxy enforcers who, nationwide, live parasitically off universities whose actual purpose is scholarship. These include Michigan's vice provost for equity and inclusion, and the director of the Office of Student Conflict Resolution. Such bureaucrats have professional stakes in finding inequities to rectify and conflicts to resolve.

A splendid new organization, Speech First, headed by Nicole Neily, is not content merely to respond after the fact to violations of students' constitutional rights. It is suing to invalidate Michigan's "elaborate investigatory and disciplinary apparatus" that exists "to suppress and punish speech that other students deem 'demeaning,' 'bothersome' or 'hurtful.'" Speech First's complaint notes that "the most sensitive student on campus effectively dictates the terms under which others may speak." The university darkly warns that "bias comes in many forms" and "the most important indication of bias is your own feelings." Speech First says that Michigan's edifice of speech regulation, with its Orwellian threats to submit offenders to "restorative justice," "individual education," and "unconscious bias training," amounts to unconstitutional prior restraint of speech and is too overbroad and vague to give anyone due notice of what is proscribed.

"Verbal conduct" that "victimizes," or jeopardizes a "social climate" that is "safe and inclusive"? Such vaporous language must have a chilling effect on humor, parody, satire, or plain speech about almost anything. What constitutes forbidden "cultural appropriation"? You will be told— after someone, encouraged by the administration to do so, has notified law enforcement.

When the *Wall Street Journal*'s Jillian Kay Melchior asked Michigan for the records of one year of bias incident reports, "the university thwarted this inquiry by imposing a fee of more than $2,400 for the public records." If this secretiveness indicates that the university is embarrassed, this is progress.

The Foundation for Individual Rights in Education says bias response teams produce "a surveillance state on campus where students and faculty must guard their every utterance for fear of being reported to and investigated" by bureaucrats. Their *profession* is the suppression and re-education of those—generally conservatives—whose attitudes and opinions constitute, as Michigan students have learned from Schlissel, "hate."

FIRE has established a grading system whereby colleges and universities are given green, yellow, or red ratings depending on their commitments to freedom of speech and inquiry. Institutions are increasingly interested in earning FIRE's green approval. FIRE gives Michigan the red rating that identifies a university that has "at least one policy that both clearly and substantially restricts freedom of speech."

Frederick M. Hess and Grant Addison of the American Enterprise Institute, writing in *National Affairs* ("Restoring Free Inquiry on Campus"), note that when, after World War II, the federal government decided to direct scientific and medical research through universities rather than government-run laboratories, there were worries that government might threaten free inquiry on campuses. Today, say Hess and Addison, "ideological homogeneity" in academia is producing "formal policies and practices" whereby "limits on speech and expression have become ingrained in campus culture." Hess and Addison have a sensible proposal:

"Taxpayer funds should not be subsidizing research at higher-education institutions where the conditions of free inquiry are compromised."

Of the thirty academic institutions that received the most research funding in 2015, six (20 percent) received $4.5 billion from the federal government (11 percent of all federal research funds)—and a red rating from FIRE. According to it, almost 40 percent of all federal research funds went to twenty-five institutions that have formal policies that restrict constitutionally protected speech.

Michigan ranks third among all universities as a recipient of federal research funding. In 2015, its $735 million in federal funding was 54 percent of the university's total R & D grants. Although Schlissel is ideologically blinkered, tone deaf, and awfully complacent about his own flagrant biases, his bias response teams probably are not worth $735 million to him.

—

After the Sixth Circuit Court of Appeals ruled against the university in Speech First, Inc. v. Schlissel, *the university disbanded its "bias response team" and modified or abandoned some of its definition of forbidden speech.*

SALUTARY LUDICROUSNESS

June 5, 2014

WASHINGTON—Colleges and universities are being educated by Washington and are finding the experience excruciating. They are learning that when they say campus victimizations are ubiquitous ("micro-aggressions," often not discernible to the untutored eye, are everywhere), and that when they make victimhood a coveted status that confers privileges, victims proliferate. And academia's progressivism has rendered it intellectually defenseless now that progressivism's achievement, the regulatory state, has decided it is academia's turn to be broken to government's saddle.

Consider the supposed campus epidemic of rape, aka "sexual assault." Herewith, a *Philadelphia* magazine report about Swarthmore College, where in 2013 a student "was in her room with a guy with whom she'd been hooking up for three months":

They'd now decided—mutually, she thought—just to be friends. When he ended up falling asleep on her bed, she changed into pajamas and climbed in next to him. Soon, he was putting his arm around her and taking off her clothes. "I basically said, 'No, I don't want to have sex with you.' And then he said, 'OK, that's fine' and stopped....And then he started again a few minutes later, taking off my panties, taking off his boxers. I just kind of laid there and didn't do anything—I had already said no. I was just tired and wanted to go to bed. I let him finish. I pulled my panties back on and went to sleep."

Six weeks later, the woman reported that she had been raped. Now the Obama administration is riding to the rescue of "sexual assault" victims. It vows to excavate equities from the ambiguities of the hookup culture, this cocktail of hormones, alcohol, and the faux sophistication of today's prolonged adolescence of especially privileged young adults.

The administration's crucial and contradictory statistics are validated the usual way, by official repetition; Joe Biden has been heard from. The statistics are: One in five women is sexually assaulted while in college, and only 12 percent of assaults are reported. Simple arithmetic demonstrates that if the 12 percent reporting rate is correct, the 20 percent assault rate is preposterous. Mark Perry of the American Enterprise Institute notes, for example, that in the four years 2009–2012 there were 98 reported sexual assaults at Ohio State. That would be 12 percent of 817 total out of a female student population of approximately 28,000, for a sexual assault rate of approximately 2.9 percent—too high but nowhere near 20 percent.

Department of Education lawyers disregard pesky arithmetic and elementary due process. Threatening to withdraw federal funding, DOE mandates adoption of a minimal "preponderance of the evidence" standard when adjudicating sexual assault charges between males and the female "survivors"—note the language of prejudgment. Combine this with capacious definitions of sexual assault that can include not only forcible sexual penetration but also nonconsensual touching. Then add the doctrine that the consent of a female who has been drinking might not protect a male from being found guilty of rape. Then comes costly litigation against institutions that have denied due process to males they accuse of what society considers serious felonies.

Now academia is unhappy about DOE's plan for government to rate every institution's educational product. But the professors need not worry. A DOE official says this assessment will be easy: "It's like rating a blender." Education, gadgets—what's the difference?

Meanwhile, the newest campus idea for preventing victimizations—an idea certain to multiply claims of them—is "trigger warnings." They would be placed on assigned readings or announced before lectures. Otherwise, traumas could be triggered in students whose tender sensibilities would be lacerated by unexpected encounters with racism, sexism, violence (dammit, Hamlet, put down that sword!), or any other facet of reality that might violate a student's entitlement to serenity. This entitlement has already bred campus speech codes that punish unpopular speech. Now the codes are begetting the soft censorship of trigger warnings to swaddle students in a "safe," "supportive," "unthreatening" environment, intellectual comfort for the intellectually dormant.

It is salutary that academia, with its adversarial stance toward limited government and cultural common sense, is making itself ludicrous. Academia is learning that its attempts to create victim-free campuses—by making everyone hypersensitive, even delusional, about victimizations—brings increasing supervision by the regulatory state that progressivism celebrates.

What government is inflicting on colleges and universities, and what they are inflicting on themselves, diminishes their autonomy, resources, prestige, and comity. Which serves them right. They have asked for this by asking for progressivism.

THE CAMPUS "RAPE CULTURE" AND THE DEATH OF DUE PROCESS

May 15, 2016

WASHINGTON—Academia's descent into perpetual hysteria and incipient tyranny is partly fueled by the fiction that one in five college students is sexually assaulted and that campuses require minute federal supervision to cure this. Encouraged by the government's misuse of discredited social science (one survey supposedly proving this one-in-five fiction), colleges and universities are implementing unconstitutional procedures mandated by the government.

The 2006 Duke lacrosse rape case fit the narrative about campuses permeated by a "rape culture." Except there was no rape. In 2014, the University of Virginia was convulsed by a magazine's lurid report of a rape that buttressed the narrative that fraternities foment the sexual predation supposedly pandemic in "male supremacist" America. Except there was no rape. Now, Colorado State University Pueblo has punished the supposed rapist of a woman who says she was not raped.

Grant Neal, a CSU Pueblo pre-med major and athlete, began a relationship with Jane Doe (as identified in Neal's lawsuit), although she, as a student in the Athletic Training Program, was not supposed to fraternize with athletes. Jane Doe texted an invitation to Neal to come to her apartment. The following is from Neal's complaint against CSU Pueblo:

> As the intimacy progressed, knowing that they both wanted to engage in sexual intercourse, Jane Doe advised Plaintiff that she was not on birth control. Accordingly, Plaintiff asked if he should put on a condom. Jane Doe clearly and unequivocally responded "yes."... They proceeded to engage in consensual sexual intercourse, during which Jane Doe... demonstrated her enjoyment both verbally and non-verbally.

The next day, one of Jane Doe's classmates, who neither witnessed nor was told of any assault, noticed a hickey on the woman's neck. Assuming an assault must have happened, the classmate told school officials that an assault had occurred. Jane Doe told school officials the sex was consensual: "I'm fine and I wasn't raped." Neal's lawsuit says she told an administrator: "Our stories are the same and he's a good guy. He's not a rapist, he's not a criminal, it's not even worth any of this hoopla!" Neal recorded on his cellphone Jane Doe saying that nothing improper had transpired, and soon the two again had intercourse.

Undeterred, CSU Pueblo mixed hearsay evidence with multiple due process violations, thereby ruining a young man's present (he has been suspended from the school for as long as Jane Doe is there) and blighting his future (his prospects for admission to another school are bleak).

Title IX of the Education Amendments enacted in 1972 merely says no person at an institution receiving federal funds shall be subjected to discrimination on the basis of sex. From this the government has concocted a right to micromanage schools' disciplinary procedures, mandating obvious violations of due process. In 2011, the Education Department's civil rights office sent "dear colleague" letters to schools directing them to convict accused persons on a mere "preponderance" of evidence rather than "clear and convincing" evidence. Schools were instructed to not allow accused students to cross-examine their accusers, but to allow accusers to appeal not-guilty verdicts, a form of double jeopardy.

Although a "dear colleague" letter is supposedly a mere "guidance document," it employs the word "must" in effectively mandating policies. While purporting to just "interpret" Title IX, these letters shred constitutional guarantees. And the letters evade the legal requirement that such significant rulemaking must be subject to comment hearings open to a properly notified public. Even were CSU Pueblo inclined to resist such dictates—academic administrators nowadays are frequently supine when challenged—it would risk a costly investigation and the potential loss of the 11 percent of its budget that comes from Washington.

The *Chronicle of Higher Education* says the case raises this "intriguing" question: "What responsibility does a college have to move ahead with a third-party complaint if the supposed victim says she consented?" This question, which in a calmer time would have a self-evident answer, will be explored in Neal's lawsuit. It should reveal what the school thought of Jane Doe's statement exculpating Neal, who says a school official "brushed off" the recording and said that Jane Doe said what she said "just because she was scared of you." Neal's lawyer says he suspects that Jane Doe might now be intimating something "inappropriate" and is perhaps scared of losing her place in the Athletic Training Program.

CSU Pueblo should be scared of joining those schools that have lost lawsuits filed by students denied due process. Such suits are remedial education for educators ignorant of constitutional guarantees.

ALL RIGHT THEN, WHAT AN *UNREASONABLE* PERSON FINDS OFFENSIVE

May 26, 2013

WASHINGTON—Barack Obama, vowing to elevate Washington to the level of his fastidiousness, came from Chicago, where the political machine inoculates itself from scandals by the proliferation of them: Many scandals mean merely cursory scrutiny of most. Now, notice the scant attention being given to an assault on civil liberties by the misconceived Education Department's misnamed Office for Civil Rights (OCR).

Responding to what it considers the University of Montana's defective handling of complaints about sexual *assaults*, OCR, in conjunction with the Department of Justice, sent the university a letter intended as a "blueprint" for institutions nationwide when handling sexual *harassment*, too. The letter, sent on May 9, *encourages* (see below) adoption of speech codes—actually, censorship regimes—to punish students who:

> Make "sexual or dirty jokes" that are "unwelcome." Or disseminate "sexual rumors" (even if true) that are "unwelcome." Or make

"unwelcome" sexual invitations. Or engage in the "unwelcome" circulation or showing of "e-mails or Web sites of a sexual nature." Or display or distribute "sexually explicit drawings, pictures, or written materials" that are "unwelcome."

UCLA law professor Eugene Volokh, a specialist in First Amendment jurisprudence, notes (on the indispensable Volokh Conspiracy blog) that the OCR-DOJ's proscriptions are "not limited to material that a *reasonable* person would find offensive." The Supreme Court has held that for speech or conduct in schools to lead to a successful sexual harassment lawsuit, it must be sufficiently severe and pervasive to create a hostile environment. And it must be "objectively offensive" to a reasonable person. But, Volokh notes, the OCR-DOJ rules would mandate punishment for any individual's "conduct of a sexual nature," conduct "verbal, nonverbal or physical," that is not objectively offensive to a normal person. This means any conduct "unwelcome" by anyone. Greg Lukianoff, president of the Foundation for Individual Rights in Education, says a single hypersensitive person could declare herself sexually harassed because she considers "unwelcome" a classroom lecture on the novel *Lolita* or a campus performance of *The Vagina Monologues*. Do not even attempt a sex education class.

Wendy Kaminer, a civil liberties lawyer who writes for the *Atlantic*, traces the pedigree of the OCR-DOJ thinking to the attempt by some feminists in the 1980s to define pornography as a form of sexual assault and hence a civil rights violation. Volokh, too, believes that the government is blurring the distinction between physical assaults and "sexually themed" speech in order to justify censoring and punishing the latter.

The OCR-DOJ "blueprint" requires, Kaminer says, colleges and universities to hear harassment complaints under quasi-judicial procedures "that favor complainants." Under 2011 rules, establishing a low standard of proof, Kaminer says, "students accused of harassment are to be convicted in the absence of clear and convincing evidence of guilt, if guilt merely seems more likely than not." And schools are enjoined to "take immediate steps to protect the complainant from further harassment," including "taking disciplinary action against the harasser" *prior to adjudication.* So the OCR-DOJ "blueprint" and related rules not only violate the First Amendment guarantee of free speech but are, to be polite, casual about due process.

Hans Bader, a former OCR lawyer now with the limited-government Competitive Enterprise Institute, notes that this *Alice in Wonderland*—"sentence first, verdict afterwards"—system "casts a cloud over academic freedom and the ability to discuss topics that are offensive to some listeners." Indeed, to *one* listener.

When the Education Department was created in 1980 (Jimmy Carter's payment to the National Education Association, the largest teachers' union, for its first presidential endorsement), conservatives warned that it would be used for ideological aggression to break state and local schools to the federal saddle. Lukianoff says: "Given that the [OCR-DOJ] letter represents an interpretation of federal law by major federal agencies, most colleges will regard it as binding. Noncompliance threatens federal funding, including Pell grants and Stafford loans."

Most of academia's leadership is too invertebrate and too soggy with political correctness to fight the OCR-DOJ mischief. But someone will. And it is so patently unconstitutional, it will be swiftly swatted down by courts. Still, it is useful idiocy because, coming right now, it underscores today's widespread government impulse for lawless coercion—the impulse that produced the Internal Revenue Service's suppression of political speech that annoys the Obama administration. Like the IRS abuses of power, the OCR-DOJ initiative demonstrates how permeated this administration is with disagreeable people with dangerous intentions. So the administration is making conservatism's case against the unlimited arrogance that is both a cause and a consequence of unlimited government.

THE COLLEGE DEGREE AS STATUS MARKER

June 10, 2012

WASHINGTON—Many parents and the children they send to college are paying rapidly rising prices for something of declining quality. This is because "quality" is not synonymous with "value."

Glenn Harlan Reynolds, University of Tennessee law professor, believes college has become, for many, merely a "status marker" signaling membership in the educated caste, and a place to meet spouses of similar status—"associative mating." Since 1961, the time students spend reading, writing, and otherwise studying has fallen from twenty-four hours a week to about fifteen—enough for a degree often desired only as an expensive signifier of rudimentary qualities (e.g., the ability to follow instructions). Employers value this signifier as an alternative to aptitude tests when evaluating potential employees because such tests can provoke lawsuits by having a "disparate impact" on this or that racial or ethnic group.

In his Encounter Books Broadside *The Higher Education Bubble*, Reynolds says this bubble exists for the same reasons the housing bubble did. The government decided that too few people owned homes/went to college, so government money was poured into subsidized and sometimes subprime mortgages/student loans, with the predictable result that housing prices/college tuitions soared and many borrowers went bust. Tuitions and fees have risen more than 440 percent in thirty years as schools happily raised prices—and lowered standards—to siphon up federal money. A recent *Wall Street Journal* headline: "Student Debt Rises by 8% as College Tuitions Climb."

Richard Vedder, an Ohio University economist, writes in the *Chronicle of Higher Education* that as many people—perhaps more—have student loan debts as have college degrees. Have you seen those T-shirts that proclaim "College: The Best Seven Years of My Life"? Twenty-nine percent of borrowers *never* graduate, and many who do graduate take decades to repay their loans.

In 2010, the *New York Times* reported on Cortney Munna, then twenty-six, a New York University graduate with almost $100,000 in debt. If her repayments were not then being deferred because she was enrolled in night school, she would have been paying $700 monthly from her $2,300 monthly after-tax income as a photographer's assistant. She says she is toiling "to pay for an education I got for four years and would happily give back." Her degree is in religious and women's studies.

The budgets of California's universities are being cut, so recently Cal State Northridge students conducted an almost-hunger strike (sustained by a blend of kale, apple, and celery juices) to protest, as usual, tuition increases and, unusually and properly, administrators' salaries. For example, in 2009 the base salary of UC Berkeley's Vice Chancellor for Equity and Inclusion was $194,000, almost four times that of starting assistant professors. And by 2006, academic administrators outnumbered faculty.

The Manhattan Institute's Heather Mac Donald notes that sinecures in academia's diversity industry are expanding as academic offerings contract. UC San Diego, while eliminating master's programs in electrical and computer engineering and comparative literature, and eliminating courses in French, German, Spanish, and English literature, added a diversity requirement for graduation to cultivate "a student's understanding of her or his identity." So, rather than study computer science and Cervantes, students can study their identities—themselves. Says Mac Donald, " 'Diversity,' it turns out, is simply a code word for narcissism."

She reports that UCSD lost three cancer researchers to Rice University, which offered them 40 percent pay increases. But UCSD found money to create a Vice Chancellorship for Equity, Diversity, and Inclusion. UC Davis has a Diversity Trainers Institute under an Administrator of Diversity Education, who presumably coordinates with the Cross-Cultural Center. It also has: a Lesbian, Gay, Bisexual, Transgender Resource Center; a Sexual Harassment Education Program; a Diversity Program Coordinator; an Early Resolution Discrimination Coordinator; a Diversity Education Series that awards Understanding Diversity Certificates in "Unpacking Oppression"; and Cross-Cultural Competency Certificates in "Understanding Diversity and Social Justice." California's budget crisis has not prevented UC San Francisco from creating a new Vice Chancellor for Diversity and Outreach to supplement UCSF's Office of Affirmative Action, Equal Opportunity, and Diversity, and the Diversity Learning Center (which teaches how to become "a Diversity Change Agent"), and the Center for LGBT Health and Equity, and the Office of Sexual Harassment Prevention & Resolution, and the Chancellor's Advisory Committees on Diversity, and on Gay, Lesbian, Bisexual, and Transgender Issues, and on the Status of Women.

So taxpayers should pay more and parents and students should borrow more to fund administrative sprawl in the service of stale political agendas? Perhaps they will, until "pop!" goes the bubble.

YALE AND OTHER INCUBATORS

November 20, 2016

WASHINGTON—Many undergraduates, their fawn-like eyes wide with astonishment, are wondering: Why didn't the dean of students prevent the election from disrupting the serenity to which my school has taught me that I am entitled? Campuses create "safe spaces" where students can shelter from discombobulating thoughts and receive spiritual balm for the trauma of micro-aggressions. Yet the presidential election came without trigger warnings?

The morning after the election, normal people rose—some elated, some despondent—and went off to actual work. But at Yale, that incubator of late-adolescent infants, a professor responded to "heartfelt notes" from students "in shock" by making that day's exam optional.

Academia should consider how it contributed to, and reflects Americans' judgments pertinent to, Donald Trump's election. The compound of childishness and condescension radiating from campuses is a constant reminder to normal Americans of the decay of protected classes—in this case, tenured faculty and cosseted students.

As "bias response teams" fanned out across campuses, an incident report was filed about a University of Northern Colorado student who wrote "free speech matters" on one of 680 "#languagematters" posters that cautioned against politically incorrect speech. Catholic DePaul University denounced as "bigotry" a poster proclaiming "Unborn Lives Matter." Bowdoin College provided counseling to students traumatized by the cultural appropriation committed by a sombrero-and-tequila party. Oberlin College students said they were suffering breakdowns because schoolwork was interfering with their political activism. Cal State University, Los Angeles established "healing" spaces for students to cope with the pain caused by a political speech delivered *three months earlier*. Indiana University experienced social-media panic ("Please PLEASE PLEASE be careful out there tonight") because a priest in a white robe, with a rope-like belt and rosary beads, was identified as someone "in a KKK outfit holding a whip."

A doctoral dissertation at the University of California, Santa Barbara uses "feminist methodologies" to understand how Girl Scout cookie sales "reproduce hegemonic gender roles." The journal *GeoHumanities* explores how pumpkins reveal "racial and class coding of rural versus urban places." Another journal's article analyzes "the relationships among gender, science and glaciers." A Vassar lecture "theorizes oscillating relations between disciplinary, pre-emptive and increasingly prehensive forms of power that shape human and non-human materialities in Palestine."

Even professors' books from serious publishers are clotted with pretentious jargon. To pick just one from innumerable examples, a recent history of the Spanish Civil War, published by the Oxford University Press, says that Franco's Spain was as "hierarchizing" as Hitler's Germany, that Catholicism "problematized" relations between Spain and the Third Reich, and that liberalism and democracy are concepts that must be "interrogated." Only the highly educated write so badly. Indeed, the point of such ludicrous prose is to signal membership in a closed clerisy that possesses a private language.

An American Council of Trustees and Alumni (ACTA) study—"No U.S. History? How College History Departments Leave the United States out of the Major," based on requirements and course offerings at seventy-five leading colleges and universities—found that "the overwhelming majority of America's most prestigious institutions do not require even the students who major in history to take a single course on United States history or government." Often "microhistories" are offered to history majors at schools that require these majors to take no U.S. history course: "Modern Addiction: Cigarette Smoking in the 20th Century" (Swarthmore College), "Lawn Boy Meets Valley Girl" (Bowdoin College), "Witchcraft and Possession" (University of Pennsylvania).

At some schools that require history majors to take at least one U.S. history course, the requirement can be fulfilled with courses like "Mad Men and Mad Women" (Middlebury College), "Hip-Hop, Politics and Youth Culture in America" (University of Connecticut), and "Jews in American Entertainment" (University of Texas). Constitutional history is an afterthought.

Small wonder, then, that a recent ACTA-commissioned survey found that less than half of college graduates knew that George Washington was the commanding general at Yorktown; that nearly half did not know that Theodore Roosevelt was important to the construction of the Panama Canal; that more than one-third could not place the Civil War in a correct twenty-year span or identify Franklin Roosevelt as the architect of the New Deal; that 58 percent did not know that the Battle of the Bulge occurred in World War II; and that nearly half did not know the lengths of the terms of U.S. senators and representatives.

Institutions of supposedly higher education are awash with hysteria, authoritarianism, obscurantism, philistinism, and charlatanry. Which must have something to do with the tone and substance of the presidential election, which took the nation's temperature.

ANOTHER YALE BURLESQUE,
"CONTEXTUALIZED"

August 31, 2017

WASHINGTON—Summer brings no respite for academics committed to campus purifications, particularly at the institution that is the leader in the silliness sweepstakes, Yale. Its Committee on Art in Public Spaces has discovered that a stone carving that has adorned an entrance to Sterling Memorial Library since it opened eighty-six years ago has become "not appropriate."

The carving, according to *Yale Alumni Magazine*, depicts "a hostile encounter: a Puritan pointing a musket at a Native American." Actually, the Native American and the Puritan are looking not hostilely at each other but into the distance. Still, one can't be too careful, so the musket has been covered with stone. This is unilateral disarmament: The Native American's weapon, a bow, has not been covered up. Perhaps Yale thinks that armed white men are more "triggering" (this academic-speak means "upsetting to the emotionally brittle") than armed people of color. National Review Online's Kyle Smith drolly worries that Yale might be perpetuating harmful stereotypes.

If such campus folderols merely added to what Samuel Johnson called "the public stock of harmless pleasure," Americans could welcome a new academic year the way they once welcomed new burlesque acts. Unfortunately, the descent of institutions of learning into ludicrousness is symptomatic of larger social distempers that Frank Furedi has diagnosed abroad as well as in America.

Furedi is a professor emeritus in England and author of *What's Happened to the University?: A Sociological Exploration of Its Infantilisation.* Writing in *The American Interest*, he cites a warning issued to Oxford University postgraduate students about the danger of "vicarious trauma," which supposedly results from "hearing about and engaging with the traumatic experiences of others." This, Furedi says, is symptomatic of the "medicalization" of almost everything in universities that strive to be "therapeutic." Universities are "promoting theories and practices that encourage people to interpret their anxieties, distress and disappointment through the language of psychological deficits." This generates self-fulfilling diagnoses of emotionally fragile students. They demand mental-health services on campuses that are replete with "trigger warnings" and "safe spaces" to insulate students from discomforts, such as the depiction of a musket. What academics perceive as "an expanded set of problems tracks right along with the exponential growth of the *Diagnostic and Statistical Manual of Mental Disorders*."

The socialization of children, which prepares them to enter the wider world, has been shifted from parents to primary and secondary schools, and now to higher education, which has embraced the task that Furedi calls "re-socialization through altering the norms that undergraduates grew up with." This is done by using speech codes and indoctrination to raise "awareness" about defects students acquired before coming to campuses that are determined to purify undergraduates.

Often, however, students arrive with little moral ballast bequeathed by parents who thought their role was, Furedi says, less to transmit values than to validate their children's feelings and attitudes: "This emphasis on validation runs in tandem with a risk-averse regime of child-rearing, the (unintended) consequence of which has been to limit opportunities for the cultivation of independence and to extend the phase of dependence of young people on adult society."

The therapeutic university's language—students are "vulnerable" to routine stresses and difficulties that are defined as "traumas"—also becomes self-fulfilling. As a result, students experience a diminished sense of capacity for moral agency—for self-determination. This can make them simultaneously passive, immersing themselves into groupthink, and volatile, like the mobs at Middlebury College, Claremont McKenna College, University of California, Berkeley, and other schools that disrupt uncongenial speakers. Hence universities provide "trigger warnings" that facilitate flights into "safe spaces." Furedi quotes an Oberlin College student who says: "There's something to be said about exposing yourself to ideas other than your own," but "I've had enough of that."

Times do, however, change, as the *Yale Alumni Magazine* delicately intimated when it said the stone now obscuring the Puritan's musket "can be removed in the future without damaging the original carving." And the future has come with strange speed to New Haven.

In a peculiar letter in Tuesday's *Wall Street Journal*, a Yale official says the university is removing the stone "that a construction project team had placed on the stonework." By clearly suggesting, implausibly, that this "team" acted on its own, the letter contradicts the magazine's report that the covering up was done because the Committee on Art in Public Spaces deemed the carving "not appropriate." The letter, which says the uncovered carving will be moved to where it can be studied and "contextualized," speaks volumes about Yale's context.

DIVERSITY: IN EVERYTHING BUT THOUGHT

October 20, 2016

WASHINGTON—A specter is haunting academia, the specter of specters—ghosts, goblins, and "cultural appropriation" through insensitive Halloween costumes. Institutions of higher education are engaged in the low comedy of avoiding the agonies of Yale.

Last October, the university was rocked to its 315-year-old foundations by the wife of a residential college master (a title subsequently expunged from Yale's vocabulary lest it trigger traumas by reminding people that slavery once existed). In response to a university memorandum urging students to wear culturally sensitive costumes—e.g., no sombreros— she wrote an email saying it should be permissible for young people to be inappropriate, provocative, or even offensive because "the ability to tolerate offense" is a hallmark of "a free and open society."

After the dust settled from this, she and her husband left the residential college. And Yale had trampled in the dust the noble legacy of its 1975 Woodward Report.

Named for the chairman of the committee that produced it, historian C. Vann Woodward, the report was written after Yale's awkward handling of some controversial speakers. Reaffirming freedom of expression's "superior importance to other laudable principles and values," the report said:

> Without sacrificing its central purpose, [a university] cannot make its primary and dominant value the fostering of friendship, solidarity, harmony, civility or mutual respect…It will never let these values, important as they are, override its central purpose.

That purpose, as Hanna Holborn Gray, a former president of the University of Chicago, once said, is not to make young adults comfortable, it is to make them think. Since 1975, however, universities have embraced the doctrine that speech that offends people actually harms them, mentally and even physically. The decision to treat young adults as fragile and perpetually vulnerable to victimization coincided with academia's turn away from the world: Fifty years ago, student assertiveness concerned momentous issues of war and civil rights. Today, students have macro-tantrums about micro-aggressions (e.g., sombreros). Time was, students rebelled against universities acting *in loco parentis*. Today, they welcome having their sexual and other social interactions minutely subjected to government regulations administered by Pecksniffs with PhDs.

Fortunately, the *Chronicle of Higher Education* reports that some schools are having second thoughts about their "bias response teams" that spring into action when someone says that someone has said something offensive. These schools have noticed the obvious: When such teams elevate campus harmony to the supreme value, they become civility enforcers with a chilling effect on speech.

America's great research universities are ornaments of Western civilization, so their descent into authoritarianism and infantilization matters. Because conservatives are largely absent from faculties, and conservative students are regarded as a rebarbative presence, many conservatives welcome academia's marginalization of itself by behavior that invites ridicule. But universities are squandering the cultural patrimony that conservatism exists to conserve.

And what happens on campuses does not stay on campuses. According to the Pew Research Center, American millennials (ages eighteen to thirty-four), fresh from academia, "are far more likely than older generations to say the government should be able to prevent people from saying offensive statements about minority groups." Forty percent of this cohort think government should be empowered to jettison much constitutional law concerning the First Amendment in order to censor speech offensive to minority groups.

Gerard Alexander, a University of Virginia political scientist, argues in *National Affairs* quarterly that a university's "permanent population," the faculty, is secure in the tenure system and maintains its monochrome intellectual culture by hiring from a PhD pipeline that young conservatives are understandably reluctant to enter. He could have added that faculties' ideological tendencies are reinforced by peer review of publications.

"Schools," Alexander notes, "have applied millions of hours of work to the priority of improving racial, ethnic and gender diversity. Viewpoint diversity could be elevated to similar prominence and urgency." This would improve scholarship, especially in the humanities and social sciences. Their research concerns economic behavior, the meaning and importance of classic literature, which social problems matter most and the evidence about ways of addressing them, how to evaluate different ethical positions and legal systems, and which aspects of history most merit study. Viewpoint diversity in faculties would, Alexander argues, at least pit one scholar's susceptibility to "confirmation bias"—the tendency to seek, and be receptive to, evidence that buttresses one's beliefs—against another's different bias.

Academia just now needs a reminder akin to Florence Nightingale's terse axiom that whatever else hospitals might do, they should not spread disease. Universities, as the word suggests, have many missions, but becoming safe spaces for faculty and student juvenility is not among them.

MANDATORY POLITICAL PARTICIPATION IN CALIFORNIA

March 12, 2020

WASHINGTON—The Free Speech Movement, an early tremor of the earthquake that shook campuses in the 1960s, began on Sproul Plaza at the University of California at Berkeley, in 1964. Today eight of the ten universities in the UC system are administering faculty hiring practices that involve coerced speech, enforced political conformity, and mandatory political participation.

Any academic seeking a position is required to write a "diversity, equity and inclusion" (DEI) statement affirming support—sometimes even "enthusiastic" support—for, and demonstrating activism in support of, a system-wide orthodoxy. In the required statement ("Demonstrating Interest in and Ability to Advance Diversity, Equity, and Inclusion"), an applicant should show that he or she has been active, and must promise to be active, in advancing the approved agenda. This process explicitly subordinates assessments of academic excellence.

Abigail Thompson, chair of the mathematics department at UC Davis, praises diversity (without explaining how ethnic, racial, and gender diversity improves teaching and research in mathematics). But she thinks mandatory DEI statements have a problematic pedigree.

In 1949, during the Cold War anxiety about communist subversion, Robert Sproul, president of the UC system, proposed that university employees sign an oath attesting that they were not members of the Communist Party or other organizations advocating violent revolution. Protests, litigation, and the firing of some non-signers ensued. Then fears of domestic communists abated, and a court ended the oath in 1967. The UC system subsequently adopted this policy: "No political test shall ever be considered in the appointment and promotion of any faculty member or employee."

Today, however, DEI statements are political litmus tests used in a baroque three-stage, five-point scoring system that winnows out applicants—sometimes most of them—*before* considering the applicants' academic qualifications. For example, eight departments in Berkeley's life sciences recently applied the DEI "rubric" in sorting through 893 eligible applicants.

First—yes, first—they were evaluated *solely* on "contributions" to diversity, equity, and inclusion. This involved assessing, among much else, candidates' "comfort" in talking about those matters. Only 214 candidates who scored well in the diversity enthusiasm sweepstakes were then evaluated as scholars.

Most of the 679 who were immediately flunked received insufficient grades—only one or two points on the category "knowledge about" DEI (e.g., insufficient discussion of "gender or ethnicity/race") or three ("strong understanding of challenges" but "little understanding of demographic data"). Most survivors scored four or five on "comfort" and enthusiasm discussing the DEI agenda.

The second test concerned demonstrating a "track record in advancing" DEI. Those who fell at this hurdle perhaps showed only "limited participation at the periphery" of officially approved activities. The third test concerned "plans for advancing" DEI. Those who failed here might have been judged "vague" about the required political "activities." The fortunate few who scored four or five, and so survived to have their scholarly credentials considered, presumably professed an impressive intention to strongly advocate the orthodoxy.

When Thompson published in the leading mathematics journal her criticism of mandatory DEI professions of loyalty, a Williams College mathematician, Chad M. Topaz, was enraged by this diversity of thought. He urged a digital mob to inflict on Thompson "some good 'ol [sic] public shame." He profits from the diversity industry: In exchange for "donations," he and associates will critique, and even help write, job candidates' diversity statements. This assistance will be "completely confidential." As befits ghostwritten political enthusiasm.

Because coast-to-coast academic culture is politically homogenized, other universities are adopting identical or similar requirements of "demonstrated commitments" to this and that, including "outreach," which presumably means something to those who speak academia's patois. Opaque language cannot, however, disguise that this is all politics.

Politics is how we organize our ideas and practices for living together. The defining characteristic of totalitarian societies is not that the individual cannot participate in politics, but that the individual cannot not participate. In such societies, politics permeates everything: Government's aim is the conquest of consciousness, and abstention from politics is subversive. Hence DEI pledges.

The Hoover Institution's John Cochrane, blogging as the Grumpy Economist, has publicized UC's practices, which he expects will become more onerous and invidious because universities continue hiring large numbers of diversity enforcers whose profession is to banish the classical liberal principle that every person should be treated as a unique individual. This banishment is a political project abetted by DEI statements, which are political tests. That they violate UC's stated policy prohibiting political tests means that the policy actually is: "Only progressive political tests shall be considered in appointments."

"SUSTAINABILITY" AS THEOLOGY

April 16, 2015

WASHINGTON—Syracuse University alumni are new additions to the lengthening list of persons who can stop contributing to their alma maters. The university has succumbed—after, one suspects, not much agonizing—to the temptation to indulge in progressive gestures. It will divest all fossil fuel stocks from its endowment. It thereby trumps Stanford, whose halfhearted exercise in right-mindedness has been to divest only coal stocks. Evidently carbon from coal is more morally disquieting than carbon from petroleum.

The effect of these decisions on consumption of fossil fuels will be nil; the effect on the growth of institutions' endowments will be negative. The effect on alumni giving should be substantial, because divesting institutions are proclaiming that the goal of expanding educational resources is less important than the striking of righteous poses—if there can be anything righteous about flamboyant futility.

The divestment movement is a manifestation of a larger phenomenon, academia's embrace of "sustainability," a development explored in "Sustainability: Higher Education's New Fundamentalism" from the National Association of Scholars (NAS). The word "fundamentalism" is appropriate, for five reasons:

Like many religions' premises, the sustainability movement's premises are more assumed than demonstrated. Second, weighing the costs of obedience to sustainability's commandments is considered unworthy. Third, the sustainability crusade supplies acolytes with a worldview that infuses their lives with purpose and meaning. Fourth, the sustainability movement uses apocalyptic rhetoric to express its eschatology. Fifth, the church of sustainability seeks converts, encourages conformity to orthodoxy, and regards rival interpretations of reality as heretical impediments to salvation.

Some subscribers to the sustainability catechism are sincerely puzzled by the accusation that it is political correctness repackaged. They see it as indisputable because it is undisputed; it is obvious, elementary, even banal. Actually, however, the term "sustainable" postulates fragility and scarcity that entail government planners and rationers to fend off planetary calamity while administering equity. The unvarying progressive agenda is for government to supplant markets in allocating wealth and opportunity. "Sustainability" swaddles this agenda in "science," as progressives understand this—"settled" findings that would be grim if they did not mandate progressivism.

Orthodoxy was enshrined in the 2006 "American College and University Presidents' Climate Commitment." Since then, the NAS study concludes, "the campus sustainability movement has gone from a minor thread of campus activism to becoming the master narrative of what 'liberal education' should seek to accomplish." Government subsidizes the orthodoxy: The Environmental Protection Agency alone has spent more than $333 million on sustainability fellowships and grants. Anticapitalism is explicit: Markets "privilege" individuals over communities. Indoctrination is relentless: Cornell has 403 sustainability courses (e.g., "The Ethics of Eating"). Sustainability pledges are common. The University of Virginia's is: "I pledge to consider the social, economic and environmental impacts of my habits and to explore ways to foster a sustainable environment during my time here at U.Va. and beyond."

Sustainability, as a doctrine of total social explanation, transforms all ills and grievances into environmental causes, cloaked in convenient science, as with: Climate change causes prostitution (warming increases poverty, which increases…). Or the "environmental racism" of the supposed warming that supposedly caused hurricane Katrina, which disproportionately impacted New Orleans blacks.

The same sort of people—sometimes the same people—who once predicted catastrophe from the exhaustion of fossil fuels now predict catastrophe because of a surfeit of such fuels. Former U.S. Senator Tim Wirth of Colorado, divestment enthusiast and possessor of astonishing knowledge, says: If we burn all known fossil fuels, we will make the planet uninhabitable, so, "Why should any rational institution invest in further exploration and development when we already have at least three times more than we can ever use?"

There is a social benefit from the sustainability mania: the further marginalization of academia. It prevents colleges and universities from trading on what they are rapidly forfeiting, their reputations for seriousness.

The divestment impulse recognizes no limiting principle. As it works its way through progressivism's thicket of moral imperatives—shedding investments tainted by involvement with Israel, firearms, tobacco, red meat, irrigation-dependent agriculture, etc.—progressivism's dream of ever-more-minute regulation of life is realized, but only in campus cocoons.

College tuitions are soaring in tandem with thickening layers of administrative bloat. So here is a proposal: Hundreds of millions could be saved, with no cost to any institution's core educational mission, by eliminating every position whose title contains the word "sustainability"—and, while we are at it, "diversity," "multicultural," or "inclusivity." The result would be higher education higher than the propaganda-saturated version we have, and more sustainable.

THE CONSEQUENCES OF ACADEMIA'S KUDZU-LIKE BUREAUCRACIES

September 13, 2018

WASHINGTON—The beginning of another academic year brings the certainty of campus episodes illustrating what Daniel Patrick Moynihan, distinguished professor and venerated politician, called "the leakage of reality from American life." Colleges and universities are increasingly susceptible to intellectual fads and political hysteria, partly because the institutions employ so many people whose talents, such as they are, are extraneous to the institutions' core mission: scholarship.

Writing last April in the *Chronicle of Higher Education*, Lyell Asher, professor of English at Lewis & Clark College, noted that "the kudzu-like growth of the administrative bureaucracy in higher education" is partly a response to two principles now widely accepted on campuses: Anything that can be construed as bigotry and hatred should be so construed, and anything construed as such should be considered evidence of an epidemic. Often, Asher noted, a majority of the academic bureaucrats directly involved with students, from dorms to "bias response teams" to freshman "orientation" (which often means political indoctrination), have graduate degrees not in academic disciplines but from education schools with "two mutually reinforcing characteristics": ideological orthodoxy and low academic standards for degrees in vaporous subjects like "educational leadership" or "higher-education management."

The problem is not anti-intellectualism but the "un-intellectualism" of a growing cohort of persons who, lacking talents for or training in scholarship, find vocations in micromanaging student behavior in order to combat imagined threats to "social justice." Can *anyone* on a campus say *anything* sensible about how the adjective modifies the noun? Never mind. As Asher said, groupthink and political intimidation inevitably result from this ever-thickening layer of people with status anxieties because they are parasitic off institutions with scholarly purposes.

The Manhattan Institute's Heather Mac Donald says that between the 1997–1998 academic year and the Great Recession year of 2008–2009, while the University of California student population grew 33 percent and tenure-track faculty grew 25 percent, senior administrators grew 125 percent. "The ratio of senior managers to professors climbed from 1 to 2.1 to near-parity of 1 to 1.1."

In her just-published book *The Diversity Delusion: How Race and Gender Pandering Corrupt the University and Undermine Our Culture*, Mac Donald writes that many students have become what tort law practitioners call "eggshell plaintiffs," people who make a cult of fragility— being "triggered" (i.e., traumatized) by this or that idea of speech. Asher correctly noted that the language of triggering "converts students into objects for the sake of rendering their reactions 'objective,' and by extension valid: A student's triggered response is no more to be questioned than an apple's falling downward or a spark's flying upward." So the number of things not to be questioned on campuses multiplies.

Students encouraged to feel fragile will learn to recoil from "micro-aggressions" so micro that few can discern them. A University of California guide to micro-aggressions gave these examples of insensitive speech: "I believe the most qualified person should get the job" and "Everyone can succeed in this society if they work hard enough." Fragile students are encouraged in "narcissistic victimhood" by administrators whose vocation is to tend to the injured. These administrators are, Mac Donald argues, "determined to preserve in many of their students the thin skin and solipsism of adolescence."

Nowadays, radical intellectuals who are eager to be "transgressive" have difficulty finding remaining social rules and boundaries to transgress: When all icons have been smashed, the iconoclast's lot is not a happy one. Similarly, academic administrators whose mission is the elimination of racism have difficulty finding any in colleges and universities whose student admissions and faculty hiring practices are shaped by the relentless pursuit of diversity.

Explicit racism having been substantially reduced in American society, a multi-billion-dollar industry for consultants (and corporate diversity officers, academic deans, etc.: UCLA's vice chancellor for equity, diversity, and inclusion earns more than $400,000) has developed around testing to detect "implicit bias." It is assumed to be ubiquitous until proven otherwise, so detecting it is steady work: Undetectable without arcane tests and expensive experts, you never know when it has been expunged, and government supervision of *everything* must be minute and unending.

And always there is a trickle of peculiar language. The associate vice chancellor and dean of students at the University of California, Berkeley—where the Division of Equity and Inclusion has a staff of 150—urges students to "listen with integrity." If you do not understand the peculiar patois spoken by the academy's administrators, try listening with more integrity.

THE HIGH COST OF OBERLIN'S "CORE VALUES"

June 20, 2019

> "You Americans do not rear children, you *incite* them; you give them food and shelter and applause."
> —Randall Jarrell, *Pictures from an Institution*

WASHINGTON—Oberlin College has an admirable liberal past and a contemptible progressive present that will devalue its degrees far into the future. This is condign punishment for the college's mendacity about helping to incite a mob mentality and collective bullying in response to "racist" behavior that never happened.

Founded in 1833, Oberlin became one of the nation's first colleges to admit African Americans, and its first coeducational liberal arts college. It has, however, long since become a byword for academic self-caricature, where students protest, among many micro-aggressions, the food service's insensitive cultural appropriation of banh mi sandwiches, sushi, and General Tso's chicken. Oberlin could have been Randall Jarrell's model for his fictional Benton College, where people "would have swallowed a porcupine, if you had dyed its quills and called it Modern Art; they longed for men to be discovered on the moon, so that they could show that *they* weren't prejudiced toward moon men."

In November 2016, a clerk in Gibson's Bakery, having seen a black Oberlin student shoplifting bottles of wine, pursued the thief. The thief and two female friends were, according to the police report, kicking and punching the clerk on the ground when the police arrived. Some social justice warriors—they evidently cut class the day critical thinking was taught, if it is taught at Oberlin—instantly accused the bakery of racially profiling the shoplifter, an accusation complicated by the fact that the shoplifter and his partners in assault pleaded guilty.

The warriors mounted a protracted campaign against the bakery's reputation and solvency. But with the cowardice characteristic of bullies, Oberlin claimed in court that it had nothing to do with what its students did when they acted on the progressive righteousness that they imbibe at the school. However, at an anti-bakery protest, according to a complaint filed by the bakery, the dean of students helped distribute fliers, produced on college machines, urging a boycott because "this is a RACIST establishment with a LONG ACCOUNT of RACIAL PROFILING and DISCRIMINATION." (There is no record of any such complaints against the bakery, from which Oberlin bought goods until the hysteria began.) According to court documents, the administration purchased pizza for the protesters and authorized the uses of student funds to buy gloves for protesters. The college also signaled support for the protests by suspending college purchases from the bakery for two months.

A jury in the defamation trial awarded the bakery $11 million from Oberlin, and $33 million more in punitive damages. The $44 million probably will be reduced because, under Ohio law, punitive damages cannot exceed double the amount of compensatory damages.

The combination of malice and mendacity precluded a free-speech defense, and the jury accepted the obvious: The college's supposed adults were complicit in this protracted smear. Such complicity is a familiar phenomenon.

As Stuart Taylor and K. C. Johnson demonstrated in their meticulous 2007 book *Until Proven Innocent: Political Correctness and the Shameful Injustices of the Duke Lacrosse Rape Case,* Duke's administration and a large swath of the faculty incited hysteria against a few young men accused of a rape that never happened. The University of Virginia's administration similarly rushed to indignant judgment in response to a facially preposterous magazine story about another fictitious rape.

The shoplifting incident occurred the day after the 2016 presidential election, which Oberlin's president and dean of students partially blamed for students' "pain and sadness" and "fears and concerns" during the "difficult few days" after the "events" at the bakery. From Oberlin's despisers of Donald Trump, the events elicited lies and, in effect, cries of "fake news," the brazenness of which the master in the White House might admire. Oberlin alumni who are exhorted to contribute to this college, which has been made stupid and mendacious by politics, should ponder where at least $22 million is going.

Continuing to do what it denies ever doing—siding against the bakery—Oberlin, in impeccable progressive-speak, accuses the bakery of an "archaic chase-and-detain" policy regarding shoplifters and insists that "the guilt or innocence of the students is irrelevant" to the—of course—"root cause" of the protests against the bakery.

Oberlin's president defiantly says "none of this will sway us from our core values." Those values—moral arrogance, ideology-induced prejudgments, indifference to evidence—are, to continue using the progressive patois, the root causes of Oberlin's descent beyond caricature and into disgrace.

ACADEMIC SUPPLY MEETS DIMINISHING DEMAND

November 14, 2019

WASHINGTON—With another academic year churning on, many people, bemused by campus excitements—trigger warnings, safe spaces, "bias response teams" in hot pursuit of the perpetrators of micro-aggressions—wonder whether higher education has become a net subtraction from the nation's stock of reasonableness. Those who read the *Chronicle of Higher Education*, a window into that world, are not reassured.

In May, the *Chronicle* published a dyspeptic report by Andrew Kay, a Wisconsin writer, on this year's meeting of the Modern Language Association, whose members teach literature to a declining number of interested students: Kay says the number of English positions on the MLA job list has shrunk 55 percent since 2008, the number of University of Michigan English majors declined from 1,000 to 200 in eight years, and adjunct (limited-term, non-tenure track) instructors now are a majority of college teachers. Kay's villains are "the avarice of universities" and "politicians and pundits" who despise "humanistic thinking, which plainly threatens them." His disparagements implicitly enlarge and celebrate him as a threat to the villains.

He is nostalgic for the 1960s and 1970s, which "brought literary-critical methods to bear on every aspect of culture, from sexuality to disability." He is impervious to the possibility that his mentality, stocked with stereotypes and luxuriating in victimhood, might be a symptom of what repels students who care about actual literature more than "literary-critical" approaches to this and that.

Also in the *Chronicle* in May, Daniel Bessner of the University of Washington and Michael Brenes of Yale deplore without defining "the neoliberalization of the university system." The definition presumably is obvious to all inhabitants of the academic bubble, where "neoliberals" are disdained as respecters of market forces—supply, demand, etc. Citing a 1972 *New York Times* report on "an oversupply of trained historians," they say "for nearly a half-century, historians have failed to organize to halt the disappearance of positions," which they blame on "unnecessary neoliberal austerity, corporatization, and adjunctification" and "boot-strappism and market-Darwinism."

Their jumble of jargon means: The fact that the supply of historians has outpaced the demand for history instruction is the fault of many things, but not of academic historians, who need to show "solidarity" to "overturn a patently unjust system" that offers "crummy and exploit-ative" jobs. Their message is clear: History doctorates are entitled to good academic positions regardless of the absence of a demand for their services. So perhaps the American Historical Association (and the MLA, the American Political Science Association, etc.) should wield its "labor power" by threatening to strike. It is a plan only academics could concoct: Because there is weak and declining demand for our labor, we should coerce our adversaries (neoliberals, market-Darwinism, the law of supply and demand) by threatening to withdraw our labor.

In the *Chronicle* in March, the University of Washington's Bessner said we are in a "crisis of capitalism," by which he seemed to mean a shortage of jobs for people like him: left-wing academics. "Given that there are almost no tenure-track jobs, the majority of the next generation of intellectuals—like my own generation—will probably have to look outside the university for employment." To him, "intellectuals" denotes left-wing aspiring academics. Again, note the absence of self-examination, and the disregard of the possibility that there are fewer teaching jobs because fewer students are drawn to the study of literature, history, and the rest of the humanities because of the way these subjects are taught.

This is a trans-Atlantic problem. The author of the *Economist*'s Bagehot column notes that although the study of history—and eminent historians—"used to hold a central position in [Britain's] national life," the number of history students has declined 10 percent in a decade. Perhaps because "the historical profession has turned in on itself," with practitioners turning away from "great matters of state" and concentrat-ing on "the marginal rather than the powerful, the poor rather than the rich, everyday life rather than Parliament." They "almost seem to be engaged in a race to discover the most marginalized subject imaginable." This reduces history's helpfulness as "a safeguard against myopia. Modernity shrinks time as well as space; people live in an eternal present of short-term stimuli and instant gratification."

Americans have a voracious appetite for serious historical writing—note the robust demand for narratives and biographies by David McCullough, Ron Chernow, Rick Atkinson, Nathaniel Philbrick, Rick Brookhiser, and many others who are not academics, who do not write about marginal subjects, and who do not tell the nation's story as a tale of embarrassments.

TAXING INDEPENDENT EXCELLENCE

November 9, 2017

WASHINGTON—Such is the federal government's sprawl, and its power to establish new governing precedents, mere Washington twitches can jeopardize venerable principles and institutions. This is illustrated by a seemingly small but actually momentous provision of the Republicans' tax bill—a 1.4 percent excise tax on the endowment earnings of approximately seventy colleges and universities with the largest per-student endowments. To raise less than $3 billion in a decade—less than 0.005 percent of projected federal spending of $53 trillion—Republicans would blur important distinctions and abandon their defining mission.

Private foundations, which are generally run by small coteries, pay a "supervisory tax" on investment income to defray the cost of IRS oversight to guarantee that their resources are used for charitable purposes. In 1984, however, Congress created a new entity, an "operating foundation." Such organizations—e.g., often museums or libraries—are exempt from the tax on investment earnings because they apply their assets directly to their charitable activities rather than making grants to other organizations, as do foundations that therefore must pay the supervisory tax.

Most university endowments are compounds of thousands of individual funds that often are restricted to particular uses, all of which further the institutions' educational purposes. Hence these endowments are akin to the untaxed "operating foundations." Yet the Republicans, without public deliberations, and without offering reasons, would arbitrarily make university endowments uniquely subject to a tax not applied to similar entities.

Are Republicans aware, for example, that Princeton's endowment earnings fund more than half its annual budget, and will support expansion of the student body? It also enables "need-blind" admissions: More than 60 percent of undergraduates receive financial assistance; those from families with incomes below $65,000 pay no tuition, room, or board; those from families with incomes below $160,000 pay no tuition. No loans are required. PhD candidates receive tuition and a stipend for living costs. Furthermore, the endowment has funded a significant increase in students from low-income families: Princeton has recently tripled to 22 percent the portion of freshmen from families with the most substantial financial needs. The idea that Princeton is largely populated by children of alumni is a canard slain by this fact: Such "legacies" are only 13 percent of this year's freshman class.

For eight centuries, surviving thickets of ecclesiastical and political interferences, the world's great research universities have enabled the liberal arts to flourish, the sciences to advance, and innovation to propel economic betterment. Increasingly, they foster upward mobility that fulfills democratic aspirations and combats the stagnation of elites. It is astonishingly shortsighted to jeopardize all this, and it is unseemly to do so in a scramble for resources to make a tax bill conform to the transitory arithmetic of a budget process that is a labyrinth of trickery.

Great universities are great because philanthropic generations have borne the cost of sustaining private institutions that seed the nation with excellence. Donors have done this in the expectation that earnings accruing from their investments will be devoted solely to educational purposes, in perpetuity. This expectation will disappear, and the generosity that it has sustained will diminish, if Republicans siphon away a portion of endowments' earnings in order to fund the federal government's general operations.

Its appetite whetted by 1.4 percent, the political class will not stop there. Once the understanding that until now has protected endowments is shredded, there will be no limiting principle to constrain governments—those of the states, too—in their unsleeping search for revenues to expand their power. Public appetites are limitless, as is the political class's desire to satisfy them. Hence there is a perennial danger that democracy will degenerate into looting—scrounging for resources, such as universities' endowments, that are part of society's seed corn for prosperous tomorrows.

Government having long ago slipped the leash of restraint, the public sector's sprawl threatens to enfeeble the private institutions of civil society that mediate between the individual and the state and that leaven society with energy and creativity that government cannot supply. Time was, conservatism's central argument for limiting government was to defend these institutions from being starved of resources and functions by government. Abandonment of this argument is apparent in the vandalism that Republicans are mounting against universities' endowments.

This raid against little platoons of independent excellence would be unsurprising were it proposed by progressives, who are ever eager to extend government's reach and to break private institutions to the state's saddle. Coming from Republicans, it is acutely discouraging.

HARVARD'S PROBLEM IS AMERICA'S, TOO

November 15, 2018

WASHINGTON—In the hierarchy of pleasures, schadenfreude ranks second only to dry martinis at dusk, so conservatives are enjoying

Harvard's entanglement with two things it has not sufficiently questioned—regulatory government and progressive sentiment. The trial that recently ended in Boston—the judge's ruling might be months away, and reach the U.S. Supreme Court—concerns whether Harvard's admissions policy regarding Asian Americans is unjust, and whether the government should respond.

Practically, the case pertains only to the few highly selective institutions that admit small portions of their applicants. But everyone, and especially conservatives, should think twice—or at least once—before hoping that government will minutely supervise how private institutions shape their student bodies.

The clearest thing about the relevant law is the absence of clear guidance. Since 1978, the Supreme Court has said that "a diverse student body" is a "constitutionally permissible goal" and a "compelling" educational interest that can be pursued using racial classifications if they are "narrowly tailored" to achieve a "critical mass" of this or that minority without "quotas" and if they do "not *unduly* harm members of any racial group" and are no more than a "'plus' factor" in a "holistic" assessment of applicants. "Distinctions between citizens *solely* because of their ancestry are by their very nature odious," and "*outright* racial balancing…is patently unconstitutional." (Emphases added.) Such open-textured language, deployed in the pursuit of "diversity" (of cultures, perspectives, experiences, etc.), leaves vast scope for practices to engineer various student bodies.

Schools should go beyond "objective" metrics—secondary school transcripts and SAT scores—because they measure only what can be quantified, which is not all that matters about individuals. Then, however, schools adopt "holistic" assessments of individual applicants. It probably is impossible for schools or government to devise rules-based assessments that tightly limit the discretion that admissions offices exercise, given the unavoidable imprecision of the open-textured legal language quoted above. And given the needs of schools' subgroups—the orchestra, the athletic teams, the classics department, etc.

Harvard's practices, say the plaintiffs, who include some aggrieved Asian Americans, constitute racial discrimination that has the intended effect of suppressing admissions of people like them: Asian-American applicants are rejected in spite of objective academic attainments that would result in admissions for African Americans, Hispanics, or whites. So, when Harvard's president is "unequivocal" that his institution "does not discriminate against anybody" in admissions, this looks like hypocrisy, understood as the tribute that vice pays to virtue.

Except that progressives and their institutions long since stopped believing that colorblind policies are virtuous. And regarding admissions, they might have a point.

Stuart Taylor, a legal analyst as temperate as he is accomplished, argues that racial preferences can ratify stereotypes when "holistic" evaluations emphasize personality traits that are supposed group attributes. There really are, however, attributes that are disproportionately prevalent among various groups at various times. Families are the primary transmitters of social capital—the habits and mores conducive to flourishing—and family cultures that produce applicants with stellar objective academic attainments should be encouraged. However, relying exclusively on objective academic metrics (Taylor notes that only Caltech does this; its student body is more than 40 percent Asian) would substantially reduce the number of blacks and Hispanics admitted. Harvard's own conclusion, in a document presented in the trial, is that admissions based solely on academic metrics would result in a student body that is 43 percent Asian-American and less than 1 percent African-American.

Eight decades ago, Harvard put itself and the nation on the path toward one understanding of meritocracy by emphasizing in admissions the Scholastic Aptitude Test. This was done partly to reduce discrimination against Jewish applicants from family cultures that stressed academic attainments, and partly to dilute favoritism toward the inherited privileges of wealthy families funneling boys through prestigious prep schools.

Harvard's problem today is a version of America's, the tension between two problematic approaches to providing opportunities—"meritocracy" that is clearly but too simply quantified, and a less tidy but more nuanced measurement of the mixture of merits that serves a university's, and society's, several purposes. The optimum result of the court case might already be occurring in voluntary, prudential adjustments of elite university practices to forestall government interventions that would serve shifting agendas of various constituencies. The adjustments would include admissions policies more welcoming to academic excellence regardless of other attributes of those who manifest it, and more sensitivity regarding the felt injustices that inevitably accompany admission disparities produced by preferences, however benignly intended.

ABOUT HARVARD: THREE HARD QUESTIONS

October 10, 2019

WASHINGTON—The judge took 130 pages to explain that Harvard's "holistic review" admissions policies—which include ascribing particular attributes to certain ethnicities, such as Asian Americans, and assessing the value to Harvard of those attributes—are, considering forty-one years of Supreme Court precedents, permissibly race-conscious. She said the policies do not discriminate against Asian Americans.

However, the suit some Asian Americans filed against Harvard correctly cited evidence from Harvard that more objective admissions policies than Harvard's would admit many more Asian Americans. What a tangled web we weave when we deceive ourselves into thinking that we can favor some groups without disfavoring others, or disfavor some without acting on the basis of stereotypes. But before disparaging Harvard's attempts to shape its student body, and before judging the judge's opinion, consider three facts:

First, Harvard admitted just 4.5 percent of the 43,330 applicants to this year's freshman class of 1,650, so it needs some sorting metrics (to serve the institution as a whole and many subconstituencies, from the athletic department to alumni relations). Second, if Harvard were to admit every applicant with a perfect grade-point average, it would increase the size of its entering class *400 percent*. Third, a Harvard document presented in the trial estimated that relying exclusively on objective academic measurements—secondary school transcripts and SAT scores—would produce a Harvard student body 43 percent Asian-American and 1 percent African-American. (Caltech, which relies much more heavily on those than other highly selective institutions, enrolled a 2018 freshman class that was 40 percent Asian.)

Now, three questions. Would you be comfortable with a legal requirement that only such objective metrics be used in college admissions? If that were required, would Harvard have to choose by lottery the 25 percent of the "perfect GPAs" to admit? Would you be comfortable with the nation's most elite institutions—very few schools are selective enough to be able to curate their student bodies for whatever diversity is desired—looking so little like the nation?

Before the discomforting reality of racial preferences was blurred by the anodyne phrase "affirmative action," the 1976 Democratic platform spoke of "compensatory opportunity," thereby presenting race-conscious policies as remediation for past social injuries. But the Supreme Court's 1978 Bakke decision, the first concerning higher education admissions, authorized schools to consider race as a small "plus" factor in admissions in order to achieve "diversity." So, "race-conscious remedies" were not to be remedial. Or of finite duration. They would be forever, for the benefit of the privileged—those admitted to, and who administer, colleges and universities.

In this fifth decade of judicial tinkering, with the Harvard case probably heading to the Supreme Court, it is clear that the admissions departments of highly selective universities will devise metrics compatible with porous judicial language in order to shape student bodies to serve what they consider institutional needs. Courts can try to confine admissions departments with porous terms like minor "plus-factors" that are "narrowly tailored" to achieve a "critical mass" of this or that minority without "unduly" harming any group. But those departments will resort to cynical evasions.

Taking race "into account" could just as well be called taking into account cultures (of communities or ethnic cohorts). Some attributes, including those conducive to academic excellence, *are* disproportionately prevalent among various groups (e.g., Asian Americans, Jews at various times).

So, a fourth question: If universities do not consciously shape their student bodies, who will? The U.S. Education Department, with criteria as variable as the nation's election results?

America's great universities, having become playthings of progressives, are now targeted by populists. Two years ago, the Republican tax bill targeted elite schools with the largest per-student endowments. This tax raises a pittance but scratches a populist itch—resentment of excellence. Last month, a Republican administration's Education Department threatened to withdraw federal funding from a joint Duke University and University of North Carolina Middle East studies program because it lacks viewpoint—wait for it—diversity. And reflects hostility to Israel, is insufficiently "positive" about Christianity and Judaism, and is saturated with extraneous progressive propaganda. These charges, and accusations of anti-Semitism, are entirely plausible, but are conservatives, supposed proponents of modest government, comfortable with bureaucrats dictating the contents of college courses?

The uninhibited District Court judge in the Harvard case, who suggested Harvard admissions officers be trained against "implicit bias," asserted that student-body diversity fosters "tolerance, acceptance and understanding." So, consider a fifth question: Is it a mere coincidence that academia's obsession with diversity has coincided with a tsunami of campus intolerance and hysteria?

THE SAT AND THE PRIVILEGE, IF SUCH IT IS, OF TRANSMITTED ADVANTAGES

January 11, 2018

WASHINGTON—During World War I, chemist James Conant was deeply involved in research on what was considered the worst imaginable weapon: poison gas. During World War II, as a science adviser to President Franklin Roosevelt, Conant was so central to the development of the atomic bomb that he was at Alamogordo on July 16, 1945. His most disruptive act, however, may have come in the interim when, as Harvard's president, he helped put the university, and the nation, on the path toward a meritocracy by advocating adoption of the Scholastic Aptitude Test.

As his granddaughter Jennet Conant explains in her new biography, *Man of the Hour: James B. Conant, Warrior Scientist*, the Harvard at which he, from a middle-class Dorchester family, matriculated in 1910 was a place of insufferable snobbery and mediocrity, devoted to passing on the inherited privileges of the families whose boys were funneled there from prestigious prep schools. To the consternation of Boston's Brahmins, Conant became Harvard's president in 1933 at age forty, hoping that standardized tests for admissions would mitigate the large degree to which enrollments at elite institutions reflected the transmission of family advantages. Ninety-two years after the SAT was first offered in 1926, it seems to have only slightly modified the advantages transmitted.

The Brookings Institution's Richard V. Reeves, writing in the *Chronicle of Higher Education's Review*, says that colleges and universities, partly because of the complexity of the admission process, are "perpetuating class divisions across generations" as America develops what the *Economist* calls a "hereditary meritocracy." It is, however, difficult to see how something like this can be avoided. Or why it should be.

Also in the *Review*, Wilfred M. McClay of the University of Oklahoma decries higher education's "dysfunctional devotion to meritocracy," which he says is subverting the ideal that one's life prospects should not be substantially predictable from facts about one's family. Meritocracy, "while highly democratic in its intentions, has turned out to be colossally undemocratic in its results" because of "the steep decline of opportunity for those Americans who must live outside the magic circle of meritocratic validation." Entrance into that circle often is substantially determined by higher education, especially at elite institutions. At two premier public universities, the University of Michigan and the University of Virginia, the percentages of students from the bottom 60 percent of households ranked by earnings (17 and 15 percent, respectively) are comparable to the percentages at Yale and Princeton (16 and 14, respectively).

In *A Theory of Justice*, the twentieth century's most influential American treatise on political philosophy, John Rawls argued that "inequalities of birth and natural endowment are undeserved." So, social benefits accruing to individuals because of such endowments are justified only if the prospering of the fortunate also improves the lot of the less fortunate. And Rawls's capacious conception of what counts as a "natural" endowment included advantages resulting from nurturing families. But as sociologist Daniel Bell warned in 1972, "There can never be a pure meritocracy because high-status parents will invariably seek to pass on their positions, either through the use of influence or simply by the cultural advantages their children inevitably possess."

Actually, the cultural advantages are so salient that the importance of crass influence is diminishing. Furthermore, to the extent that a meritocratic society measures and rewards intelligence, which is to some extent a genetic inheritance, equal opportunity becomes difficult even to define.

A meritocratic assignment of opportunity by impersonal processes and measurements might seem democratic but it can feel ruthless and can be embittering: By using ostensibly objective standards to give individuals momentum toward places high in society's inevitable hierarchies, those who do not flourish are *scientifically* stigmatized.

And as the acquisition and manipulation of information become increasingly important to social flourishing, life becomes more regressive: The benefits of information accrue disproportionately to those who are already favored by aptitudes, both natural and acquired through family nurturing and education. Add "assortative mating"—well-educated and upwardly mobile strivers marrying each other—and society's cognitive stratification reinforces itself.

Something, however, has to sort people out, and we actually want the gifted and accomplished to ascend to positions that give scope to their talents. Furthermore, we do not want to discourage families from trying to transmit advantages to their children. The challenge is to ameliorate meritocracy's severity by, among other things, nuanced admissions policies at colleges and universities that seek students whose meager family advantages can be supplemented by the schools.

MERITOCRACY AND THE SAT'S
"ADVERSITY INDEX"

June 9, 2019

WASHINGTON—The earnest improvers at the College Board, which administers the SAT, should ponder Abraham Maslow's law of the instrument. In 1966, Maslow, a psychologist, said essentially this: If the only tool you have is a hammer, every problem looks like a nail. The College Board wants to solve a complex social problem that it and its test are unsuited to solve.

The College Board has embraced a dubious idea that might have the beneficial effect of prompting college admissions officers to think of better ideas for broadening their pool of applicants. The idea is to add to the scores of some test-takers an "environmental context" bonus. Strangely, board president David Coleman told the *Wall Street Journal*'s Daniel Henninger that this is not, as the media has named it, an "adversity index." But it is: It purports to measure fifteen factors (e.g., poverty or food-stamp eligibility, crime rates, disorderly schools, broken families, families with education deficits, etc.) where these test-takers are situated. Coleman more convincingly says to the *New York Times*: "This is about finding young people who do a great deal with what they've been given."

Perhaps the board's evident discomfort with the label "adversity score" is because their more benign-sounding "environmental context" gives a social-science patina to the obverse of a category (and political accusation) currently in vogue, that of "privilege." By whatever name, however, the SAT's new metric is another step down the path of identity politics, assigning applicants to groups and categories, and another step away from evaluating individuals individually. But if the adversity metric becomes a substitute for schools emphasizing race, this will be an improvement on explicit racial categories that become implicit quotas.

343

The SAT was created partly to solve the problem of inequitable standards in college admissions. They too often rewarded nonacademic attributes (e.g., "legacies"—the children of alumni). And they facilitated the intergenerational transmission of inherited privileges. Most importantly, they were used to disfavor certain groups, particularly Jews.

By making an objective—meaning standardized—test one component of schools' assessments of applicants, it advanced the American ideal of a meritocracy open to all talents. However, it has always been the schools' prerogative to decide the importance of the SAT component relative to others. And as "diversity" (understood in various ways) becomes an increasing preoccupation of schools, the SAT becomes decreasingly important.

Any adversity index derived from this or that social "context," however refined, will be an extremely crude instrument for measuring—guessing, actually—the academic prospects of individuals in those contexts. It might, however, be a good gauge of character. Physicists speak of the "escape velocity" of particles circling in an orbit. Perhaps the adversity index can indicate individuals who, by their resilience, have achieved velocity out of challenging social environments.

But the SAT is a flimsy tool for shaping the world of social inertia. Articulate, confident parents from the professions will transmit cultural advantages to their children, advantages that, as the SAT will record them, are apt to dwarf "adversity" bonuses. As Andrew Ferguson, author of the grimly hilarious *Crazy U: One Dad's Crash Course in Getting His Kid into College*, says, America's least diverse classes are SAT prep classes.

The *Chicago Tribune* warns, plausibly, that the "secret-sauce" of the SAT's adversity score—schools will know it, applicants will not—will "breed more public mistrust" of colleges' admissions processes. But calling, as the *Tribune* does, for more "transparency" implies that the more admissions criteria are made public, the better. However, private deliberations and criteria about applicants protect the applicants' privacy interests. Furthermore, asserting a public interest in maximum transparency encourages government supervision of—and the inevitable shrinking of—schools' discretion in shaping their student bodies, and ensuring that some cohorts are not largely excluded.

Unquestionably, such discretion often is employed in unsavory ways to serve academia's fluctuating "diversity" obsessions, some of which contravene common understandings of equity and perhaps civil rights laws and norms. Soon a Boston court will render a decision, probably destined for Supreme Court review, in the case concerning Harvard's "holistic" metrics, beyond "objective" ones (secondary school transcripts, standardized tests), for—it is alleged—the purpose of restricting the admission of Asian Americans. They, like the Jews whose academic proficiency was a "problem" eight decades ago, often come from family cultures that stress academic attainments.

Caution, however, is in order. Further breaking higher education to the saddle of the state is an imprudent (and, which is much the same thing, unconservative) objective.

THE SURPLUS OF INTELLECTUAL EMPTINESS

January 29, 2017

WASHINGTON—In 2013, a college student assigned to research a deadly substance sought help via Twitter: "I can't find the chemical and physical properties of sarin gas someone please help me." An expert at a security consulting firm tried to be helpful, telling her that sarin is not gas. She replied, "yes the [expletive] it is a gas you ignorant [expletive]. sarin is a liquid & can evaporate…shut the [expletive] up."

Tom Nichols, professor at the U.S. Naval War College and the Harvard Extension School, writing in the *Chronicle Review*, says such a "storm of outraged ego" is an increasingly common phenomenon among students who, having been taught to regard themselves as peers of their teachers, "take correction as an insult." Nichols relates this to myriad intellectual viruses thriving in academia. Carried by undereducated graduates, these viruses infect the nation's civic culture.

Soon the results include the presidential megaphone being used to amplify facially preposterous assertions, e.g., that upward of 5 million illegal votes were cast in 2016. A presidential minion thinks this assertion is justified because it is the president's "long-standing belief."

"College, in an earlier time," Nichols writes, "was supposed to be an uncomfortable experience because growth is always a challenge," replacing youthful simplicities with adult complexities. Today, college involves the "pampering of students as customers," particularly by grade inflation in a context of declining academic rigor: A recent study showed "A" to be the most commonly awarded grade, 30 percent more frequent than in 1960. And a 2011 University of Chicago study found that 45 percent of students said that in the previous semester none of their courses required more than twenty pages of writing, and 32 percent had no class that required more than forty pages of reading in a week.

"Unearned praise and hollow successes," Nichols says, "build a fragile arrogance in students that can lead them to lash out at the first teacher or employer who dispels that illusion, a habit that carries over into a resistance to believe anything inconvenient or challenging in adulthood." A habit no doubt intensified when adults in high places speak breezily of "alternative facts."

"Rather than disabuse students of their intellectual solipsism," Nichols says, "the modern university reinforces it," producing students given to "taking offense at everything while believing anything." Many colleges and universities, competing for tuition dollars "too often drawn thoughtlessly from an inexhaustible well of loans," market a "college experience" rather than an education. The experience "turns into five and, increasingly, six [years]." Nichols notes that "the fragility of 21st-century students" results from "the swaddling environment of the modern university" that "infantilizes students" who demand "trigger warnings" and "safe spaces."

Much attention has been given to the non-college-educated voters who rallied to Trump. Insufficient attention is given to the role of the college miseducated. They, too, are complicit in our current condition because they emerged from their expensive "college experiences" neither disposed nor able to conduct civil, informed arguments. They are thus disarmed when confronted by political people who consider evidence, data, and reasoning to be mere conveniences and optional.

For all the talk in high places about emancipating the many from "the elites," political philosopher Walter Berns was right: The question always is not whether elites will govern but which elites will. And a republic's challenge is to increase the likelihood that the many will consent to governance by worthy elites. So, how is our republic doing?

What is most alarming about the president and his accomplices in the dissemination of factoids is not that they do not know this or that. And it is not that they do not know what they do not know. Rather, it is that they do not know what it *is* to know something.

The republican form of government rests on representation: The people do not decide issues, they decide who will decide. Who, that is, will conduct the deliberations that "refine and enlarge" public opinion (Madison, Federalist 10). This system of filtration is vitiated by a plebiscitary presidency, the occupant of which claims a direct, unmediated, almost mystical connection with "the people."

Soon, presidential enablers, when challenged about their employer's promiscuous use of "alternative facts," will routinely use last week's "justification" of the illegal voting factoid: It is the president's "long-standing belief," so there. In his intellectual solipsism, he, too, takes correction as an insult. He resembles many of his cultured despisers in the academy more than he or they realize.

A HYMN TO IMPRACTICABILITY

August 5, 2018

"Science, like the Mississippi, begins in a tiny rivulet in the distant forest."

—Abraham Flexner

WASHINGTON—In 1933, when America's most famous immigrant settled in Princeton, New Jersey, Franklin Roosevelt tried to invite Albert Einstein to the White House. Abraham Flexner, the founding director of the Institute for Advanced Study that had brought Einstein to Princeton, intercepted FDR's letter before the intended recipient saw it. Flexner declined the invitation and rebuked Roosevelt: "Professor Einstein has come to Princeton for the purpose of carrying on his scientific work in seclusion, and it is absolutely impossible to make any exception which would inevitably bring him into public notice." Robbert Dijkgraaf, the institute's current director, says that subsequently "Einstein made sure he personally answered all of his mail."

Dijkgraaf recounts this episode in a slender volume that, read in the right government places, might inoculate the nation against philistine utilitarianism. In the volume, which reprints Flexner's 1939 essay in *Harper's* magazine, *The Usefulness of Useless Knowledge*, Dijkgraaf notes that the April 1939 opening of the World's Fair in New York—Einstein was honorary chair of the fair's science advisory committee—featured such marvels as an automatic dishwasher, an air conditioner, and a fax machine. There was no intimation of electronic computers or nuclear energy. (Four months later, Einstein urgently wrote to Roosevelt about the element uranium being turned into a new and important source of energy, including bombs, which might explain why Germany had stopped the sale of uranium from Czechoslovakian mines.)

Flexner's theme, says Dijkgraaf, was the practicality of "unobstructed curiosity" that sails "against the current of practical considerations." The 1953 discovery of the structure of DNA, which led to the 1970s arrival of recombinant DNA technology and to today's biotech industry and pharmacology, was the result of scientific curiosity "without any thoughts of immediate applications."

Flexner, who died in 1959 at age ninety-two, recalled asking a great philanthropist who he considered the world's "most useful worker in science." When the philanthropist said "Marconi," Flexner responded:

Radio has enriched human life, but Guglielmo Marconi's contribution to creating it was "practically negligible." Marconi was "inevitable" and added only "the last technical detail" after the basic science (concerning magnetism and electromagnetic waves) by Heinrich Hertz, James Clerk Maxwell, and others. They had no concern whatever about "the utility of their work" that "was seized upon by a clever technician...Hertz and Maxwell were geniuses without thought of use. Marconi was a clever inventor with no thought but use."

It has been said that the great moments in science occur not when a scientist exclaims "Eureka!" but when he or she murmurs "That's strange." Flexner thought the most fertile discoveries come from scientists "driven not by the desire to be useful but merely the desire to satisfy their curiosity." He wanted to banish the word "use" in order to encourage institutions of learning to be devoted more to "the cultivation of curiosity" and less to "considerations of immediacy of application." It is axiomatic that knowledge is the only resource that increases when used, and it is a paradox of prosperity that nations only reap practical innovations from science by regarding them as afterthoughts, coming long after basic science.

The practical lesson from Flexner's hymn to impracticality is this: Indifference to immediate usefulness is a luxury central to the mission of some luxuries of our civilization—the great research universities, free from the tyranny of commercial pressures for short-term results. Only government can have the long time horizon required for the basic research that produces, in time, innovations that propel economic growth.

As 10,000 baby boomers retire each day into the embrace of the entitlement state, rapid economic growth becomes more imperative and, because of the increasing weight of the state, more difficult to maintain. Entitlement spending and the cost of servicing the surging national debt increasingly crowd out rival claims on scarce public resources, including those for basic science. Because it is politically expedient to sacrifice the future, which does not vote, to the consumption of government services by those who do, America is eating its seed corn.

The future's vital, and only, constituency is the conscience of the present. Testifying to Congress in 1969 concerning the possible Cold War utility of a particular particle accelerator, the physicist Robert Wilson said: "This new knowledge has all to do with honor and country, but it has nothing to do directly with defending our country, except to help make it worth defending."

MATTERS OF LIFE AND DEATH

BRITTANY MAYNARD: DEATH ON HER TERMS

August 27, 2015

SAN DIEGO—Brittany Maynard was soon to die. The question was whether she could do so on her own terms, as a last act of autonomy. Dr. Lynette Cederquist, who regrets that Maynard had to move to Oregon in order to do so, is working with others to change California law to allow physician assistance in dying.

Maynard, a twenty-nine-year-old newlywed, knew that her brain cancer would fill her final months with excruciating headaches, seizures, paralysis, and loss of eyesight and the ability to speak. Radiation and chemotherapy would have purchased mere months. "I'm not killing myself," she said. "Cancer is killing me." She would not put her loved ones through her cancer's depredations.

Advances in public health and medical capabilities for prolonging life—and dying—intensify interest in end-of-life issues. Reductions in heart disease and stroke have increased the number of people living to experience decrepitude's encroachments, including dementia.

"Dementia," Cederquist says, "is a whole different dilemma." Assisted suicide perhaps should be allowed only when survival is estimated at six months or less, but at that time persons suffering dementia have lost decisional capacity.

Physician-assisted dying has been done surreptitiously "as long as we have been practicing medicine," says Cederquist, professor of internal medicine at the University of California, San Diego. Today, even in the forty-six states without physician-assisted dying, doctors may legally offer "terminal sedation"—say, a life-shortening dose of morphine—when intense physical suffering cannot otherwise be satisfactorily alleviated. Some Catholic and other ethicists endorse a "double effect" standard: If the intent is to alleviate suffering but a consequence is death, the intent justifies the act.

Cederquist says the most common reason for requesting assistance in dying is not "intolerable physical suffering." Rather, it is "existential suffering," including "loss of meaning," as from the ability to relate to others. The prospect of being "unable to interact" can be as intolerable as physical suffering, and cannot be alleviated by hospice or other palliative care.

In some countries, doctors actively administer lethal injections. No U.S. jurisdiction allows doctors to go beyond writing prescriptions for life-ending drugs to be self-administered orally by persons retaining decisional capacity.

Almost 30 percent of Medicare expenditures are for patients in the last six months of life, and about 16 percent of patients die in, or soon after leaving, intensive care units. Financial reasons should be decisive in setting end-of-life policy, but Cederquist notes that reducing "expensive and inappropriate care"—costly and agonizing resistance to imminent death—"is the lowest-tech thing we can do in medicine." Hence the importance of "slow medicine geriatrics," avoiding a "rush to those interventions that build on each other" and thereby enmesh doctors and patients in ethical conundrums.

The American Medical Association remains opposed to physician assistance in dying; the California Medical Association has moved from opposition to neutrality. Litigation has been unsuccessful in seeking judicial affirmation of a right that California's legislature should establish. Legislation to do this has been authored by Assemblywoman Susan Eggman, chair of the Democratic caucus.

There are reasons for wariness. An illness's six-month trajectory can be uncertain. A right to die can become a felt obligation, particularly among bewildered persons tangled in the toils of medical technologies, or persons with meager family resources. And as a reason for ending life, mental suffering itself calls into question the existence of the requisite decisional competence.

Today's culture of casual death (see the Planned Parenthood videos) should deepen worries about a slippery slope from physician-assisted dying to a further diminution of life's sanctity. Life, however, is inevitably lived on multiple slippery slopes: Taxation could become confiscation, police could become instruments of oppression, public education could become indoctrination, etc. Everywhere and always, civilization depends on the drawing of intelligent distinctions.

Jennifer Glass, a Californian who died August 11, drew one. She said to her state legislators, "I'm doing everything I can to extend my life. No one should have the right to prolong my death."

The *Economist* reports that in the seventeen years under Oregon's pioneering 1997 law, just 1,327 people have received prescriptions for lethal medications—about seventy-four a year—and one-third of those did not use them. Possessing the option was sufficient reassurance.

There is nobility in suffering bravely borne, but also in affirming at the end the distinctive human dignity of autonomous choice. Brittany Maynard, who chose to be with loved ones when she self-administered her lethal medications, was asleep in five minutes and soon dead.

ABORTION: WHO ARE THE EXTREMISTS?

October 19, 2017

WASHINGTON—What would America's abortion policy be if the number of months in the gestation of a human infant were a prime number—say, seven or eleven? This thought experiment is germane to why the abortion issue has been politically toxic, and points to a path toward a less bitter debate. The House of Representatives has for a third time stepped onto this path. Senate Democrats will, for a third time, block this path when Majority Leader Mitch McConnell brings the House bill to the floor, allowing Democrats to demonstrate their extremism and aversion to bipartisan compromise.

Democracy, which properly is government by persuasion rather than majority bullying or executive or judicial policy fiats, is a search for splittable differences. Abortion, which supposedly is the archetypal issue that confounds efforts at compromise, has for two generations—since the Supreme Court seized custody of the issue in 1973—damaged political civility.

Pro-abortion absolutists—meaning those completely content with the post-1973 regime of essentially unrestricted abortion-on-demand at any point in pregnancy—are disproportionately Democrats who, they say, constitute the Party of Science. They are aghast that the Department of Health and Human Services now refers to protecting people at "every stage of life, beginning at conception." This, however, is elementary biology, not abstruse theology: *Something* living begins then—this is why it is called conception. And absent a natural malfunction or intentional intervention (abortion), conception results in a human birth.

In 1973, the court decreed—without basis in the Constitution's text, structure, or history, or in embryology or other science—a trimester policy. It postulated, without a scintilla of reasoning, moral and constitutional significance in the banal convenience that nine is divisible by three. The court decided that the right to abortion becomes a trifle less than absolute—in practice, not discernibly less—when the fetus reaches viability, meaning the ability to survive outside the womb. The court stipulated that viability arrived at twenty-four to twenty-eight weeks.

On October 3, the House passed (237–189) the Pain-Capable Un-born Child Protection Act banning abortions (with the usual exceptions concerning rape, incest, and the life of the mother) after the twentieth week. The act's supposition is that by then the fetus will feel pain when experiencing the violence of being aborted, and that this matters. Of course, pro-abortion absolutists consider the phrase "unborn child" oxymoronic, believing that from conception until the instant of delivery, the pre-born infant is mere "fetal material," as devoid of moral significance as would be a tumor in the (if they will pardon the provocative expression) mother.

Whether a twenty-week fetus has neurological pathways sufficient for feeling pain is surely a question that science can answer, if it has not already. Already there are myriad intrauterine medical procedures, some involving anesthesia: Doctors can heal lives that America's extremely permissive abortion law says can be terminated with impunity. Only seven nations allow unrestricted abortion after twenty weeks. Most European nations restrict abortions by at least week thirteen. France and Germany are very restrictive after twelve, Sweden after eighteen.

Getting a scientific answer to the pain question, even if it is "yes," should gratify the Party of Science. If the answer is "yes," those who think fetal suffering is irrelevant can explain why they do.

New medical technologies and techniques are lowering the age of viability. And increasingly vivid sonograms, showing beating hearts and moving fingers, make it increasingly difficult to argue that the "fetal material" is at no point, in any way, a baby. Science is presenting inconvenient truths to the Party of Science, truths that are the reasons the percentage of pregnancies aborted is the smallest since 1973.

In 1973, the court bizarrely called the fetus "potential life"; it is, of course, undeniably alive and biologically human. A large American majority is undogmatic, because uncertain, about—and the House bill does not address—the question of when the living thing that begins at conception should be held to acquire personhood protectable by law. This majority's commonsensical, prudently imprecise, split-the-difference answer is: not at conception but well before completed gestation. Hence this majority, its vocabulary provided by the court's arbitrary jurisprudence, thinks first-trimester abortions (more than 90 percent of abortions) should be legal. After which, approximately a two-thirds majority supports restricting abortions.

When—the sooner the better—the House bill comes to the Senate floor, Democrats will prevent a vote on it. This will be a tutorial on the actual extremists in our cultural conflicts.

THE WHOLESOME PROVOCATIONS OF
"HEARTBEAT BILLS"

May 5, 2019

WASHINGTON—While constitutional lawyers, ethicists, and theologians—in descending order of importance in the abortion debate—have been arguing in the forty-six years since the Supreme Court attempted to settle the debate, some technologists have been making a consequential contribution to it. They have developed machines that produce increasingly vivid sonograms of fetal development. This concreteness partially explains the intensification of the debate.

Six states have passed "heartbeat bills" to ban abortions after a fetal heartbeat is detectable, approximately six weeks after conception. Such bills are, indeed, unconstitutional given the court's Roe ukase that abortion cannot be restricted before a fetus is viable outside the womb—which means, presumably, before the fetus is a child.

But why should "viability" be the dispositive criterion? Viable means capable of surviving outside the womb, which no infant can do without constant help that others must give. Must. No infants are "viable" in that all are helpless, and the law requires that help be given by those responsible for the infant.

A *New York Times* editorial (December 28, 2018) opposing the idea that "a fetus in the womb has the same rights as a fully formed person" spoke of these living fetuses—that they are living is an elementary biological fact, not an abstruse theological deduction—as "clusters of cells that have not yet developed into viable human beings." Now, delete the obfuscating and constitutionally irrelevant adjective "viable," and look at a sonogram of a ten-week fetus. Note the eyes and lips, the moving fingers and, yes, the beating heart. Is this most suitably described as a "cluster of cells" or as a baby? The cluster-of-cells contingent resembles Chico Marx in the movie *Duck Soup*: "Who ya gonna believe, me or your own eyes?"

The "heartbeat bills" are wholesome provocations: One of their aims is to provoke thinking about the moral dimension of extinguishing a being with a visibly beating heart. Furthermore, pro-life people are being provoked in different ways.

Last month, Kansas's Supreme Court found in this from the state constitution—"All men are possessed of equal and inalienable natural rights, among which are life, liberty, and the pursuit of happiness"—a reason to overturn the state's ban on D & E (dilation-and-evacuation) abortions that involve dismemberment of the living fetus. In February, after Illinois Governor J. B. Pritzker signed an executive order to enforce taxpayer-funded abortions, Democratic legislators decided that not even that was enough. They introduced a bill to create a right to abortion for any reason at any point in a pregnancy, a bill similar to legislation enacted or advancing in other Democratic-controlled states. In February, all but three Democratic U.S. senators opposed, thereby killing, Nebraska Senator Ben Sasse's Born-Alive Abortion Survivors Protection Act that would have required, in the rare cases in which a child survives a botched abortion procedure, that the survivor receive the standard professional care that would be given to any child born alive at the same gestational age.

The 1850s debates that propelled Abraham Lincoln to greatness concerned not whether slavery should be abolished forthwith, which was neither a constitutional nor political possibility. Rather, the debates concerned two other questions: Would national policy stigmatize slavery as a tragic legacy and a moral wrong? And: Would policy confine slavery to its existing dominion by banning it from the territories, thereby, Lincoln thought, putting it on a path to ultimate extinction?

Temperate pro-life advocates, practicing Lincolnian prudence, consider the abortion debate akin to the slavery debates for three reasons: Abortion shrinks the scope of the concept of personhood. The issue has been inflamed by judicial fiat (*Roe v. Wade* as *Dred Scott v. Sandford*). And confining a morally objectionable practice is a worthy, albeit not fully satisfying, objective.

The changed composition of the Supreme Court, and the supposed imminent danger that Roe will be overturned, is the excuse that pro-abortion extremists have seized upon to do what they want to do anyway: to normalize extreme abortion practices expressive of the belief that never does fetal life have more moral significance than a tumor in a mother's stomach. (Most European nations restrict abortions by at least week thirteen. France and Germany are very restrictive after twelve, Sweden after eighteen.) The court's new composition has encouraged some pro-life advocates in their maximum hope, that Roe can be overturned, which would not proscribe abortion but would restore its pre-1973 status as a practice states can regulate. This is not a foreseeable possibility; a more nuanced abortion regime is.

"AMERICA'S BIGGEST SERIAL KILLER"

December 9, 2018

WASHINGTON—A word can be worth a thousand pictures. In the movie *Gosnell: The Trial of America's Biggest Serial Killer*, the mild word "snip" describes what the camera, demonstrating the eloquence of reticence, does not show in gory detail: Kermit Gosnell's use of scissors to cut the spinal cords of hundreds of babies that survived his late-term abortion procedures.

Directed by actor Nick Searcy (*Three Billboards Outside Ebbing, Missouri, The Shape of Water*), this gripping true-crime courtroom drama, with dialogue taken from court transcripts and police records, made it onto 670 screens, earned nearly $4 million, and soon will be available in DVD format through Netflix. This, in spite of impediments from portions of America's cultural apparatus that are reflexively hostile to examining Gosnell's career in infanticide.

The movie's makers tried to raise money on a crowdfunding website that balked at graphic—meaning accurate—descriptions of the subject, because "we are a broad website used by millions of people." However, a pluckier site gathered $2.4 million from 30,000 contributors. Almost all regular critics of movies were offered copies of the movie. A major film will receive about 270 media reviews, according to Mark Joseph, CEO of MJM Entertainment Group. *Gosnell* received twelve, even though in the October week it was released it was the top grossing independent film and cracked the top ten of all films in theaters. The critics' boycott of the film continued the journalists' indifference toward Gosnell's trial.

As the prosecutors drove to the courthouse in 2013 for the first day of Gosnell's trial on eight counts of murder (a woman who died following an abortion procedure, and seven snipped babies) and twenty-four felony counts of abortion beyond Pennsylvania's twenty-four-week limit, they anticipated a difficult maelstrom of media attention. They encountered something worse: virtually no attention. In spite of—actually, because of—its gruesome substance, the two-month trial, which ended with Gosnell sentenced to life imprisonment without parole, was not covered until, by their example, a few journalists—especially *USA Today*'s Kirsten Powers—embarrassed others into paying attention. If Gosnell's victims had been middle class instead of inner-city minorities, there surely would have been more interest in an abortion facility where babies were heard crying, and where a woman victim of Gosnell's slap-dash procedures went home with an arm and a leg of her baby still in her. According to grand jury testimony, early in Gosnell's career of carnage he used a medical device lacking federal approval, "basically plastic razors that were formed into a ball":

> They were coated into a gel, so that they would remain closed. These would be inserted into the woman's uterus. And after several hours of body temperature...the gel would melt and these 97 things would spring open, supposedly cutting up the fetus, and the fetus would be expelled.

Recently in Texas, Samuel Little, seventy-eight, has been confessing to more than ninety murders spanning thirty-five years. Now serving three life sentences for the murders of three Los Angeles women in the 1980s, he has been giving police details that seem to validate his claim to have killed in at least fourteen states. A Texas district attorney says "we anticipate that Samuel Little will be confirmed as one of the most prolific serial killers in American history," and the *New York Times* observes, "How a serial murderer could go on killing for years, apparently without anyone noticing a pattern, seems perplexing."

That Gosnell could have been a much more prolific killer than Little is not perplexing, for two reasons. People who should have known did not want to know because knowing would have forced them to answer questions about when in an infant's gestation it is preposterous to deny that a baby is present. And given that most "reproductive rights" militants oppose restrictions on late-term abortions because pre-born babies supposedly have no more moral significance than tumors, Gosnell sincerely thought he was doing nothing wrong in guaranteeing dead babies for those who paid for late-term abortions. This is why, in the movie and as actually happened, a female prosecutor is accurately warned by her supervisor that she would be characterized as "the prosecutor who went after reproductive rights."

No one knows how many—certainly hundreds, probably thousands— spinal cords Gosnell snipped before the 2010 raid on his "clinic." Law enforcement came looking for illegal drugs. They also found jars of babies' feet, fetal remains in toilets and milk cartons, and a pervasive smell of cat feces—in a facility that had not been inspected for seventeen years. Pennsylvania nail salons receive biennial inspections.

"INAPPROPRIATE"

December 4, 2016

WASHINGTON—The word "inappropriate" is increasingly used inappropriately. It is useful to describe departures from good manners or other social norms, such as wearing white after Labor Day or using the salad fork with the entrée. But the adjective has become a splatter of verbal fudge, a weasel word falsely suggesting measured seriousness.

Its misty imprecision does not disguise, it advertises, the user's moral obtuseness.

A French court has demonstrated how "inappropriate" can be an all-purpose device of intellectual evasion and moral cowardice. The court said it is inappropriate to do something that might disturb people who killed their unborn babies for reasons that were, shall we say, inappropriate.

Prenatal genetic testing enables pregnant women to be apprised of a variety of problems with their unborn babies, including Down syndrome. It is a congenital condition resulting from a chromosomal defect that causes varying degrees of mental disability and some physical abnormalities, such as low muscle tone, small stature, flatness of the back of the head, and an upward slant to the eyes. Within living memory, Down syndrome people were called Mongoloids.

Now they are included in the category called "special needs" people. What they most need is nothing special. It is for people to understand their aptitudes, and to therefore quit killing them in utero.

Down syndrome, although not common, is among the most common congenital anomalies at 49.7 per 100,000 births. In approximately 90 percent of instances when prenatal genetic testing reveals Down syndrome, the baby is aborted. Cleft lips or palates, which occur in 72.6 per 100,000 births, also can be diagnosed in utero and sometimes are the reason a baby is aborted.

In 2014, in conjunction with World Down Syndrome Day (March 21), the Global Down Syndrome Foundation prepared a two-minute video titled *Dear Future Mom* to assuage the anxieties of pregnant women who have learned that they are carrying a Down syndrome baby. More than 7 million people have seen the video online in which one such woman says, "I'm scared: what kind of life will my child have?" Down syndrome children from many nations tell the woman that her child will hug, speak, go to school, tell you he loves you, and "can be happy, just like I am—and you'll be happy, too."

The French state is not happy about this. The court has ruled that the video is—wait for it—"inappropriate" for French television. The court upheld a ruling in which the French Broadcasting Council banned the video as a commercial. The court said the video's depiction of happy Down syndrome children is "likely to disturb the conscience of women who had lawfully made different personal life choices."

So, what happens on campuses does not stay on campuses. There, in many nations, sensitivity bureaucracies have been enforcing the relatively new entitlement to be shielded from whatever might disturb, even inappropriate jokes. And now this rapidly metastasizing right has come to this: A video that accurately communicates a truthful proposition—that Down syndrome people can be happy and give happiness—should be suppressed because some people might become ambivalent, or morally queasy, about having chosen to extinguish such lives because...

This is why the video giving facts about Down syndrome people is so subversive of the flaccid consensus among those who say aborting a baby is of no more moral significance than removing a tumor from a stomach. Pictures persuade. Today's improved prenatal sonograms make graphic the fact that the moving fingers and beating heart are not mere "fetal material." They are a baby. Toymaker Fisher-Price, children's apparel manufacturer OshKosh, McDonald's, and Target have featured Down syndrome children in ads that the French court would probably ban from television.

The court has said, in effect, that the lives of Down syndrome people—and by inescapable implication, the lives of many other disabled people—matter less than the serenity of people who have acted on one or more of three vicious principles: that the lives of the disabled are not worth living. Or that the lives of the disabled are of negligible value next to the desire of parents to have a child who has no special, meaning inconvenient, needs. Or that government should suppress the voices of Down syndrome children in order to guarantee other people's right not to be disturbed by reminders that they have made lethal choices on the basis of one or both of the first two *inappropriate* principles.

ICELAND'S FINAL SOLUTION TO THE DOWN SYNDROME "PROBLEM"

March 15, 2018

WASHINGTON—Iceland must be pleased that it is close to success in its program of genocide, but before congratulating that nation on its final solution to the Down syndrome problem, perhaps it might answer a question: What is this problem? To help understand why some people might ask this question, today's column is being distributed together with two photographs. One is of Agusta, age eight, a citizen of Iceland. The other is of Lucas, age one, an American citizen in Dalton, Georgia, who recently was selected to be 2018 spokesbaby for the Gerber baby food company. They are two examples of the problem.

Now, before Iceland becomes snippy about the description of what it is doing, let us all try to think calmly about genocide, without getting judgmental about it. It is simply the deliberate, systematic attempt to erase a category of people. So, what one thinks about a genocide depends on what one thinks about the category involved. In Iceland's case, the category is people with Down syndrome.

This is a congenital condition resulting from a chromosomal defect. It involves varying degrees of mental retardation (although probably not larger variances than exist between the mental capabilities of many people who are chromosomally normal—say, Isaac Newton and some people you know). It also involves some physical abnormalities (including low muscle tone, small stature, flatness of the back of the head, an upward slant to the eyes) and some increased health risks (of heart defects, childhood leukemia, and Alzheimer's disease). Average life expectancy is now around sixty years, up from around twenty-five years four decades ago, when many Down syndrome people were institutionalized or otherwise isolated, denied education and other stimulation, and generally not treated as people.

Highly (almost but not perfectly) accurate prenatal screening tests can reveal Down syndrome in utero. The expectant couple can then decide to extinguish the fetus and try again for a normal child that might be less trouble, at least until he or she is an adolescent with hormonal turbulence and a driver's license.

In Iceland, upward of 85 percent of pregnant women opt for the prenatal testing, which has produced a Down syndrome elimination rate approaching 100 percent. Agusta was one of only three Down syndrome babies born there in 2009. Iceland could have moved one-third of the way to its goal if only Agusta had been detected and eliminated. Agusta's mother is glad the screening failed in her case.

An Iceland geneticist says "we have basically eradicated" Down syndrome people, but regrets what he considers "heavy-handed genetic counseling" that is influencing "decisions that are not medical, in a way." One Icelandic counselor "counsels" mothers as follows: "This is your life. You have the right to choose how your life will look like." She says, "We don't look at abortion as a murder. We look at it as a thing that we ended." Which makes Agusta and Lucas "things" that were not "ended."

Because Iceland's population is only about 340,000, the problem (again, see the photos of problem Agusta and problem Lucas) is more manageable there than in, say, the United Kingdom. It has approximately 40,000 Down syndrome citizens, many of whom were conceived before the development of effective search-and-destroy technologies. About 750 British Down syndrome babies are born each year, but 90 percent of women who learn that their child will have—actually, that their child does have—Down syndrome have an abortion. In Denmark the elimination rate is 98 percent.

America, where 19 percent of all pregnancies are aborted, is playing catch-up in the Down syndrome elimination sweepstakes (elimination rate of 67 percent, 1995–2011). So is France (77 percent), which seems determined to do better. In 2016, a French court ruled that it would be "inappropriate" for French television to run a two-and-a-half-minute video (*Dear Future Mom*) released for World Down Syndrome Day, which seeks to assure women carrying Down syndrome babies that their babies can lead happy lives, a conclusion resoundingly confirmed in a 2011 study "Self-perceptions from People with Down Syndrome." The court said the video is "likely to disturb the conscience of women" who aborted Down syndrome children.

So, the photos of Agusta and Lucas are probably "inappropriate." It speaks volumes about today's moral confusions that *this*—the disruption of an unethical complacency—is the real "Down syndrome problem."

JON WILL AT FORTY

May 3, 2012

WASHINGTON—When Jonathan Frederick Will was born forty years ago—on May 4, 1972, his father's thirty-first birthday—the life expectancy for people with Down syndrome was about twenty years. That is understandable.

The day after Jon was born, a doctor told Jon's parents that the first question for them was whether they intended to take Jon home from the hospital. Nonplussed, they said they thought that is what parents do with newborns. Not doing so was, however, still considered an acceptable choice for parents who might prefer to institutionalize or put up for adoption children thought to have necessarily bleak futures. Whether warehoused or just allowed to languish from lack of stimulation and attention, people with Down syndrome, not given early and continuing interventions, were generally thought to be incapable of living well, and hence usually did not live as long as they could have.

Down syndrome is a congenital condition resulting from a chromosomal defect—an extra twenty-first chromosome. It causes varying degrees of mental retardation and some physical abnormalities, including small stature, a single crease across the center of the palms, flatness of the back of the head, a configuration of the tongue that impedes articulation, and a slight upward slant of the eyes. In 1972, people with Down syndrome were still commonly called Mongoloids.

Now they are called American citizens, about 400,000 of them, and their life expectancy is now sixty. Much has improved. There has, however, been moral regression as well.

Jon was born just nineteen years after James Watson and Francis Crick published their discoveries concerning the structure of DNA, discoveries that would enhance understanding of the structure of Jon, whose every cell is imprinted with Down syndrome. Jon was born just as prenatal genetic testing, which can detect Down syndrome, was becoming common. And Jon was born eight months before *Roe v. Wade* inaugurated this era of the casual destruction of pre-born babies.

This era has coincided, not just coincidentally, with the full garish flowering of the baby boomers' vast sense of entitlement, which encompasses an entitlement to exemption from nature's mishaps, and to a perfect baby. So today science enables what the ethos ratifies, the choice of killing children with Down syndrome before birth. That is what happens to 90 percent of those whose parents have prenatal testing.

Which is unfortunate, and not just for them. Judging by Jon, the world would be improved by more people with Down syndrome, who are quite nice, as humans go. It is said we are all born brave, trusting, and greedy, and remain greedy. People with Down syndrome must remain brave in order to navigate society's complexities. They have no choice but to be trusting because, with limited understanding, and limited abilities to communicate misunderstanding, they, like Blanche DuBois in *A Streetcar Named Desire*, always depend on the kindness of strangers. Judging by Jon's experience, they almost always receive it.

Two things that have enhanced Jon's life are the Washington subway system, which opened in 1976, and the Washington Nationals baseball team, which arrived in 2005. He navigates the subway expertly, riding it to the Nationals ballpark, where he enters the clubhouse a few hours before game time and does a chore or two. The players, who have climbed to the pinnacle of a steep athletic pyramid, know that although hard work got them there, they have extraordinary aptitudes because they are winners of life's lottery. Major leaguers, all of whom understand what it is to be gifted, have been uniformly and extraordinarily welcoming to Jon, who is not.

Except he is, in a way. He has the gift of serenity, in this sense:

The oldest of four siblings, he has seen two brothers and a sister surpass him in size, and acquire cars and college educations. He, however, with an underdeveloped entitlement mentality, has been equable about life's sometimes careless allocation of equity. Perhaps this is partly because, given the nature of Down syndrome, neither he nor his parents have any tormenting sense of what might have been. Down syndrome did not alter the trajectory of his life; Jon was Jon from conception on.

This year Jon will spend his birthday where every year he spends eighty-one spring, summer, and autumn days and evenings, at Nationals Park, in his seat behind the home team's dugout. The Phillies will be in town, and Jon will be wishing them ruination, just another man, beer in hand, among equals in the republic of baseball.

DARKNESS REMEMBERED

GERMAN RESISTANCE: NEITHER NEGLIGIBLE NOR CONTEMPTIBLE

January 12, 2009

WASHINGTON—Impressed by a written report from a colonel, Adolf Hitler exclaimed, "Finally a general staff officer with imagination and intelligence!" The report's author, who had those qualities in quantities commensurate with his courage, would be repeatedly brought to Hitler's headquarters in East Prussia. He was Count Claus Schenk von Stauffenberg.

Tom Cruise portrays him in *Valkyrie*, the story of *an* attempt to assassinate Hitler. Stauffenberg's bomb that failed to kill Hitler on July 20, 1944, was one of perhaps fifteen attempts, according Joachim Fest's 1994 book *Plotting Hitler's Death: The Story of the German Resistance*. Fest does justice to the pathos, ambiguity, occasional absurdity, and ultimate dignity of the many rivulets of resistance that culminated in Stauffenberg placing a bomb in a briefcase near Hitler's feet. *Valkyrie* attempts less. Commercial imperatives incline Hollywood to avoid diluting pleasure with instruction, so *Valkyrie*, although conscientious in depicting the July 20 episode, provides scant context. By turning a complex moral drama into a mere action thriller, the movie misses a chance to revive interest in the German Resistance.

If the Munich agreements of September 29, 1938, had not given Hitler the fruits of war with Czechoslovakia without the war, some generals might have rebelled: Secret arrangements had been made to open from within the doors to Hitler's chambers so that a military force could rush in. If on November 8, 1939, Hitler had not cut short a speech scheduled for two hours in Munich, an assassination plan there might have succeeded. Two days later, with security thickened around Hitler, an officers' bomb plot was abandoned. In a March 13, 1943, attempt that *Valkyrie* does depict, explosives hidden in two bottles of Cointreau were placed aboard Hitler's plane. The fuse worked, the firing pins struck, the percussion cap evidently ignited. Still, the bomb did not detonate, perhaps because the explosive, carried in the plane's hold, was sensitive to cold.

Eight days later, as Hitler entered a military exhibit, an officer ignited a fuse on a bomb beneath his coat and stayed close to Hitler. But after just two minutes in the exhibit, Hitler, with a feral animal's instinct for danger, left through a side door. The officer dashed to a restroom to deactivate the bomb.

A highly decorated twenty-four-year-old captain, appalled by Nazi atrocities in the Ukraine, instantly agreed when Stauffenberg asked if he would kill Hitler. In November 1943, with Hitler scheduled to view a display of new uniforms, the captain, with a bomb concealed on his person, was prepared to ignite a short fuse and leap upon Hitler. But the display was canceled when the railroad car containing the uniforms was destroyed by an air raid on Berlin.

On March 11, 1944, a field marshal summoned to Obersalzberg, Hitler's Bavarian retreat, brought an adjutant, a captain, carrying in his pocket an assassination weapon—a cocked Browning revolver. An SS officer stopped the captain at the conference-room door, saying adjutants would not be allowed in.

If it had not been unusually hot on July 20, 1944, Hitler's conference with Stauffenberg and others would have been held in a concrete bunker, which would have contained the blast of Stauffenberg's bomb. Instead, they met in an aboveground wooden building, where the force dissipated. If a sergeant had not entered the room where Stauffenberg, using pliers modified to accommodate his injuries (wounds had cost him an eye, his right hand, and two fingers on his left), was arming the explosives, Stauffenberg might have armed the second bomb, or might have put it in the briefcase with the armed one, which would have detonated both with sufficient force to kill everyone in the room.

Hitler survived, and the planned coup unraveled in a few hours. Stauffenberg was executed by firing squad that night. Other conspirators were tried before Roland Freisler, whom Hitler praised as "our Vishinsky," a reference to the chief prosecutor in Stalin's show trials. Taken prisoner by the Russians during World War I, Freisler briefly became a Soviet commissar before returning to Germany and joining the Nazi Party in 1925. Among the conspirators Freisler condemned to death—many were slowly strangled by thin cords looped around butchers' hooks, their agonies filmed for Hitler's enjoyment—was the diplomat Adam von Trott, a direct descendant on his mother's side of John Jay, first chief justice of the U.S. Supreme Court. On February 3, 1945, during the largest air raid of the war, a falling beam in the courtroom killed only one person: Freisler. A doctor summoned from off the street confirmed that Freisler's injuries were fatal. The day before, Freisler had condemned to death the doctor's brother.

By July 1944, decapitation of the Nazi regime probably would not have prevented a crescendo of carnage: In the first fifty-nine months of war, 2.8 million German soldiers and civilians died; in the last nine months, 4.8 million died. Still, Stauffenberg and many others understood the need for a gesture of national purification to refute the narrative—promulgated by Hitler and embraced by the Allies as a politically useful simplification—that the German Resistance was negligible and contemptible. It was neither.

EICHMANN: NOT "TERRIFYINGLY NORMAL"

November 15, 2014

WASHINGTON—Western reflection about human nature and the politics of the human condition began with the sunburst of ancient Greece 2,500 years ago, but lurched into a new phase seventy years ago with the liberation of the Nazi extermination camps. The Holocaust is the dark sun into which humanity should stare, lest troubling lessons be lost through an intellectual shrug about "the unfathomable."

Now comes an English translation of a 2011 German book that refutes a 1963 book and rebukes those who refuse to see the Holocaust as proof of the power of the most dangerous things—ideas that denigrate reason. The German philosopher Bettina Stangneth's *Eichmann Before Jerusalem: The Unexamined Life of a Mass Murderer* responds to Hannah Arendt's extraordinarily and perversely influential *Eichmann in Jerusalem: A Report on the Banality of Evil.*

Although, or perhaps because, Arendt was a philosopher, in her report on Israel's trial of Adolf Eichmann, the organizer of industrialized murder, she accepted the façade Eichmann presented to those who could, and in 1962 would, hang him: He was a little "cog" in a bureaucratic machine. He said he merely "passed on" orders and "oversaw" compliance. Arendt agreed.

She called Eichmann "terribly and terrifyingly normal," lacking "criminal motives," "a buffoon," "a typical functionary" who was "banal" rather than "demonic" because he was not "deep," being essentially without "ideology." Arendt considered Eichmann "thoughtless," partly because, with a parochialism to which some intellectuals are prone, she could not accept the existence of a coherent and motivating ideological framework that rejected, root and branch, the universality of reason, and hence of human dignity.

It was odd for Arendt to suppose that the pride Eichmann took in his deportations—especially of the more than 430,000 Hungarian Jews when the war was already lost and even Heinrich Himmler, hoping for leniency, was urging it for the Jews—was merely pride in managerial virtuosity. Arendt, however, did not have, as Stangneth has had, access to more than 1,300 pages of Eichmann's writings and taped musings among Argentina's portion of the Nazi diaspora, before Israeli agents kidnapped him in 1960.

Eichmann was proudly prominent in preparations for the "final solution" even before the Wannsee Conference (January 20, 1942) formalized it. "His name," Stangneth notes, "appeared in David Ben-Gurion's diary only three months after the start of the war" in September

1939. On October 24, 1941, a newspaper published by German exiles in London identified Eichmann as leader of a "campaign" of "mass murder."

"I was an idealist," he told his fellow exiles, and he was. In obedience to the "morality of the Fatherland that dwells within," aka the "voice of blood," his anti-Semitism was radical *because* it was ideological. Denying that all individuals are created equal entailed affirming the irremediable incompatibility of groups, which necessitated a struggle to settle subordination and extermination.

"There are," Eichmann wrote, "a number of moralities." But because thinking is national, no morality is universal. Only war is universal as the arbiter of survival. So, Stangneth writes, "Only thinking based on ethnicity offers a chance of final victory in the battle of all living things."

Eichmann, a premature post-modernist, had a philosophy to end philosophizing. To him, Stangneth says, "philosophy in the classical sense, as the search for transcultural categories" was absurd. She says his ideology was "the fundamental authorization for his actions."

In 1996, Daniel Jonah Goldhagen's *Hitler's Willing Executioners: Ordinary Germans and the Holocaust* argued that Germany was saturated with "eliminationist anti-Semitism" that produced much voluntary participation in genocide. This made Hitler a mere product and trigger of cultural latency. But in 1992, Christopher Browning in *Ordinary Men*, a study of middle-aged German conscripts who became willing mass-murderers, had noted that the murders of millions of Cambodians by the Khmer Rouge and tens of millions of Chinese by Mao's Cultural Revolution could not be explained by centuries of conditioning by a single idea.

Martin Amis's new novel *The Zone of Interest*—set in Auschwitz, it is a study of moral vertigo—contains a lapidary afterword in which Amis abjures "epistemological rejection," the idea that an explanation of Hitler and his enthusiasts is impossible. An explanation begins with Eichmann's explanation of himself, rendered in Argentina.

Before he donned his miniaturizing mask in Jerusalem, Eichmann proclaimed that he did what he did in the service of idealism. This supposedly "thoughtless" man's devotion to ideas was such that, Stangneth says, he "was still composing his last lines when they came to take him to the gallows."

THE 442ND

April 25, 2010

WASHINGTON—Hearing about a shortage of farm laborers in California, the couple who would become Susumu Ito's parents moved from Hiroshima to become sharecroppers near Stockton. Thus began a saga that recently brought Ito, ninety-one, to the Holocaust Memorial Museum here, where he and 119 former comrades in arms were honored, during the annual Days of Remembrance, as liberators of Nazi concentration camps. While his Japanese-American Army unit was succoring survivors of Dachau, near Munich, his parents and two sisters were interned in a camp in Arkansas.

Ito attended one-room schools, graduated from high school at sixteen, and was accepted at Berkeley. His parents, however, believed Japanese Americans could not rise in the professions—even the civil service—for which the university would prepare him. So he attended community college, studying auto mechanics, although he could not join the mechanics union.

In 1940, Congress passed conscription, and Ito was content to be drafted, thinking the military would be an adventure. He got that right.

Although nearsighted and "my feet were flat as boards," he and five other Japanese Americans from around Stockton were inducted in February 1941. Because "Japanese revered their sons being in the military," the Japanese-American community threw a farewell banquet for them, and gave each thirty-five dollars. After Pearl Harbor, the Army "took our rifles away."

Soon, while he was in training at Fort Sill in Oklahoma, his parents and sisters were interned as security threats, first at a California race track where they slept in horse stalls on straw mattresses, later in Arkansas. Bored by life as a military mechanic and "gung ho about going to war," he volunteered to be a forward spotter seeking targets for the artillery, a job with a high casualty rate and a short life expectancy. Soon he was in Mississippi, from where he, wearing his country's uniform, could occasionally visit his family behind barbed wire in Arkansas.

In Mississippi, the 442nd Regimental Combat Team, composed of Japanese Americans, trained before being shipped to Europe. It included Daniel Inouye, now eighty-five, who lost an arm while winning a Medal of Honor. He is now in his eighth term as a U.S. senator.

After experiencing combat in Italy, the unit moved up through France and to the famous rescue of the "lost battalion" of the 36th Texas Division, which was cut off by Germans. The 442nd, which suffered 1,000 casualties rescuing 175 surviving Texans, became the most decorated unit for its size in American history.

By March 1945, the 442nd was in southern Germany. Soon it was at Dachau. Eddie Ichiyama of Santa Clara, California, who also was here recently, says that "even right now" he can smell the stench. The ovens were still warm. On a nearby railroad flatbed car, what looked to be a supply of cord wood was actually stacked corpses.

Nelson Akagi of Salt Lake City remembers an officer "adopting" Larry Lubetzky, a liberated Lithuanian Jew, as an interpreter. After the war, prisoner number 82123 went from Germany to Jerusalem to Canada to Mexico City, from where Akagi received a call in 1992. Akagi will search the Holocaust Memorial Museum archives for fresh information about Lubetzky.

After the war, Ito rejoined his loved ones, who had lost everything. He became a professor of cell biology and anatomy at Harvard Medical School. He retired in 1990 but still goes to the lab several days a week.

Such cheerful men, who helped to lop 988 years off the Thousand Year Reich, are serene reproaches to a nation now simmering with grievance groups that nurse their cherished resentments. The culture of complaint gets no nourishment from men like these who served their country so well while it was treating their families so ignobly. Yet it is a high tribute to this country that it is so loved by men such as these.

The Holocaust museum draws almost 2 million visitors a year, four times more than were anticipated when it opened seventeen years ago. A museum official says dryly, "Human nature has been an enormous help." She means that atrocious behavior, a constant component of the human story, continually reminds people of the museum's relevance. It is, therefore, grand that the museum also honors those, like Ito, Akagi, and Ichiyama, who exemplify the rest, and best, of that story.

"INTO ETERNITY, VILMA"

April 26, 2018

WASHINGTON—As the museum of human nature, aka the United States Holocaust Memorial Museum, marks its twenty-fifth anniversary, it continues to receive artifacts, such as a letter handwritten on a yellow scrap of paper. It was donated to the museum by Frank Grunwald, eighty-five, who lives in Indianapolis.

He was the younger of two Czechoslovakian boys who sit smiling on their mother's lap in a photograph the museum has. It was taken before this Jewish family was swept into the Nazi murder machinery. Frank, then eleven and known as Misa, is alive because, unlike his brother John, then sixteen, Frank did not limp. In July 1944, their father was segregated with male prisoners who were working in an Auschwitz factory. The boys were with their mother in the Czech family section of the camp when a Nazi noticed John's limp and selected him for gassing. Unwilling to have John face death alone, on July 11, Vilma went with him, leaving behind this letter to her husband:

You, my only one, dearest, in isolation we are waiting for darkness. We considered the possibility of hiding but decided not to do it since we felt it would be hopeless. The famous trucks are already here and we are waiting for it to begin. I am completely calm.

You—my only and dearest one, do not blame yourself for what happened, it was our destiny. We did what we could. Stay healthy and remember my words that time will heal—if not completely—then—at least partially. Take care of the little golden boy and don't spoil him too much with your love. Both of you—stay healthy, my dear ones. I will be thinking of you and Misa. Have a fabulous life, we must board the trucks.

Into eternity, Vilma.

So, the museum presents human nature's noblest as well as vilest manifestations. It has received 43 million visitors, 90 percent non-Jewish, many of whom have had opportunities to talk to survivors, such as Fanny Aizenberg, who in her 102nd year still comes most Sundays. Located just off the Mall, one of the world's most pleasant urban spaces and the epicenter of American politics, the museum inflicts an assaultive, excruciating knowing: Nothing—*nothing*—is unthinkable, and political institutions by themselves provide no permanent safety from barbarism, which permanently lurks beneath civilization's thin, brittle crust.

This is why the Holocaust is the dark sun into which this democracy should peer. Calling the Holocaust unfathomable is a moral flinch from facts that demand scholarship, which the museum enables. It has, for example, more than 900 video interviews with witnesses and collaborators. And perpetrators, such as Juozas Aleksynas, a member of a Lithuanian police battalion that committed genocide in Belarus in 1941:

We were issued Russian guns and bullets…some were exploding bullets…A person's skull opens up so fast…They would carry children—the little ones—they'd take the others by the hand. They lie down, lay the child next to them…First you shoot the father…How would the father feel if the child was shot by his side?

An album found long ago in an abandoned SS barracks contains photos of Auschwitz guards and administrators at leisure—singing, picnicking. It includes some of the few pictures of a short, dark-haired man—Dr. Josef Mengele, who escaped prosecution for his "medical" experiments, drowning in 1979 while swimming in Brazil.

In his mind-opening 2017 book *Why? Explaining the Holocaust*, Peter Hayes says the subject "continues to resist comprehension." Resist, but not defy. His many conclusions include the awesome—for better or worse—power of individual agency: No Hitler, no Holocaust. But Hitler began tentatively, with small measures. Hayes concludes his book with a German proverb: *Wehret den Anfangen*—beware the beginnings.

Today, there is an essentially fascist government in Hungary. Anti-Semitism is coming out of the closet: The Labour Party, which might form Britain's next government, is riddled with it, from the top down. Blood-and-soil tribalism—degenerate successor to throne-and-altar conservatism—is fermenting across Europe. And there is a name for what is happening to the Rohingya in Myanmar: genocide. The museum of human nature remains what it would prefer not to be: pertinent to understanding not only the past but the present.

How do those who work at the museum, immersed in the task of making us remember the unspeakable, maintain their emotional equilibrium? By also remembering Vilma.

"IT HAPPENED. THEREFORE IT CAN HAPPEN AGAIN."

November 24, 2019

NEW YORK—From the mountains of shoes that were worn by Jews when they were packed into railroad freight cars bound for Auschwitz, the Museum of Jewish Heritage: A Living Memorial to the Holocaust displays one: a woman's red dress pump with a three-inch heel. It prompts viewers to wonder: Where did she think she was going?

Perhaps she did not have time to think when she was swept into the vortex of one of Europe's innumerable roundups. She was destined for the unimaginable, where she probably vanished quickly: 900,000 of the 1.3 million people sent there were murdered shortly after their arrival.

The *New York Times* of January 28, 1945, reported on its front page the Red Army's arrival the day before at Auschwitz, which the story described, in its sixteenth paragraph, as a place where more than a million "persons" were murdered. Persons. Of them, 1 million were Jews.

A yellowed *Times* edition from that date is displayed today in the museum, which is located on Manhattan's southern tip, near the spot where, in 1654, twenty-three Jews who had come from Spain and Portugal, via Brazil, became the first Jews in what was then New Amsterdam. The museum's six-sided Core building evokes the six-pointed star of David, and the 6 million Jews killed in the Holocaust, which is the subject of a shattering exhibit, "Auschwitz. Not long ago. Not far away." The eloquence of the artifacts, which were first seen when the exhibit opened in Madrid and will be seen elsewhere in North America, is welcome testimony, in an age obsessed with new media, to the power of an old medium: the museum.

The exhibit includes Reinhard Heydrich's gift for Hermann Goering on his forty-seventh birthday. Before Heydrich was assassinated by Czech partisans in 1942, he was the "architect of the Final Solution." His gift was a piece of parchment: the original 1551 proclamation, signed by the Holy Roman Emperor Ferdinand I, requiring Jews to attach to their garments a yellow circle. The seeds of the Holocaust germinated for centuries in Europe's social soil. They did not, however, have to come to their cataclysmic fruition.

Other artifacts include Heinrich Himmler's handwriting in his annotated first edition of *Mein Kampf*. And a photo of Anne Frank's parents' wedding. And a child's shoe with a sock carefully tucked into it, waiting for the child to put it back on after the "shower" to which he had been directed, from which he did not return.

Did you know that eight of the fifteen participants in the January 20, 1942, Wannsee Conference, which finalized plans for the industrialization of murder, had doctoral degrees? Education is not necessarily an inoculation against evil. Only two participants were older than fifty:

Genocide was a project for up-and-comers, idealists who acquired the ideals from socialization under totalitarianism.

The exhibit includes grainy, black-and-white film of a passing freight train shedding notes the way a tree shed leaves in autumn, notes tossed from between the freight cars' slats by the human cargo who were desperate to scatter random traces of themselves before the final darkness. One was tossed from a train leaving Holland by seventeen-year-old Hertha Aussen: "Most likely this will be the last card you will receive from me." Three days later she was murdered on arrival at Auschwitz.

What also died at Auschwitz is—was—what is known as the Whig theory of history, which holds, or held, that there is an inevitable unfolding of history in the direction of expanding liberty under law. Just as the Holocaust was not inevitable, neither is the triumph of enlightenment: History is not a ratchet that clicks only one way. Today, in several parts of the world, including on the dark, churned, and bloody ground of central Europe, there are various forms of political regression. These are marked by a recrudescence of the blood-and-soil tribalism of degenerate nationalism, accompanied by thinly veiled, or not at all veiled, anti-Semitism.

Visitors entering "Auschwitz. Not long ago. Not far away" immediately walk past these words of Primo Levi, an Auschwitz survivor: "It happened, therefore it can happen again." Today in China's far west, concentration camps hold more than a million people who Beijing says show "symptoms" of being "infected" with the "virus" of "unhealthy thoughts." Similar medical terminology presented the Holocaust as social hygiene.

Polls indicate that a majority of millennials do not know what Auschwitz was. The future might teach them by analogies.

THE POLITICS OF MEMORY

January 19, 2020

MADRID—An hour's drive northwest of here, in the Valley of the Fallen, is a residue of Europe's past that suggests what the continent's future would have been if fascism had not been defeated in the previous century. Atop a granite mountain stands an almost 500-foot-tall stone cross, the world's tallest. An enormous basilica has been hewn deep into the mountain. The effect, surely intended, of all this gigantism is the diminution of the individual.

It was, however, conceived by, and for the apotheosis of, the individual who, from his death in 1975 until last October, was buried there. Francisco Franco's remains have been removed as part of Spain's on-going grapple with the politics of memory. Like Americans disputing about Confederate statues and other discomfiting reminders of things past, Spaniards are in the difficult process of striking a delicate balance between necessary remembering and judicious forgetting.

At thirty-three, Franco became Europe's youngest general since Napoleon. In July 1936 he ignited the civil war that, until it ended with his fascist victory in 1939, was a rehearsal for the cataclysm that engulfed the rest of Europe that year. He lacked the flamboyance of the German and Italian dictators he survived by three decades, but he had a distinctive cold cruelty: He would sign death warrants while dining, sometimes stipulating death by garroting and ordering that this method be announced to deepen the grief of the loved ones of the executed.

All civil wars are savage, but Spain's—a boiling cauldron of left and right political fanaticisms, anti-clericalism, and class hatreds—was especially so. There are mass graves not yet opened. Paul Preston, a Franco biographer, judges Franco responsible for a large majority of the 200,000 murders—non-battle deaths—during and after the war. More than 33,000 are buried in the Valley of the Fallen, the largest of Spain's many unmarked gravesites. Reportedly some from the war's losing side died there doing forced labor for the winner.

In his 2019 book *After the Fall: Crisis, Recovery and the Making of a New Spain*, Tobias Buck of the *Financial Times* reports that in 2018 there were 1,143 Spanish streets named for Franco and others in his regime, and there were villages named Caudillo, the title Franco chose for himself. Forty-five years after Franco's death, Spaniards might be embarking on a confrontation with their past akin to the one Americans are having about theirs 155 years after Appomattox.

In 1977, as Spain was beginning to tiptoe toward today's status as a normal European nation, a law granted amnesty to former members of Franco's regime, including his torturers. In September 2018, however, the tacit "pact of forgetting" was forgotten, to this extent: A socialist prime minister won the approval of a divided parliament (176 of 350 members for, 165 abstaining)—its ambivalence reflected the public's—for removing Franco's body. "I believe," he said, "that a mature European democracy like ours cannot have symbols that divide Spaniards."

Writing in the National Endowment for Democracy's *Journal of Democracy* about European "memory laws," George Soroka and Felix Krawatzek note that some are "prescriptive"in that they aim to buttress national unity and social cohesiveness—and perhaps thereby resist European homogenization—by giving official imprimaturs to certain historical judgments:

> France's 2005 Mekachera Act attempted to enshrine a more posi-tive view of that country's colonial involvement in Africa; a 2014 amendment to Russia's penal code made it illegal to denigrate the actions of the Soviet Union during the Second World War; and a 2018 Polish statute attempted to protect the "good name" of the Polish state and people against any charges of complicity in Nazi atrocities, among other potential slights.

In Spain's healthy democracy, parties heatedly debate national history. The law, however, is used lightly (as with the removal of Franco's remains) to shape the future by taking, as France, Russia, Poland, and other nations have done, normative positions about the past.

Europeans walk gingerly among their cultural inheritances. The Vienna Philharmonic always plays the "Radetzky March" at its annual New Year's Day concert, which this month was broadcast to ninety-two nations. This year, however, it played an altered version of the march because it was reminded that the usual version was arranged by an Austrian who was a member of the Nazi Party and who, the *Financial Times* reports, "also made popular arrangements of the party's anthem, the Horst-Wessel-Lied." On a continent strewn with ruins, there is much to remember to remember. Or sometimes to forget.

"FALLING SOLDIER": A WELL-INTENDED FALSIFICATION

November 15, 2009

NEW YORK—The twentieth century was one hundred years of amplitude. It overflowed with barbarous fighting faiths, wars enveloping continents, and graphic journalism assaulting global audiences with scenes of shocking immediacy. The Spanish Civil War, although small in terms of the number of combatants, was perhaps the century's emblematic conflict. As a rehearsal for the Second World War, Spain's agony became a proxy struggle between fascism and communism, with democracy crushed in the middle. And for perhaps the first time, pictures supplemented and sometimes supplanted words as primary shapers of opinion about a conflict.

According to Robert Hughes, author of *The Shock of the New* (1980), during World War I's nation-shattering and culture-shredding carnage, no photograph of a dead soldier appeared in a German, French, or British newspaper. But the September 23, 1936, issue of the French magazine *Vu* published (as did *Life* magazine ten months later) what became perhaps the century's iconic photograph—"Falling Soldier." It was taken by, and launched the remarkable career of, a twenty-two-year-old Hungarian refugee from fascism, photographer Robert Capa.

It supposedly shows a single figure, a loyalist—that is, anti-fascist—soldier, at the instant of death from a bullet fired by one of Franco's soldiers. The soldier is falling backward on a hillside, arms outstretched, his rifle being flung from his right hand. This was, surely, stunning testimony to photography's consciousness-raising and history-shaping truth-telling, the camera's indisputable accuracy, its irreducibly factual rendering of reality, its refutation of epistemological pessimism about achieving certainty based on what our eyes tell us.

Probably not. A dispute that has flared intermittently for more than thirty years has been fueled afresh, and perhaps settled, by a Spanish professor who has established that the photo could not have been taken when and where it reportedly was—September 5, 1936, near Cerro Muriano.

The photo was taken about thirty-five miles from there. The precise place has been determined by identifying the mountain range in the photo's background. The professor says there was no fighting near there at that time, and concludes that Capa staged the photo.

Could an alternative explanation be that a single fascist sniper fired the fatal shot while some loyalists were at rest? No. What was once thought to be blood spurting from the falling soldier's skull is actually a tassel on his cap. And Capa several times said the soldier was felled by machine-gun fire. In a slightly less dramatic photo of another falling soldier, taken by Capa at the same time—the cloud configuration is the same as in "Falling Soldier"—the soldier falls on the same spot.

In 1995, the controversy seemed to have been settled in Capa's favor when the fallen soldier supposedly was identified as Federico Borrell García, an anarchist militiaman. But a 2007 Spanish documentary included a written eyewitness account of Borrell dying many miles away, behind a tree. There are no trees in the many pictures Capa took when he took "Falling Soldier."

The coolly analytic professionals at the International Center of Photography in midtown Manhattan, which has the Capa archives, are commendably dispassionate about the "Falling Soldier" controversy. They also avoid postmodern mush, such as: All photographs are manipulative fabrications because the photographer chooses to point the camera here and not there, and, anyway, "Falling Soldier" is "basically" truthful because it illustrates the "essential truth" about war.

Capa was a man of the left, and "Falling Soldier" helped to alarm the world about fascism rampant. But noble purposes do not validate misrepresentations. Richard Whelan, Capa's biographer, calls it "trivializing" to insist on knowing whether this photo actually shows a soldier mortally wounded. Whelan says "the picture's greatness actually lies in its symbolic implications, not in its literal accuracy."

Rubbish. The picture's greatness evaporates if its veracity is fictitious. To argue otherwise is to endorse high-minded duplicity—and to trivialize Capa, who saw a surfeit of twentieth-century war and neither flinched from its horrors nor retreated into an "I am a camera" detachment. As a warning about well-meaning falsifications of history, "Falling Soldier" matters because Capa probably fabricated reality to serve what he called "concerned photography." But this, too, matters:

There was the integrity of constant bravery in Capa's life, which was a headlong rush toward danger. He arrived on Omaha Beach with the first soldiers early on June 6, 1944, and was only forty in 1954 when, on the move with French troops in Vietnam, he stepped on a land mine.

CHINA: CHURCHILL'S FOREBODING, REDUX

July 5, 2020

WASHINGTON—The French revolutionaries' instrument for administering the 1793–1794 Reign of Terror was the Committee of Public Safety. Today, China's totalitarians, displaying either ignorance of this unsavory history or arrogance in flaunting their emulation of it, call their new instrument for suffocating Hong Kong the Commission for Safeguarding National Security. Yet again, actual tyranny is imposed in the supposed service of safety.

Acting as communists do, the leaders of China's Communist Party, which is the bone and sinew of that nation's Leninist party-state, have, less than halfway through their commitment, shredded the 1997 agreement to respect Hong Kong's autonomy until 2047. The new law mocks the rule of law, which requires sufficient specificity to give those subject to the law due notice of what is proscribed or prohibited. The new law stipulates four major offenses: separatism, subversion, terrorism, and collusion with foreign governments. These will be defined post facto, in capricious enforcements against those whose speech is not chilled by the law's menacing vagueness. The "law" authorizing the committee to operate secretly was released at eleven p.m. Tuesday, probably to deter demonstrations on Wednesday, which was the anniversary of Beijing's 1997 agreement.

Modern technologies of communication enable the world to watch darkness descend on one of the world's most vibrant metropolises. Modern technologies of surveillance enable Beijing to refine a deep, penetrating oppression beyond what Winston Churchill could have imagined when he warned that Nazism's triumph would mean the world would "sink into the abyss of a new Dark Age made more sinister, and perhaps more protracted, by the lights of perverted science."

China's faux law, which echoes Stalin's use of randomness to intensify fear, serves two purposes: It smashes Hong Kong dissent—Leninism

brooks no challenge to the party's supremacy. And it distracts attention from reports that Beijing is pioneering a sinister fusionism that
melds Leninism and Stalinism with an ethno-nationalism reminiscent
of fascism.

The regime reportedly is employing forced abortions and sterilization to
inflict what has been called "demographic genocide" on Muslim Uighurs
and other minorities. U.S. customs officials have seized some China-made
beauty products perhaps made from human hair harvested in Xinjiang
concentration camps. China's signatures on the UN Convention on
the Prevention and Punishment of the Crime of Genocide and on the
Sino-British Joint Declaration guaranteeing Hong Kong's autonomy are
equally constraining. Next year, President Joe Biden and a Democratic-
controlled Congress should match Britain's generosity in welcoming
refugees from Hong Kong's talented, freedom-loving citizenry.

In diplomatic parlance, China is a "revisionist" power, aiming to
revise the global order. In less antiseptic language, it is a piratical
power whose crudeness, born of cultural condescension toward others,
includes special contempt for an America distracted domestically by
various hysterias, and *choosing* retreat abroad. President Biden's urgent
foreign policy tasks will include revising the longstanding U.S. policy
of "strategic ambiguity" regarding Taiwan. Beijing is demonstrating in
Hong Kong "one country, two systems" actually means one country, one
simmering stew of Leninism and Stalinism flavored with fascism.

The dictator Xi Jinping has repeatedly said that Taiwan's current
status—nationhood in all but name—is intolerable and "should not be
passed down generation after generation." A re-elected Donald Trump,
whose cramped notion of America's role in the world is confined to
commercial bookkeeping, might swap Taiwan's freedom for increased
Chinese purchases of U.S. soybeans. When at noon January 20 the
United States ends the policy of making America marginal again, Biden
should adopt strategic clarity, informing Beijing that the U.S. legal obligation to sell Taiwan weaponry needed for self-defense entails a moral
obligation to assist with that project.

The Korean War, which brought Americans into combat against
Chinese troops, began seventy years ago after Dean Acheson, President

Harry S. Truman's secretary of state, gave a speech in which he left South Korea outside his definition of America's defense perimeter. Beijing has drawn a "nine-dash line" to demarcate extravagant claims to sovereignty over the South China Sea—claims incompatible with international law and disdainful of the legal rights of various nations in the region. The Biden administration should draw a line that places Taiwan within the sphere of regional nations whose self-defense implicates vital U.S. interests.

Beijing should remember this: France's Committee on Public Safety was created in April 1793. Maximilien Robespierre, who prefigured Lenin, joined it on July 27. One year and a day later, devoured by forces he had fomented, he was guillotined in Paris's Place de la Revolution, now called Place de la Concorde. Beijing's totalitarians, who have murderous French precursors, may one day have a similarly disagreeable rendezvous with their handiwork.

FAINT ECHOES OF FASCISM

July 11, 2020

WASHINGTON—So many excitable Americans are hurling accusations of fascism, there might be more definitions of "fascism" than there are actual fascists. Fascism, one of the twentieth century's fighting faiths, has only faint echoes in twenty-first-century America's political regression.

Europe's revolutionary tradition exalted liberty, equality, and fraternity until revolutionary fascism sacrificed the first to the second and third. Fascism fancied itself as modernity armed—science translated into machines, especially airplanes, and pure energy restlessly seeking things to smash. Actually, it was a recoil against Enlightenment individualism, the idea that good societies allow reasoning, rights-bearing people to define for themselves the worthy life.

Individualism, fascists insisted, produces a human dust of deracinated people (Nietzsche's "the sand of humanity") whose loneliness and purposelessness could be cured by gusts of charismatic leadership blowing them into a vibrant national-cum-tribal collectivities. The gusts were fascist rhetoric, magnified by radio, which in its novelty was a more powerful political tool than television has ever been.

The Enlightenment exalted freedom; fascism postulated destiny for those on "the right side of history." Fascism was the youthful wave of the future: Mussolini was thirty-nine when he became Italy's youngest prime minister until then; Hitler became chancellor at forty-three; Franco was forty-three when he ignited the 1936 military insurrection in Spain. In *Three Faces of Fascism* (1965), Ernst Nolte said that Mussolini, who "had no forerunners," placed "fascism" in quotation marks as a neologism.

Fascism's celebration of unfettered leaders proclaiming "only I can fix it" entailed disparagement of "parliamentarism," the politics of incrementalism and conciliation. "Democracy," said Mussolini, "has deprived the life of the people of 'style'…the color, the strength, the picturesque, the unexpected, the mystical; in sum, all that counts in the life of the masses. We play the lyre on all its strings…"

Fascism was entertainment built around rallies—e.g., those at Nuremberg—where crowds were played as passive instruments. Success manipulating the masses fed fascist leaders' disdain for the led. Hitler described them as feminine, the ultimate fascist disparagement. Imagine the contempt a promiser feels for, say, people gulled by a promise that one nation will pay for a border wall built against it by another nation.

Mussolini, a fervent socialist until his politics mutated into a rival collectivism, distilled fascism to this: "Everything within the state, nothing outside the state, nothing against the state." The Nazi Party—the National Socialist German Workers' Party—effected a broad expansion of socialism's agenda: Rather than merely melding the proletariat into a battering ram to pulverize the status quo, fascism would conscript into tribal solidarity the entire nation—with exceptions.

Fascism based national unity on shared domestic dreads—of the media as enemies of the people, of elites, or others who prevented national homogeneity and social purification. Jews were reviled as "cosmopolitans," a precursor of today's epithet: "globalists."

In the 1920s, fascism captured Italy, in which, it has been said, the poetry of the Risorgimento—national unification achieved in 1870—was followed by "the prose of everyday existence." Mussolini, the bare-chested, jut-jawed, stallion-mounted alpha male, promised (as Vladimir Putin today does in diminished, sour Russia) derivative masculinity for men bored by humdrum life in a bourgeois "little Italy." "On to Ethiopia!" was Mussolini's hollow yelp of restored Roman grandeur.

Communism had a revolutionary doctrine; fascism was more a mood than a doctrine. It was a stance of undifferentiated truculence toward the institutions and manners of liberal democracy. "The democrats of [the newspaper] *Il Mondo* want to know our program?" said Mussolini the month he came to power in 1922. "It is to break the bones of the democrats of *Il Mondo*."

In the 1930s, Spain acquired a bland fascism—fascism without a charismatic personification: nervous nationalism, leavened by clericalism and corruption. Spain's golden age was four centuries past; what was recent was the 1898 humiliation of the Spanish-American war. Paunchy Francisco Franco, a human black hole negating excitement, would make Spain great again by keeping it distinct from modern Europe, distinct in pre-Enlightenment backwardness.

Donald Trump, an envious acolyte of today's various strongmen, appeals to those in thrall to country-music manliness: "We're truck-driving, beer-drinking, big-chested Americans too freedom-loving to let any itsy-bitsy virus make us wear masks." Trump, however, is a faux nationalist who disdains his nation's golden age of international leadership and institution-building after 1945.

Trumpism, too, is a mood masquerading as a doctrine, an entertainment genre based on contempt for its bellowing audiences. Fascism was and is more interesting.

AUTHORITARIANISM AND THE
POLITICS OF EMOTION

August 2, 2020

WASHINGTON—Campaigning to become leader of Britain's parliamentary Conservative Party, and hence prime minister, Boris Johnson, the populist from Eton and Oxford, brandished a fish. Mixing hilarity with indignation, he regaled an audience by ridiculing the gnomes of Brussels whose European Union regulations torment British producers of smoked kippers by requiring the fish to be shipped on plastic ice pillows.

The problem with Johnson's vaudevillian performance was that this regulation was written by the British government. This fact was, however, no problem for Johnson, who became prime minister. As Anne Applebaum says in her book *Twilight of Democracy*, Johnson has a "penchant for fabrication"—he was fired from the *London Times* for concocting quotes, and from a Conservative shadow cabinet for lying. This is part of what her book's subtitle calls "the seductive lure of authoritarianism," which delivers delightful liberation from the tyranny of facts.

Applebaum is a much-honored historian, long-time columnist for the *Washington Post*, now with the *Atlantic*. She lives in Europe, where Plato pioneered Western political philosophy, warning that demagogues could make democracy a springboard to tyranny. Today, the European Union's twenty-seven nations include two authoritarian regimes, Poland's and especially Hungary's, which has closed an entire university, and which operates, directly or through regime-linked companies, 90 percent of the nation's media.

Writing in the National Endowment for Democracy's *Journal of Democracy* ("Reclaiming the Politics of Emotion"), Jaroslaw Kuisz and Karolina Wigura, both Poles, note that populists have sensed "that a feeling of loss is today the dominant collective emotion." This is particularly so in Eastern Europe, where tumultuous change followed the cracking of the concrete that communism had poured over society.

But even in Britain's open society, which has experienced no comparable social disjunction, nostalgia akin to personal grief has fueled a populist politics of resentment. Nostalgia, wrote the sociologist and philosopher Robert Nisbet, is "at best a rust of memory," which picks a vanished historic epoch and bathes it in sentimentality.

Paradoxically, populist authoritarianism derives indispensable fuel from discontented intellectuals who believe, as Applebaum says, "that the wrong people have influence" in the realm of ideas. But as she says, authoritarianism "is a frame of mind, not a set of ideas."

Today it seduces the "radically lonely individual" who finds a sheltering home in an immersive political movement or environment that rejects "the hateful notions of meritocracy, political competition, and the free market, principles that, by definition, have never benefited the less successful." Authoritarianism offers not careers open to talents, but rather the populist promise of upward mobility for those whose political connections and conformity spares them the need "for competition, or for exams, or for a résumé bristling with achievements."

Authoritarianism is a temptation for people recoiling against complexity and intellectual pluralism, and yearning for social homogeneity. Applebaum says, "The noise of argument, the constant hum of disagreement—these can irritate people who prefer to live in a society tied together by a single narrative." In today's United States, such authoritarianism flourishes most conspicuously on the left, in the cancel culture's attempts to extinguish rival voices.

The current president is America's misfortune; America's good fortune has been that his mental fidgets disqualify him from mastering the means for authoritarian ends, means that, in any case, would be blocked by the nation's judiciary. Authoritarianism is, however, incubated on America's right among conservatives in the grip of cultural despair.

Applebaum notes that until recently "the most apocalyptic visions of American civilization" festered on the left, among people convinced that capitalism must breed unlovely opulence among the few, immiseration of the many, and alienation of everyone from the dignity of work. Today, however, there is a pandemic of right-wing pessimism, predictions of America's doom unless unambiguously unconstitutional measures are taken to combat secularism.

So far, authoritarian impulses on the left and right are confined to the fever swamps of social media, where, as Applebaum says, "readers and writers feel distant from one another and from the issues they describe, where everyone can be anonymous and no one needs to take responsibility for what they say."

"History," says Applebaum, "suddenly feels circular" in various European regions: "Given the right conditions, any society can turn against democracy. Indeed, if history is anything to go by, all of our societies eventually will." The good news, such as it is, is that a necessary—although not sufficient—precondition for authoritarianism's defeat is what Applebaum's book trenchantly argues for: disbelief in the defeat's inevitability.

COMPLAINTS AND APPRECIATIONS

THE PLAGUE OF DENIM

April 16, 2009

WASHINGTON—On any American street, or in any airport or mall, you see the same sad tableau: A ten-year-old boy is walking with his father, whose development was evidently arrested when he was that age, judging by his clothes. Father and son are dressed identically—running shoes, T-shirts. And jeans, always jeans. If mother is there, she, too, is draped in denim.

Writer Daniel Akst has noticed and has had a constructive conniption. He should be given the Presidential Medal of Freedom. He has earned it by identifying an obnoxious misuse of freedom. Writing in the *Wall Street Journal*, he has denounced denim, summoning Americans to soul-searching and repentance about the plague of that ubiquitous fabric, which is symptomatic of deep disorders in the national psyche.

It is, he says, a manifestation of "the modern trend toward un-differentiated dressing, in which we all strive to look equally shabby." Denim reflects "our most nostalgic and destructive agrarian longings—the ones that prompted all those exurban McMansions now sliding off their manicured lawns and into foreclosure." Jeans come prewashed and acid-treated to make them look like what they are not—authentic work clothes for horny-handed sons of toil and the soil. Denim on the bourgeoisie is, Akst says, the wardrobe equivalent of driving a Hummer to a Whole Foods store—discordant.

Long ago, when James Dean and Marlon Brando wore it, denim was, Akst says, "a symbol of youthful defiance." Today, Silicon Valley billionaires are rebels without causes beyond poses, wearing jeans when introducing new products. Akst's summa contra denim is grand as far as it goes, but it only scratches the surface of this blight on Americans' surfaces. Denim is the infantile uniform of a nation in which entertainment frequently features childlike adults (*Seinfeld, Two and a Half Men*) and cartoons for adults (*King of the Hill*). Seventy-five percent of American "gamers"—people who play video games—are older than eighteen and nevertheless are allowed to vote. In their undifferentiated dress, children and their childish parents become undifferentiated audiences for juvenilized movies (the six—so far—*Batman* adventures and *Indiana Jones and the Credit-Default Swaps*, coming soon to a cineplex near you). Denim is the clerical vestment for the priesthood of all believers in democracy's catechism of leveling—thou shalt not dress better than society's most slovenly. To do so would be to commit the sin of lookism—of believing that appearance matters. That heresy leads to denying the universal appropriateness of everything, and then to the elitist assertion that there is good and bad taste.

Denim is the carefully calculated costume of people eager to communicate indifference to appearances. But the appearances that people choose to present in public are cues from which we make inferences about their maturity and respect for those to whom they are presenting themselves.

Do not blame Levi Strauss for the misuse of Levis. When the Gold Rush began, Strauss moved to San Francisco planning to sell strong fabric for the 49ers' tents and wagon covers. Eventually, however, he made tough pants, reinforced by copper rivets, for the tough men who knelt on the muddy, stony banks of Northern California creeks, panning for gold. Today it is silly for Americans whose closest approximation of physical labor consists of loading their bags of clubs into golf carts to go around in public dressed for driving steers up the Chisholm Trail to the railhead in Abilene.

This is not complicated. For men, sartorial good taste can be reduced to one rule: If Fred Astaire would not have worn it, don't wear it. For women, substitute Grace Kelly.

Edmund Burke—what he would have thought of the denimization of America can be inferred from his lament that the French Revolution assaulted "the decent drapery of life"; it is a straight line from the fall of the Bastille to the rise of denim—said: "To make us love our country, our country ought to be lovely." Ours would be much more so if supposed grown-ups would heed St. Paul's first letter to the Corinthians, and St. Barack's inaugural sermon to the Americans, by putting away childish things, starting with denim.

(A confession: The author owns one pair of jeans. Wore them once. Had to. Such was the dress code for former Senator Jack Danforth's seventieth birthday party, where Jerry Jeff Walker sang his classic "Up Against the Wall, Redneck Mother." Music for a jeans-wearing crowd.)

DROWNING IN A RIVER OF PUBLIC WORDS

October 27, 2011

WASHINGTON—You step onto an airport's moving walkway, a flat metal conveyor belt that conveys travelers down an airport concourse, sparing them the indignity of burning a few calories by walking a bit. And soon a recorded voice says: "The moving sidewalk is coming to an end. Please look down."

Well, yes. Pretty much everything does come to an end, doesn't it? Besides, we can actually *see* what we already knew—the moving walkway does not go on forever. So, is that announcement about it ending really necessary? Whatever happened to the rule, "Do not speak unless you can improve the silence"?

Passing through an American airport is an immersion in a merciless river of words. They are intended to be helpful but clearly they flow from an assumption that increasingly animates our government in its trans-actions with us. The assumption is that we are all infants or imbeciles in need of constant kindly supervision and nudging, lest we allow ourselves to be flung off a moving walkway and over the edge of the world.

In Denver, underground trains take passengers to and from the ticketing area and departure concourses. As a train arrives, an announcement slightly louder than the noise of the arriving train says: "A train is arriving." Do tell.

At Kansas City's airport, a recurring announcement tells travelers: "Designated smoking areas are located outside, away from doors." That means the designated smoking areas *are* pretty much the entire Midwest and everything contiguous to it—all of Creation that is "away from" this airport's doors.

Perhaps some silly warnings are "necessary" to fend off the Fourth Branch of government, aka trial lawyers. But this merely underscores the fact that all this noise is symptomatic of modern derangements. Solemn warnings about nonexistent risks and information intended to spare us the slightest responsibility for passing through life with a modicum of attention and intelligence—these express, among other things, an entitlement mentality the nanny state foments: If something bad or even inconvenient or merely annoying happens to us, even if it results from our foolishness, daydreaming, or brooding about the meaning of life, we are entitled to sue *someone* for restitution.

These minatory pronouncements pouring from public address systems would drive us mad if we made the mistake of paying attention to them. Fortunately, Americans' adaptive response to the ubiquity of advertising has caused them to develop mental filters that reduce public pronouncements to audible wallpaper—there but not noticed. Perhaps this is why the Department of Homeland Security no longer bothers to tell travelers it has set the terrorist threat level at burnt umber, or whatever.

And while we are at this, let us, as lawyers say, stipulate that Wolf Blitzer is a prince of a fellow and CNN is an ornament to civilization. Still, is it bad citizenship to wish one could sit in an airport without enduring journalism?

The drizzle of superfluous words continues on the plane, beginning with "this is a no-smoking flight"—please tell us something we don't already know: smoking on planes has been banned for more than a decade—and ending with the admonition that deplaning passengers should "make sure you have all your belongings." Shoes? Check. Trousers? Check.

In the Augusta, Georgia, airport, soft chimes—a pleasant Southern touch—warn travelers that the eighty-six-word announcement they heard just ten minutes ago is about to belabor them again: "May I have your attention please. All travelers. If any unknown person attempts to give you any item…No liquids, aerosol cans or gels…There are a few exceptions such as insulin and baby formula." Every ten minutes, never mind the Eighth Amendment to the Constitution.

"If we had a keen vision and feeling of all ordinary human life," wrote George Eliot in *Middlemarch*, "it would be like hearing the grass grow and the squirrel's heartbeat, and we should die of that roar which lies on the other side of silence." What silence? Where? One would fly there, were it not necessary to run the gantlet of airport words.

More and more public spaces are like airports, places where we are assaulted by instructions, advice, warnings, and unwanted information. Almost none of this noise is necessary for people mature enough to be allowed to walk around the block, let alone fly around the country. This is the way the world will end, not with a bang but with an environmental blitzkrieg of blather.

HOBBES AT WHOLE FOODS

October 11, 2009

WASHINGTON—Consider nature. Not the placid nature that Constable painted, but nature as Tennyson saw it, "red in tooth and claw." To glimpse a state of nature as Hobbes imagined it, where human life is "nasty, brutish and short," visit the Whole Foods store on River Road in Bethesda, Maryland. There, and—let the political profiling begin—probably at many Whole Food stores and other magnets for liberals, nationwide, you will see proof of this social equation: Four Priuses + three parking spaces = angry anarchy.

Anger is one of the seven deadly sins. Therefore advanced thinkers are agreed that conservatives are especially susceptible to it. As everyone knows, all liberals are advanced thinkers and all advanced thinkers are liberals. And yet...

If you think the health care town halls in August cornered the market on anger, come to Bethesda and watch the private security force—normal men in an abnormal situation—wage a losing struggle to keep the lid on liberal anger. When parking lot congestion impedes the advance of responsible eaters toward the bin of heirloom tomatoes, you see that anger comes in many flavors.

You also see the problem with founding a nation, as America is founded, on the principle that human beings are rights-bearing creatures. That they are. But if that is all they are, batten down the hatches.

If our vocabulary is composed exclusively of references to rights, aka entitlements, we are condemned to endless jostling among elbow-throwing individuals irritably determined to protect, or enlarge, the boundaries of their rights. Among such people, all political discourse tends to be distilled to what Mary Ann Glendon of Harvard Law School calls "rights talk."

Witness the inability of people nowadays to recommend this or that health care policy as merely wise or just. Each proposal must be invested with the dignity of a *right*. And since not all proposals are compatible, you have not merely differences of opinion but apocalyptic clashes of rights.

Rights talk is inherently aggressive, even imperial; it tends toward moral inflation and militates against accommodation. Rights talkers, with their inner monologues of pre-emptive resentments, work themselves into a simmering state of annoyed vigilance against any limits on their willfulness. To rights talkers, life—always and everywhere—is unbearably congested with insufferable people impertinently rights talking, and behaving, the way you and I of course have a real right to.

Recently Paul Schwartzman, a war correspondent for the Metro section of the *Washington Post*, ventured into the combat zone that is the Chevy

Chase neighborhood in the District of Columbia. It is not a neighborly place nowadays. Residents are at daggers drawn over...speed humps.

Chevy Chase, D.C., is, Schwartzman says, "a community that views itself as the essence of worldly sophistication." Some cars there express their owner's unassuageable anger by displaying faded "Kerry/Edwards" and even "Gore/Lieberman" bumper stickers. Neighborhood zoning probably excludes Republicans, other than the few who are bused in for "diversity."

Speed humps—the lumps on the pavement that force traffic to go slow—have, Schwartzman reports, precipitated "a not-so-civil war...among the lawyers, journalists, policymakers and wonks" of Chevy Chase—and Cleveland Park, another D.C. habitat for liberals. The problem is that a goal of liberal urbanists has been achieved: Families with young children are moving into such neighborhoods. They worry about fast-flowing traffic. Hence speed humps.

And street rage. Some people who think speed humps infringe their rights protest by honking when they drive over one. The purpose is to make life unpleasant for the people who live on the street and think they have a right to have the humps. One resident, who Schwartzman identifies as the husband of a former campaign manager for Hillary Clinton, recently sat on his porch and videotaped an angry driver who honked *thirty times*. Other honkers "gave residents the finger as they drove by."

Can't liberals play nicely together? Not, evidently, when they are bristling, like furious porcupines, with spiky rights that demand respect because the rights-bearers' dignity is implicated in them.

Fortunately, it is a short drive from Chevy Chase to the mellow oasis of the River Road Whole Foods store, where comity can be rebuilt on the firm foundation of a shared reverence for heirloom tomatoes. And if you, you seething liberal, will put the pedal to the metal you can seize the store's last parking place. So damn the humps, full speed ahead.

A CAR UNDER A CLOUD OF SMUG

May 13, 2012

> "You have a Prius...You probably compost, sort all your re-
> cycling, and have a reusable shopping bag for your short drive
> to Whole Foods. You are the best! So, do we really need the
> Obama sticker?"
>
> — *The Portland Mercury*, 2008

WASHINGTON—Prius, which is Latin for "to go before" or "lead the
way," is the perfect name for the car whose owners are confident they
are leading the way for the benighted. "Prius preening," an almost erotic
pleasure, is, however, a perishable delight because the status derived from
enlightened exclusivity evaporates if the hoi polloi crash the party.

The connection between cars and self-image is as American as the
anti-Prius, the F-150 pickup truck. This connection is the subject of
the entertaining and instructive book *Engines of Change: A History
of the American Dream in Fifteen Cars* by Paul Ingrassia, a journalist
knowledgeable about the automobile industry. He thinks the hinge
of our history was the 1920s, when General Motors' LaSalle was
introduced as a conspicuous-consumption alternative to Henry Ford's
pedestrian, so to speak, Model T. Since then, Ingrassia says, American
culture has been a tug of war "between the practical and the pretentious,
the frugal versus the flamboyant, haute cuisine versus hot wings."

The Model T, born in 1908, was priced at $850. By 1924, it was
offered only in black but cost just $260 and had America on the
move. Three years later—the year Babe Ruth hit sixty home runs and
Charles Lindbergh flew the Atlantic—the LaSalle, a Cadillac sibling, announced Detroit's determination to join Hollywood as a manufacturer
of visual entertainment, but working in chrome rather than celluloid.
The phrase "It's a Duesie" became an American encomium in tribute

to the Duesenberg, which sold for upward of $20,000, or $245,000 in today's dollars.

In 1953, after almost twenty-five years of Depression and war, the Korean armistice signaled the restoration of the pleasure principle, as did the December appearance of two first editions—of Hugh Hefner's *Playboy* magazine and Chevrolet's Corvette. The so-called "Father of the Corvette" Zora Arkus-Duntov—English was his fourth language— explained: "In our age where the average person is a cog wheel who gets pushed in the subways, elevators, department stores, cafeterias...the ownership of a different car provides the means to ascertain his individuality to himself and everybody around." Ere long, Supreme Court Justice Clarence Thomas's Corvette license plate read "RES IPSA," lawyer's Latin for "It speaks for itself." And loudly.

The 1950s brought tail fins (justified as safety devices—"directional stabilizers") on land yachts such as the twenty-one-foot-long 1959 Cadillac. A small-is-beautiful reaction came in the form of a car originally named the Kraft durch Freude Wagen ("Strength through Joy Car"), a clunky name no one criticized, because it was bestowed by the Volkswagen's progenitor, Adolf Hitler, the unlikely father of the emblematic vehicle of 1960s hippies, the VW Microbus. (Steve Jobs sold his for startup capital for his business.)

Thanks to Ralph Nader, Chevrolet's small Corvair begat a growth industry—lawsuits—and a president. (The Corvair made Nader famous, and thirty-five years later his 97,000 Florida votes gave George W. Bush the presidency.) Baby boomers had babies so they had to buy minivans, but got revenge against responsibilities by buying "the ultimate driving machine." This is from a 1989 *Los Angeles Times* restaurant review: "There they are, the men with carefully wrinkled $800 sports jackets...the BMW cowboys...they're all here, grazing among the arugula."

Boomers, says Ingrassia, "had to buy to live, just as sharks had to swim to breathe." They bought stuff that screamed: "Cognoscenti!" Dove bars—the ultimate ice cream bar?—not Eskimo Pies. Anchor Steam, not Budweiser. Starbucks, not Dunkin' Donuts. And Perrier, when gas cost less than designer water. In 1978, an early reaction against all this made Ford's F-150 pickup what it still is, America's best-selling vehicle.

In 2003, Toyota previewed its second-generation Prius at Whole Foods supermarkets and an international yoga convention. And in the cartoon town of South Park, Priuses became so popular the town developed a huge cloud of "smug." Prius, vehicle of the vanguard of the intelligentsia, does not have the most obnoxious name ever given an automobile. In 1927, Studebaker, which anticipated the Prius mentality, named one of its models the Dictator. The car supposedly dictated standards that the unwashed would someday emulate. In the mid-1930s, Studebaker canceled the name.

FRANK SINATRA'S REMINDER

December 10, 2015

WASHINGTON—In today's culture of hyperbole, born of desperate attempts to be noticed amid the Niagara of Internet and other outpourings, the label "genius" is affixed promiscuously to evanescent popular entertainers, fungible corporate CEOs, and other perishable phenomena. But it almost fits the saloon singer—his preferred description of himself—who was born one hundred years ago, on December 12, 1915, in Hoboken, New Jersey.

It is, however, more precise and, in a way, more flattering to say that Frank Sinatra should be celebrated for his craftsmanship. Of geniuses, we have, it seems, a steady stream. Actual craftsmen are rarer and more useful because they are exemplary for anyone with a craft, be it surgery or carpentry. Sinatra was many things, some of them—libertine, bully, gangster groupie—regrettable. But he unquestionably was the greatest singer of American songs.

How should an artist's character and private life condition our appreciation of his or her art? How, say, should knowledge of T. S. Eliot's anti-Semitism condition one's admiration for his poetry? With Sinatra, tune out the public personality and listen to his music as Miles Davis, Duke Ellington, Benny Goodman, Gerry Mulligan, and Oscar Peterson did. They all, according to the culture critic Terry Teachout, named Sinatra their most admired singer.

For decades he was, Teachout says, "the fixed star in the crowded sky of American popular culture." It speaks well of Sinatra, and reveals the prickly pride that sometimes made him volcanic, that he refused to adopt a less Italian name when ethnicity was problematic in the waning days of America's Anglo-Saxon ascendancy. Anthony Dominick Benedetto (Tony Bennett) and Dino Paul Crocetti (Dean Martin) adjusted. Sinatra was an unadjusted man.

In spite of the spectacular vulgarity of Sinatra's choices of friends and fun, he bequeathed to postwar America a sense of style, even male elegance. His Las Vegas cavorting with "The Rat Pack" (Martin, Sammy Davis Jr., Joey Bishop, Peter Lawford) was an embarrassing manifestation of 1950s arrested-development masculinity—adolescence forever. But never mind his toupees and elevator shoes, his loutish flunkies and violent bodyguards, his many awful movies and public brawls, his pimping for Camelot. And never mind that the comedian Shecky Greene was not altogether joking when he said: "Sinatra saved my life in 1967. Five guys were beating me up, and I heard Frank say, 'That's enough.'"

Never mind the tawdriness so abundantly reported in the just-published second volume of James Kaplan's 1,765-page biography (*Sinatra: The Chairman*). But you must remember this: In a recording studio, Sinatra, who could not read music, was a meticulous collaborator with great musicians—including the Hollywood String Quartet—and arrangers.

For Sinatra, before a song was music, it was words alone. He studied lyrics, internalized them, then sang, making music from poems. His good fortune was that he had one of the nation's cultural treasures, the Great American Songbook, to interpret. It was the good fortune of that book's authors—Cole Porter, the Gershwins, Johnny Mercer, and many others—that Sinatra came along to remind some Americans and inform others of that book's existence.

This is one kind of popular music:

I can't get no satisfaction,
I can't get no girl reaction

This is Sinatra's kind:

The summer wind came blowin' in from across the sea
It lingered there, to touch your hair and walk with me
All summer long we sang a song and then we strolled that golden sand
Two sweethearts and the summer wind
Like painted kites, those days and nights, they went flyin' by
The world was new beneath a blue umbrella sky
Then softer than a piper man, one day it called to you
I lost you, I lost you to the summer wind
The autumn wind, and the winter winds, they have come and gone
And still the days, those lonely days, they go on and on
And guess who sighs his lullabies through nights that never end
My fickle friend, the summer wind.

Frequent performing, and too much Jack Daniel's, and too many unfiltered Camel cigarettes took their toll before he acknowledged this and left the road, much too late. However, his reputation is preserved by the short-term memory loss of a nation that will forever hear the Sinatra of the 1940s, 1950s, and 1960s.

Kaplan reports, according to "legend," that Sinatra's casket in a Palm Springs cemetery contains some Jack Daniel's and Camels. If so, even in death, Sinatra did it his way.

APPROPRIATION INDIGNATION:
ELVIS, HOW COULD YOU!

May 14, 2017

WASHINGTON—In July 1954, a nineteen-year-old Memphis truck driver recorded at Sun Studio the song "That's All Right." When a local disc jockey promised to play it, the truck driver tuned his parents' radio to the station and went to a movie. His mother pulled him from the theater because the DJ was playing the record repeatedly and wanted to interview the singer immediately. The DJ asked where the singer had gone to high school. He answered, "Humes," an all-white school. The DJ asked because many callers "who like your record think you must be colored, singing the way you do." Elvis Presley from Tupelo, Mississippi, had committed "cultural appropriation."

According to Ray Connolly in *Being Elvis*, Arthur "Big Boy" Crudup, a black Mississippian, had popularized "That's All Right." When Presley first entered the recording studio, he was asked, "Who do you sound like?" He replied, "I don't sound like nobody." Actually, he sounded like someone melding the sounds of gospel, country, and what was then called "race music"—music by Southern blacks—to make something new.

The hysteria du jour, on campuses and elsewhere, against "appropriation" illustrates progressivism's descent into authoritarianism leavened by philistinism. This "preening silliness"—the phrase is from The Federalist's David Marcus—is by people oblivious to the fact that, as Marcus says, "culture blending is central to the development of, well, everything."

Indignation about appropriation is a new frontier in the ever-expanding empire of cultivated victimhood: "Marginalized" persons from a particular culture supposedly are somehow wounded when "privileged" people—those who are unvictimized or less victimized—express or even just enjoy the culture of more pure victims without their permission.

The wearing of sombreros at tequila-themed parties triggered—to speak the language of the exquisitely sensitive—the anti-appropriation constabulary at Bowdoin College. Oberlin College's palate police denounced as "appropriative" an allegedly inauthentic preparation of General Tso's chicken. Such nonsense is harmless—until it morphs into attempts to regulate something serious, like writing fiction: Do not write about cultures other than your own.

With characteristic tartness, novelist Lionel Shriver responded to this "climate of scrutiny" when, at a writers' conference, she clapped a sombrero on her head and said: We're not supposed to try on other people's hats? That's what we're paid to do. Instead, "any tradition, any experience, any costume, any way of doing and saying things, that is associated with a minority or disadvantaged group is ring-fenced: look-but-don't-touch."

Eugene Volokh, law professor and maestro of the Volokh Conspiracy blog, drolly says: If only there were a word for "telling people that they mustn't do something because of their race or ethnic origin." Asks Franklin Einspruch, writing in The Federalist, "Where does new culture come from? It is copied, with alterations, from existing culture. The process is reproductive. Sexy, even. So of course, the outrage-as-a-lifestyle wing of the progressive left wants to dictate rules for its proper enjoyment."

The Federalist's Robert Tracinski says appropriation is actually learning through admiration, adding: "The left loudly promotes its flattering self-image as…more culturally open and advanced—more intellectual, artistic, and cosmopolitan," but its "appropriation" tantrums reveal how its fixation with "racial identity and resentments ends up imposing the narrowest kinds of parochialism."

The University of Pennsylvania's Jonathan Zimmerman, writing in the *Chronicle of Higher Education*, says "the mostly left-wing quest for cultural purity bears an eerie echo to the right-wing fantasy of national purity, which peaked during the so-called 100-percent-American campaigns of the early 20th century." Of Chuck Berry, Zimmerman writes: "His first big hit, 'Maybellene,' adapted an old melody that had been recorded by country-music performers like Bob Wills and His Texas Playboys. Berry combined the 'hillbilly' sound of white country with the African-American rhythm and blues that he imbibed in his native St. Louis." For this, he was heckled in Harlem.

John Lennon said, "Before Elvis, there was nothing." Not really: There was Crudup, and before him there was a long, creatively tangled line of precursors. Elvis, said Mick Jagger, was "an original in an area of imitators." Actually, no cultural figure is entirely original.

Listening to Radio Luxembourg late one night, teenaged Keith Richards heard "Heartbreak Hotel," and "when I woke up the next day I was a different guy." Bob Dylan, a freewheeling cultural appropriator himself, said, "Hearing Elvis for the first time was like busting out of jail." Those who would wall off cultures from "outsiders" are would-be wardens.

BOB DYLAN'S TWO PROPOSITIONS

December 11, 2016

WASHINGTON—There has been ferment among the literati since Bob Dylan was awarded the Nobel Prize in Literature. Many say that however well Dylan does what he does, it is not literature. Dylan did not go to Stockholm Saturday to collect his prize, which the Swedish Academy says was awarded "for having created new poetic expressions within the great American song tradition." Well, then:

God said to Abraham, "Kill me a son"
Abe says, "Man, you must be puttin' me on."

or:

Einstein, disguised as Robin Hood
With his memories in a trunk
Passed this way an hour ago
With his friend, a jealous monk
He looked so immaculately frightful
As he bummed a cigarette
Then he went off sniffing drainpipes
And reciting the alphabet
Now you would not think to look at him
But he was famous long ago
For playing the electric violin
On Desolation Row.

The *New York Times* primly notes that the academy is famous for "its at times almost willful perversity in picking winners." Scottish novelist Irvine Welsh (*Trainspotting*) professes himself "a Dylan fan" but tweeted that the Nobel is "an ill-conceived nostalgia award wrenched from the rancid prostates of senile, gibbering hippies." Strong letter to follow.

One critic says that the more than 150 books on Dylan are "a library woozy with humid overstatement and baby boomer mythology." A sample of the humidity is: "Dylan seemed less to occupy a turning point in cultural space and time than to be that turning point." But Dylan should not be blamed for the hyperventilating caused by DDS—Dylan Derangement Syndrome. Besides, Dylan has collected a Pulitzer Prize for "lyrical compositions of extraordinary poetic power," so there.

Now seventy-five, he was born Robert Zimmerman in Duluth, Minnesota, and lived in Hibbing, Minnesota, 150 miles from Sauk Centre, Minnesota, home of Sinclair Lewis, who won the 1930 Nobel for literature (*Babbitt, Elmer Gantry*). This was evidence of abruptly defining literature down: Thomas Mann won in 1929. If you recognize even one-third of the 113 literature prize winners since 1901, you need to get out of the house more. Philip Roth has not won, a fact that would cost the Swedish Academy its reputation for seriousness, if it had one.

The *Weekly Standard*'s Andrew Ferguson would win the Nobel Prize for Common Sense, if there were one. He notes that by not taking himself too seriously or encouraging others to do so, Dylan has "proved two propositions that seemed increasingly unlikely in the age of media-saturation: You can shun publicity and still be hugely famous, and you can be hugely famous and not be obnoxious about it." For this, Dylan deserves some sort of prize. Ferguson laments that it is evidently impossible to take Dylan "for what he is, an impressive man worthy of admiration, affection and respect, and leave it at that."

Impossible. In an age of ever more extravagant attention-getting yelps about everything, people have tumbled over one another reaching for encomia, such as this from a Harvard professor: "Dylan has surpassed Walt Whitman as the defining American artist."

(Hawthorne, Melville, Dickinson, Wharton, Fitzgerald, Faulkner?)

If song lyrics are literature, why did the academy discover this with Dylan and not Stephen Sondheim (from *West Side Story* on)? Last year, the literature prize was won by Belarus's Svetlana Alexievich, whose specialty is interviews woven into skillfully wrought books (e.g.,

Secondhand Time). They are highly informative, even moving, but are they literature?

Sean Wilentz, Princeton professor of American history, grew up in New York City near the end of its red-tinged folk revival and was thirteen when he attended Dylan's 1964 concert at Manhattan's Philharmonic Hall. Wilentz's book *Bob Dylan in America*, which would better have been titled *America in Bob Dylan*, interestingly locates him in the stream of American culture and celebrates him for expanding his range as relentlessly as he has toured—more than 1,400 shows in this century. Wilentz recalls how Dylan "going electric" at the 1965 Newport Folk Festival scandalized "the fetishists of authenticity," but Dylan did not look back. "He sees," Wilentz says, "a kind of literature in performance." If that is so, then is Mike Trout, baseball's best performer, doing literature for the Los Angeles Angels? Literature is becoming a classification that no longer classifies.

Never mind. Just enjoy the music of the surprising man who in 1961 arrived in Greenwich Village and who once said "my favorite politician was Arizona Senator Barry Goldwater."

THE BEACH BOYS AND THE BOOMERS' MUSIC-CUED NOSTALGIA

June 21, 2012

COLUMBIA, Md.—Three hours before showtime, Brian Wilson says: "There is no Rhonda." Sitting backstage, gathering strength for the evening's forty-eight-song, 150-minute concert, Wilson was not asked about her, he just volunteered this fact. The other members of the Beach Boys seem mildly surprised to learn that the 1965 song "Help Me, Rhonda" was about no one in particular.

Not that it matters; the sound is everything. Attention must be paid to baby boomer music-cued nostalgia, and no one pays it better than the Beach Boys. They are currently on a fiftieth-anniversary tour that has more than sixty concerts scheduled and others still being booked. Their new album, *That's Why God Made the Radio*, debuted at number three in *Billboard*'s listing, and with this the Beach Boys topped the Beatles for most weeks on *Billboard*'s top-ten album chart.

Their band began in 1961 in Hawthorne, in Los Angeles County, when the parents of Brian, Dennis, and Carl Wilson went away for a weekend, leaving the boys with meal money they used to rent instruments and record a song called "Surfin'." They rode a wave of fascination with California to the top of pop music.

Given California's dystopian present, it is difficult to recall that the Beach Boys' appeal derived not just from their astonishing harmonies (which derived from the Four Freshmen) but also from their embodiment of a happy Southern California that beckoned to the rest of the nation. Political scientist James Q. Wilson grew up there, and in 1967, the year after the Beach Boys' "Good Vibrations," he wrote a seminal essay on the political vibrations that produced California's new governor: "A Guide to Reagan Country." Wilson's conclusion was that Ronald Reagan represented the political culture of a region where social structure nurtured individualism.

Southern Californians had, Wilson wrote, "no identities except their personal identities, no obvious group affiliations to make possible any reference to them by collective nouns. I never heard the phrase 'ethnic group' until I was in graduate school." Eastern teenagers had turf. Their Southern California counterparts had cars, the subject of so many Beach Boys songs ("Little Deuce Coupe," "409," "Shut Down," etc.). They hung out in places reached by car and with lots of parking, particularly drive-in restaurants. "The Eastern lifestyle," Wilson wrote, "produced a feeling of territory, the Western lifestyle a feeling of *property*." The East was defined less by cold weather than social congestion—apartments in ethnic neighborhoods. Southern Californians lived in single-dwelling homes and had almost no public transportation, so their movements within the city were unconfined to set corridors. Houses and cars— the "Sunday afternoon drive" was often just to look at others' homes— strengthened, Wilson wrote, "a very conventional and bourgeois sense of property and responsibility."

When James Watt, Reagan's secretary of the interior, barred the Beach Boys from playing a Fourth of July concert on the National Mall in 1983 because he thought they attracted "the wrong element," Reagan invited them to the White House. This was almost a generation after the Beach Boys were dethroned but invigorated by the challenge of the British Invasion, particularly the Beatles.

Brian Wilson has long been troubled by mental illness, but he responded to the challenge of the Beatles album *Rubber Soul* with *Pet Sounds*, including "God Only Knows," which Paul McCartney called "the greatest song ever written." The Beatles' *Sgt. Pepper* was a response to *Pet Sounds*. Leonard Bernstein called Brian Wilson, the Beach Boys' creative engine, "one of today's most important musicians," and the Joffrey Ballet danced to Wilson's music.

Dennis and Carl Wilson died long ago, but today's band includes three original members—Brian, Al Jardine, and Mike Love—plus David Marks, who grew up down the street from the Wilsons, and Bruce Johnston, "the new guy" who first joined the group in 1965. The Beatles dissolved in 1970; the Beach Boys are the first American band to enter a second half-century.

Boomers must be served, so Mick Jagger, who long ago said, "I'd rather be dead than sing 'Satisfaction' when I'm forty-five," is singing it at sixty-eight. In 1966, the thirty-one-year-old Elvis Presley asked the Beach Boys for advice about touring; he has been dead for nearly thirty-five years but they play on, all of them approaching or past seventy, singing "When I Grow Up (to Be a Man)" without a trace of irony. Southern California in their formative years was not zoned for irony.

DOWNTON ABBEY AND NOSTALGIA GLUTTONY

February 13, 2014

WASHINGTON—Many *Downton Abbey* watchers are nostalgia gluttons who grieved when Lord Grantham lost his fortune in Canadian railroad shares. There are, however, a discerning few whose admirable American sensibilities caused them to rejoice about Grantham's loss: "Now perhaps this amiable but dilettantish toff will get off his duff and get a job."

This drama's verisimilitude extends to emphasizing that his lordship had a fortune to squander only because he married an American heiress. By battening on what they disdained, this republic's commercial culture, many British aristocrats could live beyond their inherited means—actual work being, of course, unthinkable.

The deserved decline of Downton's finances demonstrates why estate taxes are unnecessary: Even when Balzac's axiom is accurate ("At the bottom of every great fortune without apparent source, there's always some crime") and fortunes are ill-gotten, subsequent generations often soon fritter them away. Call this Darwinian redistribution.

Americans have an unslakable appetite for British artistic syrup. Charles Dickens, although a noble spirit and literary genius, could be so insufferably saccharine that his flinty Mr. Gradgrind in *Hard Times* ("The Good Samaritan was a Bad Economist") seemed like a breath of fresh air. In 1841, when Dickens was serializing *The Old Curiosity Shop*, the ship arriving in America carrying the latest installment reportedly was greeted by dockworkers shouting, "Is Nell still alive?"

But Oscar Wilde was right: "One must have a heart of stone to read the death of little Nell without laughing." And one must have a head of stone to enjoy the *Downton Abbey* scene when Matthew, a fragment of the upper crust whose war wound had left him in a wheelchair, sees that Lavinia, another chip off the old crust, is about to trip while carrying a heavy tray. Gallantry propels Matthew up from his chair and he is ambulatory once again and ever more.

It is fitting that PBS offers *Downton Abbey* to its disproportionately progressive audience. This series is a languid appreciation of a class structure supposedly tempered by the paternalism of the privileged. And if progressivism prevails, America will *be* Downton Abbey: Upstairs, the administrators of the regulatory state will, with a feudal sense of noblesse oblige, assume responsibility for the lower orders downstairs, gently protecting them from "substandard" health insurance policies, school choice, gun ownership, large sodas, and other decisions that experts consider naughty or calamitous.

Why, however, does a normally wise and lucid conservative such as Peter Augustine Lawler, professor of government at Berry College, celebrate the "astute nostalgia" of *Downton Abbey*? Writing in *Intercollegiate Review*, he interprets the Abbey as a welfare state conservatives can revere:

> Everyone—aristocrat or servant—knows his place, his relational responsibilities...The characters aren't that burdened by the modern individualistic freedom of figuring out one's place in the world...Many of the customs that seem pointlessly expensive and time consuming, such as dressing for every dinner, are employment programs for worthy servants given secure, dignified places in a world where most ordinary people struggle...The nobility of living in service to a lord...What aristocracy offers us at its best is a proud but measured acceptance of the unchangeable relationship between privileges and responsibilities in the service of those whom we know and love.

Good grief. Americans do not call the freedom to figure out one's place in the world a burden; they call it the pursuit of happiness. And to be "given" a "secure" place amid "unchangeable" relationships is not dignified, it is servitude.

One reason Thomas Jefferson, a child of Virginia's gentry, preferred an agricultural society to one in which people are "piled upon one another in large cities" ("let our workshops remain in Europe") is that he valued social stasis, as the privileged are wont to do. One reason his rival Alexander Hamilton, an immigrant striver thriving in Manhattan, wanted a restless market society of ample and volatile capital was as a solvent of the entrenched hierarchies that impede upward mobility. *Downton Abbey* viewers should remember the following rhapsodic hymn to capitalism's unceasing social churning:

> Constant revolutionizing of production, uninterrupted disturbance of all social conditions...All fixed, fast-frozen relations, with their

train of ancient and venerable prejudices and opinions, are swept away, all new-formed ones become antiquated before they can ossify. All that is solid melts into air.

This (from *The Communist Manifesto*) explains why capitalism liberates. And why American conservatives should understand that some people smitten by *Downton Abbey* hope to live upstairs during a future reign of gentry progressivism.

TRUTH DECAY AND HEALTHY DISTRUST

January 25, 2018

WASHINGTON—It cannot be a sign of social health that the number of tweets per day worldwide exploded from 5,000 in 2007 to 500 million six years later. And this might be related, by a few degrees of separation, to the fact that whereas in the 1992 presidential election more than one-third of America's 3,113 counties or their equivalents had a single-digit margin of victory, in 2016 presidential, fewer than 10 percent did. And to the fact that in 2016, 1,196 counties—about 2.5 times the average over the preceding twenty years—were decided by margins larger than 50 percent. All of which are perhaps related to rising skepticism, without scientific warrant, about the safety of vaccinations and genetically modified foods. And to the fact that newspaper subscriptions have declined about 38 percent in the last twenty years. And that between 1974 and 2016, the percentage of Americans who said they spent significant time with a neighbor declined from 30 percent to 19 percent.

These developments and others worry two of the virtuoso worriers at the Rand Corporation, the research institution now celebrating its seventieth birthday. Michael D. Rich, Rand's president, and his colleague Jennifer Kavanagh, are not feeling celebratory in their 255-page report "Truth Decay: An Initial Exploration of the Diminishing Role of Facts and Analysis in American Public Life." They suggest that the public's mental bandwidth is being stressed by today's torrent of information pouring from the Internet, social media, cable television, and talk radio, all of which might be producing—partly because the media's audience has difficulty sorting fact from opinions—a net subtraction from the public's stock of truth and trust.

The authors discern four trends inimical to fact-based discourse and policy making: increasing disagreement about facts and the interpretation of them (e.g., "The fact that immigrants are actually less likely to commit crimes than people born in the United States"); the blurring of the line between fact and opinion; the increasing quantity of opinion relative to facts; and declining trust in formerly respected sources of factual information. The volume and velocity of the information flow, combined with the new ability to curate à la carte information menus, erode society's assumption of a shared set of facts. They also deepen the human proclivity for "confirmation bias" and "motivated reasoning"—people inhabiting information silos, seeking and receiving only congenial facts.

Gerrymandering, "assortative mating" (people from the same socio-cultural backgrounds marrying each other), geographic segregation of the like-minded—all these are both causes and effects of living in echo chambers, which produces polarization. Furthermore, when, on social media and elsewhere, filters and gatekeepers are dispensed with, barriers to entry into public discourse become negligible, so being intemperate or ignorant—or both, in the service of partisanship—are not barriers, and toxic digital subcultures proliferate. Kavanagh and Rich say that not only do new media technologies exacerbate cognitive biases, they promote "the permeation of partisanship throughout the media landscape." They dryly say, "When the length of news broadcasts increased from two to 24 hours per day, there was not a 12-fold increase in the amount of reported facts."

Kavanagh and Rich are earnest social scientists with a long list of policy dentistry to combat truth decay. Their suggestions range from the anodyne (schools that teach critical reasoning; imagine that) to the appalling ("public money to support long-form and investigative jour-nalism"). But their main purpose is, appropriately, to suggest research projects that will yield facts about the consequences of the new media and intellectual landscape. Unfortunately, truth decay also spreads because campuses have become safe spaces for dime-store Nietzscheans (there are no facts, only interpretations), and that what happens on campuses does not stay on campuses.

Also, there is simple mendacity: Social justice warriors at Google probably think they are clever and heroic in saying that Lincoln was a member not of the Republican Party but of the National Union Party (the name the national Republican Party, but not most state parties, chose for the exigencies of the wartime 1864 election).

We should regret only unjust distrust; distrust of the untrustworthy is healthy. The preceding fifty years, from Watergate and the Pentagon Papers, through Iraq's missing weapons of mass destruction and "if you like your health care plan you can keep it," a default position of skepticism is defensible. And consumers of media products should remember Jerry Seinfeld's oblique skepticism: "It's amazing that the amount of news that happens in the world every day always just exactly fits the newspaper."

IN PRAISE OF BINGE READING

April 19, 2020

WASHINGTON—Long before today's coronavirus lockdown provided occasions for the vice that the phrase denotes, "binge watching" had entered Americans' lexicon. Few, however, speak of binge reading. To understand why this is regrettable, mute Netflix long enough to read Adam Garfinkle's "The Erosion of Deep Literacy" in *National Affairs*. He believes that because of the displacement of reading by digital, usually pictorial, entertainment and communication, "something neurophysiological" is happening to individuals, and especially to the "neural pathways" of the young. And something vital to democratic culture is waning.

Garfinkle, founding editor of the *American Interest*, elaborates on Maryanne Wolf's idea of "deep literacy" from her 2018 book *Reader, Come Home*. Garfinkle defines this (or "deep reading") as engagement with "an extended piece of writing" in a way that draws the reader into "a dialectical process with the text." This involves the reader in anticipation of the author's "direction and meaning."

Few scientists doubt that heavy dependency on electronic screens has shortened attention spans. "We know," Garfinkle says, "that prolonged and repetitive exposure to digital devices changes the way we think and behave in part because it changes us physically."

The brain is continuously rewiring itself in response to changing stimuli, and 200,000 years of evolution did not suit it to process today's torrents of fleeting stimuli.

"More items vie for our attention in a given hour," Garfinkle says, "than our ancestors had to handle in a day or even a week." Becoming comfortable with shallow attention to everything, people become transfixed by the present, unable to remember, or to plan well. He reports that high school guidance counselors say most students lack the social skills to speak one-on-one with college admissions personnel. This, Garfinkle believes, reflects "acquired social autism."

People immersed in digital torrents acquire "self-inflicted attention deficits." They become incapable of the "quality attention" that deep literacy requires. Such literacy is, in evolutionary terms, a recent innovation that changed brain circuitry. Garfinkle says, "We are or become, cognitively speaking, what we do with language." Printed words, presented sequentially in sentences and paragraphs, are demanding, but rewarding: Only they can present the reasoning required to establish complicated truths.

Garfinkle's surmise is that government's problem-solving failures reflect not just hyper-partisanship and polarization but the thin thinking of a political class of non-deep readers who are comfortable only with the shallowness of tweets. Instantaneous digital interactions encourage superficiality, insularity, and tribalism.

Deep reading, like deep writing, is difficult, hence unnatural. It is unpleasant to those who, tethered to their devices, have become accustomed to lives that are surface straight through. Garfinkle worries that "cognitively sped-up and multitasking young brains may not acquire sufficient capacities for critical thinking, personal reflection, imagination, and empathy, and hence will become easy prey for charlatans and demagogues."

Modernity's greatest blessing—individualism: the celebration of individual agency—depends on a sense of one's interior, of *self*-consciousness. This is facilitated by deep literacy that, unlike the oral communication of premodern groups, requires solitude for the reader's private repose. Modernity, and eventually democracy, advanced through Protestantism's emphasis of individual engagement with writing—the Bible made accessible to personal reading in various languages.

Integral to liberal-democratic politics are, Garfinkle says, abstract ideas—"representation; the virtues of doubt, dissent, and humility; and the concept of a depersonalized constitutional order." A society that loses the ballast of deep literacy is apt to become less thoughtful, more emotional and volatile. It will become impatient with the pace of refined, impersonal governance through institutions. It will seek "a less abstract, re-personalized form of social and political authority concentrated in a 'great' authoritarian leader."

Deep literacy has always been a minority taste and attainment, but is always necessary, especially among elites, to leaven majoritarian politics. But because of today's social-media technologies, Garfinkle believes, there is increased, if superficial and emotive, participation in political discourse. Yet even among young people in higher education, many professors will not assign entire books, or substantial portions of challenging ones.

Deep readers can "deploy shields of skepticism" against those who, lacking the reading habit, are "locked in perpetual intellectual adolescence." And then? "Populism of the illiberal nationalist kind is," Garfinkle believes, "what happens in a mass-electoral democracy when a decisive percentage of mobilized voters drops below a deep-literacy standard."

Garfinkle's essay—mental calisthenics for a confined nation—deserves at least the grudging gratitude of even the most egalitarian Americans. It requires what it describes—deep literacy—and might be a spur to binge reading.

GAMES

ARE YOU READY FOR SOME AUTOPSIES?

August 5, 2012

WASHINGTON—Are you ready for some football? First, however, are you ready for some autopsies?

The opening of the NFL training camps coincided with the closing of the investigation into the April suicide by gunshot of Ray Easterling, sixty-two, an eight-season NFL safety in the 1970s. The autopsy found moderately severe chronic traumatic encephalopathy (CTE), progressive damage to the brain associated with repeated blows to the head. CTE was identified as a major cause of Easterling's depression and dementia.

In February 2011, Dave Duerson, fifty, an eleven-year NFL safety, committed suicide by shooting himself in the chest to spare his brain tissue for research, which has found evidence of CTE. Brain tissue of twenty-season linebacker Junior Seau, who was forty-three when he killed himself the same way in May, is being studied. The NFL launched a mental health hotline developed and operated with the assistance of specialists in suicide prevention.

Football is bigger than ever, in several senses. Bear Bryant's 1966 undefeated Alabama team had only nineteen players who weighed more than 200 pounds. The heaviest weighed 223. The linemen averaged 194. The quarterback weighed 177. Today, many high school teams are much bigger. In 1980, only three NFL players weighed 300 or more pounds. In 2011, according to pro-football-reference.com, there were 352, including three 350-pounders. Thirty-one of the NFL's thirty-two offensive lines averaged more than 300.

Various unsurprising studies indicate high early mortality rates among linemen resulting from cardiovascular disease. For all players who play five or more years, life expectancy is less than sixty; for linemen it is much less.

After twenty years of caring for her husband, Easterling's widow is one of more than 3,000 plaintiffs—former players, spouses, relatives—in a lawsuit charging that the NFL inadequately acted on knowledge it had, or should have had, about hazards such as CTE. We are, however, rapidly reaching the point where playing football is like smoking cigarettes: The risks are well known.

Not that this has prevented smokers from successfully suing tobacco companies. But, then, smoking is an addiction. Football is just an increasingly guilty pleasure. Might Americans someday feel as queasy enjoying it as sensible people now do watching boxing and wondering how the nation was once enamored of a sport the *point* of which is brain trauma?

That is unlikely. Degenerate prize fighting, or prize fighting for degenerates—called mixed martial arts or "ultimate fighting"—is booming.

Still, football has bigger long-term problems than lawsuits. Football is entertainment in which the audience is expected to delight in gladiatorial action that a growing portion of the audience knows may cause the players degenerative brain disease. Not even football fans, a tribe not known for savoring nuance, can forever block that fact from their excited brains.

Furthermore, in this age of bubble-wrapped children, when parents put helmets on wee *tricycle* riders, many children are going to be steered away from youth football, diverting the flow of talent to the benefit of other sports.

In the NFL, especially, football is increasingly a spectacle, a game surrounded by manufactured frenzy, on the grass and in the increasingly unpleasant ambiance of the fans in the stands. Football on the field is a three-hour adrenaline-and-testosterone bath. For all its occasional elegance and beauty, it is basically violence for, among other purposes, inflicting intimidating pain. (Seau said his job was "to inflict pain on my opponent and have him quit.") The New Orleans Saints' "bounty" system of cash payments to players who knocked opposing players out of games crossed a line distinguishing the essence of the game from the perversion of it. This is, however, an increasingly faint line.

Decades ago, this column lightheartedly called football a mistake because it combines two of the worst features of American life—violence, punctuated by committee meetings, which football calls huddles. Now, however, accumulating evidence about new understandings of the human body—the brain, especially, but not exclusively—compel the conclusion that football is a mistake because the body is not built to absorb, and cannot be adequately modified by training or protected by equipment to absorb, the game's kinetic energies.

After eighteen people died playing football in 1905, even President Theodore Roosevelt, who loved war and gore generally, flinched and forced some rules changes. Today, however, the problem is not the rules; it is the fiction that football can be fixed and still resemble the game fans relish.

THE MORALITY OF ENJOYING FOOTBALL

September 3, 2017

WASHINGTON—Autumn, which is bearing down upon us like a menacing linebacker, is, as John Keats said, a season of mists and mellow fruitfulness and chronic traumatic encephalopathy (CTE). Actually, Keats, a romantic, did not mention that last part. He died before the birth of the subject of a waning American romance, football. This sport will never die but it will never again be, as it was until recently, the subject of uncomplicated national enthusiasm.

CTE is a degenerative brain disease confirmable only after death, and often caused by repeated blows to the head that knock the brain against the skull. The cumulative impacts of hundreds of supposedly minor blows can have the cumulative effect of many concussions. The *New York*

Times recently reported Stanford researchers' data showing "that one college offensive lineman sustained 62 of these hits in a single game. Each one came with an average force on the player's head equivalent to what you would see if he had driven his car into a brick wall at 30 mph."

Boston University researchers found CTE in 110 of 111 brains of deceased NFL players. In fifty-three other brains from college players, forty-eight had CTE. There was significant selection bias: Many of the brains came from families who had noticed CTE symptoms, including mood disorders and dementia. A BU researcher says, however, that a ten-year NFL linebacker could receive more than 15,000 sub-concussive blows.

Football's kinetic energy—a function of the masses and velocities of the hurtling bodies—has increased dramatically in fifty years. On Alabama's undefeated 1966 team, only 21 percent of the players weighed more than 200 pounds. The heaviest weighed 223; the linemen averaged 194. The quarterback, who weighed 177, was Ken Stabler, who went on to a Hall of Fame NFL career—and to "moderately severe" CTE before death from cancer. Today, many high school teams are much beefier than the 1966 Crimson Tide. Of the 114 members of Alabama's 2016 squad, just twenty-five weighed less than 200, and twenty weighed more than 300. In 1980, only three NFL players weighed 300 or more pounds. Last season, 390 weighed 300 pounds or more, and six topped 350.

Players love football, and a small minority will have lucrative post-college NFL careers. Many will make increasingly informed choices to accept the risk-reward calculus. But because today's risk-averse middle-class parents put crash helmets on their tykes riding *tricycles*, football participation will skew to the uninformed and economically desperate. But will informed spectators become queasy about deriving pleasure from an entertainment with such human costs?

No. They will say: Players know the risks that they, unlike the baited bears, voluntarily embrace, just as smokers do. Notice, however, that smoking, which is increasingly a choice of those least receptive to public health information, is banned in all NFL stadiums and is severely discouraged on all college campuses, including those that are football factories. And football fans will say: Better equipment will solve the problem of body parts, particularly the one in the skull's brain pan, that are unsuited to the game.

Perhaps evolving standards of decency will reduce football to a marginalized spectacle, like boxing. But the UFC's (Ultimate Fighting Championship) burgeoning popularity is (redundant) evidence that "evolving" is not a synonym for "improving."

Besides, as disturbing scientific evidence accumulates, NFL franchise values soar (*Forbes* says the most valuable is the Dallas Cowboys at $4.2 billion, and the least valuable is the $1.5 billion Buffalo Bills) and annual revenues reach $14 billion. The league distributes $244 million to each team—$77 million more than each team's salary cap. Local revenues are gravy. The appendage of higher education that is called college football also is a big business: The Southeastern Conference's cable television channel is valued at almost $5 billion. Universities, who find and develop the NFL's players, pay their head coaches well for performing this public service: Twenty head coaches make more than $4 million a year. Michigan's Jim Harbaugh earns $9 million.

It has been said (by Thomas Babington Macaulay) that the Puritans banned bear baiting—unleashing fierce dogs on a bear chained in a pit—not because it gave pain to bears but because it gave pleasure to Puritans. But whatever the Puritans' motives, they understood that there are degrading enjoyments. Football is becoming one, even though Michigan's $9 million coach has called it "the last bastion of hope in America for toughness in men." That thought must amuse the Marines patrolling Afghanistan's Helmand Province.

SUPER BOWL SUNDAY: A ROMAN HOLIDAY

February 7, 2016

WASHINGTON—Settling unhappily into his Super Bowl seat, Himalayan high behind the end zone, Joe spots an empty seat low and on the fifty-yard line. He descends to it and asks the man seated next to him why the wonderful seat is unoccupied. The man says, "It's mine. I was supposed to come with my wife, but she died. This is the first Super Bowl since 1967 we have not attended together." Joe says: "But couldn't you find a friend or relative to come with you today?" The man replies: "No, they're all at the funeral."

This story (from *Heidegger and a Hippo Walk Through Those Pearly Gates: Using Philosophy (and Jokes!) to Explore Life, Death, the Afterlife, and Everything in Between*, by Thomas Cathcart and Daniel Klein) prepares you for gathering around the national campfire that is the annual Super Bowl telecast. Super Bowls are so august they are usually denoted with Roman numerals. This year's, however, is designated Super Bowl 50 because Super Bowl L looks weird. It should be called the 50th (or Lth) Chronic Traumatic Encephalopathy Bowl.

Last week, the *New York Times* reported that after Ken Stabler died of colon cancer in July at sixty-nine, his brain was sent, as he had directed, to scientists in Massachusetts. His mind, according to his daughter, "was definitely in a pretty quick downward spiral." The scientists determined that Stabler, the Oakland Raiders quarterback in Super Bowl XI (1977), who played fifteen seasons in the NFL, had, on a scale of 1 to 4, "high Stage 3" CTE, a degenerative brain disease associated with repeated blows to the head, including blows not severe enough to produce immediate symptoms of concussion. Stabler probably will be voted into the Pro Football Hall of Fame, making him the eighth member among the more than one hundred former players known to have had CTE.

Quarterbacks are somewhat protected, by their offensive line and by NFL rules, from football's worst violence. But the *Times* also reported that Earl Morrall, the Miami Dolphins' quarterback in Super Bowl VII (1973), had Stage 4 CTE when he died in 2014 at seventy-nine. And last month, Jim McMahon, fifty-six, another fifteen-season NFL quarterback, said he considers medicinal marijuana a "godsend" as he copes with headaches and difficulties associated with his diagnosis of early onset dementia. He played for the victorious Chicago Bears in Super Bowl XX (1986).

How many deceased players had, and how many former players have, or how many current players will have, CTE is unknown because it can only be confirmed by autopsy. Its symptoms, however, are similar to those of dementia.

Football's kinetic energy is increasing as the players become bigger and even the biggest become faster. In 1980, only three NFL players weighed 300 or more pounds. This season, 354 did, including seven 350-pounders.

Sunday's game will be sixty minutes of football—an adrenaline-and-testosterone bath stretched by commercial breaks (two of them called "two minute warnings"), replay challenges, and other delays to about 200 minutes—embedded in an all-day broadcast of manufactured frenzy. It would be nice, but probably fanciful, to think that even 1 percent of tonight's expected television audience of more than 110 million will have qualms about the ethics of their enjoyment.

The NFL's fondness for Roman numerals is appropriate because the game is gladiatorial, as Romans enjoyed entertainment featuring people maiming and being maimed for the entertainment of spectators. But things change.

Capital punishment was not considered among the "cruel and unusual punishments" in 1791 when the Eighth Amendment was ratified; every state used the death penalty and the Fifth Amendment assumes its existence. In 1958, the Supreme Court held that the Eighth Amendment "must draw its meaning from the evolving standards of decency that mark the progress of a maturing society." Our society would emphatically say the Eighth Amendment forbids ear-cropping, branding, and the pillory, punishments used in 1791.

Standards evolve concerning amusements, too. Someday, boxing might seem as repugnant as bearbaiting and cockfighting now do. Or maybe not, given the growing popularity of "mixed martial arts" cage fighting, which is degenerative prizefighting. The phrase "evolving standards" is synonymous with "improving standards."

Are today's parents, who put crash helmets on tykes before they put the tykes on tricycles, going to allow these children to play football? Not likely. This game will be different, or much less popular—or perhaps both—when in 2066 the national campfire is lit for Super Bowl C.

RALLY 'ROUND THE MATH CLASS!

September 9, 2012

WASHINGTON—With two extravagant entertainments under way, it is instructive to note the connection between the presidential election and the college football season: Barack Obama represents progressivism, a doctrine whose many blemishes on American life include universities as football factories, which progressivism helped to create.

Higher education embraced athletics in the first half of the nineteenth century, when most colleges were denominational and most instruction was considered mental and moral preparation for a small minority—clergy and other professionals. Physical education had nothing to do with spectator sports entertaining people from outside the campus community. Rather, it was individual fitness—especially gymnastics—for the moral and pedagogic purposes of muscular Christianity—*mens sana in corpore sano*, a sound mind in a sound body.

The collective activity of team sports came after a great collective exertion, the Civil War, and two great social changes, urbanization and industrialization. This story is told well in *The Rise of Gridiron University: Higher Education's Uneasy Alliance with Big-Time Football* (University Press of Kansas) by Brian M. Ingrassia, a Middle Tennessee State University historian.

Intercollegiate football began when Rutgers played Princeton in 1869, four years after Appomattox. In 1878, one of Princeton's two undergraduate student managers was Thomas—he was called Tommy—Woodrow Wilson. For the rest of the nineteenth century, football appealed as a venue for valor for collegians whose fathers' venues had been battlefields. Stephen Crane, author of the Civil War novel *The Red Badge of Courage* (1895)—the badge was a wound—said: "Of course, I have never been in a battle, but I believe that I got my sense of the rage of conflict on the football field."

Harvard philosopher William James then spoke of society finding new sources of discipline and inspiration in "the moral equivalent of war." Society found football, which like war required the subordination of the individual, and which would relieve the supposed monotony of workers enmeshed in mass production.

College football became a national phenomenon because it supposedly served the values of progressivism, in two ways. It exemplified specialization, expertise, and scientific management. And it would reconcile the public to the transformation of universities, especially public universities, into something progressivism desired but the public found alien. Replicating industrialism's division of labor, universities introduced the fragmentation of the old curriculum of moral instruction into increasingly specialized and arcane disciplines. These included the recently founded social sciences—economics, sociology, political science—that were supposed to supply progressive governments with the expertise to manage the complexities of the modern economy and the simplicities of the uninstructed masses.

Football taught the progressive virtue of subordinating the individual to the collectivity. Inevitably, this led to the cult of one individual, the coach. Today, in almost every state, at least one public university football coach is paid more than the governor.

As universities multiplied, football fueled the competition for prestige and other scarce resources. Shortly after it was founded, the University of Chicago hired as football coach the nation's first tenured professor of physical culture and athletics, Amos Alonzo Stagg, who had played at Yale for Walter Camp, an early shaper of the rules and structure of intercollegiate football. Camp also was president of the New Haven Clock Company. Clocks were emblematic of modernity—workers punching time clocks, time-and-motion efficiency studies. Camp saw football as basic training for the managerial elites demanded by corporations.

Progressives saw football as training managers for the modern regulatory state. Ingrassia says a Yale professor, the Social Darwinist William Graham Sumner (who was Camp's brother-in-law), produced one academic acolyte who thought the "English race" was establishing hegemony because it played the "sturdiest" sports.

Reinforced concrete and other advancements in construction were put to use building huge stadiums to bring the public onto campuses that, to many, seemed increasingly unintelligible. Ingrassia says "Harvard Stadium was the prototype" for dozens of early twentieth-century stadiums. In 1914, the inaugural game in the Yale Bowl drew 70,055 spectators. The Alabama, LSU, and Southern California football programs are the children of Harvard's, Yale's, and Princeton's.

"It's kind of hard," said Alabama's Bear Bryant, "to rally 'round a math class." And today college football is said to give vast, fragmented universities a sense of community through shared ritual. In this year's first "game of the century," Alabama's student-athletes played those from Michigan in Cowboys Stadium in Arlington, Texas, which is 605 miles and 1,191 miles from Tuscaloosa and Ann Arbor, respectively.

COLLEGE FOOTBALL AND THE QUESTION OF COOKIE CORRUPTION

September 19, 2013

WASHINGTON—Like baby birds with yawning beaks, college football fans clamor to be fed. So fasten the chin strap on your helmet— ignore the warning label on it ("No helmet system can protect you from serious brain and/or neck injuries including paralysis or death. To avoid these risks, do not engage in the sport of football.") and enjoy the seasonal festival of physical carnage, institutional derangement, and moral seaminess.

LSU offensive tackle Josh Williford, twenty-two, will, however, leave his helmet off, having just retired rather than risk another concussion. A third concussion triples the risk of clinical depression for those with no prior symptoms, and autopsies performed on 334 deceased NFL players "found that they were three times more likely than the general population to suffer from neurodegenerative diseases such as Alzheimer's and ALS (Lou Gehrig's disease)." These figures are from a *Wall Street Journal* essay *defending* football from critics. These critics must admit that big-time college football, although a peculiar appendage of institutions of higher learning, is at least adding to our knowledge of brains by fueling studies of chronic traumatic encephalopathy (CTE), the cumulative effect of repeated small "subconcussive" blows to the head.

Football's doughty defenders note that other recreational activities, such as bicycling, injure more participants. But only in football is long-term injury the result not of accidents but of the game played properly, meaning within the rules. Rules could be changed by, for example, eliminating kickoffs with their high-velocity collisions and barring the three-point stance whereby linemen begin each play with their heads down and helmet-to-helmet collisions are likely. But such changes could be made only over the dead bodies of fans who relish mayhem from safe distances.

The broadcast and cable organizations that pay billions for the rights to televise football have an incentive to not call attention to health problems. Gushers of money are generated by football's amateurs, who enable other people to get rich while getting fired.

Gregg Easterbrook, an intelligent journalist who nevertheless loves football, has a new book (*The King of Sports: Football's Impact on America*) that is hardly a love letter. "At many big-college sports programs," he writes, "the athletic department is structured as an independent organization that leases campus space and school logos, then operates a tax-exempt business over which the school's president and board of trustees have little control."

Easterbrook notes that when Auburn won the 2010 national championship, its net football income was $37 million, just a bit less than the $43 million of that season's NFL champion, the Green Bay Packers. Auburn's head coach, Gene Chizik, was paid $3.5 million that year (in most states, the highest paid person on the public payroll is a university coach), a sum justified because, said Auburn's $600,000 athletic director, "Coach Chizik is a great mentor to our student-athletes."

Two years later, Chizik's mentoring greatness counted for less than his 3–9 record. He was fired, the blow cushioned by a $7.5 million buyout, more than the approximately $5 million Auburn had paid to buy out

Chizik's predecessor. In 2012, the University of Tennessee fired its losing coach with a $5 million severance—and the athletic department (annual revenue, more than $70 million) was given a three-year exemption from its annual $6 million contribution to the university's academic side. In 2011, Michigan paid $1 million to San Diego State University so Michigan could hire SDSU's coach, paying him $3.3 million (plus up to $500,000 in bonuses for victories) to replace the fired coach to whom Michigan had paid a $2.5 million severance. That was the same sum Michigan had paid in a buyout to pry the coach it was firing away from West Virginia. In 2011, Texas Tech gave its head coach a $500,000 raise while freezing faculty salaries.

Payoffs can be financed by selling *everything*, including the naming rights to football *positions*. The 2007 North Carolina State media guide thanked people for "scholarship endowments," including the "Ed 'Scooter' Mooney Nose Guard Scholarship," the "Longley Family Punter Scholarship," and twelve others.

Meanwhile, to preserve college football's purity, the NCAA has approximately seventy pages of stern rules about dealing with recruits: "An institution may provide fruit, nuts and bagels to a student-athlete at any time." Cookies? See the relevant regulation. In 2008, Easterbrook notes, the *Raleigh News & Observer* "reported that University of North Carolina football and men's basketball players were enrolled in email Swahili 'courses' that had no instructors and never met and always led to A's." There was, however, no evidence of cookie corruption.

THE WAGES OF AMATEURISM

April 4, 2019

WASHINGTON—Appropriately, during the crescendo of this college basketball season, in which the most significant event was a shoe malfunction, a lawyer whose best-known client was a pornographic actress was indicted for threatening to shrink a shoe company's market capitalization by making allegations about the company misbehaving in the meat market for a small number of tall "student-athletes." What counts as misbehavior in this swamp is a murky subject.

Zion Williamson is a "one-and-done" superstar at Duke, a university (one can lose sight of this fact) that aspires to be worthy of its basketball program. There Williamson is spending the obligatory year before becoming eligible to rake in riches in the NBA, which forbids its teams to sign players directly out of high school, thereby giving institutions of higher education a year to refine future NBA talent.

In a February game, one of Williamson's Nike shoes blew apart under the torque of his 285 pounds. This injured him, not seriously but enough to furrow the brows of those who ponder the ethics of college athletics—in a sense, a small subject. They wondered: While Williamson is serving his one-year sentence as an unpaid student-athlete, helping Duke and the National Collegiate Athletic Association make millions and more than a billion, respectively (he has 3 million followers on Instagram), an injury could ruin his prospects as a professional. So, perhaps he should be a paid student-athlete.

Nike pays Duke serious money, but not a penny—heaven forfend—to Williamson, to wear its stuff. (Duke, a private institution, can keep such transactions secret, but a comparable basketball factory, the University of Kentucky, recently extended its marriage to Nike for $30.6 million over eight years.) Williamson's defective shoe briefly knocked $1.1 billion off Nike's market capitalization. Michael Avenatti, former lawyer for Stormy Daniels, was apparently nine times more ambitious.

He was arrested after being recorded, according to the U.S. attorney for the Southern District of New York, threatening to release—on the eve of March Madness and of a Nike earnings call—evidence that Nike has participated in a particular practice of sports apparel companies (Adidas and Under Armour also supposedly compete). They sluice money, through third parties, to "blue chip" recruits, or their families, to steer players to schools that are paid to wear the companies' goods. To lawyers for Nike, Avenatti said: "I'll go take ten billion dollars off your client's market cap…I'm not f—ing around."

Recently three men were convicted of fraud and conspiracy for directing recruits to Adidas schools, on the amusing theory that the schools who welcomed these players had never noticed any of the money sloshing around, and so were somehow victims. Pure as the driven slush. Louisiana State University reached the Sweet Sixteen in 2019's March Madness without its coach, who was suspended by LSU after refusing to talk to the university about transcripts of colorful telephone conversations. The coach spoke about "a hell of a [expletive] offer" and "a [expletive] strong-ass offer"—to whom was unclear—concerning prospective recruits. Conceivably, the offers were not for NCAA-permitted benefits for the athlete.

The judge in another recent case compounded the comedy, ruling that although the NCAA has no "coherent definition of amateurism," it can continue to sharply limit financial aid to athletes because the judge accepts the NCAA's convenient theory about "the importance to consumer demand of maintaining a distinction between college sports and professional sports."

About the importance of equity, Representative Mark Walker, a Republican from basketball-crazed North Carolina, has an idea: Tweak the tax code to say that "amateur sports organizations" cannot "substantially [restrict] the use of an athlete's name, image or likeness." So the NCAA, epicenter of the college-sports industry, would forfeit its tax-exempt status—let's not dwell on *that* absurdity—if it continues forbidding athletes from making money from their names.

An ordained minister, Walker understands mankind's fallen nature, so he knows that rivers of money from boosters and others might flow to star players for, say, endorsing a local car dealership. A believer in redemption, perhaps Walker understands that improvement of the multibillion-dollar entertainment industry that is parasitic off educational institutions must begin by forcing it to confront its foundational hypocrisy about amateurism.

In 1957, Queen Elizabeth, attending a Maryland–North Carolina football game, asked Maryland's governor, "Where do you get all those enormous players?" He replied, "Your majesty, that's a very embarrassing question." In college basketball there are many such questions.

MARCH MADNESS AFTER ALL

March 29, 2020

> "Nine out of ten schools are cheating. The other one is in last place."
>
> —Jerry Tarkanian

WASHINGTON—When Tark the Shark was basketball coach at the University of Nevada at Las Vegas, 1973–1992, his win-loss record was 509–105, and he took the Runnin' Rebels to the NCAA's Final Four four times and won the national championship in 1990. His refreshing refusal to obfuscate tells us that UNLV was not a tenth place school.

Those words ascribed to Tarkanian introduce HBO's *The Scheme*, which airs Tuesday evening, when fans would have been anticipating the Final Four, if the coronavirus had not shuttered the college basketball industry. HBO's documentary is a darkly hilarious story of government squandering resources to concoct preposterous crimes whose supposed victims are enriched by pretending to be oblivious to them. The victims are fabulously remunerated coaches and the universities that profit from unpaid "student athletes."

HBO's through-the-looking-glass tale revolves around Christian Dawkins, a now-twenty-seven-year-old African American who is an almost admirable rascal as well as an unrepentant felon. Growing up in basketball-mad Saginaw, Michigan, he realized he was not NBA material so he decided to monetize his mania in college basketball's netherworld. This is the meat market at the intersection of shoe companies (Nike, Adidas, Under Armour) and college basketball factories (e.g., Kansas, Louisville, North Carolina) that turn high school "blue chippers" into NBA prospects who hope to soon need agents, who will themselves become wealthy negotiating enormous NBA contracts.

An aspiring agent, Dawkins became a minor operator in the business of spotting rising stars, often in middle school or even before, and cultivating them and their families in order to grease, with shoe companies' money, the path of such prodigies to certain universities. These are schools whose basketball and other athletic programs have multiyear contracts paying them to wear Adidas (Kansas, $196 million), Nike (Ohio State, $252 million), or Under Armour (UCLA, $280 million) stuff.

This racket revolving around tall and talented adolescents is relationship roulette: Many relationships fail, either because the player's talent turns out to be insufficient or because the player ditches one agent, who has gambled much time and money on him, for another agent. But one player who wins a giant contract is a jackpot that more than repays an agent's investment in a dozen failures.

In one criminal trial, Dawkins was convicted of directing a recruit to a school that supposedly was "defrauded." The prosecution's theory was—seriously—that the school was a victim because the player, coveted by the school as a stupendous revenue generator, falsely attested to his amateur status after taking cash from Dawkins. So the school wasted a scholarship, which is sofa-cushion change compared with the apparel contracts and other basketball bonanzas. But the stern ethic is that schools and coaches may fill their pails from the Niagara of money, but never players. Dawkins declines to feel guilty about helping players and their families, often inner-city African Americans, get a thimbleful.

In another trial, Dawkins was convicted of bribing public officials: assistant coaches, whose quid pro quo was supposed to be that they would steer stars to Dawkins's sports management business, after the stars had enriched the school. Public officials? Why, yes: Such is America's devotion to higher education, in forty states the highest-paid public employee works for a public university. He is a football or basketball coach.

LSU's coach, Will Wade, and Arizona's coach, Sean Miller, multimillionaires who were wiretapped talking with Dawkins about recruiting, claim to barely know him. They prosper while he is appealing his sentence.

The Scheme details how the FBI rented a yacht in Manhattan and suites in Las Vegas where undercover agents encouraged the commission of crimes that are difficult to describe with a straight face. An FBI squad brandishing assault rifles crashed into a suite to encourage Dawkins to cooperate. He didn't. After three years of investigations, two trials produced paltry results for the nation's premier law enforcement agency and the legendarily potent federal prosecutors of the Southern District of New York, who evidently have no more urgent business.

Don't blink during *The Scheme* because the jaw-dropping incidents unfold so fast that you might miss some dandies, such as "escorts" and strippers reportedly brought to a Louisville athletic dorm twenty-two times between 2010 and 2014. Although this perk supposedly astonished head coach Rick Pitino, it contributed to his being fired. This month, however, he was hired as coach at Iona, a Catholic college. There is some March Madness after all.

COOPERSTOWN: MUSEUM OR SHRINE?

January 22, 2017

WASHINGTON—Many Americans are more thoughtful when choosing appliances than when choosing presidents, but the baseball writers whose ballots decide who is "enshrined"—more about that verb anon—in Cooperstown's Hall of Fame are mostly conscientious voters struggling to unravel a knotty puzzle: How to treat retired players who are known or suspected to have used performance enhancing drugs (PEDs) while compiling gaudy numbers?

Such chemicals increase muscle mass, thereby increasing hitters' bat speeds, pitchers' velocities, and recovery from the strain of training and competing. On Wednesday, two highly probable users, Roger Clemens (third-most career strikeouts, seven Cy Young awards) and Barry Bonds (career and season home run records, seven MVP awards) reached 54.1 percent and 53.8 percent, respectively, up from 45.2 percent and 44.3 percent last year and approaching the 75 percent threshold for admission. Only three players have reached 50 percent without eventually being admitted (Jack Morris, Gil Hodges, Lee Smith).

Cooperstown's administrators—it is not run by Major League Baseball—and the writers-cum-gatekeepers must decide what the institution is. Its title—the National Baseball Hall of Fame and Museum—implies that the hall containing the players' plaques is somehow apart from and other than the museum. The *Oxford English Dictionary* defines "museum" as where "objects of historical, scientific, artistic or cultural interest are stored and exhibited." A "shrine" contains "memorabilia of a particular revered person or thing." Cooperstown stipulates that "voting shall be based upon the player's record, playing ability, integrity, sportsmanship, character and contributions to the team(s) on which the player played."

Some players' records reflect abilities enhanced by acts of bad character—surreptitious resorts to disreputable chemistry that traduces sportsmanship. But as younger writers who did not cover baseball during the PED era become Hall of Fame voters, the electorate is becoming less interested in disqualifying PED users. These writers should, however, consider why PEDs matter.

They subvert the central idea of sport—athletes competing on equal terms. Distinguishing legitimate from illegitimate athletic enhancement can be complex: The body produces testosterone and human growth hormone (HGH) that are components of some potent PEDs. Enhancements improve performance without devaluing it only if they involve methods and materials (e.g., better training and nutrition) that help the body perform unusually rather than unnaturally well.

PEDs mock the idea that winning is a just reward for praiseworthy behavior—submission to an exacting training regimen and the mental mastery of pressure, pain, and exhaustion. Drugs that make sport exotic make it less exemplary; they drain sport of admirable excellence, which elevates spectators as well as competitors.

Beyond this civic interest in honest athletics, there is a matter of justice. Many former ballplayers missed having major league careers, or longer major league careers with larger contracts, because they competed honestly against cheating opponents, or lost playing time to cheating teammates. These handicapped-because-honorable players could have leveled the playing field only by using dangerous PEDs, thereby jeopardizing their physical and mental health and forfeiting their integrity.

And consider Fred McGriff, who in nineteen sterling seasons during the steroid era hit 493 home runs, seven short of the 500 mark that has generally opened Cooperstown's doors to eligible players (retired five years) not suspected of PED use. There is no suspicion that McGriff used PEDs, and if he had he certainly would have hit many more than seven additional home runs. The closest he has come to Cooperstown's 75 percent is 23.9 percent in 2012. (He received 21.7 percent Wednesday.) And there are players in Cooperstown whose careers were enhanced by amphetamines, which once were ubiquitous in baseball but now are banned.

Until baseball's steroid parenthesis, only one demarcation had disrupted the game's continuity, that between the dead ball era and, beginning around 1920, the live ball era. The parenthesis has been closed, although the financial incentives to cheat are such that there always will be sinister chemists competing to concoct PEDs that defeat the efforts of other chemists to detect them. The incentives can, however, be decisively reordered by sufficiently severe penalties, which almost all players would favor.

If Cooperstown is content, as perhaps it should be, to be merely a museum—not a negligible thing—then Bonds and Clemens belong there as important elements of the game's story, and their story should be candidly told on their plaques. If, however, Cooperstown wants admission to mean enshrinement, it must embrace and articulate the Hall's ethic. America has never more urgently needed the insistence that real success must be honorably achieved.

BASEBALL'S COMMON LAW

April 4, 2010

WASHINGTON—The 2006 summit that preserved the peace occurred in a laundry room in the Minneapolis Metrodome after the Twins beat the Red Sox 8–1. Twins manager Ron Gardenhire, with center fielder Torii Hunter in tow, met with Red Sox manager Terry Francona to assure him that Hunter had not intentionally sinned.

With the Twins seven runs ahead in the bottom of the eighth, with two outs and no one on and a 3–0 count, Hunter had swung hard at a pitch. According to baseball's common law, he should not have swung at all.

This episode is recounted in Jason Turbow's *The Baseball Codes* about the game's unwritten rules. Just as the common law derives from ancient precedents—judges' decisions—rather than statutes, baseball's codes are the game's distilled mores. Their unchanged purpose is to show respect for opponents and the game.

In baseball, as in the remainder of life, the most important rules are unwritten. But not unenforced.

With the Red Sox down seven runs with three outs remaining, it was, according to the codes, time to "play soft." With the count 3–0, Hunter knew a fastball strike was coming from a struggling pitcher whose job was just to end the mismatch. Over 162 games, every team is going to get drubbed, so every team favors an ethic that tells when to stop stealing bases, when to not tag at third and try to score on a medium deep fly ball, when not to bunt a runner from first to second.

But, Turbow notes, the codes require judgments conditioned by contingencies. Although the team on top late in a lopsided game does not stop trying to hit, it stops pressing to manufacture runs. But how big a lead is "big enough"? Well, how bad is the leading team's bullpen? Does the losing team score runs in bunches? Where is the game being played?

In launching pads such as Wrigley Field and Fenway Park? In the thin air of Denver's Coors Field?

The codes are frequently enforced from the pitcher's mound. When a fastball hits a batter's ribs, he is reminded to stop peeking to see where—inside or outside—the catcher is preparing to receive the pitch. In 1946, Dodger Hugh Casey threw at Cardinals shortstop Marty Marion while Marion was standing out of the batter's box—but closer to it than Casey thought proper—in order to time Casey's warm-up pitches.

Traditionally, baseball punishes preening. In a society increasingly tolerant of exhibitionism, it is splendid when a hitter is knocked down because in his last at bat he lingered at the plate to admire his home run. But it was, Turbow suggests, proper for the Cardinals' Albert Pujols, after hitting a home run, to flip his bat high in the air to show up Pirates pitcher Oliver Perez, who earlier in the game had waved his arms to celebrate getting Pujols out.

The consensus was that the codes were not violated when, during Joe DiMaggio's fifty-six-game hitting streak in 1941, with one out in the bottom of the eighth and a Yankee runner on first and DiMaggio, who was hitless, on deck, Tommy Henrich bunted just to avoid a double play and assure DiMaggio another chance to extend the streak. Which he did.

In the codes, as in law generally, dogmatism can be dumb. The rule is that late in a no-hitter, the first hit must not be a bunt. So the Padres' Ben Davis was denounced for his eighth-inning bunt that broke up Curt Schilling's no-hitter. But the score was 2–0; the bunt brought to the plate the potential tying run.

Cheating by pitchers often operates under a "don't ask, don't tell" code. When George Steinbrenner demanded during a game that Yankees manager Lou Piniella protest that Don Sutton of the Angels was scuffing the ball, Piniella said, "The guy (Tommy John) who taught Don Sutton everything he knows about cheating is the guy pitching for us tonight." When a reporter asked Gaylord Perry's five-year-old daughter if her father threw a spitball, she replied, "It's a hard slider."

When the Yankees' Deion ("Neon Deion") Sanders barely moved toward first after popping up to short, White Sox catcher Carlton Fisk, forty-two, a keeper of the codes, screamed: "Run the (expletive) ball out, you piece of (expletive)—that's not the way we do things up here!" Were Fisk and his standards out of date? As has been said, standards are always out of date—that is why we call them standards.

AUTUMN FOR SOME BOYS OF LONG AGO SUMMERS

January 12, 2012

CHARLESTON, S.C.—They are nearing seventy now, the eleven men who were twelve-year-old boys in 1955 and who are remembered for the baseball games they could not play. They were—actually, with their matching blue blazers and striped ties, they still are—members of the Cannon Street All Stars.

The Cannon Street YMCA is near the Ashley River, which flows toward the harbor and Fort Sumter. The unpleasantness that started there in 1861 had left pertinent questions unsettled ninety-four years later when the All Stars, all African Americans, decided to enter this city's Little League tournament. Charleston canceled the tournament because blacks and whites simply did not play together. Actually, they did, all the time, in informal settings, on vacant lots. "Kids do not mess up the world, adults do," says Leroy Major, sixty-nine, the All Stars' pitcher and a retired schoolteacher.

Never mind, said the All Stars' coach, who entered them in the state tournament in Greenville. That was too much for the sixty-one white teams, who withdrew. Well, then, said the coach, we will head for Rome, Georgia, and the regional tournament where the winners of eight Southern state tournaments would compete to see which would go to the Little League World Series in Williamsport, Pennsylvania.

Those running things at Rome said the Cannon Street team could not compete because it had advanced by forfeit. But the national Little

League organization decided it wasn't the Cannon Street All Stars' fault that no one would play them, so it invited them to Williamsport as honored guests. For many of them, it was their first venture away from Charleston, exciting and a bit worrisome, because the route north passed through areas where the Ku Klux Klan was restive.

When the All Stars settled into the stands at Williamsport, the crowd began to chant, "Let them play!" Vermont Brown, sixty-eight, an Army veteran and former Lockheed Martin employee, who still is about the size of a Little Leaguer, remembers that when he and his teammates saw the teams warming up on the field, "We knew we would have kicked their butts." They probably would have, given the pitching of Major. He is a former Marine who is about twice Brown's size. A mountain of Christian serenity, he works with his church, practicing what the summer of 1955 taught him: "Move on."

The spring chicken among the Cannon Street All Stars organization is Augustus Holt, sixty-five. He was too young to play with them but is now the team historian. He became interested in the events of 1955 when his son played Dixie Youth Baseball, whose uniforms had the Confederate battle flag on their sleeves.

Dixie Youth Baseball, which has removed the flag, came into existence when Little League organizations in eight Southern states seceded from the national Little League after 1955. Its Official Rule Guide stated: "The Organizers hereof are of the opinion it is for the best interest of all concerned that this program be on a racially segregated basis; they believe that mixed teams and competition between the races would create regrettable conditions and destroy the harmony and tranquility which now exists." Dixie Youth Baseball, which in 1967 removed that from its charter, has produced major leaguers Bo Jackson, Tom Gordon, Reggie Sanders, and Otis Nixon, all African Americans.

The year the Cannon Street All Stars won without playing was the year after *Brown v. Board of Education*, and the summer before the December when, 370 miles from here, Rosa Parks refused to move to the back of a Montgomery, Alabama, bus. As the boys were on the night bus trip back from Pennsylvania, a fourteen-year-old Chicago boy,

Emmett Till, visiting his relatives in Mississippi, was seized from his bed and murdered.

"We haven't seen the best of it yet," says John Rivers, sixty-nine, the All Stars' shortstop who later studied architecture at Hampton Institute and Columbia University and today has offices in Atlanta and Columbus, Georgia. "The country's always getting better." It speaks well of these spry gentlemen of nearly three score and ten that, without a trace of bitterness, they are determined to keep telling their story for the benefit of old people who only dimly remember it, and for the edification of young people who cannot imagine it. It speaks well of the nation that, without gentle reminders by people like the men in the blue blazers, it has difficulty remembering the way things were.

VIN SCULLY, CRAFTSMAN

September 4, 2016

> Irish poets learn your trade
> Sing whatever is well made....
> —William Butler Yeats, "Under Ben Bulben"

LOS ANGELES—For sixty-seven years, the son of Vincent and Bridget Scully, immigrants who came to New York City from County Cavan, Ireland, has been plying his trade. For eight years on the East Coast and fifty-nine on the West Coast, on radio and television, he has strolled with Brooklyn Dodgers fans and then Los Angeles Dodgers fans down the long, winding road of baseball's seasons. In an era with a surfeit of shoddiness, two things are well-made—major league baseball and Vin Scully's broadcasts of it.

Although he uses language fluently and precisely, he is not a poet. He is something equally dignified and exemplary but less celebrated: He is a craftsman. Scully, the most famous and beloved person in Southern

California, is not a movie star, but has the at-ease, old-shoe persona of Jimmy Stewart. With his shock of red hair and maple syrup voice, Scully seems half his eighty-eight years.

"[America's] most widespread age-related disease," Tom Wolfe has written, "was not senility but juvenility. The social ideal was to look 23 and dress 13." It is not Scully's fault that he looks unreasonably young. It is to his credit that he comes to work in a coat and tie, and *prepared*—stocked with information.

Aristotle defined human beings as language-using creatures. They are not always as well-behaved as wolves but everything humane depends on words—love, promise-keeping, story-telling, democracy. And baseball.

A game of episodes, not of flow, it leaves time for, and invites, conversation, rumination, and speculation. And storytelling, by which Scully immerses his audience in baseball's rich history, and stories that remind fans that players "are not wind-up dolls."

In recent years, Scully has not accompanied the Dodgers on the road. Hence this recent tweet quoting an eight-year-old Dodgers fan, Zoe: "I hate when the Dodgers have away games. They don't tell stories."

When the Baltimore Orioles visited Dodger Stadium in July, Scully's listeners learned that the father of Orioles manager Buck Showalter fought from North Africa to Italy to Normandy to the Battle of the Bulge. Whenever the Orioles come to town, Scully dispenses nuggets about the War of 1812. On June 6 broadcasts, they learned something about D-Day. His neighbor once was Ronald Reagan.

This is how Franklin Roosevelt began his first Fireside Chat (March 12, 1933): "I want to talk for a few minutes with the people of the United States about banking..." For many years now Scully has worked alone because he wants to talk not to someone seated next to him but to each listener, which was FDR's talent. A free society—a society of persuasion, exhortation, and neighborliness—resonates with familiar voices, such as FDR's and Reagan's. And Scully's.

On Opening Day this year, before the season's first pitch, Scully was the center of attention on the center of Dodger Stadium's diamond, standing on the pitcher's mound with various retired Dodger stars, including pitcher Don Newcombe. Newcombe, now ninety, was the starter in the first game Scully participated in broadcasting—Opening Day, 1950, in Philadelphia. Scully knew players who knew Ty Cobb. Scully's listeners today include the great-great-grandchildren of earlier listeners. Baseball, more than any other American institution, and Scully, more than any other baseball person, braid America's generations.

In this year of few blessings, one is the fact that Scully's final season coincides with a presidential campaign of unprecedented coarseness. The nation winces daily from fresh exposure to sullied politics, which surely is one reason so many people are paying such fond attention to Scully's sunset. It is easy to disregard or even disparage gentility—until confronted, as Americans now are, with its utter absence.

In late September, Scully will drive up Vin Scully Avenue to Dodger Stadium, settle himself in front of a mic in the Vin Scully Press Box, and speak five familiar words: "It's time for Dodger baseball." Later, as the sun sets on the San Gabriel Mountains, he will accompany the Dodgers for their final regular-season series, with the San Francisco Giants, who came west when Scully and the Dodgers did in 1957.

Then, or perhaps after a postseason game, he will stride away, toward his tenth decade. In this era of fungible and forgettable celebrities, he is a rarity: For millions of friends he never met, his very absence will be a mellow presence.

SECTION 12

FAREWELLS, MOSTLY FOND

"THE SMARTEST MAN IN THE UNITED STATES"

March 3, 2012

WASHINGTON—The most accomplished social scientist of the last half-century would occasionally visit his friend and Harvard colleague Pat Moynihan at the White House when Moynihan was President Nixon's domestic policy adviser. Once Moynihan took him to Nixon and said: "Mr. President, James Q. Wilson is the smartest man in the United States. The president of the United States should pay attention to what he has to say." Moynihan was right on both counts.

Wilson, who has died at eighty, understood America's unending argument about how freedom both depends upon government and is threatened by it, and how freedom competes with other values. He also understood that although social science cannot tell us what to do, it can tell us what is not working, which has included a lot since the radical expansion of what is considered political.

New Deal liberalism, Wilson said, was concerned with who got what, when, where, and how; since the 1960s, liberalism has been concerned with who thinks what, who acts when, who lives where, and who feels how: "Once politics was about only a few things; today, it is about nearly everything." Until the 1960s, "the chief issue in any congressional argument over new policies was whether it was legitimate for the federal government to do something at all." But since the "legitimacy barrier" fell, "no program is any longer 'new'—it is seen, rather, as an extension, a modification, or an enlargement of something the government is already doing."

The normal dynamic of politics, Wilson warned, is a process of addition, candidates promising to add to government's menu of benefits. Hence today's problem of collective choice: Can Washington, acknowledging no limit to its scope and responding to clamorous factions that proliferate because of its hyperactivity, make difficult choices? With government no longer constrained by either the old constitutional understanding of its limits or by the old stigma against deficit spending, hard choices can be deferred, and are.

Try, he wrote, to think "of a human want or difficulty that is not now defined as a 'public policy problem.'" The defining is done by elites to whose ideas the political system has become so open that changes of policy often result not from changes of public opinion but from changes in the way elites think. Liberal elites define problems as amenable to government engineering of new social structures. Conservative elites emphasize the cultural roots of many problems and hence their intractability.

America, Wilson said, increasingly faces "problems that do not seem to respond, or to respond enough, to changes in incentives." This is because culture is often determinative, is harder to change than incentives, and impedes individuals' abilities to respond to incentives. If Wilson was right, and the memory of man runneth not to when he wasn't, his wisdom should inform America's worries about increasing inequality:

Largely because of genetic factors, and partly because of advantages of nurturing that cannot be redistributed by government, people differ in aptitudes. Society tends to reward useful aptitudes. This produces hierarchies of pay and power that are resistant to rearrangement by government, including government attempts to redistribute income. Such attempts often ignore how income differences are necessary to reward activities, and ignore history, which suggests that economic growth, which redistribution often inhibits, does more than redistributionist measures to narrow inequalities.

Wilson warned that we should be careful about what we think we are, lest we become that. Human nature, he said, is not infinitely plastic; we cannot be socialized to accept anything. We do not recoil from Auschwitz only because our culture has so disposed us. Children,

Wilson thought, are intuitive moralists, but instincts founded in nature must be nurtured in families. The fact that much of modern life, from family disintegration to scabrous entertainment, is shocking is evidence for, not against, the moral sense, which is what is shocked. And the highest purpose of politics is to encourage the flourishing of a culture that nurtures rather than weakens the promptings of the moral sense.

Elegant in bearing, voracious for learning, eloquent in advocacy, and amiable in disputation, Wilson was a prophet honored in his own country, including with the presidency of the American Political Science Association and the Presidential Medal of Freedom. Every contemporary writer about American society and politics knows how Mel Tormé must have felt being a singer in Frank Sinatra's era. Everyone else has competed for the silver medal. Wilson won the gold.

THE ROMAN CANDLE JURIST

February 15, 2016

WASHINGTON—Antonin Scalia, who combined a zest for intellectual combat with a vast talent for friendship, was a Roman candle of sparkling jurisprudential theories leavened by acerbic witticisms. The serrated edges of his most passionate dissents sometimes strained the court's comity and occasionally limited his ability to proclaim what the late Justice William Brennan called the most important word in the court's lexicon: "Five." Scalia was, however, one of the most formidable thinkers among the 112 justices who have served on the court, and he often dissented in the hope of shaping a future replete with majorities steeped in principles he honed while in the minority.

Those principles include textualism and originalism: A justice's job is to construe the text of the Constitution or of statutes by discerning and accepting the original meaning the words had to those who ratified or wrote them. These principles of judicial modesty were embraced by a generation of conservatives who recoiled from what they considered the unprincipled creation of rights by results-oriented Supreme Court justices and other jurists pursuing their preferred policy outcomes.

Today, however, America's most interesting and potentially consequential argument about governance is not between conservatives and progressives but among conservatives. It concerns the proper scope of the judicial supervision of democracy.

Scalia worried more than some other conservatives do about the "counter-majoritarian dilemma" supposedly posed by judicial review—the power of appointed justices to overturn the work of elected legislators. Many Scalia-style conservatives distill their admiration into a familiar phrase of praise: "judicial restraint." Increasing numbers of conservatives, however, reason as follows:

Democracy's drama derives from the tension between the natural rights of individuals and the constructed right of the majority to have its way. Natural rights are affirmed by the Declaration of Independence; majority rule, circumscribed and modulated, is constructed by the Constitution. But as the Goldwater Institute's Timothy Sandefur argues, the Declaration is logically as well as chronologically prior to the Constitution. The latter enables majority rule. It is, however, the judiciary's duty to prevent majorities from abridging natural rights. After all, it is for the securing of such rights, the Declaration declares, that "governments are instituted among men."

Scalia's death will enkindle a debate missing from this year's presidential campaign, a debate discomfiting for some conservatives: Do they want a passive court that is deferential to legislative majorities and to presidents who claim untrammeled powers deriving from national majorities? Or do they want a court actively engaged in defending liberty's borders against unjustified encroachments by majorities?

This is an overdue argument that conservatism is now prepared for because of Scalia's elegant mind. He was crucial to the creation of an alternative intellectual infrastructure for conservative law students. The Federalist Society, founded in 1982, has leavened the often monochrome liberalism of law schools, and Scalia has been the jurisprudential lodestar for tens of thousands of students in society chapters coast to coast.

Students of the court understand that, given Harry Reid's demonstrated disdain for Senate rules, if Republicans had not won Senate control in the 2014 elections, he as majority leader would very likely now extend the institutional vandalism he committed in 2013. Then he changed Senate rules, by a simple majority vote and in the middle of a session, to prevent filibusters of judicial nominees other than Supreme Court nominees. This enabled Obama to pack the nation's second-most important court, that of the U.S. Circuit for the District of Columbia. Were Reid still majority leader, the Senate's only rule would be the whim of the majority of the moment, and his caucus would promptly proscribe filibusters of Supreme Court nominees.

One consequence would be this: America today is one Supreme Court vote away from a radical truncation of the First Amendment's protection of freedom of speech. A Democratic president in 2017 will nominate to replace Scalia someone pledged to construe the amendment as permitting Congress to regulate political campaign speech, which would put First Amendment jurisprudence on a slippery slope to regarding *all* speech as eligible for regulation by the administrative state.

Scalia lived twenty-seven years after the person who nominated him left office, thereby extending the reach of Ronald Reagan's presidency and reminding voters of the long-lasting ripples that radiate from their presidential choices. A teacher, wrote Henry Adams, attains a kind of immortality because one never knows where a teacher's influence ends. Scalia, always a teacher, will live on in the law and in the lives of unnumbered generations who will write, teach, and construe it.

WILLIAM F. BUCKLEY'S HIGH-SPIRITED ROMP

June 1, 2017

WASHINGTON—In 1950, the year before William F. Buckley burst into the national conversation, the literary critic Lionel Trilling revealed why the nation was ripe for Buckley's high-spirited romp through its political and cultural controversies. Liberalism, Trilling declared, was "not only the dominant but even the sole intellectual tradition" in mid-century America because conservatism was expressed merely in "irritable mental gestures." Buckley would change that by infusing conservatism with brio, bringing elegance to its advocacy and altering the nation's trajectory while having a grand time.

Today, conservatism is soiled by scowling primitives whose irritable gestures lack mental ingredients. America needs a reminder of conservatism before vulgarians hijacked it, and a hint of how it became susceptible to hijacking. Both are in Alvin S. Felzenberg's *A Man and His Presidents: The Political Odyssey of William F. Buckley Jr.* Yale University Press publishes this biography of the man who first challenged the liberal consensus in 1951 with an excoriation of his alma mater, *God and Man at Yale*.

Influenced by his isolationist father, Buckley was precociously opinionated. He named his first sailboat *Sweet Isolation*. While at school in England in September 1938, the twelve-year-old Buckley saw Prime Minister Neville Chamberlain deplane from the Munich Conference proclaiming "peace for our time." On May 23, 1941, Buckley, then fifteen, attended an America First rally in Madison Square Garden addressed by Charles Lindbergh. As a soldier stationed in Georgia in April 1945, Buckley was a young officer selected for the honor guard for Franklin Roosevelt's casket en route to the train from Warm Springs to Washington.

In the *Yale Daily News*, Buckley inveighed against the 1948 presidential campaign of leftist Henry Wallace because, Felzenberg writes, Buckley's "reading of history persuaded him that ideas advanced in the course of elections could outlast losing campaigns, capture the imagination of budding intellectuals and, under the right circumstances, gain acceptance over time." So, *National Review*, founded by Buckley in 1955, functioned, Felzenberg says, as Barry Goldwater's "unofficial headquarters and policy shop" during the 1964 presidential campaign. Goldwater lost forty-four states but put the Republican Party on the path to Ronald Reagan.

Some Buckley judgments were dotty (Goldwater should offer the vice presidential nomination to the retired Dwight Eisenhower), puerile (Eisenhower was "a miserable president"; Douglas MacArthur was "the last of the great Americans"), or worse (the name of the National Association for the Advancement of Colored People conceded that its constituents were "less advanced"). But Buckley's ebullience, decency, and enthusiasm for learning propelled him up from sectarianism.

He had the courage of his convictions that were costly. Although one of *National Review*'s staunchest benefactors was Roger Milliken, a protectionist textile magnate, Buckley supported the North American Free Trade Agreement, urging conservatives "to stand steady, joyful in our faith in the basic propositions of a free society."

Said the novelist Edna Buchanan, "Friends are the family we choose for ourselves." Buckley, with his talent for friendship, had an extraordinarily extended family that included Democrat Daniel Patrick Moynihan, who in the 1970s wrote that something momentous had happened: The Republican Party had become the party of ideas. Some, however, were incompatible, producing the dissonance that currently is crippling conservatism.

Buckley famously said he would rather be governed by the first 2,000 names in the Boston telephone directory than by Harvard's faculty, but he briskly defended the Council on Foreign Relations from "those American right-wingers who specialize in ignorance."

"All his life," Felzenberg writes, "Buckley walked a tightrope between elitism and populism," never resolving the tension between them. If only he had.

He, to his credit, befriended Whittaker Chambers, whose autobiography *Witness* became a canonical text of conservatism. Unfortunately, it injected conservatism with a sour, whiny, complaining, crybaby populism. It is the screechy and dominant tone of the loutish faux conservatism that today is erasing Buckley's legacy of infectious cheerfulness and unapologetic embrace of high culture.

Chambers wallowed in cloying sentimentality and curdled resentment about "the plain men and women"—"my people, humble people, strong in common sense, in common goodness"—enduring the "musk of snobbism" emanating from the "socially formidable circles" of the "nicest people" produced by "certain collegiate eyries." Buckley, a Bach aficionado from Yale and ocean mariner from the New York Yacht Club, was unembarrassed about having good taste and without guilt about savoring the good life.

"His true ideal," Felzenberg writes, "was governance by a new conservative elite in which he played a prominent role." And for which he would play the harpsichord.

THE TWENTIETH CENTURY'S MOST CONSEQUENTIAL JOURNALIST

February 29, 2008

WASHINGTON—Those who think Jack Nicholson's neon smile is the last word in smiles never saw William F. Buckley's. It could light up an auditorium; it did light up half a century of elegant advocacy that made him an engaging public intellectual and the twentieth century's most consequential journalist.

Before there could be Ronald Reagan's presidency, there had to be Barry Goldwater's candidacy. It made conservatism confident and placed the Republican Party in the hands of its adherents.

Before there could be Goldwater's insurgency, there had to be *National Review* magazine. From the creative clutter of its Manhattan offices flowed the ideological electricity that powered the transformation of American conservatism from a mere sensibility into a fighting faith and a blueprint for governance.

Before there was *National Review*, there was Buckley, spoiling for a philosophic fight, to be followed, of course, by a flute of champagne with his adversaries. He was twenty-nine when, in 1955, he launched *National Review* with the vow that it "stands athwart history, yelling Stop." Actually, it helped Bill take history by the lapels, shake it to get its attention, and then propel it in a new direction. Bill died Wednesday in his home, in his study, at his desk, diligent at his lifelong task of putting words together well, and to good use.

Before his intervention—often laconic in manner, always passionate in purpose—in the plodding political arguments within the flaccid liberal consensus of the post–World War II intelligentsia, conservatism's face was that of another Yale man, Robert Taft, somewhat dour, often sour, three-piece suits, wire-rim glasses. The word "fun" did not spring to mind.

The fun began when Bill picked up his clipboard, and conservatives' spirits, by bringing his distinctive brio and elan to political skirmishing. When young Goldwater decided to give politics a fling, he wrote to his brother: "It ain't for life and it might be fun." He was half right: Politics became his life and it was fun, all the way. Politics was not Bill's life—he had many competing and compensating enthusiasms—but it mattered to him, and he mattered to the course of political events.

One clue to Bill's talent for friendship surely is his fondness for this thought of Harold Nicolson's: "Only one person in a thousand is a bore, and *he* is interesting because he is one person in a thousand." Consider this from Bill's introduction to a collection of his writings titled *The Jeweler's Eye: A Book of Irresistible Political Reflections*:

The title is, of course, a calculated effrontery, the relic of an impromptu answer I gave once to a tenacious young interviewer who, toward the end of a very long session, asked me what opinion did I have of myself. I replied that I thought of myself as a perfectly average middle-aged American, with, however, a jeweler's eye for political truths. I suppressed a smile—and watched him carefully record my words in his notebook. Having done so, he looked up and asked, "Who gave you your jeweler's eye?" "God," I said, tilting my head skyward just a little. He wrote *that* down—the journalism schools warn you not to risk committing anything to memory. "Well,"—he rose to go, smiling at last—"that settles *that!*" We have become friends.

Pat, Bill's beloved wife of fifty-six years, died last April. During the memorial service for her at New York's Metropolitan Museum of Art, a friend read lines from "Vitae Summa Brevis" by a poet she admired, Ernest Dowson:

They are not long, the days of wine and roses:
Out of a misty dream
Our path emerges for a while, then closes
Within a dream.

Bill's final dream was to see her again, a consummation of which his faith assured him. He had an aptitude for love—of his son, his church, his harpsichord, language, wine, skiing, sailing.

He began his sixty-year voyage on the turbulent waters of American controversy by tacking into the wind with a polemical book, *God and Man at Yale* (1951), that was a lovers' quarrel with his alma mater. And so at Pat's service the achingly beautiful voices of Yale's Whiffenpoofs were raised in their signature song about the tables down at Mory's, "the place where Louis dwells":

We will serenade our Louis
While life and voice shall last
Then we'll pass and be forgotten with the rest

Bill's distinctive voice permeated, and improved, his era. It will be forgotten by no one who had the delight of hearing it.

CHARLES KRAUTHAMMER: "FIRST, YOU GO TO MEDICAL SCHOOL"

June 22, 2018

WASHINGTON—When he was asked how to become a columnist, Charles Krauthammer would say, with characteristic drollery, "First, you go to medical school." He did, with psychiatry as his specialty because, he said with characteristic felicity, it combined the practicality of medicine and the elegance of philosophy. But he also came to the columnist craft by accident. Because of one.

It has been said that if we had to think about tying our shoes or combing our hair we would never get out of the house in the morning. Life is mostly habitual—do you actually remember any details of driving home last evening? The more of life's functions that are routinely performed without thinking, the more thinking we can do. That, however, is not how life was for Charles after his accident.

In 1972, when he was a twenty-two-year-old student at Harvard Medical School, he was swimming in a pool. Someone pushed the diving board out, extending over a shallower part of the pool. Charles, not realizing this, dove and broke his neck. At the bottom of the pool, "I knew exactly what happened. I knew why I wasn't able to move, and I knew what that meant." It meant that life was going to be different than he and Robyn had anticipated when they met at Oxford.

He left two books at the pool. One was a text on the spinal cord. The other was André Malraux's novel *Man's Fate*.

Paralyzed from the neck down, he completed medical school, did an internship and, one thing leading to another, as life has a way of doing, became not a jewel in the crown of the medical profession, which he would have been, but one of America's foremost public intellectuals. Nothing against doctors, but the nation needed Charles more as a diagnostician of our public discontents.

During the 1980 presidential campaign, Charles wrote speeches for the Democratic vice presidential candidate, Walter Mondale, who did not realize—neither did Charles—that the campaign harbored a thinker who soon would be a leading light of contemporary conservatism. Dictating columns when not driving himself around Washington in a specially designed van that he operated while seated in his motorized wheelchair, crisscrossing the country to deliver speeches to enthralled audiences, Charles drew on reserves of energy and willpower to overcome a multitude of daily challenges, any one of which would cause most people to curl up in a fetal position. Fortunately, with more brain cells to spare than the rest us have to use, he could think about doing what was no longer habitual, and about national matters, too.

Charles died at sixty-eight, as did, nineteen years ago, Meg Greenfield, the editor of the *Washington Post*'s editorial page. For many years, Meg, Charles, and this columnist met for Saturday lunches with a guest—usually someone then newsworthy; now completely forgotten—at a Washington greasy spoon whose name, the Chevy Chase Lounge, was grander than the place. Like Meg, Charles was one of those vanishingly rare Washingtonians who could be both likable and logical. This is not easy in a town where the local industry, politics—unlike, say, engineering; get things wrong and the bridges buckle—thrives on unrefuted errors.

Medicine made Charles intimate with finitude—the skull beneath the skin of life; the fact that expiration is written into the lease we have on our bodies. And his accident gave him a capacity for sympathy, as Rick Ankiel knows.

Ankiel was a can't-miss, Cooperstown-bound pitching phenomenon for the St. Louis Cardinals—until, suddenly and inexplicably, he could not find the plate. Starting the opening game of a playoff series at age twenty-one, the prodigy threw five wild pitches, and his career rapidly spiraled far down to...resurrection as a twenty-eight-year-old major league outfielder, for a short but satisfying stint in defiance of F. Scott Fitzgerald's dictum that there are no second acts in a life. As Charles wrote, Ankiel's saga illustrated "the catastrophe that awaits everyone from a single false move, wrong turn, fatal encounter. Every life has such a moment. What distinguishes us is whether—and how—we ever come back."

The health problems that would end Charles's life removed him from the national conversation nine months ago, so his legion of admirers already know that he validated this axiom: Some people are such a large presence while living that they still occupy space even when they are gone.

THE CATCHER AT DAGO HILL

September 24, 2015

WASHINGTON—The eighteen-year-old U.S. Navy enlistee, thinking it sounded less boring than the dull training he was doing in 1944, volunteered for service on what he thought an officer had called "rocket ships." Actually, they were small, slow, vulnerable boats used as launching pads for rockets to give close-in support for troops assaulting beaches.

The service on those boats certainly was not boring. At dawn on June 6, 1944, that sailor was a few hundred yards off Omaha Beach. Lawrence Peter Berra, who died Tuesday at ninety, had a knack for being where the action was.

Because he stood—when he stood; as a catcher, he spent a lot of time at baseball's most physically and mentally demanding position—five feet seven inches, he confirmed the axiom that the beauty of baseball is that a player does not need to be seven feet tall or seven feet wide. The shortstop during Yogi's first Yankee years was an even smaller Italian American, 150-pound Phil Rizzuto, listed at a generous five feet six.

Yogi had, sportswriter Allen Barra says (in *Yogi Berra: Eternal Yankee*), "the winningest career in the history of American sports." He played on Yankee teams that went to the World Series fourteen times in seventeen years. He won ten World Series rings; no other player has more than nine. He won three MVP awards; only Barry Bonds has more, with seven, but four of them are probably tainted by performance-enhancing drugs. In seven consecutive seasons (1950–1956) Yogi finished in the top four in MVP voting. Only Bill Russell of the Boston Celtics (eleven NBA championships, five MVP awards) and Henri Richard (eleven NHL championships) have records of winning that exceed Yogi's.

He grew up in what he and others called the Dago Hill section of St. Louis, when the Italian Americans who lived there did not take offense at the name. They had bigger problems. Allen Barra notes that an 1895 advertisement seeking labor to build a New York reservoir said whites would be paid $1.30 to $1.50 a day, "colored" workers $1.25 to $1.40, and Italians $1.15 to $1.25. The term "wop" may have begun as an acronym for "without papers," as many Italians were when they arrived at Ellis Island.

American sports and ethnicity have been interestingly entangled. The nickname "Fighting Irish" was originally a disparagement by opponents of Notre Dame, which for many years had problems filling its football schedule because of anti-Catholic bigotry. But sports also have been solvents of a sense of apartness felt by ethnic groups.

In 1923, the *Sporting News*, which for many decades was described as "the Bible of baseball" (except by baseball fans, who described the Bible as "the *Sporting News* of religion"), called the national pastime the essence of the nation: "In a democratic, catholic, real American game like baseball, there has been no distinction raised except tacit understanding that a player of Ethiopian descent is ineligible.... The Mick, the Sheeny, the Wop, the Dutch and the Chink, the Cuban, the Indian, the Jap or the so-called Anglo-Saxon—his 'nationality' is never a matter of moment if he can pitch, hit or field."

Ah, diversity. In 1908, the *Sporting News* said this about a Giants rookie, Charley "Buck" Herzog:

The long-nosed rooters are crazy whenever young Herzog does anything noteworthy. Cries of "Herzog! Herzog! Goot poy, Herzog!" go up regularly, and there would be no let-up even if a million ham sandwiches suddenly fell among these believers in percentages and bargains.

David Maraniss, in his biography of the Pirates' Roberto Clemente, the first Puerto Rican superstar, notes that as late as 1971, Clemente's seventeenth season, one sportswriter still quoted him in phonetic English: "Eef I have my good arm thee ball gets there a leetle quicker." In 1962, Alvin Dark, manager of the San Francisco Giants, banned the speaking of Spanish in the clubhouse. Today, with three of the most common surnames in baseball being Martinez, Rodriguez, and Gonzalez, some managers speak Spanish.

Yogi's great contemporary, Dodgers' catcher Roy Campanella (another three-time MVP), was the son of an African-American mother and Italian-American father. Today, with two Italian Americans on the Supreme Court, it is difficult to imagine how delighted Italian Americans were with their first national celebrity—the elegant center fielder on baseball's most glamorous team, Joe DiMaggio, the son of a San Francisco fisherman.

DiMaggio was "Big Dago" to his teammates. Yogi was "Little Dago" and became the nation's most beloved sports figure. As Yogi said when Catholic Dublin elected a Jewish mayor, "Only in America."

FIDEL CASTRO AND UTOPIANISM, BOTH DEAD

November 27, 2016

WASHINGTON—With the end of Fidel Castro's nasty life Friday night, we can hope, if not reasonably expect, to have seen the last of charismatic totalitarians worshiped by political pilgrims from open societies. Experience suggests there will always be tyranny tourists in flight from what they consider the boring banality of bourgeois society and eager for the excitement of sojourns in "progressive" despotisms that they are free to admire and then leave.

During the 1930s, there were many apologists for Josef Stalin's brutalities, which he committed in the name of building a workers' paradise fit for an improved humanity. The apologists complacently said, "You can't make an omelet without breaking eggs." To which George Orwell acidly replied: "Where's the omelet?" With Castro, the problem was lemonade.

Soon after Castro seized power in 1959, Jean-Paul Sartre, the French intellectual whose Stalinist politics were as grotesque as his philosophy was opaque, left Les Deux Magots cafe in Paris to visit Cuba. During a drive, he and Castro stopped at a roadside stand. They were served warm lemonade, which Castro heatedly said "reveals a lack of revolutionary consciousness." The waitress shrugged, saying the refrigerator was broken. Castro "growled" (Sartre's approving description): "Tell your people in charge that if they don't take care of their problems, they will have problems with me." Sartre swooned:

> This was the first time I understood—still quite vaguely—what I called "direct democracy." Between the waitress and Castro, an immediate secret understanding was established. She let it be seen by her tone, her smiles, by a shrug of the shoulders, that she was without illusion. And the prime minister…in expressing himself before her without circumlocution, calmly invited her to join the rebellion.

Another political innovator, Benito Mussolini, called his regime "ennobled democracy," and as the American columnist Murray Kempton mordantly noted in 1982, photographs of Castro "cutting sugar cane evoke the bare-chested Mussolini plunged into the battle for wheat." Castro's direct democracy was parsimonious regarding elections but permissive of shrugs. It did, however, forbid "acts of public destruction," meaning criticism of communism.

This charge condemned Armando Valladares, then twenty-three, to twenty-two years in Castro's prisons. Stalin's terror was too high a price to pay for a great novel, but at least the world got from it Arthur Koestler's *Darkness at Noon*. And although Castro's regime, saturated with sadism, should never have existed, because of it the world got Valladares's testament to human endurance, his prison memoir *Against All Hope*. Prison food was watery soup laced with glass, or dead rats, or cows' intestines filled with feces, and Castro's agents had special uses for the ditch filled with the sewage from 8,000 people.

On April 15, 1959, fifteen weeks after capturing Havana, Castro, then thirty-two, landed in Washington at what is now Reagan National Airport. He had been in America in 1948, when he studied English and bought a Lincoln. This time, on April 16, in a concession to bourgeois expectations, he dispatched an aide to buy a comb and toothbrush. His connections to communism? "None," he said. He endorsed a free press as "the first enemy of dictatorship," and said free elections were coming soon. Then he was off to a Princeton seminar and a lecture in the chapel at Lawrenceville prep school, well received at both places.

By July red stars were being painted on Cuban military vehicles. Three years later, Soviet ballistic missiles were arriving. A year after that, a Castro admirer murdered the U.S. president whose administration had been interested in, indeed almost obsessed with, removing Castro.

U.S. flings at "regime change" in distant lands have had, to say no more, uneven results, but the most spectacular futility has been ninety miles from Florida. Castro was the object of various and sometimes unhinged U.S. attempts to remove him. After the Bay of Pigs debacle, the Kennedy administration doubled down with Operation Mongoose, which included harebrained assassination plots and a plan skeptics called "elimination by illumination"—having a U.S. submarine surface in Havana harbor and fire star shells into the night sky to convince Catholic Cubans that the Second Coming had come, causing them to rebel against Castro the anti-Christ. Nevertheless, Castro ruled Cuba during eleven U.S. presidencies and longer than the Soviet Union ruled Eastern Europe.

Socialism is bountiful only of slogans, and a Castro favorite was "socialism or death." The latter came to him decades after the former had made Cuba into a gray museum for a dead utopianism.

BILLY GRAHAM: NEITHER PROPHET NOR THEOLOGIAN

February 21, 2018

WASHINGTON—Asked in 1972 if he believed in miracles, Billy Graham answered: Yes, Jesus performed some and there are many "miracles around us today, including television and airplanes." Graham was no theologian.

'Neither was he a prophet. Jesus said "a prophet hath no honor in his own country." Prophets take adversarial stances toward their times, as did the twentieth century's two greatest religious leaders, Martin Luther King Jr. and Pope John Paul II. Graham did not. Partly for that reason, his country showered him with honors.

So, the subtitle of Grant Wacker's 2014 book *America's Pastor: Billy Graham and the Shaping of a Nation* (Harvard University Press) is inapposite. When America acquired television and a celebrity culture, this culture shaped Graham. Professor Wacker of Duke's Divinity School judges Graham sympathetically as a man of impeccable personal and business probity.

Americans respect quantification, and Graham was a marvel of quantities. He spoke, Wacker says, to more people directly—about 215 million—than any person in history. In 1945, at age twenty-six, he addressed 65,000 in Chicago's Soldier Field. The 1949 crusade in Los Angeles, promoted by the not notably devout William Randolph Hearst, had a cumulative attendance of 350,000. In 1957, a May-to-September rally in New York had attendance of 2.4 million, including 100,000 on one night at Yankee Stadium. A five-day meeting in Seoul, South Korea, in 1973 drew 3 million.

Graham's effects are impossible to quantify. His audiences were exhorted to make a "decision" for Christ, but a moment of volition might be (in theologian Dietrich Bonhoeffer's phrase) an exercise in "cheap grace." Graham's preaching, to large rallies and broadcast audiences, gave comfort to many people and probably improved some.

Regarding race, this North Carolinian was brave, telling a Mississippi audience in 1952 that, in Wacker's words, "there was no room for segregation at the foot of the cross." In 1953, he personally removed the segregating ropes at a Chattanooga crusade. After the Supreme Court's 1954 desegregation ruling, Graham abandoned the practice of respecting local racial practices. Otherwise, he rarely stepped far in advance of the majority. His 1970 *Ladies' Home Journal* article "Jesus and the Liberated Woman" was, Wacker says, "a masterpiece of equivocation."

The first preacher with a star on Hollywood's Walk of Fame was an entrepreneurial evangelical who consciously emulated masters of secular communication such as newscasters Drew Pearson, Walter Winchell, and H. V. Kaltenborn. Wielding the adverbs "nearly" and "only," Graham, says Wacker, would warn that all is nearly lost and the only hope is Christ's forgiveness.

Graham frequently vowed to abstain from partisan politics, and almost as frequently slipped this self-imposed leash, almost always on behalf of Republicans. Before the 1960 election, Graham, displaying some cognitive dissonance, said that if John Kennedy were a true Catholic, he would be a president more loyal to the Pope than to the Constitution but would fully support him if elected.

Graham's dealings with presidents mixed vanity and naiveté. In 1952, he said he wanted to meet with all the candidates "to give them the moral side of the thing." He was thirty-three. He applied flattery with a trowel, comparing Dwight Eisenhower's first foreign policy speech to the Sermon on the Mount and calling Richard Nixon "the most able and the best trained man for the job probably in American history." He told Nixon that God had given him, Nixon, "supernatural wisdom." Graham should have heeded the psalmist's warning about putting one's faith in princes.

On February 1, 1972, unaware of Nixon's Oval Office taping system, when Nixon ranted about how Jews "totally dominated" the media, Graham said "this stranglehold has got to be broken or this country is going down the drain." He also told Nixon that Jews are "the ones putting out the pornographic stuff." One can reasonably acquit Graham of anti-Semitism only by convicting him of toadying. When Graham read transcripts of Nixon conspiring to cover up crimes, Graham said that what "shook me most" was Nixon's vulgar language.

Of the My Lai massacre of Vietnamese civilians by U.S. troops, Graham said, "we have all had our My Lais in one way or another, perhaps not with guns, but we have hurt others with a thoughtless word, an arrogant act or a selfish deed." Speaking in the National Cathedral three days after 9/11, he said "it's so glorious and wonderful" that the victims were in heaven and would not want to return.

Graham, Wacker concludes, had an attractively sunny personality and was "invincibly extrospective." This precluded "irony" but also "contemplativeness."

GEORGE MCGOVERN: HE CAME BY THE HORROR OF WAR HONORABLY

February 17, 2008

WASHINGTON—The former bomber pilot's spry walk belies his eighty-five years, he dresses like a boulevardier—gray slacks, blue blazer, shirt with bright-red stripes and white collar—and tucks into a robust breakfast. Long ago, he began shaping the Democrats' presidential nomination process into the one that has his party's two contenders locked in a long march to Pennsylvania's April primary. He has seen important aspects of American politics move in his direction in the thirty-six years since he lost forty-nine states to Richard Nixon.

The belittling of George McGovern, especially by Democrats, only waned as memory of him faded after he lost his bid for a fourth Senate term in the 1980 Reagan landslide. But his story is fascinating, and pertinent to current events.

This minister's son was raised on South Dakota's parched prairies during the Depression. He remembers hiking home to the town of Mitchell by following the railroad tracks in a blinding dust storm. He was only the second major-party nominee with a PhD (Woodrow Wilson was the first), which he earned at Northwestern University under Arthur Link, Wilson's foremost biographer.

Like Wilson, a minister's son, McGovern was a political moralist. He also was a tenacious politician, who, inspired by the untenacious Adlai Stevenson's presidential campaign the year before, went to work for the South Dakota Democratic Party in 1953, when it held only two of 110 seats in the state legislature. Just four years later McGovern was in Congress, where his first roll-call vote was in opposition to granting

President Eisenhower broad authority for military intervention in the Middle East.

In tumultuous 1968, with the Tet Offensive and two assassinations (of Martin Luther King Jr. and Robert Kennedy) in five months, two insurgent candidates, Eugene McCarthy and Robert Kennedy, sought the Democratic nomination. It was won by Vice President Hubert Humphrey, who competed in no primaries. More than one third of the delegates to the riotous convention in Chicago had been selected in 1967, months before President Lyndon Johnson decided to retire.

McGovern was named chairman of a commission to reform the nomination process, which put the party on a path to the proliferation of caucuses and primaries allocating delegates proportionally rather than winner-take-all—the long, winding path Obama and Clinton are on. In 1972, McGovern became the first winner under the democratized process. Then he was buried by the demos, Nixon vs. McGovern.

Nixon was, McGovern notes, running nationally for the fifth time (only FDR had done that) and was at his pre-Watergate apogee, fresh from the opening to China and a strategic-arms agreement with Moscow. McGovern was bitterly opposed all the way to the Miami convention by the Democratic constituencies he was displacing. He says Barry Goldwater had warned him, "Don't get fatigued," but he reached Miami exhausted, lost control of the convention (he delivered his acceptance speech at 2:30 a.m.), and disastrously selected a running mate, Missouri Senator Tom Eagleton, who did not disclose previous psychiatric problems and was forced off the ticket.

Still, McGovern thinks he could have won with a running mate then called "the most trusted man in America"—Walter Cronkite. Before choosing Eagleton, McGovern considered asking Cronkite, who recently indicated he would have accepted.

Bruce Miroff, a political scientist and admirer of McGovern, argues in his new book, *The Liberals' Moment: The McGovern Insurgency and the Identity Crisis of the Democratic Party*, that although McGovern's domestic proposals featured redistributions of wealth, this was Ivy League, not prairie, populism. Branded the candidate of "acid, amnesty and abortion" (the Democrats' platform, adopted six months before the

Supreme Court in *Roe v. Wade* legislated a liberal abortion policy, did not mention abortion), McGovern became the first candidate since the New Deal to lose the Catholic and labor union vote. So 1972, more than 1968, was the hinge of the party's history. In 1972, Miroff writes, "college-educated issue activists" supplanted the "labor/urban machine coalition."

George Meany, head of the AFL-CIO, had dropped out of high school at age fourteen. Speaking about McGovern's 1972 convention, where 39 percent of the delegates had advanced degrees, he said: "We heard from people who look like Jacks, acted like Jills and had the odor of Johns about them." The Reagan Democrats of 1980 were incubated eight years earlier.

McGovern won only 14 percent of Southern white Protestants. This, Miroff notes, made Democrats susceptible four years later to the appeal of a pious Southerner. Thus did a disaster compound itself.

In September 1963, McGovern became the only senator who opposed U.S. involvement in Vietnam during the Kennedy administration. He came by his horror of war honorably in 35 B-24 missions over Germany, where half the B-24 crews did not survive—they suffered a higher rate of fatalities than did Marines storming Pacific islands. McGovern was awarded a Distinguished Flying Cross with three oak-leaf clusters. In his seventies he lost a forty-five-year-old daughter to alcoholism. Losing a presidential election, he says softly, "was not the saddest thing in my life." Time confers a comforting perspective, giving consolations to old age, which needs them.

GERALD FORD: THE BENEVOLENT ACCIDENT

June 3, 2018

WASHINGTON—Within seventeen days in the autumn of 1975—first in Sacramento, then in San Francisco—two separate handgun-wielding women attempted to assassinate the president. Had either succeeded, and each was close enough to have done so, the nation would have had a third president in fourteen months, and a second consecutive one who had never been on a national ticket. Gerald Ford survived to continue with an 895-day presidency during which the nation regained its equilibrium after Watergate and Vietnam.

The only president never to appear on a ballot for either vice president or president, Ford became vice president (under the Twenty-fifth Amendment) when scandals forced Richard Nixon's vice president, Spiro Agnew, to resign. Ford became president when Nixon resigned. Had Ford been assassinated, his vice president, Nelson Rockefeller (also confirmed by Congress under the Twenty-fifth Amendment), would have become president. Today, with the nation seemingly more irritable and depressed than at any time since then, it is well to fondly remember the thirty-eighth president, which Donald Rumsfeld does in *When the Center Held: Gerald Ford and the Rescue of the American Presidency*. Readers can tickle from this book a reason for looking on the bright side of, or at least for an inadvertent benefit from, the forty-fifth president.

Ford was the most accomplished athlete ever to hold the nation's highest elective office: For three seasons he was the center (hence Rumsfeld's title) on University of Michigan's football teams, two of which were undefeated national champions. Yet because of a few public stumbles related to a football-weakened knee, he is remembered as awkward. His lack of rhetorical nimbleness, one instance of which might have cost him the 1976 election, elicited condescension from critics, few of whom were, as he was, graduates of Yale Law School.

When he was sworn in as president on August 9, 1974, only 36 percent of Americans expressed trust in government, down from 77 percent in 1964. And the inflation rate was 10.9 percent, the highest since 1919: *Nothing* destroys faith in government faster than its currency failing as a store of value. To cauterize the Watergate wound, Ford pardoned Nixon, an act both statesmanlike—it spared the nation additional years of rancor—and politically damaging: Ford's job approval plunged thirty-one points. And he was clueless about inflation, urging people to drive less and buy cheaper groceries. Rumsfeld, who served as Ford's White

House chief of staff and then secretary of defense, delicately says this "perplexed a number of our country's top economists."

In January 1975, in his first State of the Union address, delivered three months before the last helicopters lifted the remnants of the U.S. presence in Vietnam off the roof of the Saigon embassy, Ford said: "The state of the Union is not good." Ronald Reagan agreed and began planning his attempt to wrest the 1976 Republican nomination from Ford.

That fate had dealt Ford a miserable hand of cards did not discombobulate him, largely because, as Rumsfeld says, he had not "come to the Oval Office with an outsized view of himself." Never having campaigned other than in Michigan's Fifth Congressional District (Grand Rapids), he nevertheless won the 1976 GOP nomination, and probably would have won the election if, during a debate with Jimmy Carter, he had inserted the word "permanently" in his statement that Eastern European peoples did not "consider themselves dominated by the Soviet Union."

Rumsfeld, who calls Ford "the president we always wanted that we didn't know we had," tiptoes up to a comparison with today's Washington when he says the city "can be a magnet for sizable personalities" and that Ford's "saving grace" was that he was not like that: "His calm, thoughtful and steadfast nature was remarkable in Washington, D.C., even in his own day, and some might assert even more so now." Do tell.

The current president's contribution—unintended but not insignificant—to America's civic health might be to help cure the country of unreasonable fastidiousness regarding presidential aspirants. For a while, at least, many voters will be less inclined than they once were to measure candidates with a political micrometer that encourages voters to be excessively finicky, rejecting candidates for minor blemishes, only to wind up with one who is all blemish. More than four decades on from Ford's accidental presidency, this man who wore plaid trousers and wore power lightly is a reminder that the nation can always do worse than to embrace normality.

GEORGE H. W. BUSH: "I AM NOT A MYSTIC"

December 2, 2018

WASHINGTON—At the beginning of his long and well-lived life, George Herbert Walker Bush, who in politics was always prosaic, acquired, by way of a grandfather, the name of a British poet and priest (George Herbert, 1593–1633). He acquired much else from family inheritance.

The future forty-first president was descended from a governor of the Federal Reserve Bank of Cleveland—from financier George Herbert Walker, whose name is on golf's Walker Cup—and from a U.S. senator— his father Prescott, of Brown Brothers Harriman, the Wall Street investment house whose partners included Robert Lovett, a future secretary of defense.

This was the world from which Bush came into a life whose trajectory often left him caught between the worlds of the old East Coast Republicanism of banks, railroads, and good works of noblesse oblige, and the New Right Republicanism of the Sun Belt. He had an easy social grace imparted by Greenwich Country Day School, Andover, and Yale, yet seemed forever uneasy about where he was and how he got there.

Rejecting family entreaties that he go to Yale before going to war, he enlisted on his eighteenth birthday and promptly became the Navy's youngest commissioned aviator, compiling 126 carrier landings and fifty-eight missions. After Yale, he spurned a Wall Street career and with his wife—the former Barbara Pierce, a descendant of the fourteenth president, Franklin Pierce—headed in his Studebaker for the West Texas oil patch. But he took Wall Street with him in the form of connections and capital that helped launch the Bush-Overbey Oil Development Company.

Business success brought him to Houston; boredom with business brought him to politics. He was thirty-nine when he announced he would seek the Republican nomination to oppose Senator Ralph Yarborough in 1964, the year Barry Goldwater, harbinger of the Republicans' future, would be at the top of the ticket.

Bush took on the coloration of Texas's first generation of Republicanism. He endorsed right-to-work laws and denounced Medicare—it was coming in 1965—as "socialistic." He opposed the 1964 civil rights bill on the grounds that it would "make the Department of Justice the most powerful police force in the nation." He said the bill's public accommodations provisions were unconstitutional, and whereas the law might "protect 14 percent of the people," he was equally concerned about "the other 86 percent."

While Bush criticized Walter Reuther of the United Auto Workers because he had "donated $50 to the militant Dr. Martin Luther King Jr.," Bush's campaign supporters sang, "The sun's going to shine in the Senate someday/George Bush is going to chase them liberals away." He lost.

And he repented and revised himself. Running successfully for Congress in 1965–1966, he endorsed Lyndon Johnson's Great Society agenda as meaning "a better life for all."

Richard Nixon considered Bush as a running mate in 1968, but chose Spiro Agnew. In 1970, Bush's plans for a rematch with Yarborough crashed when Lloyd Bentsen defeated Yarborough in the Democratic primary. So Bush ran to Bentsen's left—e.g., supporting gun control—and again lost. He was forty-six, twice defeated, and his political future, if any, depended on the patronage of others, beginning with Nixon, who made him ambassador to the United Nations and then chairman of the Republican National Committee when the job involved defending Nixon against Watergate accusations, which Bush dutifully did. President Gerald Ford considered Bush as his vice president, but chose Nelson Rockefeller. He became chief envoy to China when Secretary of State Henry Kissinger's close attention to that country made the envoy's job merely ceremonial. Then, by becoming CIA director, Bush removed himself from consideration as Ford's 1976 running mate.

Seeking the 1980 Republican presidential nomination, Bush ran as the moderate alternative to Reagan, who nevertheless then positioned Bush, as his vice president, for a 1988 candidacy. Announcing it, Bush said: "I am not a mystic and I do not yearn to lead a crusade." Having lost to Robert Dole in Iowa, Bush saved his candidacy by winning New Hampshire with yet more role playing—driving an eighteen-wheeler around a truck stop's parking lot.

In 1989, as president, he could at last be himself. He was, by then, an Eisenhower Republican, whose prudence was displayed first when the Berlin Wall came down, next when Saddam Hussein invaded Kuwait and Bush, when expelling him, stopped short of invading Iraq. Presiding over the orderly end of the Cold War and the vast coalition for Desert Storm, Bush earned the lasting admiration of a discerning posterity, a judgment more important than the one rendered by the undiscerning electorate that in 1992 limited him to one term.

"THEN ALONG CAME NANCY"

March 8, 2016

WASHINGTON—They were just four words, but they denoted something that led to a wonderful swerve in world history. They were words Ronald Reagan repeatedly used when referring to something that happened long before he spoke his most famous four words: "Tear down this wall." The other four words described the most important event in his eventful life, an event without which Reagan probably would never have been in a position to bring down the Berlin Wall: "Then along came Nancy." If she had not come along, he would not have come to the place he now occupies in history and in the hearts of his countrymen.

When filling out forms that ask if one is married, many people perfunctorily check that box. The Reagans should have put not a check mark but an exclamation point: They were the most married couple imaginable. Ronald was a reproach to every husband who does not write love notes to his wife as they sit together in evening repose. It was a remarkable woman who could elicit such private devotion from a public man with presidential preoccupations.

Reagan's strength was reflected in his preternatural cheerfulness, which flowed from his marriage. Politics requires the patience, endurance, and serenity that a happy marriage can confer. In a democracy, politics is a team sport. Parties are teams; congressional caucuses are teams; campaigns are teams. But often the most important team is the smallest, a harmonious marriage. The presidency has had three especially history-shaping partnerships: Abigail and John Adams, Dolley and James Madison, Nancy and Ronald Reagan.

Much, but not too much, has been made of Nancy's protectiveness, her steely devotion to her husband's interests. With her in mind, one occasionally wonders whether the reason most societies have refused to allow women in combat is not that women are too frail for combat but that they are too fierce for it: They would not obey the rules.

Ronald Reagan was a friendly man who used friendliness as a buffer, keeping the world at a distance from his sphere of privacy. He had one true friend, and he married her. She understood his amiable propensity for thinking the best of everybody, a mistake she did not make.

Her cool public persona and occasionally icy decisiveness sometimes obscured her warmth, her capacity for fun, and her sly wit. She revealed the latter, for example, when describing a problem of Hollywood manners.

What should you do, she asked, when you are invited to the home of an actor or director for a private screening of his newest movie—and the movie is dreadful? What do you say to your anxious host when he asks your opinion of his handiwork? Nancy impishly explained: You fix your host with an earnest gaze and exclaim, "You've done it again!" Her husband was not the only master politician living on the second floor of the White House.

Nancy bore the brunt of much criticism from people who were inclined but reluctant to assail her husband. She did not enjoy these slings and arrows, but she was shrewd enough to be stoical about her role as alternative target. Today, in the midst of an unusually unseemly political season, it is salutary to remember that Nancy was faulted for what some considered her excessive interest in decorum and elegance in public life.

Now she goes to a grave on a hill, where she joins the love of her life. Atop that hill sits the Ronald Reagan Presidential Foundation and Library. Emerson said that any institution is the lengthening shadow of a man. This library is the lengthening shadow of the woman who channeled through it her devotion that was undimmed through twelve years without her husband.

He spoke often of America as a shining city on a hill, words first used long ago to describe the American aspiration at a time when the nascent nation was a few hardy people on the continent's rocky Atlantic shore. The hill to which Nancy now goes overlooks the sun-dappled Pacific shore of a nation grown great not just in size but in moral stature because of its fidelity to principles that the Reagans defended together.

For generations to come, Americans will continue to climb that hill in Simi Valley to renew their devotion to the nation. And to one another, moved by the luminous example of two people who changed the world as, and because, they moved through it as one.

"THE EYES OF CALIGULA AND THE LIPS OF MARILYN MONROE"

April 8, 2013

WASHINGTON—She had the eyes of Caligula and the lips of Marilyn Monroe. So said François Mitterrand, the last serious socialist to lead a major European nation, speaking of Margaret Thatcher, who helped bury socialism as a doctrine of governance.

She had the smooth, cold surface of a porcelain figurine, but her decisiveness made her the most formidable woman in twentieth-century politics, and England's most formidable woman since its greatest sovereign, Elizabeth I. The Argentine junta learned of her decisiveness when it seized the Falklands. The British, too, learned. A Tory MP said, "She cannot see an institution without hitting it with her handbag."

She aimed to be the moral equivalent of military trauma, shaking her nation into vigor through rigor. As stable societies mature, they resemble long-simmering stews—viscous and lumpy with organizations resistant to change and hence inimical to dynamism. Her program was sound money, laissez faire, social fluidity, and upward mobility through self-reliance and other "vigorous virtues." She is the only prime minister whose name came to denote a doctrine—Thatcherism. ("Churchillian" denotes not a political philosophy but a leadership style.) When she left office in 1990, the trade unions had been tamed by democratizing them, the political argument was about how to achieve economic growth rather than redistribute wealth, and individualism and nationalism were revitalized.

And the Labour Party, shellacked three times, was ready for a post-socialist leader. Tony Blair was part of Thatcher's legacy.

Time was, Labour considered itself the party of ideas, and Tories preferred balancing interests to implementing political philosophy. But by the 1970s, Labour was a creature of a single interest group, the unions, and the Tories, who made Thatcher their leader in 1975, were becoming, as America's Republicans were becoming, a party of ideas.

Britain has periodically been a laboratory for economic ideas—those of Adam Smith, John Maynard Keynes, the socialism of postwar Labour. Before the ascendancy of Thatcher—a disciple of Milton Friedman and Friedrich Hayek—Tories tried to immunize Britain against socialism by administering prophylactic doses of the disease. But by 1979, Britain's fundamental political arrangements were at issue: Such was the extortionate power of the unions to paralyze the nation, the writ of Parliament often seemed not to run beyond a few acres along the Thames.

In 1979, she won the most lopsided election since 1945, when there had not been an election for ten years. In 1983, she became the first Tory since 1924 to win two consecutive elections. In 1987, she won a third. Her twelve consecutive years were an achievement without precedent since the 1832 Reform Act moved Britain, gingerly, toward mass democracy. The most consequential peacetime prime minister since Disraeli, by 1990 she had become the first prime minister to govern through an entire decade since the Earl of Liverpool from 1812 to 1827.

In Britain and America in the 1960s and 1970s, government's hubris expanded as its competence shrank. Like her soul mate, Ronald Reagan, Thatcher practiced the politics of psychotherapy, giving her nation a pride transplant. Reagan was responding to seventeen lacerating years—Dallas, Vietnam, Watergate, stagflation, the Iranian hostage crisis. She was sick and tired of three decades of Britain being described as the Ottoman Empire once was, as "the sick man of Europe." She set about disrupting settled attitudes and arrangements by enlarging and energizing the middle class, the great engine of social change in every modern society.

Before Thatcher, Britain's economic problems often were ascribed to national character, and hence were thought immune to remediation. Thatcher thought national character was part of the problem, but that national character is malleable, given bracing economic medicine. Marx's ghost, hovering over his grave in London's Highgate Cemetery, must have marveled at this Tory variant of economic determinism.

When Nature was serving up charm and convictions, Thatcher took a double serving of the latter, leaving little room on her plate for the former. But by what has been called her "matriarchal machismo" she usefully demonstrated that a soothing personality is not always necessary in democracy.

Like de Gaulle, she was a charismatic conservative nationalist who was properly resistant to what she called the European federalists' attempts to "suppress nationhood and concentrate power at the center of a European conglomerate." She left the British this ongoing challenge: "We have not successfully rolled back the frontiers of the state in Britain, only to see them reimposed at a European level." As long as her brave heart beat, she knew there are no final victories.

THE LAST DOUGHBOY

May 25, 2008

CHARLES TOWN, W.Va.—Numbers come precisely from the agile mind and nimble tongue of Frank Buckles, who seems bemused to say that 4,734,991 Americans served in the military during America's involvement in the First World War and 4,734,990 are gone. He is feeling fine, thank you for asking.

The eyes of the last doughboy are still sharp enough for him to be a keen reader, and his voice is still deep and strong at age 107. He must have been a fine broth of a boy when, at sixteen, persistence paid off and he found, in Oklahoma City, an Army recruiter who believed, or pretended to, the fibs he had unavailingly told to Marine and Navy recruiters in Kansas about being eighteen. He grew up on a Missouri farm, not far from where two eminent generals were born—John "Black Jack" Pershing and Omar Bradley.

"Boys in the country," says Buckles, "read the papers," so he was eager to get into the fight over there. He was told that the quickest way was to train for casualty retrieval and ambulance operations. Soon he was headed for England aboard the passenger ship *Carpathia*, which was celebrated for having, five years earlier, rescued survivors from the *Titanic*.

Buckles never saw combat but "I saw the results." He seems vague about only one thing: What was the First World War about?

Before leaving England for France, he was stationed near Winchester College, where he noticed "Buckles" among the names that boys had carved in their desks. This ignited his interest in genealogy, which led him to discover that his ancestor Robert Buckles, born in Yorkshire on May 15, 1702, arrived at age thirty in what is now West Virginia.

After Corporal Buckles was mustered out of the Army in 1920 with $143.90 in his pocket, he went to business school in Oklahoma City for five months, then rented a typewriter for three dollars a month and sent out job applications. One landed him work in the steamship business, which took him around the world—Latin America, China, Manchuria. And Germany, where, he says, in 1928 "two impressive gentlemen" told him, "We are preparing for another war."

Behind glass in a cabinet in his small sitting room are mementos from his eventful life: a German army belt with a buckle bearing words all nations believe, "Gott Mit Uns (God Is With Us)." The tin cup from which he ate all his meals, such as they were, during the thirty-nine months he was a prisoner of the Japanese—because he was working for a shipping company in Manila on December 7, 1941.

Widowed in 1999, this man who was born during the administration of the twenty-fifth president recently voted in West Virginia's primary to select a candidate to be the forty-fourth. His favorite president of his lifetime? The oldest, Ronald Reagan.

Buckles is reading David McCullough's *1776*. That date is just eighteen years more distant from his birth than today is.

This Memorial Day, Buckles will be feted back in Missouri, at the annual parade and fireworks in Kansas City. Perhaps he will journey to Bethany, to the house on whose porch he sat at age three, 104 years ago.

He was born in February 1901, seven months before President William McKinley was assassinated. If Buckles had been born fourteen months earlier, he would have lived in three centuries. He has lived through 46 percent of the nation's life, a percentage that rises each morning when he does.

On June 28, 1914, an assassin's bullet in Sarajevo killed the heir to the throne of the Austro-Hungarian empire. The war that followed took more than 116,000 American lives—more than all of America's wars after the Second World War. And in a sense, the First World War took many more American lives because it led to the Second World War and beyond.

The First World War is still taking American lives because it destroyed the Austro-Hungarian, Romanoff, and Ottoman empires. A shard of the latter is called Iraq.

The twentieth century's winds of war blew billions of ordinary people hither and yon. One of them sits here in a cardigan sweater in an old wood-and-stone house on a rise on a 330-acre cattle farm. In this case, and probably in every case, the word "ordinary" is inappropriate.

—

Buckles died February 27, 2011.

LIEUTENANT COLONEL JIM WALTON

July 6, 2008

"The curtains pull away. They come to the door. And they know. They always know."

—Major Steve Beck,
U.S. Marine Corps

WASHINGTON—Sometimes Beck would linger in his vehicle in front of an American home, like that of the parents of Lance Corporal Kyle Burns in Laramie, Wyoming. Beck knew that, as Jim Sheeler writes, every second he waited "was one more tick of his wristwatch that, for the family inside the house, everything remained the same."

Beck—now Lieutenant Colonel Beck—was a CACO, a casualty assistance calls officer, whose duty was to inform a spouse or parents that their Marine had been killed. He is the scarlet thread—like the stripes on Marines' dress-blue trousers, symbolizing shed blood—that connects the heart-rending stories in Sheeler's *Final Salute: A Story of Unfinished Lives*. The book, which proves that the phrase "literary journalism" is not an oxymoron, expands the meticulous and marvelously modulated reporting that he did for the *Rocky Mountain News* and for which he received a Pulitzer Prize. His subject is how America honors fallen warriors.

More precisely, it is about how the military honors them. The nation, as Marine Sergeant Damon Cecil says, "has changed the channel." Still,

Sheeler sees civilians getting glimpses of those who have sacrificed everything. The glimpses come as the fallen are escorted home. When an airline passenger, noting an escort's uniform, asked if the sergeant was going to or coming from the war, he repeated words the military had told him to say: "I'm escorting a fallen Marine home to his family from the situation in Iraq."

The situation. Sheeler:

When the plane landed in Nevada, the sergeant was allowed to disembark alone. Outside, a procession walked toward the cargo hold. The airline passengers pressed their faces against the windows.

From their seats in the plane they saw a hearse and a Marine extending a white-gloved hand into a limousine. In the plane's cargo hold, Marines readied the flag-draped casket and placed it on the luggage conveyor belt.

Inside the plane, the passengers couldn't hear the screams.

The knock on the survivors' door is, Beck says, "not a period at the end of their lives. It's a semicolon." Deployed military personnel often leave behind, or write in the war zone, "just in case" letters. Army Private First Class Jesse Givens of Fountain, Colorado: "My angel, my wife, my love, my friend. If you're reading this, I won't be coming home...Please find it in your heart to forgive me for leaving you alone." To his son Dakota: "I will always be there in our park when you dream so we can still play together...I'll be in the sun, shadows, dreams, and joys of your life." To his unborn son: "You were conceived of love and I came to this terrible place for love."

The manual for CACOs says, "It is helpful if the [next of kin] is seated prior to delivering the news...Speak naturally and at a normal pace." Sometimes, however, things do not go by the book.

Doyla Lundstrom, a Lakota Sioux, was away from her house when she learned that men in uniform had been to her door. She called the father of her two sons—each serving in Iraq; one as a Marine, one as a soldier—and screamed into her cellphone, "Which one was it?" It was the Marine.

Sheeler says that troops in war zones often have email and satellite telephones, so when someone is killed, communication from the area is stopped lest rumors reach loved ones before notification officers do. "As soon as we receive the call," Beck says, "we are racing the electron."

When the Army CACOs came to the Arlington door of Sarah Walton, my assistant, she was not there. She rarely forgot the rule that a spouse of a soldier in a combat zone is supposed to inform the Army when he or she will be away from home. This time Sarah forgot, so it took the Army awhile to locate her at her parents' home in Richmond.

Her husband, Lieutenant Colonel Jim Walton, West Point Class of 1989, was killed in Afghanistan on June 21. This week he will be back in Arlington, among the remains of the more than 300,000 men and women who rest in the more than 600 acres where it is always Memorial Day. This is written in homage to him, and to Sarah, full sharer of his sacrifices.

Acknowledgments

For forty-seven years my columns have been subject to the exacting editorial standards of the *Washington Post* Writers Group. To its superb professionals, I give thanks. The writings in this volume have benefitted from the diligence of five research assistants: Greg Reed, Greg Collins, Todd Shaw, Jessica Cruzan, and Elayne Allen. The production of this volume owes much to Alexa Secrest. As always, Sarah Walton has been the indispensable constant in my office.

Index